GW00771367

The Classic Plays

The Classic Plays

All My Sons
Death of a Salesman
The Crucible
A View from the Bridge

ARTHUR MILLER

PENGUIN CLASSICS

PENGUIN CLASSICS

UK | USA | Canada | Ireland | Australia
India | New Zealand | South Africa

Penguin Classics is part of the Penguin Random House group of companies
whose addresses can be found at global.penguinrandomhouse.com.

All My Sons first published in 1947
Copyright 1947 by Arthur Miller

Death of a Salesman first published in 1949
Copyright 1949 by Arthur Miller

The Crucible first published in 1953
Copyright 1952, 1953 by Arthur Miller

A View from the Bridge first published in 1955
Copyright © Arthur Miller, 1955, 1957, 1960
Copyright renewed Arthur Miller, 1983, 1985, 1988

This collection first published in Great Britain by Penguin Classics 2015
001

Set in 12/14.75 pt Dante MT Std
Typeset by Jouve (UK), Milton Keynes
Printed in Great Britain by Clays Ltd, St Ives plc

A CIP catalogue record for this book is available from the British Library

ISBN: 978-0-141-98161-1

www.greenpenguin.co.uk

MIX
Paper from
responsible sources
FSC
www.fsc.org
FSC® C018179

Penguin Random House is committed to a
sustainable future for our business, our readers
and our planet. This book is made from Forest
Stewardship Council® certified paper.

Contents

All My Sons

FOR ELIA KAZAN

All My Sons was first presented by Elia Kazan, Harold Clurman, and Walter Fried (in association with Herbert Harris), at the Coronet Theatre on the evening of 29 January 1947, with the following cast:

JOE KELLER	*Ed Begley*
KATE KELLER	*Beth Merrill*
CHRIS KELLER	*Arthur Kennedy*
ANN DEEVER	*Lois Wheeler*
GEORGE DEEVER	*Karl Malden*
DR JIM BAYLISS	*John McGovern*
SUE BAYLISS	*Peggy Meredith*
FRANK LUBEY	*Dudley Sadler*
LYDIA LUBEY	*Hope Cameron*
BERT	*Eugene Steiner*

The production was directed by ELIA KAZAN
The setting was designed by MORDECAI GORELIK

SYNOPSIS OF SCENES

Act One
The back yard of the Keller home in the outskirts of an American town. August of our era.

Act Two
Scene, as before. The same evening, as twilight falls.

Act Three
Scene, as before. Two o'clock the following morning.

Act One

The back yard of the KELLER home in the outskirts of an American town. August of our era.

The stage is hedged on R. and L. by tall, closely planted poplars which lend the yard a secluded atmosphere. Upstage is filled with the back of the house and its open, unroofed porch which extends into the yard some six feet. The house is two storeys high and has seven rooms. It would have cost perhaps fifteen thousand in the early twenties when it was built. Now it is nicely painted, looks tight and comfortable, and the yard is green with sod, here and there plants whose season is gone. At the R., beside the house, the entrance of the driveway can be seen, but the poplars cut off view of its continuation downstage. In the L. corner, downstage, stands the four-foot-high stump of a slender apple tree whose upper trunk and branches lie toppled beside it, fruit still clinging to its branches. Downstage R. is a small, trellised arbour, shaped like a sea-shell, with a decorative bulb hanging from its forward-curving roof. Garden chairs and a table are scattered about. A garbage pail on the ground next to the porch steps, a wire leaf-burner near it.

ON THE RISE: It is early Sunday morning. JOE KELLER is sitting in the sun reading the want ads of the Sunday paper, the other sections of which lie neatly on the ground beside him. Behind his back, inside the arbour, DOCTOR JIM BAYLISS is reading part of the paper at the table.

KELLER is nearing sixty. A heavy man of stolid mind and build, a business man these many years, but with the imprint of the machine-shop worker and boss still upon him. When he reads, when he speaks, when he listens, it is with the terrible concentration of the uneducated man for whom there is still wonder in many commonly known things, a man whose judgements must be dredged out of experience and a peasant-like common sense. A man among men.

5

DOCTOR BAYLISS *is nearing forty. A wry self-controlled man, an easy talker, but with a wisp of sadness that clings even to his self-effacing humour.*

AT CURTAIN, JIM *is standing at* L., *staring at the broken tree. He taps a pipe on it, blows through the pipe, feels in his pockets for tobacco, then speaks.*

JIM: Where's your tobacco?

KELLER: I think I left it on the table. [JIM *goes slowly to table on the arbour at* R., *finds a pouch, and sits there on the bench, filling his pipe.*] Gonna rain tonight.

JIM: Paper says so?

KELLER: Yeah, right here.

JIM: Then it can't rain.

[FRANK LUBEY *enters, from* R., *through a small space between the poplars.* FRANK *is thirty-two but balding. A pleasant, opinionated man, uncertain of himself, with a tendency toward peevishness when crossed, but always wanting it pleasant and neighbourly. He rather saunters in, leisurely, nothing to do. He does not notice* JIM *in the arbour. On his greeting,* JIM *does not bother looking up.*]

FRANK: Hya.

KELLER: Hello, Frank. What's doin'?

FRANK: Nothin'. Walking off my breakfast. [*Looks up at the sky*] That beautiful? Not a cloud.

KELLER [*looks up*]: Yeah, nice.

FRANK: Every Sunday ought to be like this.

KELLER [*indicating the sections beside him*]: Want the paper?

FRANK: What's the difference, it's all bad news. What's today's calamity?

KELLER: I don't know, I don't read the news part any more. It's more interesting in the want ads.

FRANK: Why, you trying to buy something?

KELLER: No, I'm just interested. To see what people want, y'know? For instance, here's a guy is lookin' for two Newfoundland dogs. Now what's he want with two Newfoundland dogs?

FRANK: That is funny.

KELLER: Here's another one. Wanted – Old Dictionaries. High prices paid. Now what's a man going to do with an old dictionary?

FRANK: Why not? Probably a book collector.

KELLER: You mean he'll make a living out of that?

FRANK: Sure, there's a lot of them.

KELLER [*shakes his head*]: All the kind of business goin' on. In my day, either you were a lawyer, or a doctor, or you worked in a shop. Now . . .

FRANK: Well, I was going to be a forester once.

KELLER: Well, that shows you; in my day, there was no such thing. [*Scanning the page, sweeping it with his hand*] You look at a page like this you realize how ignorant you are. [*Softly, with wonder, as he scans page*] Psss!

FRANK [*noticing tree*]: Hey, what happened to your tree?

KELLER: Ain't that awful? The wind must've got it last night. You heard the wind, didn't you?

FRANK: Yeah, I got a mess in my yard, too. [*Goes to tree*] What a pity. [*Turns to* KELLER] What'd Kate say?

KELLER: They're all asleep yet. I'm just waiting for her to see it.

FRANK [*struck*]: You know? – It's funny.

KELLER: What?

FRANK: Larry was born in August. He'd been twenty-seven this month. And his tree blows down.

KELLER [*touched*]: I'm surprised you remember his birthday, Frank. That's nice.

FRANK: Well, I'm working on his horoscope.

KELLER: How can you make him a horoscope? That's for the future, ain't it?

FRANK: Well, what I'm doing is this, see. Larry was reported missing on November 25th, right?

KELLER: Yeah?

FRANK: Well, then, we assume that if he was killed it was on November 25th. Now, what Kate wants . . .

KELLER: Oh, Kate asked you to make a horoscope?

FRANK: Yeah, what she wants to find out is whether November 25th was a favourable day for Larry.

KELLER: What is that, favourable day?

FRANK: Well, a favourable day for a person is a fortunate day, according to his stars. In other words it would be practically impossible for him to have died on his favourable day.

KELLER: Well, was that his favourable day? – November 25th?

FRANK: That's what I'm working on to find out. It takes time! See, the point is, if November 25th was his favourable day, then it's completely possible he's alive somewhere, because . . . I mean it's possible. [*He notices* JIM *now.* JIM *is looking at him as though at an idiot. To* JIM *– with an uncertain laugh*] I didn't even see you.

KELLER [*to* JIM]: Is he talkin' sense?

JIM: Him? He's all right. He's just completely out of his mind, that's all.

FRANK [*peeved*]: The trouble with you is, you don't *believe* in anything.

JIM: And your trouble is that you believe in *anything*. *You* didn't see my kid this morning, did you?

FRANK: No.

KELLER: Imagine? He walked off with his thermometer. Right out of his bag.

JIM [*gets up*]: What a problem. One look at a girl and he takes her temperature. [*Goes to driveway, looks upstage toward street.*]

FRANK: That boy's going to be a real doctor; he's smart.

JIM: Over my dead body he'll be a doctor. A good beginning, too.

FRANK. Why? It's an honourable profession.

JIM [*looks at him tiredly*]: Frank, will you stop talking like a civics book?

[KELLER *laughs.*]

FRANK: Why, I saw a movie a couple of weeks ago, reminded me of you. There was a doctor in that picture . . .

KELLER: Don Ameche!

FRANK: I think it was, yeah. And he worked in his basement discovering things. That's what you ought to do; you could help humanity, instead of . . .

JIM: I would love to help humanity on a Warner Brothers salary.

KELLER [*points at him, laughing*]: That's very good, Jim.

JIM [*looks toward house*]: Well, where's the beautiful girl was supposed to be here?

FRANK [*excited*]: Annie came?

KELLER: Sure, sleepin' upstairs. We picked her up on the one o'clock train last night. Wonderful thing. Girl leaves here, a scrawny kid. Couple of years go by, she's a regular woman. Hardly recognized her, and she was running in and out of this yard all her life. That was a very happy family used to live in your house, Jim.

JIM: Like to meet her. The block can use a pretty girl. In the whole neighbourhood there's not a damned thing to look at. [*Enter* SUE, JIM's *wife, from* L. *She is rounding forty, an overweight woman who fears it. On seeing her* JIM *wryly adds*] . . . Except my wife, of course.

SUE [*in same spirit*]: Mrs Adams is on the phone, you dog.

JIM [*to* KELLER]: Such is the condition which prevails [*going to his wife*], my love, my light . . .

SUE: Don't sniff around me. [*Points to their house,* L.] And give her a nasty answer. I can smell her perfume over the phone.

JIM: What's the matter with her now?

SUE: I don't know, dear. She sounds like she's in terrible pain – unless her mouth is full of candy.

JIM: Why don't you just tell her to lay down?

SUE: She enjoys it more when you tell her to lay down. And when are you going to see Mr Hubbard?

JIM: My dear; Mr Hubbard is not sick, and I have better things to do than to sit there and hold his hand.

SUE: It seems to me that for ten dollars you could hold his hand.

JIM [*to* KELLER]: If your son wants to play golf tell him I'm ready. [*Going* L.] Or if he'd like to take a trip around the world for about thirty years. [*He exits* L.]

KELLER: Why do you needle him? He's a doctor, women are supposed to call him up.

SUE: All I said was Mrs Adams is on the phone. Can I have some of your parsley?

KELLER: Yeah, sure. [*She goes* L. *to parsley box and pulls some parsley.*]
   You were a nurse too long, Susie. You're too . . . too . . . realistic.
SUE [*laughing, points at him*]: Now you said it!

   [*Enter* LYDIA LUBEY *from* R. *She is a robust, laughing girl of
   twenty-seven.*]

LYDIA: Frank, the toaster . . . [*Sees the others*] Hya.
KELLER: Hello!
LYDIA [*to* FRANK]: The toaster is off again.
FRANK: Well, plug it in, I just fixed it.
LYDIA [*kindly, but insistently*]: Please, dear, fix it back like it was
   before.
FRANK: I don't know why you can't learn to turn on a simple thing
   like a toaster! [FRANK *exits* R.]
SUE [*laughs*]: Thomas Edison.
LYDIA [*apologetically*]: He's really very handy. [*She sees broken tree*]
   Oh, did the wind get your tree?
KELLER: Yeah, last night.
LYDIA: Oh, what a pity. Annie get in?
KELLER: She'll be down soon. Wait'll you meet her, Sue, she's a
   knockout.
SUE: I should've been a man. People are always introducing me to
   beautiful women. [*To* JOE] Tell her to come over later; I imagine
   she'd like to see what we did with her house. And thanks. [SUE
   exits L.]
LYDIA: Is she still unhappy, Joe?
KELLER: Annie? I don't suppose she goes around dancing on her
   toes, but she seems to be over it.
LYDIA: She going to get married? Is there anybody . . . ?
KELLER: I suppose . . . say, it's a couple years already. She can't
   mourn a boy forever.
LYDIA: It's so strange . . . Annie's here and not even married. And I've
   got three babies. I always thought it'd be the other way around.
KELLER: Well, that's what a war does. I had two sons, now I got one.
   It changed all the tallies. In my day when you had sons it was an

honour. Today a doctor could make a million dollars if he could figure out a way to bring a boy into the world without a trigger finger.

LYDIA: You know, I was just reading . . .

[*Enter* CHRIS KELLER *from house, stands in doorway.*]

LYDIA: Hya, Chris . . .

[FRANK *shouts from off* R.]

FRANK: Lydia, come in here! If you want the toaster to work don't plug in the malted mixer.

LYDIA [*embarrassed, laughs*]: Did I . . . ?

FRANK: And the next time I fix something don't tell me I'm crazy! Now come in here!

LYDIA [*to* KELLER]: I'll never hear the end of this one.

KELLER [*calling to* FRANK]: So what's the difference? Instead of toast have a malted!

LYDIA: Sh! sh! [*She exits* R. *laughing.*]

[CHRIS *watches her off. He is thirty-two; like his father, solidly built, a listener. A man capable of immense affection and loyalty. He has a cup of coffee in one hand, part of a doughnut in the other.*]

KELLER: You want the paper?

CHRIS: That's all right, just the book section. [*He bends down and pulls out part of paper on porch floor.*]

KELLER: You're always reading the book section and you never buy a book.

CHRIS [*coming down to settee*]: I like to keep abreast of my ignorance. [*He sits on settee.*]

KELLER: What is that, every week a new book comes out?

CHRIS: Lot of new books.

KELLER: All different.

CHRIS: All different.

KELLER [*shakes his head, puts knife down on bench, takes oilstone up to the cabinet*]: Psss! Annie up yet?

CHRIS: Mother's giving her breakfast in the dining-room.

KELLER [*crosses*, D.S. *of stool, looking at broken tree*]: See what happened to the tree?

CHRIS [*without looking up*]: Yeah.

KELLER: What's Mother going to say?

[BERT *runs on from driveway. He is about eight. He jumps on stool, then on* KELLER's *back.*]

BERT: You're finally up.

KELLER [*swinging him around and putting him down*]: Ha! Bert's here! Where's Tommy? He's got his father's thermometer again.

BERT: He's taking a reading.

CHRIS: What!

BERT: But it's only oral.

KELLER: Oh, well, there's no harm in oral. So what's new this morning, Bert?

BERT: Nothin'. [*He goes to broken tree, walks around it.*]

KELLER: Then you couldn't've made a complete inspection of the block. In the beginning, when I first made you a policeman you used to come in every morning with something new. Now, nothin's ever new.

BERT: Except some kids from Thirtieth Street. They started kicking a can down the block, and I made them go away because you were sleeping.

KELLER: Now you're talkin', Bert. Now you're on the ball. First thing you know I'm liable to make you a detective.

BERT [*pulls him down by the lapel and whispers in his ear*]: Can I see the jail now?

KELLER: Seein' the jail ain't allowed, Bert. You know that.

BERT: Aw, I betcha there isn't even a jail. I don't see any bars on the cellar windows.

KELLER: Bert, on my word of honour, there's a jail in the basement. I showed you my gun, didn't I?

BERT: But that's a hunting gun.

KELLER: That's an arresting gun!

BERT: Then why don't you ever arrest anybody? Tommy said another dirty word to Doris yesterday, and you didn't even demote him.

KELLER [*he chuckles and winks at* CHRIS, *who is enjoying all this*]: Yeah, that's a dangerous character, that Tommy. [*Beckons him closer*] What word does he say?

BERT [*backing away quickly in great embarrassment*]: Oh, I can't say that.

KELLER [*grabs him by the shirt and pulls him back*]: Well, gimme an idea.

BERT: I can't. It's not a nice word.

KELLER: Just whisper it in my ear. I'll close my eyes. Maybe I won't even hear it.

BERT [*on tiptoe, puts his lips to* KELLER'*s ear, then in unbearable embarrassment steps back*]: I can't, Mr Keller.

CHRIS [*laughing*]: Don't make him do that.

KELLER: Okay, Bert. I take your word. Now go out, and keep both eyes peeled.

BERT [*interested*]: For what?

KELLER: For what! Bert, the whole neighbourhood is depending on you. A policeman don't ask questions. Now peel them eyes!

BERT [*mystified, but willing*]: Okay. [*He runs off* R. *back of arbour.*]

KELLER [*calling after him*]: And mum's the word, Bert.

BERT [*stops and sticks his head through the arbour*]: About what?

KELLER: Just in general. Be v-e-r-y careful.

BERT [*nods in bewilderment*]: Okay. [BERT *exits* D.R.]

KELLER [*laughs*]: I got all the kids crazy!

CHRIS: One of these days, they'll all come in here and beat your brains out.

KELLER: What's she going to say? Maybe we ought to tell her before she sees it.

CHRIS: She saw it.

KELLER: How could she see it? I was the first one up. She was still in bed.

CHRIS: She was out here when it broke.

KELLER: When?

CHRIS: About four this morning. [*Indicating window above them*] I heard it cracking and I woke up and looked out. She was standing right here when it cracked.

KELLER: What was she doing out here four in the morning?

CHRIS: I don't know. When it cracked she ran back into the house and cried in the kitchen.

KELLER: Did you talk to her?

CHRIS: No, I . . . I figured the best thing was to leave her alone.

[*Pause.*]

KELLER [*deeply touched*]: She cried hard?

CHRIS: I could hear her right through the floor of my room.

KELLER [*slight pause*]: What was she doing out here at that hour? [CHRIS *silent. An undertone of anger showing.*] She's dreaming about him again. She's walking around at night.

CHRIS: I guess she is.

KELLER: She's getting just like after he died. [*Slight pause.*] What's the meaning of that?

CHRIS: I don't know the meaning of it. [*Slight pause.*] But I know one thing, Dad. We've made a terrible mistake with Mother.

KELLER: What?

CHRIS: Being dishonest with her. That kind of thing always pays off, and now it's paying off.

KELLER: What do you mean, dishonest?

CHRIS: You know Larry's not coming back and I know it. Why do we allow her to go on thinking that we believe with her?

KELLER: What do you want to do, argue with her?

CHRIS: I don't want to argue with her, but it's time she realized that nobody believes Larry is alive any more. [KELLER *simply moves away, thinking, looking at the ground.*] Why shouldn't she dream of him, walk the nights waiting for him? Do we contradict her? Do we say straight out that we have no hope any more? That we haven't had any hope for years now?

KELLER [*frightened at the thought*]: You can't say that to her.

CHRIS: We've got to say it to her.

KELLER: How're you going to prove it? Can you prove it?

CHRIS: For God's sake, three years! Nobody comes back after three years. It's insane.

KELLER: To you it is, and to me. But not to her. You can talk yourself blue in the face, but there's no body and there's no grave, so where are you?

CHRIS: Sit down, Dad. I want to talk to you.

KELLER [looks at him searchingly a moment, and sitting . . .]: The trouble is the Goddam newspapers. Every month some boy turns up from nowhere, so the next one is going to be Larry, so . . .

CHRIS: All right, all right, listen to me. [Slight pause. KELLER sits on settee.] You know why I asked Annie here, don't you?

KELLER [he knows, but . . .]: Why?

CHRIS: You know.

KELLER: Well, I got an idea, but . . . What's the story?

CHRIS: I'm going to ask her to marry me.

[Slight pause.]

KELLER [nods]: Well, that's only your business, Chris.

CHRIS: You know it's not only my business.

KELLER: What do you want me to do? You're old enough to know your own mind.

CHRIS [asking, annoyed]: Then it's all right, I'll go ahead with it?

KELLER: Well, you want to be sure Mother isn't going to . . .

CHRIS: Then it isn't just my business.

KELLER: I'm just sayin' . . .

CHRIS: Sometimes you infuriate me, you know that? Isn't it your business, too, if I tell this to Mother and she throws a fit about it? You have such a talent for ignoring things.

KELLER: I ignore what I gotta ignore. The girl is Larry's girl . . .

CHRIS: She's not Larry's girl.

KELLER: From Mother's point of view he is not dead and you have no right to take his girl. [Slight pause.] Now you can go on from there if you know where to go, but I'm tellin' you I don't know where to go. See? I don't know. Now what can I do for you?

CHRIS: I don't know why it is, but every time I reach out for something I want, I have to pull back because other people will suffer. My whole bloody life, time after time after time.

KELLER: You're a considerate fella, there's nothing wrong in that.

CHRIS: To hell with that.

KELLER: Did you ask Annie yet?

CHRIS: I wanted to get this settled first.

KELLER: How do you know she'll marry you? Maybe she feels the same way Mother does?

CHRIS: Well, if she does, then that's the end of it. From her letters I think she's forgotten him. I'll find out. And then we'll thrash it out with Mother? Right? Dad, don't avoid me.

KELLER: The trouble is, you don't see enough women. You never did.

CHRIS: So what? I'm not fast with women.

KELLER: I don't see why it has to be Annie . . .

CHRIS: Because it is.

KELLER. That's a good answer, but it don't answer anything. You haven't seen her since you went to war. It's five years.

CHRIS. I can't help it. I know her best. I was brought up next door to her. These years when I think of someone for my wife, I think of Annie. What do you want, a diagram?

KELLER. I don't want a diagram . . . I . . . I'm . . . She thinks he's coming back, Chris. You marry that girl and you're pronouncing him dead. Now what's going to happen to Mother? Do you know? I don't!

[*Pause.*]

CHRIS: All right, then, Dad.

KELLER [*thinking* CHRIS *has retreated*]: Give it some more thought.

CHRIS: I've given it three years of thought. I'd hoped that if I waited, Mother would forget Larry and then we'd have a regular wedding and everything happy. But if that can't happen here, then I'll have to get out.

KELLER: What the hell is *this*?

CHRIS: I'll get out. I'll get married and live someplace else. Maybe in New York.

KELLER: Are you crazy?

CHRIS: I've been a good son too long, a good sucker. I'm through with it.

KELLER: You've got a business here, what the hell is this?

CHRIS: The business! The business doesn't inspire me.

KELLER: Must you be inspired?

CHRIS: Yes. I like it an hour a day. If I have to grub for money all day long at least at evening I want it beautiful. I want a family, I want some kids, I want to build something I can give myself to. Annie is in the middle of that. Now . . . where do I find it?

KELLER: You mean . . . [*Goes to him*] Tell me something, you mean you'd leave the business?

CHRIS: Yes. On this I would.

KELLER [*pause*]: Well . . . you don't want to think like that.

CHRIS: Then help me stay here.

KELLER: All right, but . . . but don't think like that. Because what the hell did I work for? That's only for you, Chris, the whole shootin'-match is for you!

CHRIS: I know that, Dad. Just you help me stay here.

KELLER [*puts a fist up to* CHRIS's *jaw*]: But don't think that way, you hear me?

CHRIS: I am thinking that way.

KELLER [*lowering his hand*]: I don't understand you, do I?

CHRIS: No, you don't. I'm a pretty tough guy.

KELLER: Yeah. I can see that.

[MOTHER *appears on porch. She is in her early fifties, a woman of uncontrolled inspirations, and an overwhelming capacity for love.*]

MOTHER: Joe?

CHRIS [*going toward porch*]: Hello, Mom.

MOTHER [*indicating house behind her. To* KELLER]: Did you take a bag from under the sink?

KELLER: Yeah, I put it in the pail.

MOTHER: Well, get it out of the pail. That's my potatoes.

[CHRIS *bursts out laughing – goes up into alley.*]

KELLER [*laughing*]: I thought it was garbage.

MOTHER: Will you do me a favour, Joe? Don't be helpful.

KELLER: I can afford another bag of potatoes.

MOTHER: Minnie scoured that pail in boiling water last night. It's cleaner than your teeth.

KELLER: And I don't understand why, after I worked forty years and I got a maid, why I have to take out the garbage.

MOTHER: If you would make up your mind that every bag in the kitchen isn't full of garbage you wouldn't be throwing out my vegetables. Last time it was the onions.

[CHRIS *comes on, hands her bag.*]

KELLER: I don't like garbage in the house.

MOTHER: Then don't eat. [*She goes into the kitchen with bag.*]

CHRIS: That settles you for today.

KELLER: Yeah, I'm in last place again. I don't know, once upon a time I used to think that when I got money again I would have a maid and my wife would take it easy. Now I got money, and I got a maid, and my wife is workin' for the maid. [*He sits in one of the chairs.* MOTHER *comes out on last line. She carries a pot of stringbeans.*]

MOTHER: It's her day off, what are you crabbing about?

CHRIS [*to* MOTHER]: Isn't Annie finished eating?

MOTHER [*looking around preoccupiedly at yard*]: She'll be right out. [*Moves*] That wind did some job on this place. [*Of the tree*] So much for that, thank God.

KELLER [*indicating chair beside him*]: Sit down, take it easy.

MOTHER [*she presses her hand to top of her head*]: I've got such a funny pain on the top of my head.

CHRIS: Can I get you an aspirin?

MOTHER [*picks a few petals off ground, stands there smelling them in her hand, then sprinkles them over plants*]: No more roses. It's so funny . . . everything decides to happen at the same time. This month is his birthday; his tree blows down, Annie comes. Everything that happened seems to be coming back. I was just down the cellar, and what do I stumble over? His baseball glove. I haven't seen it in a century.

CHRIS: Don't you think Annie looks well?

MOTHER: Fine. There's no question about it. She's a beauty . . . I still don't know what brought her here. Not that I'm not glad to see her, but . . .

CHRIS: I just thought we'd all like to see each other again. [MOTHER *just looks at him, nodding ever so slightly – almost as though admitting something.*] And I wanted to see her myself.

MOTHER [*her nods halt. To* KELLER]: The only thing is I think her nose got longer. But I'll always love that girl. She's one that didn't jump into bed with somebody else as soon as it happened with her fella.

KELLER [*as though that were impossible for* ANNIE]: Oh, what're you . . . ?

MOTHER: Never mind. Most of them didn't wait till the telegrams were opened. I'm just glad she came, so you can see I'm not *completely* out of my mind. [*Sits, and rapidly breaks stringbeans in the pot.*]

CHRIS: Just because she isn't married doesn't mean she's been mourning Larry.

MOTHER [*with an undercurrent of observation*]: Why then isn't she?

CHRIS [*a little flustered*]: Well . . . it could've been any number of things.

MOTHER [*directly at him*]: Like what, for instance?

CHRIS [*embarrassed, but standing his ground*]: I don't know. Whatever it is. Can I get you an aspirin? [MOTHER *puts her hand to her head.*]

MOTHER [*she gets up and goes aimlessly toward the trees on rising*]: It's not like a headache.

KELLER: You don't sleep, that's why. She's wearing out more bedroom slippers than shoes.

MOTHER: I had a terrible night. [*She stops moving.*] I never had a night like that.

CHRIS [*looks at* KELLER]: What was it, Mom? Did you dream?

MOTHER: More, more than a dream.

CHRIS [*hesitantly*]: About Larry?

MOTHER: I was fast asleep, and . . . [*Raising her arm over the audience*] Remember the way he used to fly low past the house when he was in training? When we used to see his face in the cockpit going by? That's the way I saw him. Only high up. Way, way up, where the clouds are. He was so real I could reach out and touch him. And suddenly he started to fall. And crying, crying to me . . . Mom, Mom! I could hear him like he was in the room. Mom! . . . it was his voice! If I could touch him I knew I could stop him, if I could only . . . [*Breaks off, allowing her outstretched hand to fall*] I woke up and it was so funny . . . The wind . . . it was like the roaring of his engine. I came out here . . . I must've still been half asleep. I could hear that roaring like he was going by. The tree snapped right in front of me . . . and I like . . . came awake. [*She is looking at tree. She suddenly realizes something, turns with a reprimanding finger shaking slightly at* KELLER.] See? We should never have planted that tree. I said so in the first place; it was too soon to plant a tree for him.

CHRIS [*alarmed*]: Too soon!

MOTHER [*angering*]: We rushed into it. Everybody was in such a hurry to bury him. I *said* not to plant it yet. [*To* KELLER] I *told* you to . . . !

CHRIS: Mother, Mother! [*She looks into his face.*] The wind blew it down. What significance has that got? What are you talking about? Mother, please . . . Don't go through it all again, will you? It's no good, it doesn't accomplish anything. I've been thinking, y'know? – maybe we ought to put our minds to forgetting him?

MOTHER: That's the third time you've said that this week.

CHRIS: Because it's not right; we never took up our lives again. We're like at a railroad station waiting for a train that never comes in.

MOTHER [*presses top of her head*]: Get me an aspirin, heh?

CHRIS: Sure, and let's break out of this, heh, Mom? I thought the four of us might go out to dinner a couple of nights, maybe go dancing out at the shore.

MOTHER: Fine. [*To* KELLER] We can do it tonight.

KELLER: Swell with me!

CHRIS: Sure, let's have some fun. [*To* MOTHER] You'll start with this aspirin. [*He goes up and into house with new spirit. Her smile vanishes.*]

MOTHER [*with an accusing undertone*]: Why did he invite her here?

KELLER: Why does that bother you?

MOTHER: She's been in New York three and a half years, why all of a sudden . . . ?

KELLER: Well, maybe . . . maybe he just wanted to see her . . .

MOTHER: Nobody comes seven hundred miles 'just to see'.

KELLER: What do you mean? He lived next door to the girl all his life, why shouldn't he want to see her again? [MOTHER *looks at him critically.*] Don't look at me like that, he didn't tell me any more than he told you.

MOTHER [*a warning and a question*]: He's not going to marry her.

KELLER: How do you know he's even thinking of it?

MOTHER: It's got that about it.

KELLER [*sharply watching her reaction*]: Well? So what?

MOTHER [*alarmed*]: What's going on here, Joe?

KELLER: Now listen, kid . . .

MOTHER [*avoiding contact with him*]: She's not his girl, Joe; she knows she's not.

KELLER: You can't read her mind.

MOTHER: Then why is she still single? New York is full of men, why isn't she married? [*Pause.*] Probably a hundred people told her she's foolish, but she's waited.

KELLER: How do you know why she waited?

MOTHER: She knows what I know, that's why. She's faithful as a rock. In my worst moments, I think of her waiting, and I know again that I'm right.

KELLER: Look, it's a nice day. What are we arguing for?

MOTHER [*warningly*]: Nobody in this house dast take her faith away, Joe. Strangers might. But not his father, not his brother.

KELLER [*exasperated*]: What do you want me to do? What do you want?

MOTHER: I want you to act like he's coming back. Both of you. Don't think I haven't noticed you since Chris invited her. I won't stand for any nonsense.

KELLER: But, Kate . . .

MOTHER: Because if he's not coming back, then I'll kill myself! Laugh. Laugh at me. [*She points to tree*] But why did that happen the very night she came back? Laugh, but there are meanings in such things. She goes to sleep in his room and his memorial breaks in pieces. Look at it; look. [*She sits on bench at his* L.] Joe . . .

KELLER: Calm yourself.

MOTHER: Believe with me, Joe. I can't stand all alone.

KELLER: Calm yourself.

MOTHER: Only last week a man turned up in Detroit, missing longer than Larry. You read it yourself.

KELLER: All right, all right, calm yourself.

MOTHER: You above all have got to believe, you . . .

KELLER [*rises*]: Why me above all?

MOTHER: . . . Just don't stop believing . . .

KELLER: What does that mean, me above all?

[BERT *comes rushing on from* L.]

BERT: Mr Keller! Say, Mr Keller . . . [*Pointing up driveway*] Tommy just said it again!

KELLER [*not remembering any of it*]: Said what? . . . Who? . . .

BERT: The dirty word.

KELLER: Oh. Well . . .

BERT: Gee, aren't you going to arrest him? I warned him.

MOTHER [*with suddenness*]: Stop that, Bert. Go home. [BERT *backs up, as she advances.*] There's no jail here.

KELLER [*as though to say, 'Oh-what-the-hell-let-him-believe-there-is'*]: Kate . . .

MOTHER [*turning on* KELLER, *furiously*]: There's no jail here! I want you to stop that jail business! [*He turns, shamed, but peeved.*]

BERT [*past her to* KELLER]: He's right across the street . . .

MOTHER: Go home, Bert. [BERT *turns around and goes up driveway. She is shaken. Her speech is bitten off, extremely urgent.*] I want you to stop that, Joe. That whole jail business!

KELLER [*alarmed, therefore angered*]: Look at you, look at you shaking.

MOTHER [*trying to control herself, moving about clasping her hands*]: I can't help it.

KELLER: What have I got to hide? What the hell is the matter with you, Kate?

MOTHER: I didn't say you had anything to hide, I'm just telling you to stop it! Now stop it! [*As* ANN *and* CHRIS *appear on porch.* ANN *is twenty-six, gentle but despite herself capable of holding fast to what she knows.* CHRIS *opens door for her.*]

ANN: Hya, Joe! [*She leads off a general laugh that is not self-conscious because they know one another too well.*]

CHRIS [*bringing* ANN *down, with an outstretched, chivalric arm*]: Take a breath of that air, kid. You never get air like that in New York.

MOTHER [*genuinely overcome with it*]: Annie, where did you get that dress!

ANN: I couldn't resist. I'm taking it right off before I ruin it. [*Swings around*] How's that for three weeks' salary?

MOTHER [*to* KELLER]: Isn't she the most . . . ? [*To* ANN] It's gorgeous, simply gor . . .

CHRIS [*to* MOTHER]: No kidding, now, isn't she the prettiest gal you ever saw?

MOTHER [*caught short by his obvious admiration, she finds herself reaching out for a glass of water and aspirin in his hand, and . . .*]: You gained a little weight, didn't you, darling? [*She gulps pill and drinks.*]

ANN: It comes and goes.

KELLER: Look how nice her legs turned out!

ANN [*she runs to fence, L.*]: Boy, the poplars got thick, didn't they?

KELLER [*moves U. to settee and sits*]: Well, it's three years, Annie. We're gettin' old, kid.

MOTHER: How does Mom like New York? [ANN *keeps looking through trees.*]

ANN [*a little hurt*]: Why'd they take our hammock away?

KELLER: Oh, no, it broke. Couple of years ago.

MOTHER: What broke? He had one of his light lunches and flopped into it.

ANN [*she laughs and turns back toward* JIM's *yard . . .*]: Oh, excuse me! [JIM *has come to fence and is looking over it. He is smoking a cigar. As she cries out, he comes on around on stage.*]

JIM: How do you do. [*To* CHRIS] She looks very intelligent!

CHRIS: Ann, this is Jim . . . Doctor Bayliss.

ANN [*shaking* JIM's *hand*]: Oh sure, he writes a lot about you.

JIM: Don't believe it. He likes everybody. In the Battalion he was known as Mother McKeller.

ANN: I can believe it . . . You know—? [*To* MOTHER] It's so strange seeing him come out of that yard. [*To* CHRIS] I guess I never grew up. It almost seems that Mom and Pop are in there now. And you and my brother doing Algebra, and Larry trying to copy my home-work. Gosh, those dear dead days beyond recall.

JIM: Well, I hope that doesn't mean you want me to move out?

SUE [*calling from off* L.]: Jim, come in here! Mr Hubbard is on the phone!

JIM: I told you I don't want . . .

SUE [*commandingly sweet*]: Please, dear! Please!!

JIM [*resigned*]: All right, Susie, [*trailing off*] all right, all right . . . [*To* ANN] I've only met you, Ann, but if I may offer you a piece of advice – When you marry, never – even in your mind – never count your husband's money.

SUE [*from off*]: Jim?!

JIM: At once! [*Turns and goes* L.] At once. [*He exits* L.]

MOTHER [ANN *is looking at her. She speaks meaningfully*]: I told her to take up the guitar. It'd be a common interest for them. [*They laugh.*] Well, he loves the guitar!

ANN [*as though to overcome* MOTHER, *she becomes suddenly lively, crosses to* KELLER *on settee, sits on his lap*]: Let's eat at the shore tonight! Raise some hell around here, like we used to before Larry went!

MOTHER [*emotionally*]: You think of him! You see? [*Triumphantly*] She thinks of him!

ANN [*with an uncomprehending smile*]: What do you mean, Kate?

MOTHER: Nothing. Just that you . . . remember him, he's in your thoughts.

ANN: That's a funny thing to say; how could I help remembering him?

MOTHER [*it is drawing to a head the wrong way for her; she starts anew. She rises and comes to* ANN]: Did you hang up your things?

ANN: Yeah . . . [*To* CHRIS] Say, you've sure gone in for clothes. I could hardly find room in the closet.

MOTHER: No, don't you remember? That's Larry's room.

ANN: You mean . . . they're Larry's?

MOTHER: Didn't you recognize them?

ANN [*slowly rising, a little embarrassed*]: Well, it never occurred to me that you'd . . . I mean the shoes are all shined.

MOTHER: Yes, dear. [*Slight pause.* ANN *can't stop staring at her.* MOTHER *breaks it by speaking with the relish of gossip, putting her arm around* ANN *and walking* S.L. *with her.*] For so long I've been aching for a nice conversation with you, Annie. Tell me something.

ANN: What?

MOTHER: I don't know. Something nice.

CHRIS [*wryly*]: She means do you go out much?

MOTHER: Oh, shut up.

KELLER: And are any of them serious?

MOTHER [*laughing, sits in her chair*]: Why don't you both choke?

KELLER: Annie, you can't go into a restaurant with that woman any more. In five minutes thirty-nine strange people are sitting at the table telling her their life story.

MOTHER: If I can't ask Annie a personal question . . .

KELLER: Askin' is all right, but don't beat her over the head. You're beatin' her, you're beatin' her. [*They are laughing.*]

ANN [*to* MOTHER. *Takes pan of beans off stool, puts them on floor under chair and sits*]: Don't let them bulldoze you. Ask me anything you like. What do you want to know, Kate? Come on, let's gossip.

MOTHER [*to* CHRIS *and* KELLER]: She's the only one is got any sense. [*To* ANN] Your mother . . . she's not getting a divorce, heh?

ANN: No, she's calmed down about it now. I think when he gets out they'll probably live together. In New York, of course.

MOTHER: That's fine. Because your father is still . . . I mean he's a decent man after all is said and done.

ANN: I don't care. She can take him back if she likes.

MOTHER: And you? You . . . [*shakes her head negatively*] . . . go out much?

[*Slight pause.*]

ANN [*delicately*]: You mean am I still waiting for him?

MOTHER: Well, no, I don't expect you to wait for him but . . .

ANN [*kindly*]: But that's what you mean, isn't it?

MOTHER: . . . Well . . . yes.

ANN: Well, I'm not, Kate.

MOTHER [*faintly*]: You're not?

ANN: Isn't it ridiculous? You don't really imagine he's . . . ?

MOTHER: I know, dear, but don't say it's ridiculous, because the papers were full of it; I don't know about New York, but there was half a page about a man missing even longer than Larry, and he turned up from Burma.

CHRIS [*coming to* ANN]: He couldn't have wanted to come home very badly, Mom.

MOTHER: Don't be so smart.

CHRIS: You can have a helluva time in Burma.

ANN [*rises and swings around in back of* CHRIS]: So I've heard.

CHRIS: Mother, I'll bet you money that you're the only woman in the country who after three years is still . . .

MOTHER: You're sure?

CHRIS: Yes, I am.

MOTHER: Well, if you're sure then you're sure. [*She turns her head away an instant.*] They don't say it on the radio but I'm sure that in the dark at night they're still waiting for their sons.

CHRIS: Mother, you're absolutely—

MOTHER [*waving him off*]: Don't be so damned smart! Now stop it! [*Slight pause.*] There are just a few things you *don't* know. All of you. And I'll tell you one of them, Annie. Deep, deep in your heart you've always been waiting for him.

ANN [*resolutely*]: No, Kate.

MOTHER [*with increasing demand*]: But deep in your heart, Annie!

CHRIS: She ought to know, shouldn't she?

MOTHER: Don't let them tell you what to think. Listen to your heart. Only your heart.

ANN: Why does your heart tell you he's alive?

MOTHER: Because he has to be.

ANN: But why, Kate?

MOTHER [*going to her*]: Because certain things have to be, and certain things can never be. Like the sun has to rise, it has to be. That's why there's God. Otherwise anything could happen. But there's God, so certain things can never happen. I would know, Annie – just like I knew the day he [*indicates* CHRIS] went into that terrible battle. Did he write me? Was it in the papers? No, but that morning I couldn't raise my head off the pillow. Ask Joe. Suddenly, I knew! I knew! And he was nearly killed that day. Ann, you *know* I'm right!

ANN [*she stands there in silence, then turns trembling, going upstage*]: No, Kate.

MOTHER: I have to have some tea.

[FRANK *appears from* L. *carrying ladder.*]

FRANK: Annie! [*Coming down*] How are you, gee whiz!

ANN [*taking his hand*]: Why, Frank, you're losing your hair.

KELLER: He's got responsibility.

FRANK: Gee whiz!

KELLER: Without Frank the stars wouldn't know when to come out.

FRANK [*laughs. To* ANN]: You look more womanly. You've matured. You . . .

KELLER: Take it easy, Frank, you're a married man.

ANN [*as they laugh*]: You still haberdashering?

FRANK: Why not? Maybe I too can get to be president. How's your brother? Got his degree, I hear.

ANN: Oh, George has his own office now!

FRANK: Don't say! [*Funereally*] And your dad? Is he . . . ?

ANN [*abruptly*]: Fine. I'll be in to see Lydia.

FRANK [*sympathetically*]: How about it, does Dad expect a parole soon?

ANN [*with growing ill-ease*]: I really don't know, I . . .

FRANK [*staunchly defending her father for her sake*]: I mean because I feel, y'know, that if an intelligent man like your father is put in prison, there ought to be a law that says either you execute him, or let him go after a year.

CHRIS [*interrupting*]: Want a hand with that ladder, Frank?

FRANK [*taking cue*]: That's all right, I'll . . . [*Picks up ladder*] I'll finish the horoscope tonight, Kate. [*Embarrassed*] See you later, Ann, you look wonderful. [*He exits* R. *They look at* ANN.]

ANN [*to* CHRIS, *as she sits slowly on stool*]: Haven't they stopped talking about Dad?

CHRIS [*comes down and sits on arm of chair*]: Nobody talks about him any more.

KELLER [*rises and comes to her*]: Gone and forgotten, kid.

ANN: Tell me. Because I don't want to meet anybody on the block if they're going to . . .

CHRIS: I don't want you to worry about it.

ANN [*to* KELLER]: Do they still remember the case, Joe? Do they talk about you?

KELLER: The only one still talks about it is my wife.

MOTHER: That's because you keep on playing policeman with the kids. All their parents hear out of you is jail, jail, jail.

KELLER: Actually what happened was that when I got home from the penitentiary the kids got very interested in me. You know kids. I was [*laughs*] like the expert on the jail situation. And as time passed they got it confused and . . . I ended up a detective. [*Laughs.*]

MOTHER: Except that *they* didn't get it confused. [*To* ANN] He hands out police badges from the Post Toasties boxes. [*They laugh.*]

ANN [*looking wondrously at them, happily. She rises and comes to* KELLER, *putting her arm around his shoulder*]: Gosh, it's wonderful to hear you laughing about it.

CHRIS: Why, what'd you expect?

ANN: The last thing I remember on this block was one word – 'Murderers!' Remember that, Kate? . . . Mrs Hammond standing in front of our house and yelling that word . . . She's still around, I suppose?

MOTHER: They're all still around.

KELLER: Don't listen to her. Every Saturday night the whole gang is playin' poker in this arbour. All the ones who yelled murderer takin' my money now.

MOTHER: Don't Joe, she's a sensitive girl, don't fool her. [*To* ANN]

They still remember about Dad. It's different with him – [*indicates* JOE] – he was exonerated, your father's still there. That's why I wasn't so enthusiastic about your coming. Honestly, I know how sensitive you are, and I told Chris, I said . . .

KELLER: Listen, you do like I did and you'll be all right. The day I come home, I got out of my car; – but not in front of the house . . . on the corner. You should've been here, Annie, and you too, Chris; you'd-a seen something. Everybody knew I was getting out that day; the porches were loaded. Picture it now; none of them believed I was innocent. The story was, I pulled a fast one getting myself exonerated. So I get out of my car, and I walk down the street. But very slow. And with a smile. The beast! I was the beast; the guy who sold cracked cylinder heads to the Army Air Force; the guy who made twenty-one P-40's crash in Australia. Kid, walkin' down the street that day I was guilty as hell. Except I wasn't, and there was a court paper in my pocket to prove I wasn't, and I walked . . . past . . . the porches. Result? Fourteen months later I had one of the best shops in the state again, a respected man again; bigger than ever.

CHRIS [*with admiration*]: Joe McGuts.

KELLER [*now with great force*]: That's the only way you lick 'em is guts! [*To* ANN] The worst thing you did was to move away from here. You made it tough for your father when he gets out. That's why I tell you, I like to see him move back right on this block.

MOTHER [*pained*]: How could they move back?

KELLER: It ain't gonna end *till* they move back! [*To* ANN] Till people play cards with him again, and talk with him, and smile with him – you play cards with a man you know he can't be a murderer. And the next time you write him I like you to tell him just what I said. [ANN *simply stares at him.*] You hear me?

ANN [*surprised*]: Don't you hold anything against him?

KELLER: Annie, I never believed in crucifying people.

ANN [*mystified*]: But he was your partner, he dragged you through the mud . . .

KELLER: Well, he ain't my sweetheart, but you gotta forgive, don't you?

ANN: You, either, Kate? Don't you feel any . . . ?

KELLER [*to* ANN]: The next time you write Dad . . .

ANN: I don't write him.

KELLER [*struck*]: Well every now and then you . . .

ANN [*a little ashamed, but determined*]: No, I've *never* written to him. Neither has my brother. [*To* CHRIS] Say, do you feel this way, too?

CHRIS: He murdered twenty-one pilots.

KELLER: What the hell kinda talk is that?

MOTHER: That's not a thing to say about a man.

ANN: What else can you say? When they took him away I followed him, went to him every visiting day. I was crying all the time. Until the news came about Larry. Then I realized. It's wrong to pity a man like that. Father or no father, there's only one way to look at him. He knowingly shipped out parts that would crash an airplane. And how do you know Larry wasn't one of them?

MOTHER: I was waiting for that. [*Going to her*] As long as you're here, Annie, I want to ask you never to say that again.

ANN: You surprise me. I thought you'd be mad at him.

MOTHER: What your father did had nothing to do with Larry. Nothing.

ANN: But we can't know that.

MOTHER [*striving for control*]: As long as you're here!

ANN [*perplexed*]: But, Kate . . .

MOTHER: Put that out of your head!

KELLER: Because . . .

MOTHER [*quickly to* KELLER]: That's all, that's enough. [*Places her hand on her head.*] Come inside now, and have some tea with me. [*She turns and goes up steps.*]

KELLER [*to* ANN]: The one thing you . . .

MOTHER [*sharply*]: He's not dead, so there's no argument! Now come!

KELLER [*angrily*]: In a minute! [MOTHER *turns and goes into house.*] Now look, Annie . . .

CHRIS: All right, Dad, forget it.

KELLER: No, she dasn't feel that way. Annie . . .

CHRIS: I'm sick of the whole subject, now cut it out.

KELLER: You want her to go on like this? [*To* ANN] Those cylinder heads went into P-40's only. What's the matter with you? You know Larry never flew a P-40.

CHRIS: So who flew those P-40's, pigs?

KELLER: The man was a fool, but don't make a murderer out of him. You got no sense? Look what it does to her! [*To* ANN] Listen, you gotta appreciate what was doin' in that shop in the war. The both of you! It was a madhouse. Every half hour the Major callin' for cylinder heads, they were whippin' us with the telephone. The trucks were hauling them away hot, damn near. I mean just try to see it human, see it human. All of a sudden a batch comes out with a crack. That happens, that's the business. A fine, hairline crack. All right, so . . . so he's a little man, your father, always scared of loud voices. What'll the Major say? – Half a day's production shot . . . What'll I say? You know what I mean? Human. [*He pauses.*] So he takes out his tools and he . . . covers over the cracks. All right . . . that's bad, it's wrong, but that's what a little man does. If I could have gone in that day I'd a told him – junk 'em, Steve, we can afford it. But alone he was afraid. But I know he meant no harm. He believed they'd hold up a hundred percent. That's a mistake, but it ain't murder. You mustn't feel that way about him. You understand me? It ain't right.

ANN [*she regards him a moment*]: Joe, let's forget it.

KELLER: Annie, the day the news came about Larry he was in the next cell to mine . . . Dad. And he cried, Annie . . . he cried half the night.

ANN [*touched*]: He shoulda cried all night.

[*Slight pause.*]

KELLER [*almost angered*]: Annie, I do not understand why you . . . !

CHRIS [*breaking in – with nervous urgency*]: Are you going to stop it?!

ANN: Don't yell at him. He just wants everybody happy.

KELLER [*clasps her around waist, smiling*]: That's my sentiments. Can you stand steak?

CHRIS: And champagne!

KELLER: Now you're operatin'! I'll call Swanson's for a table! Big time tonight, Annie!

ANN: Can't scare me.

KELLER [*to* CHRIS, *pointing at* ANN]: I like that girl. Wrap her up. [*They laugh. Goes up porch.*] You got nice legs, Annie! . . . I want to see everybody drunk tonight. [*Pointing to* CHRIS] Look at him, he's blushin'! [*He exits, laughing, into house.*]

CHRIS [*calling after him*]: Drink your tea, Casanova. [*He turns to* ANN.] Isn't he a great guy?

ANN: You're the only one I know who loves his parents!

CHRIS: I know. It went out of style, didn't it?

ANN [*with a sudden touch of sadness*]: It's all right. It's a good thing. [*She looks about.*] You know? It's lovely here. The air is sweet.

CHRIS [*hopefully*]: You're not sorry you came?

ANN: Not sorry, no. But I'm . . . not going to stay . . .

CHRIS: Why?

ANN: In the first place, your mother as much as told me to go.

CHRIS: Well . . .

ANN: You saw that . . . and then you . . . you've been kind of . . .

CHRIS: What?

ANN: Well . . . kind of embarrassed ever since I got here.

CHRIS: The trouble is I planned on kind of sneaking up on you over a period of a week or so. But they take it for granted that we're all set.

ANN: I knew they would. Your mother anyway.

CHRIS: How did you know?

ANN: From *her* point of view, why else would I come?

CHRIS: Well . . . would you want to? [ANN *studies him.*] I guess you know this is why I asked you to come.

ANN: I guess this is why I came.

CHRIS: Ann, I love you. I love you a great deal. [*Finally*] I love you. [*Pause. She waits.*] I have no imagination . . . that's all I know to tell you. [ANN, *waiting, ready*] I'm embarrassing you. I didn't want to tell it to you here. I wanted some place we'd never been; a place where we'd be brand new to each other . . . You feel it's wrong here, don't you? This yard, this chair? I want you to be ready for me. I don't want to win you away from anything.

ANN [*putting her arms around him*]: Oh, Chris, I've been ready a long, long time!

CHRIS: Then he's gone forever. You're sure.

ANN: I almost got married two years ago.

CHRIS: . . . why didn't you?

ANN: You started to write to me . . .

[*Slight pause.*]

CHRIS: You felt something that far back?

ANN: Every day since!

CHRIS: Ann, why didn't you let me know?

ANN: I was waiting for you, Chris. Till then you never wrote. And when you did, what did you say? You sure can be ambiguous, you know.

CHRIS [*he looks towards house, then at her, trembling*]: Give me a kiss, Ann. Give me a . . . [*They kiss.*] God, I kissed you, Annie, I kissed Annie. How long, how long I've been waiting to kiss you!

ANN: I'll never forgive you. Why did you wait all these years? All I've done is sit and wonder if I was crazy for thinking of you.

CHRIS: Annie, we're going to live now! I'm going to make you so happy. [*He kisses her, but without their bodies touching.*]

ANN [*a little embarrassed*]: Not like that you're not.

CHRIS: I kissed you . . .

ANN: Like Larry's brother. Do it like you, Chris. [*He breaks away from her abruptly.*] What is it, Chris?

CHRIS: Let's drive some place . . . I want to be alone with you.

ANN: No . . . what is it, Chris, your mother?

CHRIS: No . . . nothing like that . . .

ANN: Then what's wrong? . . . Even in your letters, there was something ashamed.

CHRIS: Yes. I suppose I have been. But it's going from me.

ANN: You've got to tell me –

CHRIS: I don't know how to start. [*He takes her hand. He speaks quietly, factually at first.*]

ANN: It wouldn't work this way.

[*Slight pause.*]

CHRIS: It's all mixed up with so many other things . . . You remember, overseas, I was in command of a company?

ANN: Yeah, sure.

CHRIS: Well, I lost them.

ANN: How many?

CHRIS: Just about all.

ANN: Oh, gee!

CHRIS: It takes a little time to toss that off. Because they weren't just men. For instance, one time it'd been raining several days and this kid came to me, and gave me his last pair of dry socks. Put them in my pocket. That's only a little thing . . . but . . . that's the kind of guys I had. They didn't die; they killed themselves for each other. I mean that exactly; a little more selfish and they'd've been here today. And I got an idea – watching them go down. Everything was being destroyed, see, but it seemed to me that one new thing was made. A kind of . . . responsibility. Man for man. You understand me? – To show that, to bring that on to the earth again like some kind of a monument and everyone would feel it standing there, behind him, and it would make a difference to him. [*Pause.*] And then I came home and it was incredible. I . . . there was no meaning in it here; the whole thing to them was a kind of a – bus accident. I went to work with Dad, and that rat-race again. I felt . . . what you said . . . ashamed somehow. Because nobody was changed at all. It seemed to make suckers out of a lot of guys. I felt wrong to be alive, to open the bank-book, to drive the new car, to see the new refrigerator. I mean you can take those things out of a war, but when you drive that car you've got to know that it came out of the love a man can have for a man, you've got to be a little better because of that. Otherwise what you have is really loot, and there's blood on it. I didn't want to take any of it. And I guess that included you.

ANN: And you still feel that way?

CHRIS: I want you now, Annie.

ANN: Because you mustn't feel that way any more. Because you have a right to whatever you have. Everything, Chris, understand that? To me, too . . . And the money, there's nothing wrong in your money. Your father put hundreds of planes in the air, you should be proud. A man should be paid for that . . .

CHRIS: Oh Annie, Annie . . . I'm going to make a fortune for you!

KELLER [*offstage*]: Hello . . . Yes. Sure.

ANN [*laughing softly*]: What'll I do with a fortune . . . ?

[*They kiss.* KELLER *enters from house.*]

KELLER [*thumbing toward house*]: Hey, Ann, your brother . . . [*They step apart shyly.* KELLER *comes down, and wryly* . . .] What is this, Labor Day?

CHRIS [*waving him away, knowing the kidding will be endless*]: All right, all right . . .

ANN: You shouldn't burst out like that.

KELLER: Well, nobody told me it was Labor Day. [*Looks around*] Where's the hot dogs?

CHRIS [*loving it*]: All right. You said it once.

KELLER: Well, as long as I know it's Labor Day from now on, I'll wear a bell around my neck.

ANN [*affectionately*]: He's so subtle!

CHRIS: George Bernard Shaw as an elephant.

KELLER: George! – hey, you kissed it out of my head – your brother's on the phone.

ANN [*surprised*]: My brother?

KELLER: Yeah, George. Long distance.

ANN: What's the matter, is anything wrong?

KELLER: I don't know, Kate's talking to him. Hurry up, she'll cost him five dollars.

ANN [*she takes a step upstage, then comes down toward* CHRIS]: I wonder if we ought to tell your mother yet? I mean I'm not very good in an argument.

CHRIS: We'll wait till tonight. After dinner. Now don't get tense, just leave it to me.

KELLER: What're you telling her?

CHRIS: Go ahead, Ann. [*With misgivings,* ANN *goes up and into house.*]

We're getting married, Dad. [KELLER *nods indecisively.*] Well, don't you say anything?

KELLER [*distracted*]: I'm glad, Chris, I'm just . . . George is calling from Columbus.

CHRIS: Columbus!

KELLER: Did Annie tell you he was going to see his father today?

CHRIS: No, I don't think she knew anything about it.

KELLER [*asking uncomfortably*]: Chris! You . . . you think you know her pretty good?

CHRIS [*hurt and apprehensive*]: What kind of a question . . . ?

KELLER: I'm just wondering. All these years George don't go to see his father. Suddenly he goes . . . and she comes here.

CHRIS: Well, what about it?

KELLER: It's crazy, but it comes to my mind. She don't hold nothin' against me, does she?

CHRIS [*angry*]: I don't know what you're talking about.

KELLER [*a little more combatively*]: I'm just talkin'. To his last day in court the man blamed it all on me; and this is his daughter. I mean if she was sent here to find out something?

CHRIS [*angered*]: Why? What is there to find out?

ANN [*on phone, offstage*]: Why are you so excited, George? What happened there?

KELLER: I mean if they want to open up the case again, for the nuisance value, to hurt us?

CHRIS: Dad . . . how could you think that of her? ⎱

ANN [*still on phone*]: But what did he say to you, ⎰ [*Together*]
for God's sake?

KELLER: It couldn't be, heh. You know.

CHRIS: Dad, you amaze me . . .

KELLER [*breaking in*]: All right, forget it, forget it. [*With great force, moving about*] I want a clean start for you, Chris. I want a new sign over the plant – Christopher Keller, Incorporated.

CHRIS [*a little uneasily*]: J. O. Keller is good enough.

KELLER: We'll talk about it. I'm going to build you a house, stone, with a driveway from the road. I want you to spread out, Chris, I want you to use what I made for you . . . [*He is close to him now.*] . . . I mean, with joy, Chris, without shame . . . with joy.

CHRIS [*touched*]: I will, Dad.

KELLER [*with deep emotion*]: . . . Say it to me.

CHRIS: Why?

KELLER: Because sometimes I think you're . . . ashamed of the money.

CHRIS: No, don't feel that.

KELLER: Because it's good money, there's nothing wrong with that money.

CHRIS [*a little frightened*]: Dad, you don't have to tell me this.

KELLER [*with overriding affection and self-confidence now. He grips* CHRIS *by the back of the neck, and with laughter between his determined jaws*]: Look, Chris, I'll go to work on Mother for you. We'll get her so drunk tonight we'll all get married! [*Steps away, with a wide gesture of his arm*] There's gonna be a wedding, kid, like there never was seen! Champagne, tuxedoes . . . !

[*He breaks off as* ANN's *voice comes out loud from the house where she is still talking on phone.*]

ANN: Simply because when you get excited you don't control yourself . . . [MOTHER *comes out of house.*] Well, what did he tell you for God's sake? [*Pause.*] All right, come then. [*Pause.*] Yes, they'll all be here. Nobody's running away from you. And try to get hold of yourself, will you? [*Pause.*] All right, all right. Goodbye. [*There is a brief pause as* ANN *hangs up receiver, then comes out of kitchen.*]

CHRIS: Something happen?

KELLER: He's coming here?

ANN: On the seven o'clock. He's in Columbus. [*To* MOTHER] I told him it would be all right.

KELLER: Sure, fine! Your father took sick?

ANN [*mystified*]: No, George didn't say he was sick. I . . . [*Shaking it off*] I don't know, I suppose it's something stupid, you know my brother . . . [*She comes to* CHRIS.] Let's go for a drive, or something . . .

CHRIS: Sure. Give me the keys, Dad.

MOTHER: Drive through the park. It's beautiful now.

CHRIS: Come on, Ann. [*To them*] Be back right away.

ANN [*as she and* CHRIS *exit up driveway*]: See you.

[MOTHER *comes down toward* KELLER, *her eyes fixed on him.*]

KELLER: Take your time. [*To* MOTHER] What does George want?

MOTHER: He's been in Columbus since this morning with Steve. He's gotta see Annie right away, he says.

KELLER: What for?

MOTHER: I don't know. [*She speaks with warning.*] He's a lawyer now, Joe. George is a lawyer. All these years he never even sent a postcard to Steve. Since he got back from the war, not a postcard.

KELLER: So what?

MOTHER [*her tension breaking out*]: Suddenly he takes an airplane from New York to see him. An airplane!

KELLER: Well? So?

MOTHER [*trembling*]: Why?

KELLER: I don't read minds. Do you?

MOTHER: Why, Joe? What has Steve suddenly got to tell him that he takes an airplane to see him?

KELLER: What do I care what Steve's got to tell him?

MOTHER: You're sure, Joe?

KELLER [*frightened, but angry*]: Yes, I'm sure.

MOTHER [*she sits stiffly in a chair*]: Be smart now, Joe. The boy is coming. Be smart.

KELLER [*desperately*]: Once and for all, did you hear what I said? I said I'm sure!

MOTHER [*she nods weakly*]: All right, Joe. [*He straightens up.*] Just . . . be smart. [KELLER, *in hopeless fury, looks at her, turns around, goes up to porch and into house, slamming screen door violently behind him.* MOTHER *sits in chair downstage, stiffly, staring, seeing.*]

CURTAIN

Act Two

As twilight falls, that evening.

ON THE RISE: CHRIS *is discovered at* R., *sawing the broken-off tree, leaving stump standing alone. He is dressed in good pants, white shoes, but without a shirt. He disappears with tree up the alley when* MOTHER *appears on porch. She comes down and stands watching him. She has on a dressing-gown, carries a tray of grape-juice drink in a pitcher, and glasses with sprigs of mint in them.*

MOTHER [*calling up alley*]: Did you have to put on good pants to do that? [*She comes downstage and puts tray on table in the arbour. Then looks around uneasily, then feels pitcher for coolness.* CHRIS *enters from alley brushing off his hands.*] You notice there's more light with that thing gone?

CHRIS: Why aren't you dressing?

MOTHER: It's suffocating upstairs. I made a grape drink for Georgie. He always liked grape. Come and have some.

CHRIS [*impatiently*]: Well, come on, get dressed. And what's Dad sleeping so much for? [*He goes to table and pours a glass of juice.*]

MOTHER: He's worried. When he's worried he sleeps. [*Pauses. Looks into his eyes*] We're dumb, Chris. Dad and I are stupid people. We don't know anything. You've got to protect us.

CHRIS: You're silly; what's there to be afraid of?

MOTHER: To his last day in court Steve never gave up the idea that Dad made him do it. If they're going to open the case again I won't live through it.

CHRIS: George is just a damn fool, Mother. How can you take him seriously?

MOTHER: That family hates us. Maybe even Annie . . .

CHRIS: Oh, now, Mother . . .

MOTHER: You think just because you like everybody, they like you!

CHRIS: All right, stop working yourself up. Just leave everything to me.

MOTHER: When George goes home tell her to go with him.

CHRIS [*noncommittally*]: Don't worry about Annie.

MOTHER: Steve is her father, too.

CHRIS: Are you going to cut it out? Now, come.

MOTHER [*going upstage with him*]: You don't realize how people can hate, Chris, they can hate so much they'll tear the world to pieces . . .

[ANN, *dressed up, appears on porch.*]

CHRIS: Look! She's dressed already. [*As he and* MOTHER *mount porch*] I've just got to put on a shirt.

ANN [*in a preoccupied way*]: Are you feeling well, Kate?

MOTHER: What's the difference, dear. There are certain people, y'know, the sicker they get the longer they live. [*She goes into house.*]

CHRIS: You look nice.

ANN: We're going to tell her tonight.

CHRIS: Absolutely, don't worry about it.

ANN: I wish we could tell her now. I can't stand scheming. My stomach gets hard.

CHRIS: It's not scheming, we'll just get her in a better mood.

MOTHER [*offstage, in the house*]: Joe, are you going to sleep all day!

ANN [*laughing*]: The only one who's relaxed is your father. He's fast asleep.

CHRIS: I'm relaxed.

ANN: Are you?

CHRIS: Look. [*He holds out his hand and makes it shake.*] Let me know when George gets here. [*He goes into the house. She moves aimlessly, and then is drawn toward tree stump. She goes to it, hesitantly touches broken top in the hush of her thoughts. Offstage* LYDIA *calls, 'Johnny! Come get your supper!'* SUE *enters from L., and halts, seeing* ANN.]

SUE: Is my husband . . . ?

ANN [*turns, startled*]: Oh!

SUE: I'm terribly sorry.

ANN: It's all right, I . . . I'm a little silly about the dark.

SUE [*looks about*]: It is getting dark.

ANN: Are you looking for your husband?

SUE: As usual. [*Laughs tiredly*] He spends so much time here, they'll be charging him rent.

ANN: Nobody was dressed so he drove over to the depot to pick up my brother.

SUE: Oh, your brother's in?

ANN: Yeah, they ought to be here any minute now. Will you have a cold drink?

SUE: I will, thanks. [ANN *goes to table and pours.*] My husband. Too hot to drive me to beach. – Men are like little boys; for the neighbours they'll always cut the grass.

ANN: People like to do things for the Kellers. Been that way since I can remember.

SUE: It's amazing. I guess your brother's coming to give you away, heh?

ANN [*giving her drink*]: I don't know. I suppose.

SUE: You must be all nerved up.

ANN: It's always a problem getting yourself married, isn't it?

SUE: That depends on your shape, of course. I don't see why you should have had a problem.

ANN: I've had chances –

SUE: I'll bet. It's romantic . . . it's very unusual to me, marrying the brother of your sweetheart.

ANN: I don't know. I think it's mostly that whenever I need somebody to tell me the truth I've always thought of Chris. When he tells you something you know it's so. He relaxes me.

SUE: And he's got money. That's important, you know.

ANN: It wouldn't matter to me.

SUE: You'd be surprised. It makes all the difference. I married an intern. On my salary. And that was bad, because as soon as a woman supports a man he owes her something. You can never owe somebody without resenting them. [ANN *laughs.*] That's true, you know.

ANN: Underneath, I think the doctor is very devoted.

SUE: Oh, certainly. But it's bad when a man always sees the bars in front of him. Jim thinks he's in jail all the time.

ANN: Oh . . .

SUE: That's why I've been intending to ask you a small favour, Ann . . . it's something very important to me.

ANN: Certainly, if I can do it.

SUE: You can. When you take up housekeeping, try to find a place away from here.

ANN: Are you fooling?

SUE: I'm very serious. My husband is unhappy with Chris around.

ANN: How is that?

SUE: Jim's a successful doctor. But he's got an idea he'd like to do medical research. Discover things. You see?

ANN: Well, isn't that good?

SUE: Research pays twenty-five dollars a week minus laundering the hair shirt. You've got to give up your life to go into it.

ANN: How does Chris . . . ?

SUE [*with growing feeling*]: Chris makes people want to be better than it's possible to be. He does that to people.

ANN: Is that bad?

SUE: My husband has a family, dear. Every time he has a session with Chris he feels as though he's compromising by not giving up everything for research. As though Chris or anybody else isn't compromising. It happens with Jim every couple of years. He meets a man and makes a statue out of him.

ANN: Maybe he's right. I don't mean that Chris is a statue, but . . .

SUE: Now darling, you know he's not right.

ANN: I don't agree with you. Chris . . .

SUE: Let's face it, dear. Chris is working with his father, isn't he? He's taking money out of that business every week in the year.

ANN: What of it?

SUE: You ask me what of it?

ANN: I certainly do ask you. [*She seems about to burst out.*] You oughtn't cast aspersions like that, I'm surprised at you.

SUE: You're surprised at me!

ANN: He'd never take five cents out of that plant if there was anything wrong in it.

SUE: You know that.

ANN: I know it. I resent everything you've said.

SUE [*moving toward her*]: You know what I resent, dear?

ANN: Please, I don't want to argue.

SUE: I resent living next door to the Holy Family. It makes me look like a bum, you understand?

ANN: I can't do anything about that.

SUE: Who is he to ruin a man's life? Everybody knows Joe pulled a fast one to get out of jail.

ANN: That's not true!

SUE: Then why don't you go out and talk to people? Go on, talk to them. There's not a person on the block who doesn't know the truth.

ANN: That's a lie. People come here all the time for cards and . . .

SUE: So what? They give him credit for being smart. I do, too, I've got nothing against Joe. But if Chris wants people to put on the hair shirt let him take off his broadcloth. He's driving my husband crazy with that phony idealism of his, and I'm at the end of my rope on it! [CHRIS *enters on porch, wearing shirt and tie now. She turns quickly, hearing. With a smile.*] Hello, darling. How's Mother?

CHRIS: I thought George came.

SUE: No, it was just us.

CHRIS [*coming down to them*]: Susie, do me a favour, heh? Go up to Mother and see if you can calm her. She's all worked up.

SUE: She still doesn't know about you two?

CHRIS [*laughs a little*]: Well, she senses it, I guess. You know my mother.

SUE [*going up to porch*]: Oh, yeah, she's psychic.

CHRIS: Maybe there's something in the medicine chest.

SUE: I'll give her one of everything. [*On porch*] Don't worry about Kate; couple of drinks, dance her around a little . . . she'll love

43

Ann. [*To* ANN] Because you're the female version of him. [CHRIS *laughs.*] Don't be alarmed, I said version. [*She goes into house.*]

CHRIS: Interesting woman, isn't she?

ANN: Yeah, she's very interesting.

CHRIS: She's a great nurse, you know, she . . .

ANN [*in tension, but trying to control it*]: Are you still doing that?

CHRIS [*sensing something wrong, but still smiling*]: Doing what?

ANN: As soon as you get to know somebody you find a distinction for them. How do you know she's a great nurse?

CHRIS: What's the matter, Ann?

ANN: The woman hates you. She despises you!

CHRIS: Hey . . . what's hit you?

ANN: Gee, Chris . . .

CHRIS: What happened here?

ANN: You never . . . Why didn't you tell me?

CHRIS: Tell you what?

ANN: She says they think Joe is guilty.

CHRIS: What difference does it make what they think?

ANN: I don't care what they think, I just don't understand why you took the trouble to deny it. You said it was all forgotten.

CHRIS: I didn't want you to feel there was anything wrong in you coming here, that's all. I know a lot of people think my father was guilty, and I assumed there might be some question in your mind.

ANN: But I never once said I suspected him.

CHRIS: Nobody says it.

ANN: Chris, I know how much you love him, but it could never . . .

CHRIS: Do you think I could forgive him if he'd done that thing?

ANN: I'm not here out of a blue sky, Chris. I turned my back on my father, if there's anything wrong here now . . .

CHRIS: I know that, Ann.

ANN: George is coming from Dad, and I don't think it's with a blessing.

CHRIS: He's welcome here. You've got nothing to fear from George.

ANN: Tell me that . . . just tell me that.

CHRIS: The man is innocent, Ann. Remember he was falsely accused once and it put him through hell. How would you behave if you were faced with the same thing again? Annie, believe me, there's nothing wrong for you here, believe me, kid.

ANN: All right, Chris, all right. [*They embrace as* KELLER *appears quietly on porch.* ANN *simply studies him.*]

KELLER: Every time I come out here it looks like Playland! [*They break and laugh in embarrassment.*]

CHRIS: I thought you were going to shave?

KELLER [*sitting on bench*]: In a minute. I just woke up, I can't see nothin'.

ANN: You look shaved.

KELLER: Oh, no. [*Massages his jaw*] Gotta be extra special tonight. Big night, Annie. So how's it feel to be a married woman?

ANN [*laughs*]: I don't know, yet.

KELLER [*to* CHRIS]: What's the matter, you slippin'? [*He takes a little box of apples from under the bench as they talk.*]

CHRIS: The great roué!

KELLER: What is that, roué?

CHRIS: It's French.

KELLER: Don't talk dirty. [*They laugh.*]

CHRIS [*to* ANN]: You ever meet a bigger ignoramus?

KELLER: Well, somebody's got to make a living.

ANN [*as they laugh*]: That's telling him.

KELLER: I don't know, everybody's gettin' so Goddam educated in this country there'll be nobody to take away the garbage. [*They laugh.*] It's gettin' so the only dumb ones left are the bosses.

ANN: You're not so dumb, Joe.

KELLER: I know, but you go into our plant, for instance. I got so many lieutenants, majors, and colonels that I'm ashamed to ask somebody to sweep the floor. I gotta be careful I'll insult somebody. No kiddin'. It's a tragedy: you stand on the street today and spit, you're gonna hit a college man.

CHRIS: Well, don't spit.

KELLER [*breaks apple in half, passing it to* ANN *and* CHRIS]: I mean to

say, it's comin' to a pass. [*He takes a breath.*] I been thinkin',
Annie . . . your brother, George. I been thinkin' about your
brother George. When he comes I like you to *brooch* something
to him.

CHRIS: Broach.

KELLER: What's the matter with brooch?

CHRIS [*smiling*]: It's not English.

KELLER: When I went to night school it was brooch.

ANN [*laughing*]: Well, in day school it's broach.

KELLER: Don't surround me, will you? Seriously, Ann . . . You say
he's not well. George, I been thinkin', why should he knock himself out in New York with that cut-throat competition, when I
got so many friends here; I'm very friendly with some big lawyers
in town. I could set George up here.

ANN: That's awfully nice of you, Joe.

KELLER: No, kid, it ain't nice of me. I want you to understand me.
I'm thinking of Chris. [*Slight pause.*] See . . . this is what I mean.
You get older, you want to feel that you . . . accomplished something. My only accomplishment is my son. I ain't brainy. That's
all I accomplished. Now, a year, eighteen months, your father'll
be a free man. Who is he going to come to, Annie? His baby. You.
He'll come, old, mad, into your house.

ANN: That can't matter any more, Joe.

KELLER: I don't want that hate to come between us. [*Gestures between*
CHRIS *and himself.*]

ANN: I can only tell you that that could never happen.

KELLER: You're in love now, Annie, but believe me, I'm older than
you and I know – a daughter is a daughter, and a father is a father.
And it could happen. [*He pauses.*] I like you and George to go to
him in prison and tell him . . . 'Dad, Joe wants to bring you into
the business when you get out.'

ANN [*surprised, even shocked*]: You'd have him as a partner?

KELLER: No, no partner. A good job. [*Pause. He sees she is shocked, a
little mystified. He gets up, speaks more nervously.*] I want him to
know, Annie . . . while he's sitting there I want him to know that

when he gets out he's got a place waitin' for him. It'll take his bitterness away. To know you got a place . . . it sweetens you.

ANN: Joe, you owe him nothing.

KELLER: I owe him a good kick in the teeth, but he's your father . . .

CHRIS: Then kick him in the teeth! I don't want him in the plant, so that's that! You understand? And besides, don't talk about him like that. People misunderstand you!

KELLER: And I don't understand why she has to crucify the man.

CHRIS: Well, it's her father, if she feels . . .

KELLER: No, no . . .

CHRIS [*almost angrily*]: What's it to you? Why . . . ?

KELLER [*a commanding outburst in his high nervousness*]: A father is a father! [*As though the outburst had revealed him, he looks about, wanting to retract it. His hand goes to his cheek.*] I better . . . I better shave. [*He turns and a smile is on his face. To* ANN] I didn't mean to yell at you, Annie.

ANN: Let's forget the whole thing, Joe.

KELLER: Right. [*To* CHRIS] She's likable.

CHRIS [*a little peeved at the man's stupidity*]: Shave, will you?

KELLER: Right again.

[*As he turns to porch* LYDIA *comes hurrying from her house,* R.]

LYDIA: I forgot all about it . . . [*Seeing* CHRIS *and* ANN] Hya. [*To* JOE] I promised to fix Kate's hair for tonight. Did she comb it yet?

KELLER: Always a smile, hey, Lydia?

LYDIA: Sure, why not?

KELLER [*going up on porch*]: Come on up and comb my Katie's hair. [LYDIA *goes up on porch.*] She's got a big night, make her beautiful.

LYDIA: I will.

KELLER [*he holds door open for her and she goes into kitchen. To* CHRIS *and* ANN]: Hey, that could be a song. [*He sings softly.*]
'Come on up and comb my Katie's hair . . .
Oh, come on up, 'cause she's my lady fair –'

[*To* ANN] How's that for one year of night school? [*He continues singing as he goes into kitchen.*]

'Oh, come on up, come on up, and comb my lady's hair—'

[JIM BAYLISS *rounds corner of driveway, walking rapidly.* JIM *crosses to* CHRIS, *motions him up and pulls him down to stage* L., *excitedly.* KELLER *stands just inside kitchen door, watching them.*]

CHRIS: What's the matter? Where is he?

JIM: Where's your mother?

CHRIS: Upstairs, dressing.

ANN [*crossing to them rapidly*]: What happened to George?

JIM: I asked him to wait in the car. Listen to me now. Can you take some advice? [*They wait.*] Don't bring him in here.

ANN: Why?

JIM: Kate is in bad shape, you can't explode this in front of her.

ANN: Explode what?

JIM: You know why he's here, don't try to kid it away. There's blood in his eye; drive him somewhere and talk to him alone.

[ANN *turns to go up drive, takes a couple of steps, sees* KELLER *and stops. He goes quietly on into house.*]

CHRIS [*shaken, and therefore angered*]: Don't be an old lady.

JIM: He's come to take her home. What does that mean? [*To* ANN] You know what that means. Fight it out with him someplace else.

ANN [*she comes back down toward* CHRIS]: I'll drive . . . him somewhere.

CHRIS [*goes to her*]: No.

JIM: Will you stop being an idiot?

CHRIS: Nobody's afraid of him here. Cut that out! [*He starts for driveway, but is brought up short by* GEORGE, *who enters there.* GEORGE *is* CHRIS*'s age, but a paler man, now on the edge of his self-restraint. He speaks quietly, as though afraid to find himself screaming. An instant's hesitation and* CHRIS *steps up to him, hand extended, smiling.*] Helluva way to do; what're you sitting out there for?

GEORGE: Doctor said your mother isn't well, I . . .

CHRIS: So what? She'd want to see you, wouldn't she? We've been waiting for you all afternoon. [*He puts his hand on* GEORGE'*s arm, but* GEORGE *pulls away, coming across toward* ANN.]

ANN [*touching his collar*]: This is filthy, didn't you bring another shirt?

[GEORGE *breaks away from her, and moves down and* L., *examining the yard. Door opens, and he turns rapidly, thinking it is* KATE, *but it's* SUE. *She looks at him, he turns away and moves on* L., *to fence. He looks over it at his former home.* SUE *comes downstage.*]

SUE [*annoyed*]: How about the beach, Jim?

JIM: Oh, it's too hot to drive.

SUE: How'd you get to the station – Zeppelin?

CHRIS: This is Mrs Bayliss, George. [*Calling, as* GEORGE *pays no attention, staring at house off* L.] George! [GEORGE *turns.*] Mrs Bayliss.

SUE: How do you do.

GEORGE [*removing his hat*]: You're the people who bought our house, aren't you?

SUE: That's right. Come and see what we did with it before you leave.

GEORGE [*he walks down and away from her*]: I liked it the way it was.

SUE [*after a brief pause*]: He's frank, isn't he?

JIM [*pulling her off* L.] See you later . . . Take it easy, fella. [*They exit,* L.]

CHRIS [*calling after them*]: Thanks for driving him! [*Turning to* GEORGE] How about some grape juice? Mother made it especially for you.

GEORGE [*with forced appreciation*]: Good old Kate, remembered my grape juice.

CHRIS: You drank enough of it in this house. How've you been, George? – Sit down.

GEORGE [*he keeps moving*]: It takes me a minute. [*Looking around*] It seems impossible.

CHRIS: What?

GEORGE: I'm back here.

CHRIS: Say, you've gotten a little nervous, haven't you?

GEORGE: Yeah, toward the end of the day. What're you, big executive now?

CHRIS: Just kind of medium. How's the law?

GEORGE: I don't know. When I was studying in the hospital it seemed sensible, but outside there doesn't seem to be much of a law. The trees got thick, didn't they? [*Points to stump*] What's that?

CHRIS: Blew down last night. We had it there for Larry. You know.

GEORGE: Why, afraid you'll forget him?

CHRIS [*starts for* GEORGE]: Kind of a remark is that?

ANN [*breaking in, putting a restraining hand on* CHRIS]: When did you start wearing a hat?

GEORGE [*discovers hat in his hand*]: Today. From now on I decided to look like a lawyer, anyway. [*He holds it up to her.*] Don't you recognize it?

ANN: Why? Where . . . ?

GEORGE: Your father's . . . he asked me to wear it.

ANN: . . . How is he?

GEORGE: He got smaller.

ANN: Smaller?

GEORGE: Yeah, little. [*Holds out his hand to measure*] He's a little man. That's what happens to suckers, you know. It's good I went to him in time – another year there'd be nothing left but his smell.

CHRIS: What's the matter, George, what's the trouble?

GEORGE: The trouble? The trouble is when you make suckers out of people once, you shouldn't try to do it twice.

CHRIS: What does that mean?

GEORGE [*to* ANN]: You're not married yet, are you?

ANN: George, will you sit down and stop –?

GEORGE: Are you married yet?

ANN: No, I'm not married yet.

GEORGE: You're not going to marry him.

ANN: Why am I not going to marry him?

GEORGE: Because his father destroyed your family.

CHRIS: Now look, George . . .

GEORGE: Cut it short, Chris. Tell her to come home with me. Let's not argue, you know what I've got to say.

CHRIS: George, you don't want to be the voice of God, do you?

GEORGE: I'm . . .

CHRIS: That's been your trouble all your life, George, you dive into things. What kind of a statement is that to make? You're a big boy now.

GEORGE: I'm a big boy now.

CHRIS: Don't come bulling in here. If you've got something to say, be civilized about it.

GEORGE: Don't civilize me!

ANN: Shhh!

CHRIS [*ready to hit him*]: Are you going to talk like a grown man or aren't you?

ANN [*quickly, to forestall an outburst*]: Sit down, dear. Don't be angry, what's the matter? [*He allows her to seat him, looking at her.*] Now what happened? You kissed me when I left, now you . . .

GEORGE [*breathlessly*]: My life turned upside down since then. I couldn't go back to work when you left. I wanted to go to Dad and tell him you were going to be married. It seemed impossible not to tell him. He loved you so much . . . [*He pauses.*] Annie . . . we did a terrible thing. We can never be forgiven. Not even to send him a card at Christmas. I didn't see him once since I got home from the war! Annie, you don't know what was done to that man. You don't know what happened.

ANN [*afraid*]: Of course I know.

GEORGE: You can't know, you wouldn't be here. Dad came to work that day. The night foreman came to him and showed him the cylinder heads . . . they were coming out of the process with defects. There was something wrong with the process. So Dad went directly to the phone and called here and told Joe to come down right away. But the morning passed. No sign of Joe. So Dad called again. By this time he had over a hundred defectives. The Army was screaming for stuff and Dad didn't have anything to ship. So Joe told him . . . on the phone he told him to weld, cover up the cracks in any way he could, and ship them out.

CHRIS: Are you through now?

GEORGE [*surging up at him*]: I'm not through now! [*Back to* ANN] Dad was afraid. He wanted Joe there if he was going to do it. But Joe can't come down . . . he's sick. Sick! He suddenly gets the flu! Suddenly! But he promised to take responsibility. Do you understand what I'm saying? On the telephone you can't have responsibility! In a court you can always deny a phone call and that's exactly what he did. They knew he was a liar the first time, but in the appeal they believed that rotten lie and now Joe is a big shot and your father is the patsy. [*He gets up.*] Now what're you going to do? Eat his food, sleep in his bed? Answer me; what're you going to do?

CHRIS: What're you going to do, George?

GEORGE: He's too smart for me, I can't prove a phone call.

CHRIS: Then how dare you come in here with that rot?

ANN: George, the court . . .

GEORGE: The court didn't know your father! But you know him. You know in your heart Joe did it.

CHRIS [*whirling him around*]: Lower your voice or I'll throw you out of here!

GEORGE: She knows. She knows.

CHRIS [*to* ANN]: Get him out of here, Ann. Get him out of here.

ANN: George, I know everything you've said. Dad told that whole thing in court, and they . . .

GEORGE [*almost a scream*]: The court did not know him, Annie!

ANN: Shhh! – But he'll say anything, George. You know how quick he can lie.

GEORGE [*turning to* CHRIS, *with deliberation*]: I'll ask you something, and look me in the eye when you answer me.

CHRIS: I'll look you in the eye.

GEORGE: You know your father . . .

CHRIS: I know him well.

GEORGE: And he's the kind of boss to let a hundred and twenty-one cylinder heads be repaired and shipped out of his shop without even knowing about it?

CHRIS: He's that kind of boss.

GEORGE: And that's the same Joe Keller who never left his shop without first going around to see that all the lights were out.

CHRIS [*with growing anger*]: The same Joe Keller.

GEORGE: The same man who knows how many minutes a day his workers spend in the toilet.

CHRIS: The same man.

GEORGE: And my father, that frightened mouse who'd never buy a shirt without somebody along – that man would dare do such a thing on his own?

CHRIS: On his own. And because he's a frightened mouse this is another thing he'd do; – throw the blame on somebody else because he's not man enough to take it himself. He tried it in court but it didn't work, but with a fool like you it works!

GEORGE: Oh, Chris, you're a liar to yourself!

ANN [*deeply shaken*]: Don't talk like that!

CHRIS [*sits facing* GEORGE]: Tell me, George. What happened? The court record was good enough for you all these years, why isn't it good now? Why did you believe it all these years?

GEORGE [*after a slight pause*]: Because you believed it . . . That's the truth, Chris. I believed everything, because I thought you did. But today I heard it from his mouth. From his mouth it's altogether different than the record. Anyone who knows him, and knows your father, will believe it from his mouth. Your Dad took everything we have. I can't beat that. But she's one item he's not going to grab. [*He turns to* ANN.] Get your things. Everything they have is covered with blood. You're not the kind of a girl who can live with that. Get your things.

CHRIS: Ann . . . you're not going to believe that, are you?

ANN [*she goes to him*]: You know it's not true, don't you?

GEORGE: How can he tell you? It's his father. [*To* CHRIS] None of these things ever even cross your mind?

CHRIS: Yes, they crossed my mind. Anything can cross your mind!

GEORGE: *He knows*, Annie. He knows!

CHRIS: The Voice of God!

GEORGE: Then why isn't your name on the business? Explain that to her!

CHRIS: What the hell has that got to do with . . . ?

GEORGE: Annie, why isn't his name on it?

CHRIS: Even when I don't own it!

GEORGE: Who're you kidding? Who gets it when he dies? [*To* ANN] Open your eyes, you know the both of them, isn't that the first thing they'd do, the way they love each other? – J. O. Keller & Son? [*Pause.* ANN *looks from him to* CHRIS.] I'll settle it. Do you want to settle it, or are you afraid to?

CHRIS: . . . What do you mean?

GEORGE: Let me go up and talk to your father. In ten minutes you'll have the answer. Or are you afraid of the answer?

CHRIS: I'm not afraid of the answer. I know the answer. But my mother isn't well and I don't want a fight here now.

GEORGE: Let me go to him.

CHRIS: You're not going to start a fight here now.

GEORGE [*to* ANN]: What more do you want!!!

[*There is a sound of footsteps in the house.*]

ANN [*turns her head suddenly toward house*]: Someone's coming.

CHRIS [*to* GEORGE, *quietly*]: You won't say anything now.

ANN: You'll go soon. I'll call a cab.

GEORGE: You're coming with me.

ANN: And don't mention marriage, because we haven't told her yet.

GEORGE: You're coming with me.

ANN: You understand? Don't . . . George, you're not going to start anything now! [*She hears footsteps.*] Shsh!

[MOTHER *enters on porch. She is dressed almost formally, her hair is fixed. They are all turned toward her. On seeing* GEORGE *she raises both hands, comes down toward him.*]

MOTHER: Georgie, Georgie.

GEORGE [*he has always liked her*]: Hello, Kate.

MOTHER [*she cups his face in her hands*]: They made an old man out of you. [*Touches his hair*] Look, you're grey.

GEORGE [*her pity, open and unabashed, reaches into him, and he smiles sadly*]: I know, I . . .

MOTHER: I told you when you went away, don't try for medals.

GEORGE [*he laughs, tiredly*]: I didn't try, Kate. They made it very easy for me.

MOTHER [*actually angry*]: Go on. You're all alike. [*To* ANN] Look at him, why did you say he's fine? He looks like a ghost.

GEORGE [*relishing her solicitude*]: I feel all right.

MOTHER: I'm sick to look at you. What's the matter with your mother, why don't she feed you?

ANN: He just hasn't any appetite.

MOTHER: If he ate in my house he'd have an appetite. [*To* ANN] I pity your husband! [*To* GEORGE] Sit down. I'll make you a sandwich.

GEORGE [*sits with an embarrassed laugh*]: I'm really not hungry.

MOTHER: Honest to God, it breaks my heart to see what happened to all the children. How we worked and planned for you, and you end up no better than us.

GEORGE [*with deep feeling for her*]: You . . . you haven't changed at all, you know that, Kate?

MOTHER: None of us changed, Georgie. We all love you. Joe was just talking about the day you were born and the water got shut off. People were carrying basins from a block away – a stranger would have thought the whole neighbourhood was on fire! [*They laugh. She sees the juice. To* ANN] Why didn't you give him some juice!

ANN [*defensively*]: I offered it to him.

MOTHER [*scoffingly*]: You offered it to him! [*Thrusting glass into* GEORGE'*s hand*] Give it to him! [*To* GEORGE, *who is laughing*] And now you're going to sit here and drink some juice . . . and look like something!

GEORGE [*sitting*]: Kate, I feel hungry already.

CHRIS [*proudly*]: She could turn Mahatma Gandhi into a heavy-weight!

MOTHER [*to* CHRIS, *with great energy*]: Listen, to hell with the restaurant! I got a ham in the icebox, and frozen strawberries, and avocados, and . . .

ANN: Swell, I'll help you!

GEORGE: The train leaves at eight-thirty, Ann.

MOTHER [*to* ANN]: You're leaving?

CHRIS: No, Mother, she's not . . .

ANN [*breaking through it, going to* GEORGE]: You hardly got here; give yourself a chance to get acquainted again.

CHRIS: Sure, you don't even know us any more.

MOTHER: Well, Chris, if they can't stay, don't . . .

CHRIS: No, it's just a question of George, Mother, he planned on . . .

GEORGE [*he gets up politely, nicely, for* KATE'*s sake*]: Now wait a minute, Chris ∴ . .

CHRIS [*smiling and full of command, cutting him off*]: If you want to go, I'll drive you to the station now, but if you're staying, no arguments while you're here.

MOTHER [*at last confessing the tension*]: Why should he argue? [*She goes to him, and with desperation and compassion, stroking his hair*] Georgie and us have no argument. How could we have an argument, Georgie? We all got hit by the same lightning, how can you . . . ? Did you see what happened to Larry's tree, Georgie? [*She has taken his arm, and unwillingly he moves across stage with her.*] Imagine? While I was dreaming of him in the middle of the night, the wind came along and . . .

[LYDIA *enters on porch. As soon as she sees him*]

LYDIA: Hey, Georgie! Georgie! Georgie! Georgie! Georgie! [*She comes down to him eagerly. She has a flowered hat in her hand, which* KATE *takes from her as she goes to* GEORGE.]

GEORGE [*they shake hands eagerly, warmly*]: Hello, Laughy. What'd you do, grow?

LYDIA: I'm a big girl now.

MOTHER [*taking hat from her*]: Look what she can do to a hat!

ANN [*to* LYDIA, *admiring the hat*]: Did you make that?

MOTHER: In ten minutes! [*She puts it on.*]

LYDIA [*fixing it on her head*]: I only rearranged it.

GEORGE: You still make your own clothes?

CHRIS [*of* MOTHER]: Ain't she classy! All she needs now is a Russian wolfhound.

MOTHER [*moving her head from* L. *to* R.]: It feels like somebody is sitting on my head.

ANN: No, it's beautiful, Kate.

MOTHER [*kisses* LYDIA – *to* GEORGE]: She's a genius! You should've married her. [*They laugh.*] This one can feed you!

LYDIA [*strangely embarrassed*]: Oh, stop that, Kate.

GEORGE [*to* LYDIA]: Didn't I hear you had a baby?

MOTHER: You don't hear so good. She's got three babies.

GEORGE [*a little hurt by it – to* LYDIA]: No kidding, three?

LYDIA: Yeah, it was one, two, three – You've been away a long time, Georgie.

GEORGE: I'm beginning to realize.

MOTHER [*to* CHRIS *and* GEORGE]: The trouble with you kids is you *think* too much.

LYDIA: Well, we think, too.

MOTHER: Yes, but not all the time.

GEORGE [*with almost obvious envy*]: They never took Frank, heh?

LYDIA [*a little apologetically*]: No, he was always one year ahead of the draft.

MOTHER: It's amazing. When they were calling boys twenty-seven Frank was just twenty-eight, when they made it twenty-eight he was just twenty-nine. That's why he took up astrology. It's all in when you were born, it just goes to show.

CHRIS: What does it go to show?

MOTHER [*to* CHRIS]: Don't be so intelligent. Some superstitions are very nice! [*To* LYDIA] Did he finish Larry's horoscope?

LYDIA: I'll ask him now, I'm going in. [*To* GEORGE, *a little sadly, almost embarrassed*] Would you like to see my babies? Come on.

GEORGE: I don't think so, Lydia.

LYDIA [*understanding*]: All right. Good luck to you, George.

GEORGE: Thanks. And to you . . . And Frank.

[*She smiles at him, turns and goes off* R. *to her house.* GEORGE *stands staring after her.*]

LYDIA [*as she runs off*]: Oh, Frank!

MOTHER [*reading his thoughts*]: She got pretty, heh?

GEORGE [*sadly*]: Very pretty.

MOTHER [*as a reprimand*]: She's beautiful, you damned fool!

GEORGE [*looks around longingly; and softly, with a catch in his throat*]: She makes it seem so nice around here.

MOTHER [*shaking her finger at him*]: Look what happened to you because you wouldn't listen to me! I told you to marry that girl and stay out of the war!

GEORGE [*laughs at himself*]: She used to laugh too much.

MOTHER: And you didn't laugh enough. While you were getting mad about Fascism Frank was getting into her bed.

GEORGE [*to* CHRIS]: He won the war, Frank.

CHRIS: All the battles.

MOTHER [*in pursuit of this mood*]: The day they started the draft, Georgie, I told you you loved that girl.

CHRIS [*laughs*]: And truer love hath no man!

MOTHER: I'm smarter than any of you.

GEORGE [*laughing*]: She's wonderful!

MOTHER: And now you're going to listen to me, George. You had big principles, Eagle Scouts the three of you; so now I got a tree, and this one, [*indicating* CHRIS] when the weather gets bad he can't stand on his feet; and that big dope [*pointing to* LYDIA's *house*] next door who never reads anything but Andy Gump has three children and his house paid off. Stop being a philosopher, and look after yourself. Like Joe was just saying – you move back here, he'll help you get set, and I'll find you a girl and put a smile on your face.

GEORGE: Joe? Joe wants me here?

ANN [*eagerly*]: He asked me to tell you, and I think it's a good idea.

MOTHER: Certainly. Why must you make believe you hate us? Is that another principle? – that you have to hate us? You don't hate us, George, I know you, you can't fool me, I diapered you. [*Suddenly to* ANN] You remember Mr Marcy's daughter?

ANN [*laughing, to* GEORGE]: She's got you hooked already! [GEORGE *laughs, is excited.*]

MOTHER: You look her over, George; you'll see she's the most beautiful . . .

CHRIS: She's got warts, George.

MOTHER [*to* CHRIS]: She hasn't got warts! [*To* GEORGE] So the girl has a little beauty mark on her chin . . .

CHRIS: And two on her nose.

MOTHER: You remember. Her father's the retired police inspector.

CHRIS: Sergeant, George.

MOTHER: He's a very kind man!

CHRIS: He looks like a gorilla.

MOTHER [*to* GEORGE]: He never shot anybody. [*They all burst out laughing, as* KELLER *appears in doorway.* GEORGE *rises abruptly, stares at* KELLER, *who comes rapidly down to him.*]

KELLER [*the laughter stops. With strained joviality*]: Well! Look who's here! [*Extending his hand*] Georgie, good to see ya.

GEORGE [*shakes hands – sombrely*]: How're you, Joe?

KELLER: So-so. Gettin' old. You comin' out to dinner with us?

GEORGE: No, got to be back in New York.

ANN: I'll call a cab for you. [*She goes up into the house.*]

KELLER: Too bad you can't stay, George. Sit down. [*To* MOTHER] He looks fine.

MOTHER: He looks terrible.

KELLER: That's what I said, you look terrible, George. [*They laugh.*] I wear the pants and she beats me with the belt.

GEORGE: I saw your factory on the way from the station. It looks like General Motors.

KELLER: I wish it was General Motors, but it ain't. Sit down, George. Sit down. [*Takes cigar out of his pocket*] So you finally went to see your father, I hear?

GEORGE: Yes, this morning. What kind of stuff do you make now?

KELLER: Oh, little of everything. Pressure cookers, an assembly for washing machines. Got a nice, flexible plant now. So how'd you find Dad? Feel all right?

GEORGE [*searching* KELLER, *he speaks indecisively*]: No, he's not well, Joe.

KELLER [*lighting his cigar*]: Not his heart again, is it?

GEORGE: It's everything, Joe. It's his soul.

KELLER [*blowing out smoke*]: Uh huh –

CHRIS: How about seeing what they did with your house?

KELLER: Leave him be.

GEORGE [*to* CHRIS, *indicating* KELLER]: I'd like to talk to him.

KELLER: Sure, he just got here. That's the way they do, George. A little man makes a mistake and they hang him by the thumbs; the big ones become ambassadors. I wish you'd-a told me you were going to see Dad.

GEORGE [*studying him*]: I didn't know you were interested.

KELLER: In a way, I am. I would like him to know, George, that as far as I'm concerned, any time he wants, he's got a place with me. I would like him to know that.

GEORGE: He hates your guts, Joe. Don't you know that?

KELLER: I imagined it. But that can change, too.

MOTHER: Steve was never like that.

GEORGE: He's like that now. He'd like to take every man who made money in the war and put him up against a wall.

CHRIS: He'll need a lot of bullets.

GEORGE: And he'd better not get any.

KELLER: That's a sad thing to hear.

GEORGE [*with bitterness dominant*]: Why? What'd you expect him to think of you?

KELLER [*the force of his nature rising, but under control*]: I'm sad to see he hasn't changed. As long as I know him, twenty-five years, the man never learned how to take the blame. You know that, George.

GEORGE [*he does*]: Well, I . . .

KELLER: But you do know it. Because the way you come in here you don't look like you remember it. I mean like in 1937 when we had the shop on Flood Street. And he damn near blew us all up with that heater he left burning for two days without water. He wouldn't admit that was his fault, either. I had to fire a mechanic to save his face. You remember that.

GEORGE: Yes, but . . .

KELLER: I'm just mentioning it, George. Because this is just another one of a lot of things. Like when he gave Frank that money to invest in oil stock.

GEORGE [*distressed*]: I know that, I . . .

KELLER [*driving in, but restrained*]: But it's good to remember those things, kid. The way he cursed Frank because the stock went down. Was that Frank's fault? To listen to him Frank was a swindler. And all the man did was give him a bad tip.

GEORGE [*gets up, moves away*]: I know those things . . .

KELLER: Then remember them, remember them. [ANN *comes out of house.*] There are certain men in the world who rather see everybody hung before they'll take blame. You understand me, George? [*They stand facing each other,* GEORGE *trying to judge him.*]

ANN [*coming downstage*]: The cab's on its way. Would you like to wash?

MOTHER [*with the thrust of hope*]: Why must he go? Make the midnight, George.

KELLER: Sure, you'll have dinner with us!

ANN: How about it? Why not? We're eating at the lake, we could have a swell time.

GEORGE [*long pause, as he looks at* ANN, CHRIS, KELLER, *then back to her*]: All right.

MOTHER: Now you're talking.

CHRIS: I've got a shirt that'll go right with that suit.

MOTHER: Size fifteen and a half, right, George?

GEORGE: Is Lydia . . . ? I mean – Frank and Lydia coming?

MOTHER: I'll get you a date that'll make her look like a . . . [*She starts upstage.*]

GEORGE [*laughs*]: No, I don't want a date.

CHRIS: I know somebody just for you! Charlotte Tanner! [*He starts for the house.*]

KELLER: Call Charlotte, that's right.

MOTHER: Sure, call her up. [CHRIS *goes into house.*]

ANN: You go up and pick out a shirt and tie.

GEORGE [*he stops, looks around at them and the place*]: I never felt at home anywhere but here. I feel so . . . [*He nearly laughs, and turns away from them.*] Kate, you look so young, you know? You didn't change at all. It . . . rings an old bell. [*Turns to* KELLER] You too, Joe, you're amazingly the same. The whole atmosphere is.

KELLER: Say, I ain't got time to get sick.

MOTHER: He hasn't been laid up in fifteen years . . .

KELLER: Except my flu during the war.

MOTHER: Huhh?

KELLER: My flu, when I was sick during . . . the war.

MOTHER: Well, sure . . . [*To* GEORGE] I meant except for that flu. [GEORGE *stands perfectly still.*] Well, it slipped my mind, don't look at me that way. He wanted to go to the shop but he couldn't lift himself off the bed. I thought he had pneumonia.

GEORGE: Why did you say he's never . . . ?

KELLER: I know how you feel, kid, I'll never forgive myself. If I could've gone in that day I'd never allow Dad to touch those heads.

GEORGE: She said you've never been sick.

MOTHER: I said he was sick, George.

GEORGE [*going to* ANN]: Ann, didn't you hear her say . . . ?

MOTHER: Do you remember every time you were sick?

GEORGE: I'd remember pneumonia. Especially if I got it just the day my partner was going to patch up cylinder heads . . . What happened that day, Joe?

FRANK [*enters briskly from driveway, holding Larry's horoscope in his hand. He comes to* KATE]: Kate! Kate!

MOTHER: Frank, did you see George?

FRANK [*extending his hand*]: Lydia told me, I'm glad to . . . you'll have to pardon me. [*Pulling* MOTHER *over* R.] I've got something amazing for you, Kate, I finished Larry's horoscope.

MOTHER: You'd be interested in this, George. It's wonderful the way he can understand the . . .

CHRIS [*entering from house*]: George, the girl's on the phone . . .

MOTHER [*desperately*]: He finished Larry's horoscope!

CHRIS: Frank, can't you pick a better time than this?

FRANK: The greatest men who ever lived believed in the stars!

CHRIS: Stop filling her head with that junk!

FRANK: Is it junk to feel that there's a greater power than ourselves? I've studied the stars of his life! I won't argue with you, I'm telling you. Somewhere in this world your brother is alive!

MOTHER [*instantly to* CHRIS]: Why isn't it possible?

CHRIS: Because it's insane.

FRANK: Just a minute now. I'll tell you something and you can do as you please. Just let me say it. He was supposed to have died on November twenty-fifth. But November twenty-fifth was his favourable day.

CHRIS: Mother!

MOTHER: Listen to him!

FRANK: It was a day when everything good was shining on him, the kind of day he should've married on. You can laugh at a lot of it, I can understand you laughing. But the odds are a million to one that a man won't die on his favourable day. That's known, that's known, Chris!

MOTHER: Why isn't it possible, why isn't it possible, Chris!

GEORGE [*to* ANN]: Don't you understand what she's saying? She just told you to go. What are you waiting for now?

CHRIS: Nobody can tell her to go. [*A car horn is heard.*]

MOTHER [*to* FRANK]: Thank you, darling, for your trouble. Will you tell him to wait, Frank?

FRANK [*as he goes*]: Sure thing.

MOTHER [*calling out*]: They'll be right out, driver!

CHRIS: She's not leaving, Mother.

GEORGE: You heard her say it, he's never been sick!

MOTHER: He misunderstood me, Chris! [CHRIS *looks at her, struck.*]

GEORGE [*to* ANN]: He simply told your father to kill pilots, and covered himself in bed!

CHRIS: You'd better answer him, Annie. Answer him.

MOTHER: I packed your bag, darling . . .

CHRIS: What?

MOTHER: I packed your bag. All you've got to do is close it.

ANN: I'm not closing anything. He asked me here and I'm staying till he tells me to go. [*To* GEORGE] Till Chris tells me!

CHRIS: That's all! Now get out of here, George!

MOTHER [*to* CHRIS]: But if that's how he feels . . .

CHRIS: That's all, nothing more till Christ comes, about the case or Larry as long as I'm here! [*To* GEORGE] Now get out of here, George!

GEORGE [*to* ANN]: You tell me. I want to hear you tell me.

ANN: Go, George! [*They disappear up the driveway,* ANN *saying 'Don't take it that way, George! Please don't take it that way.'*]

[CHRIS *turns to his mother.*]

CHRIS: What do you mean, you packed her bag? How dare you pack her bag?

MOTHER: Chris . . .

CHRIS: How dare you pack her bag?

MOTHER: She doesn't belong here.

CHRIS: Then I don't belong here.

MOTHER: She's Larry's girl.

CHRIS: And I'm his brother and he's dead, and I'm marrying his girl.

MOTHER: Never, never in this world!

KELLER: You lost your mind?

MOTHER: You have nothing to say!

KELLER [*cruelly*]: I got plenty to say. Three and a half years you been talking like a maniac –

MOTHER [*she smashes him across the face*]: Nothing. You have nothing to say. Now I say. He's coming back, and everybody has got to wait.

CHRIS: Mother, Mother . . .

MOTHER: Wait, wait . . .

CHRIS: How long? How long?

MOTHER [*rolling out of her*]: Till he comes; forever and ever till he comes!

CHRIS [*as an ultimatum*]: Mother, I'm going ahead with it.

MOTHER: Chris, I've never said no to you in my life, now I say no!

CHRIS: You'll never let him go till I do it.

MOTHER: I'll never let him go and you'll never let him go . . . !

CHRIS: I've let him go. I've let him go a long . . .

MOTHER [*with no less force, but turning from him*]: Then let your father go.

[*Pause.* CHRIS *stands transfixed.*]

KELLER: She's out of her mind.

MOTHER: Altogether! [*To* CHRIS, *but not facing them*] Your brother's alive, darling, because if he's dead, your father killed him. Do you understand me now? As long as you live, that boy is alive. God does not let a son be killed by his father. Now you see, don't you? Now you see. [*Beyond control, she hurries up and into house.*]

KELLER [CHRIS *has not moved. He speaks insinuatingly, questioningly*]: She's out of her mind.

CHRIS [*a broken whisper*]: Then . . . you did it?

KELLER [*the beginning of plea in his voice*]: He never flew a P-40 –

CHRIS [*struck. Deadly*]: But the others.

KELLER [*insistently*]: She's out of her mind. [*He takes a step toward* CHRIS, *pleadingly.*]

CHRIS [*unyielding*]: Dad . . . you did it?

KELLER: He never flew a P-40, what's the matter with you?

CHRIS [*still asking, and saying*]: Then you did it. To the others. [*Both hold their voices down.*]

KELLER [*afraid of him, his deadly insistence*]: What's the matter with you? What the hell is the matter with you?

CHRIS [*quietly, incredibly*]: How could you do that? How?

KELLER: What's the matter with you!

CHRIS: Dad . . . Dad, you killed twenty-one men!

KELLER: What, killed?

CHRIS: You killed them, you murdered them.

KELLER [*as though throwing his whole nature open before* CHRIS]: How could I kill anybody?

CHRIS: Dad! Dad!

KELLER [*trying to hush him*]: I didn't kill anybody!

CHRIS: Then explain it to me. What did you do? Explain it to me or I'll tear you to pieces!

KELLER [*horrified at his overwhelming fury*]: Don't, Chris, don't . . .

CHRIS: I want to know what you did, now what did you do? You had a hundred and twenty cracked engine-heads, now what did you do?

KELLER: If you're going to hang me then I . . .

CHRIS: I'm listening, God Almighty, I'm listening!

KELLER [*their movements now are those of subtle pursuit and escape.* KELLER *keeps a step out of* CHRIS*'s range as he talks*]: You're a boy, what could I do! I'm in business, a man is in business; a hundred and twenty cracked, you're out of business; you got a process, the process don't work you're out of business; you don't know how to operate, your stuff is no good; they close you up, they tear up your contracts, what the hell's it to them? You lay forty years into a business and they knock you out in five minutes, what could I do, let them take forty years, let them take my life away? [*His voice cracking*] I never thought they'd install them. I swear to God. I thought they'd stop 'em before anybody took off.

CHRIS: Then why'd you ship them out?

KELLER: By the time they could spot them I thought I'd have the process going again, and I could show them they needed me and they'd let it go by. But weeks passed and I got no kick-back, so I was going to tell them.

CHRIS: Then why didn't you tell them?

KELLER: It was too late. The paper, it was all over the front page, twenty-one went down, it was too late. They came with hand-cuffs into the shop, what could I do? [*He sits on bench at* C.] Chris . . . Chris, I did it for you, it was a chance and I took it for you. I'm sixty-one years old, when would I have another chance to make something for you? Sixty-one years old you don't get another chance, do ya?

CHRIS: You even knew they wouldn't hold up in the air.

KELLER: I didn't say that . . .

CHRIS: But you were going to warn them not to use them . . .

KELLER: But that don't mean . . .

CHRIS: It means you knew they'd crash.

KELLER: It don't mean that.

CHRIS: Then you *thought* they'd crash.

KELLER: I was afraid maybe . . .

CHRIS: You were afraid maybe! God in heaven, what kind of a man are you? Kids were hanging in the air by those heads. You knew that!

KELLER: For you, a business for you!

CHRIS [*with burning fury*]: For me! Where do you live, where have you come from? For me! – I was dying every day and you were killing my boys and you did it for me? What the hell do you think I was thinking of, the Goddam business? Is that as far as your mind can see, the business? What is that, the world – the business? What the hell do you mean, you did it for me? Don't you have a country? Don't you live in the world? What the hell are you? You're not even an animal, no animal kills his own, what are you? What must I do to you? I ought to tear the tongue out of your mouth, what must I do? [*With his fist he pounds down upon his father's shoulder. He stumbles away, covering his face as he weeps.*] What must I do, Jesus God, what must I do?

KELLER: Chris . . . My Chris . . .

CURTAIN

Act Three

Two o'clock the following morning, MOTHER is discovered on the rise, rocking ceaselessly in a chair, staring at her thoughts. It is an intense, slight sort of rocking. A light shows from upstairs bedroom, lower floor windows being dark. The moon is strong and casts its bluish light.

Presently JIM, dressed in jacket and hat, appears from L., and seeing her, goes up beside her.

JIM: Any news?

MOTHER: No news.

JIM [*gently*]: You can't sit up all night, dear, why don't you go to bed?

MOTHER: I'm waiting for Chris. Don't worry about me, Jim, I'm perfectly all right.

JIM: But it's almost two o'clock.

MOTHER: I can't sleep. [*Slight pause.*] You had an emergency?

JIM [*tiredly*]: Somebody had a headache and thought he was dying. [*Slight pause.*] Half of my patients are quite mad. Nobody realizes how many people are walking around loose, and they're cracked as coconuts. Money. Money-money-money-money. You say it long enough it doesn't mean anything. [*She smiles, makes a silent laugh.*] Oh, how I'd love to be around when that happens!

MOTHER [*shakes her head*]: You're so childish, Jim! Sometimes you are.

JIM [*looks at her a moment*]: Kate. [*Pause.*] What happened?

KATE: I told you. He had an argument with Joe. Then he got in the car and drove away.

JIM: What kind of an argument?

MOTHER: An argument, Joe . . . he was crying like a child, before.

JIM: They argued about Ann?

MOTHER [*slight hesitation*]: No, not Ann. Imagine? [*Indicates lighted window above*] She hasn't come out of that room since he left. All night in that room.

JIM [*looks at window, then at her*]: What'd Joe do, tell him?

MOTHER [*she stops rocking*]: Tell him what?

JIM: Don't be afraid, Kate, I know. I've always known.

MOTHER: How?

JIM: It occurred to me a long time ago.

MOTHER: I always had the feeling that in the back of his head, Chris . . . almost knew. I didn't think it would be such a shock.

JIM [*gets up*]: Chris would never know how to live with a thing like that. It takes a certain talent . . . for lying. You have it, and I do. But not him.

MOTHER: What do you mean . . . he's not coming back?

JIM: Oh, no, he'll come back. We all come back, Kate. These private little revolutions always die. The compromise is always made. In a peculiar way, Frank is right – every man does have a star. The star of one's honesty. And you spend your life groping for it, but once it's out it never lights again. I don't think he went very far. He probably just wanted to be alone to watch his star go out.

MOTHER: Just as long as he comes back.

JIM: I wish he wouldn't, Kate. One year I simply took off, went to New Orleans; for two months I lived on bananas and milk, and studied a certain disease. It was beautiful. And then she came, and she cried. And I went back home with her. And now I live in the usual darkness; I can't find myself; it's even hard sometimes to remember the kind of man I wanted to be. I'm a good husband; Chris is a good son – he'll come back. [KELLER *comes out on porch in dressing-gown and slippers. He goes upstage – to alley.* JIM *goes to him.*]

JIM: I have a feeling he's in the park. I'll look around for him. Put her to bed, Joe; this is no good for what she's got. [JIM *exits up driveway.*]

KELLER [*coming down*]: What does he want here?

MOTHER: His friend is not home.

KELLER [*his voice is husky. Comes down to her*]: I don't like him mixing in so much.

MOTHER: It's too late, Joe. He knows.

KELLER [*apprehensively*]: How does he know?

MOTHER: He guessed a long time ago.

KELLER: I don't like that.

MOTHER [*laughs dangerously, quietly into the line*]: What you don't like . . .

KELLER: Yeah, what I don't like.

MOTHER: You can't bull yourself through this one, Joe, you better be smart now. This thing – this thing is not over yet.

KELLER [*indicating lighted window above*]: And what is she doing up there? She don't come out of the room.

MOTHER: I don't know, what is she doing? Sit down, stop being mad. You want to live? You better figure out your life.

KELLER: She don't know, does she?

MOTHER: She saw Chris storming out of here. It's one and one – she knows how to add.

KELLER: Maybe I ought to talk to her?

MOTHER: Don't ask me, Joe.

KELLER [*almost an outburst*]: Then who do I ask? But I don't think she'll do anything about it.

MOTHER: You're asking me again.

KELLER: I'm askin' you. What am I, a stranger? I thought I had a family here. What happened to my family?

MOTHER: You've got a family. I'm simply telling you that I have no strength to think any more.

KELLER: You have no strength. The minute there's trouble you have no strength.

MOTHER: Joe, you're doing the same thing again; all your life whenever there's trouble you yell at me and you think that settles it.

KELLER: Then what do I do? Tell me, talk to me, what do I do?

MOTHER: Joe . . . I've been thinking this way. If he comes back . . .

KELLER: What do you mean 'if'? . . . he's comin' back!

MOTHER: I think if you sit him down and you . . . explain yourself. I mean you ought to make it clear to him that you know you did a terrible thing. [*Not looking into his eyes*] I mean if he saw that you realize what you did. You see?

KELLER: What ice does that cut?

MOTHER [*a little fearfully*]: I mean if you told him that you want to pay for what you did.

KELLER [*sensing . . . quietly*]: How can I pay?

MOTHER: Tell him . . . you're willing to go to prison.

[*Pause.*]

KELLER [*struck, amazed*]: I'm willing to . . . ?

MOTHER [*quickly*]: You wouldn't go, he wouldn't ask you to go. But if you told him you wanted to, if he could feel that you wanted to pay, maybe he would forgive you.

KELLER: He would forgive me! For what?

MOTHER: Joe, you know what I mean.

KELLER: I don't know what you mean! You wanted money, so I made money. What must I be forgiven? You wanted money, didn't you?

MOTHER: I didn't want it that way.

KELLER: I didn't want it that way, either! What difference is it what you want? I spoiled the both of you. I should've put him out when he was ten like I was put out, and make him earn his keep. Then he'd know how a buck is made in this world. Forgiven! I could live on a quarter a day myself, but I got a family so I . . .

MOTHER: Joe, Joe . . . it don't excuse it that you did it for the family.

KELLER: It's got to excuse it!

MOTHER: There's something bigger than the family to him.

KELLER: Nothin' is bigger!

MOTHER: There is to him.

KELLER: There's nothin' he could do that I wouldn't forgive. Because he's my son. Because I'm his father and he's my son.

MOTHER: Joe, I tell you . . .

KELLER: Nothin's bigger than that. And you're goin' to tell him, you understand? I'm his father and he's my son, and if there's something bigger than that I'll put a bullet in my head!

MOTHER: You stop that!

KELLER: You heard me. Now you know what to tell him. [*Pause. He moves from her – halts.*] But he wouldn't put me away though . . . He wouldn't do that . . . Would he?

MOTHER: He loved you, Joe, you broke his heart.

KELLER: But to put me away . . .

MOTHER: I don't know. I'm beginning to think we don't really know him. They say in the war he was such a killer. Here he was always afraid of mice. I don't know him. I don't know what he'll do.

KELLER: Goddam, if Larry was alive he wouldn't act like this. He understood the way the world is made. He listened to me. To him the world had a forty-foot front, it ended at the building line. This one, everything bothers him. You make a deal, overcharge two cents, and his hair falls out. He don't understand money. Too easy, it came too easy. Yes sir. Larry. That was a boy we lost. Larry. Larry. [*He slumps on chair in front of her.*] What am I gonna do, Kate . . .

MOTHER: Joe, Joe, please . . . you'll be all right, nothing is going to happen . . .

KELLER [*desperately, lost*]: For you, Kate, for both of you, that's all I ever lived for . . .

MOTHER: I know, darling, I know . . .

[ANN *enters from house. They say nothing, waiting for her to speak.*]

ANN: Why do you stay up? I'll tell you when he comes.

KELLER [*rises, goes to her*]: You didn't eat supper, did you? [*To* MOTHER] Why don't you make her something?

MOTHER: Sure, I'll . . .

ANN: Never mind, Kate, I'm all right. [*They are unable to speak to each other.*] There's something I want to tell you. [*She starts, then halts.*] I'm not going to do anything about it . . .

MOTHER: She's a good girl! [*To* KELLER] You see? She's a . . .

ANN: I'll do nothing about Joe, but you're going to do something for me. [*Directly to* MOTHER] You made Chris feel guilty with me. Whether you wanted to or not, you've crippled him in front of me. I'd like you to tell him that Larry is dead and that you know it. You understand me? I'm not going out of here alone.

There's no life for me that way. I want you to set him free. And then I promise you, everything will end, and we'll go away, and that's all.

KELLER: You'll do that. You'll tell him.

ANN: I know what I'm asking, Kate. You had two sons. But you've only got one now.

KELLER: You'll tell him . . .

ANN: And you've got to say it to him so he knows you mean it.

MOTHER: My dear, if the boy was dead, it wouldn't depend on my words to make Chris know it . . . The night he gets into your bed, his heart will dry up. Because he knows and you know. To his dying day he'll wait for his brother! No, my dear, no such thing. You're going in the morning, and you're going alone. That's your life, that's your lonely life. [*She goes to porch, and starts in.*]

ANN: Larry is dead, Kate.

MOTHER [*she stops*]: Don't speak to me.

ANN: I said he's dead. I know! He crashed off the coast of China November twenty-fifth! His engine didn't fail him. But he died. I know . . .

MOTHER: How did he die? You're lying to me. If you know, how did he die?

ANN: I loved him. You know I loved him. Would I have looked at anyone else if I wasn't sure? That's enough for you.

MOTHER [*moving on her*]: What's enough for me? What're you talking about? [*She grasps* ANN*'s wrists.*]

ANN: You're hurting my wrists.

MOTHER: What are you talking about! [*Pause. She stares at* ANN *a moment, then turns and goes to* KELLER.]

ANN: Joe, go in the house . . .

KELLER: Why should I . . .

ANN: Please go.

KELLER: Lemme know when he comes. [KELLER *goes into house.*]

MOTHER [*she sees* ANN *take a letter from her pocket*]: What's that?

ANN: Sit down . . . [MOTHER *moves L. to chair, but does not sit.*] First you've got to understand. When I came, I didn't have any idea that Joe . . . I had nothing against him or you. I came to get married. I hoped . . . So I didn't bring this to hurt you. I thought I'd show it to you only if there was no other way to settle Larry in your mind.

MOTHER: Larry? [*Snatches letter from* ANN's *hand.*]

ANN: He wrote it to me just before he – [MOTHER *opens and begins to read letter.*] I'm not trying to hurt you, Kate. You're making me do this, now remember you're— Remember. I've been so lonely, Kate . . . I can't leave here alone again. [*A long, low moan comes from* MOTHER's *throat as she reads.*] You made me show it to you. You wouldn't believe me. I told you a hundred times, why wouldn't you believe me!

MOTHER: Oh, my God . . .

ANN [*with pity and fear*]: Kate, please, please . . .

MOTHER: My God, my God . . .

ANN: Kate, dear, I'm so sorry . . . I'm so sorry. [CHRIS *enters from driveway. He seems exhausted.*]

CHRIS: What's the matter . . . ?

ANN: Where were you? . . . you're all perspired. [MOTHER *doesn't move.*] Where were you?

CHRIS: Just drove around a little. I thought you'd be gone.

ANN: Where do I go? I have nowhere to go.

CHRIS [*to* MOTHER]: Where's Dad?

ANN: Inside lying down.

CHRIS: Sit down, both of you. I'll say what there is to say.

MOTHER: I didn't hear the car . . .

CHRIS: I left it in the garage.

MOTHER: Jim is out looking for you.

CHRIS: Mother . . . I'm going away. There are a couple of firms in Cleveland, I think I can get a place. I mean, I'm going away for good. [*To* ANN *alone*] I know what you're thinking, Annie. It's true. I'm yellow. I was made yellow in this house because I suspected my father and I did nothing about it, but if I knew that night when I came home what I know now, he'd be in the district attorney's office by this time, and I'd have brought him there. Now if I look at him, all I'm able to do is cry.

MOTHER: What are you talking about? What else can you do?

CHRIS: I could jail him! I could jail him, if I were human any more. But I'm like everybody else now. I'm practical now. You made me practical.

MOTHER: But you have to be.

CHRIS: The cats in that alley are practical, the bums who ran away when we were fighting were practical. Only the dead ones weren't practical. But now I'm practical, and I spit on myself. I'm going away. I'm going now.

ANN [*goes up to stop him*]: I'm coming with you . . .

CHRIS: No, Ann.

ANN: Chris, I don't ask you to do anything about Joe.

CHRIS: You do, you do . . .

ANN: I swear I never will.

CHRIS: In your heart you always will.

ANN: Then do what you have to do!

CHRIS: Do what? What is there to do? I've looked all night for a reason to make him suffer.

ANN: There's reason, there's reason!

CHRIS: What? Do I raise the dead when I put him behind bars? Then what'll I do it for? We used to shoot a man who acted like a dog, but honour was real there, you were protecting something. But here? This is the land of the great big dogs, you don't love a man here, you eat him! That's the principle; the only one we live by – it just happened to kill a few people this time, that's all. The world's that way, how can I take it out on him? What sense does that make? This is a zoo, a zoo!

ANN [*to* MOTHER]: You know what he's got to do! Tell him!

MOTHER: Let him go.

ANN: I won't let him go. You'll tell him what he's got to do . . .

MOTHER: Annie!

ANN: Then I will! [KELLER *enters from house.* CHRIS *sees him, goes down* R. *near arbour.*]

KELLER: What's the matter with you? I want to talk to you.

CHRIS: I've got nothing to say to you.

KELLER [*taking his arm*]: I want to talk to you!

CHRIS [*pulling violently away from him*]: Don't do that, Dad. I'm going to hurt you if you do that. There's nothing to say, so say it quick.

KELLER: Exactly what's the matter? What's the matter? You got too much money? Is that what bothers you?

CHRIS [*with an edge of sarcasm*]: It bothers me.

KELLER: If you can't get used to it, then throw it away. You hear me? Take every cent and give it to charity, throw it in the sewer. Does that settle it? In the sewer, that's all. You think I'm kidding? I'm tellin' you what to do, if it's dirty then burn it. It's your money, that's not my money. I'm a dead man, I'm an old dead man, nothing's mine. Well, talk to me! – what do you want to do!

CHRIS: It's not what I want to do. It's what you want to do.

KELLER: What should I want to do? [CHRIS *is silent.*] Jail? You want me to go to jail? If you want me to go, say so! Is that where I belong? – then tell me so! [*Slight pause.*] What's the matter, why can't you tell me? [*Furiously*] You say everything else to me, say that! [*Slight pause.*] I'll tell you why you can't say it. Because you know I don't belong there. Because you know! [*With growing emphasis and passion, and a persistent tone of desperation*] Who worked for nothin' in that war? When they work for nothin', I'll work for nothin'. Did they ship a gun or a truck outa Detroit before they got their price? Is that clean? It's dollars and cents, nickels and dimes; war and peace, it's nickels and dimes, what's clean? Half the Goddam country is gotta go if I go! That's why you can't tell me.

CHRIS: That's exactly why.

KELLER: Then . . . why am *I* bad?

CHRIS: *I* know you're no worse than most men but I thought you were better. I never saw you as a man. I saw you as my father. [*Almost breaking*] I can't look at you this way, I can't look at myself! [*He turns away unable to face* KELLER. ANN *goes quickly to* MOTHER, *takes letter from her and starts for* CHRIS. MOTHER *instantly rushes to intercept her.*]

MOTHER: Give me that!

ANN: He's going to read it! [*She thrusts letter into* CHRIS*'s hand.*] Larry. He wrote it to me the day he died . . .

KELLER: Larry!?

MOTHER: Chris, it's not for you. [*He starts to read.*] Joe . . . go away . . .

KELLER [*mystified, frightened*]: Why'd she say, Larry, what . . . ?

MOTHER [*she desperately pushes him toward alley, glancing at* CHRIS]: Go to the street, Joe, go to the street! [*She comes down beside* KELLER.] Don't, Chris . . . [*Pleading from her whole soul*] Don't tell him . . .

CHRIS [*quietly*]: Three and one half years . . . talking, talking. Now you tell me what you must do . . . This is how he died, now tell me where you belong.

KELLER [*pleading*]: Chris, a man can't be a Jesus in this world!

CHRIS: I know all about the world. I know the whole crap story. Now listen to this, and tell me what a man's got to be! [*Reads*] 'My dear Ann: . . .' You listening? He wrote this the day he died. Listen, don't cry . . . listen! 'My dear Ann: It is impossible to put down the things I feel. But I've got to tell you something. Yesterday they flew in a load of papers from the States and I read about Dad and your father being convicted. I can't express myself. I can't tell you how I feel – I can't bear to live any more. Last night I circled the base for twenty minutes before I could bring myself in. How could he have done that? Every day three or four men never come back and he sits back there doing business . . . I don't know how to tell you what I feel . . . I can't face anybody . . . I'm going out on a mission in a few minutes. They'll probably report me missing. If they do, I want you to know that you mustn't wait for me. I tell you, Ann, if I had him here now I could kill him –' [KELLER *grabs letter from* CHRIS*'s hand and reads it. After a long pause*] Now blame the world. Do you understand that letter?

KELLER [*he speaks almost inaudibly*]: I think I do. Get the car, I'll put on my jacket. [*He turns and starts slowly for the house.* MOTHER *rushes to intercept him.*]

MOTHER: Why are you going? You'll sleep, why are you going?

KELLER: I can't sleep here. I'll feel better if I go.

MOTHER: You're so foolish. Larry was your son too, wasn't he? You know he'd never tell you to do this.

KELLER [*looking at letter in his hand*]: Then what is this if it isn't telling me? Sure, he was my son. But I think to him they were all my sons. And I guess they were, I guess they were. I'll be right down. [*Exits into house.*]

MOTHER [*to* CHRIS, *with determination*]: You're not going to take him!

CHRIS: I'm taking him.

MOTHER: It's up to you, if you tell him to stay he'll stay. Go and tell him!

CHRIS: Nobody could stop him now.

MOTHER: You'll stop him! How long will he live in prison? – are you trying to kill him?

CHRIS [*holding out letter*]: I thought you read this!

MOTHER [*of Larry, the letter*]: The war is over! Didn't you hear?— it's over!

CHRIS: Then what was Larry to you? A stone that fell into the water? It's not enough for him to be sorry. Larry didn't kill himself to make you and Dad sorry.

MOTHER: What more can we be!

CHRIS: You can be better! Once and for all you can know there's a universe of people outside and you're responsible to it, and unless you know that you threw away your son because that's why he died.

[*A shot is heard in the house. They stand frozen for a brief second.* CHRIS *starts for porch, pauses at step, turns to* ANN.]

CHRIS: Find Jim! [*He goes on into the house and* ANN *runs up driveway.* MOTHER *stands alone, transfixed.*]

MOTHER [*softly, almost moaning*]: Joe . . . Joe . . . Joe . . . Joe . . .
[CHRIS *comes out of house, down to* MOTHER's *arms.*]

CHRIS [*almost crying*]: Mother, I didn't mean to . . .

MOTHER: Don't, dear. Don't take it on yourself. Forget now. Live. [CHRIS *stirs as if to answer.*] Shhh . . . [*She puts his arms down gently and moves towards porch.*] Shhh . . . [*As she reaches porch steps she begins sobbing, as*]

THE CURTAIN FALLS

———

Property List

I

Garbage pail
Leaf burner
Sunday paper
Paper bag
Flower petals
Glass of water and aspirins
Ladder
Pot of raw stringbeans

II

Limb of broken-off tree
Tray with grape juice, pitcher, glasses
Scrap of paper
Hat (for George)
Flowered hat (for Lydia)
Sheet of paper
About 6 apples in small fruit box
Saw

III

Letter

1. Arthur Miller on stage at the original Broadway production of *All My Sons*, directed by Elia Kazan at the Coronet Theatre, New York, 1947. Photograph by Eileen Darby.

2. Playbill for the first production.

3. Cast of the original Broadway production, starring Beth Miller, Arthur Kennedy and Karl Malden. Photograph by Eileen Darby.

4. Poster for the Lyric Theatre production in London, 1948.

5. (*below*) Miller at the time he was staging *All My Sons*. Photograph by Arnold Newman.

6. (*top*) Burt Lancaster, Mady Christians and Edward G. Robinson in the 1948 film directed by Irving Reis.

7. (*bottom*) Colin Blakely (*left*) in the 1981 production at the Wyndham's Theatre, London. Photograph by Frazer Ashford.

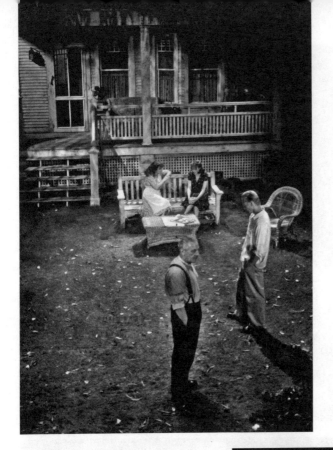

8. (*above*) Howard Davies' Olivier Award–winning production at the National Theatre, London, 2000. Photograph by Chris Parker.

9. (*right*) Julie Walters as Kate Keller in the National Theatre revival. Photograph by Colin Willoughby.

10. (*above*) Madeleine Potter, Ben Daniels and Charles Edward at the National Theatre, 2001. Photograph by Elliot Franks.

11. (*right*) John Lithgow and Katie Holmes in a Broadway revival in 2008. Photograph by Joan Marcus.

12. (*above*) John Lithgow,
Dianne Wiest, Patrick Wilson
and Katie Holmes on Broadway.
Photograph by Joan Marcus.

13. (*left*) Cast of the Apollo
Theatre production in London,
2010. Photograph by
Tristram Kenton.

14. (*top*) Zoë Wanamaker and David Suchet in the Apollo Theatre revival. Photograph by Robbie Jack.

15. (*bottom*) A 2013 production at the Royal Exchange Theatre in Manchester. Photograph by Jonathan Keenan.

Death of a Salesman

First presented in England at the Phoenix Theatre, London, on 28 July 1949, with the following cast:

WILLY LOMAN	*Paul Muni*
LINDA	*Katherine Alexander*
BIFF	*Kevin McCarthy*
HAPPY	*Frank Maxwell*
BERNARD	*Sam Main*
THE WOMAN	*Bessie Love*
CHARLEY	*Ralph Theodore*
UNCLE BEN	*Henry Oscar*
HOWARD WAGNER	*J. Anthony La Penna*
JENNY	*Joan MacArthur*
STANLEY	*George Margo*
MISS FORSYTHE	*Mary Laura Wood*
LETTA	*Barbara Cummings*
WAITER	*Ronald Frazer*

Produced by ELIA KAZAN

CHARACTERS

WILLY LOMAN	CHARLEY
LINDA	UNCLE BEN
BIFF	HOWARD WAGNER
HAPPY	JENNY
BERNARD	STANLEY
THE WOMAN	MISS FORSYTHE
LETTA	WAITER

The action takes place in Willy Loman's house and yard and in various places he visits in the New York and Boston of today.

Act One

A melody is heard, played upon a flute. It is small and fine, telling of grass and trees and the horizon. The curtain rises.

Before us is the SALESMAN'S *house. We are aware of towering, angular shapes behind it, surrounding it on all sides. Only the blue light of the sky falls upon the house and forestage; the surrounding area shows an angry glow of orange. As more light appears, we see a solid vault of apartment houses around the small, fragile-seeming home. An air of the dream clings to the place, a dream rising out of reality. The kitchen at centre seems actual enough, for there is a kitchen table with three chairs, and a refrigerator. But no other fixtures are seen. At the back of the kitchen there is a draped entrance, which leads to the living-room. To the right of the kitchen, on a level raised two feet, is a bedroom furnished only with a brass bedstead and a straight chair. On a shelf over the bed a silver athletic trophy stands. A window opens on to the apartment house at the side.*

Behind the kitchen, on a level raised six and a half feet, is the boys' bedroom, at present barely visible. Two beds are dimly seen, and at the back of the room a dormer window. (This bedroom is above the unseen living-room.) At the left a stairway curves up to it from the kitchen.

The entire setting is wholly or, in some places, partially transparent. The roof-line of the house is one-dimensional; under and over it we see the apartment buildings. Before the house lies an apron, curving beyond the forestage into the orchestra. This forward area serves as the back yard as well as the locale of all WILLY'S *imaginings and of his city scenes. Whenever the action is in the present the actors observe the imaginary wall-lines, entering the house only through its door at the left. But in the scenes of the past these boundaries are broken, and characters enter or leave a room by stepping 'through' a wall on to the forestage.*

From the right, WILLY LOMAN, *the Salesman, enters, carrying two large sample cases. The flute plays on. He hears but is not aware of it. He is past sixty years of age, dressed quietly. Even as he crosses the stage to the doorway of the house, his exhaustion is apparent. He unlocks the door, comes into the kitchen, and thankfully lets his burden down, feeling the soreness of his palms. A word-sigh escapes his lips – it might be 'Oh, boy, oh, boy.' He closes the door, then carries his cases out into the living-room, through the draped kitchen doorway.* LINDA, *his wife, has stirred in her bed at the right. She gets out and puts on a robe, listening. Most often jovial, she has developed an iron repression of her exceptions to* WILLY's *behaviour – she more than loves him, she admires him, as though his mercurial nature, his temper, his massive dreams and little cruelties, served her only as sharp reminders of the turbulent longings within him, longings which she shares but lacks the temperament to utter and follow to their end.*

LINDA [*hearing* WILLY *outside the bedroom, calls with some trepidation*]: Willy!

WILLY: It's all right. I came back.

LINDA: Why? What happened? [*Slight pause.*] Did something happen, Willy?

WILLY: No, nothing happened.

LINDA: You didn't smash the car, did you?

WILLY [*with casual irritation*]: I said nothing happened. Didn't you hear me?

LINDA: Don't you feel well?

WILLY: I'm tired to the death. [*The flute has faded away. He sits on the bed beside her, a little numb.*] I couldn't make it. I just couldn't make it, Linda.

LINDA [*very carefully, delicately*]: Where were you all day? You look terrible.

WILLY: I got as far as a little above Yonkers. I stopped for a cup of coffee. Maybe it was the coffee.

LINDA: What?

WILLY [*after a pause*]: I suddenly couldn't drive any more. The car kept going off on to the shoulder, y'know?

LINDA [*helpfully*]: Oh. Maybe it was the steering again. I don't think Angelo knows the Studebaker.

WILLY: No, it's me, it's me. Suddenly I realize I'm goin' sixty miles an hour and I don't remember the last five minutes. I'm – I can't seem to – keep my mind to it.

LINDA: Maybe it's your glasses. You never went for your new glasses.

WILLY: No, I see everything. I came back ten miles an hour. It took me nearly four hours from Yonkers.

LINDA [*resigned*]: Well, you'll just have to take a rest, Willy, you can't continue this way.

WILLY: I just got back from Florida.

LINDA: But you didn't rest your mind. Your mind is over-active, and the mind is what counts, dear.

WILLY: I'll start out in the morning. Maybe I'll feel better in the morning. [*She is taking off his shoes.*] These goddam arch supports are killing me.

LINDA: Take an aspirin. Should I get you an aspirin? It'll soothe you.

WILLY [*with wonder*]: I was driving along, you understand? And I was fine. I was even observing the scenery. You can imagine, me looking at scenery, on the road every week of my life. But it's so beautiful up there, Linda, the trees are so thick, and the sun is warm. I opened the windshield and just let the warm air bathe over me. And then all of a sudden I'm going' off the road! I'm tellin' ya, I absolutely forgot I was driving. If I'd've gone the other way over the white line I might've killed somebody. So I went on again – and five minutes later I'm dreamin' again, and I nearly – [*He presses two fingers against his eyes.*] I have such thoughts, I have such strange thoughts.

LINDA: Willy, dear. Talk to them again. There's no reason why you can't work in New York.

WILLY: They don't need me in New York. I'm the New England man. I'm vital in New England.

LINDA: But you're sixty years old. They can't expect you to keep travelling every week.

WILLY: I'll have to send a wire to Portland. I'm supposed to see Brown and Morrison tomorrow morning at ten o'clock to show the line. Goddammit, I could sell them! [*He starts putting on his jacket.*]

LINDA [*taking the jacket from him*]: Why don't you go down to the place tomorrow and tell Howard you've simply got to work in New York? You're too accommodating, dear.

WILLY: If old man Wagner was alive I'd a been in charge of New York now! That man was a prince, he was a masterful man. But that boy of his, that Howard, he don't appreciate. When I went north the first time, the Wagner Company didn't know where New England was!

LINDA: Why don't you tell those things to Howard, dear?

WILLY [*encouraged*]: I will, I definitely will. Is there any cheese?

LINDA: I'll make you a sandwich.

WILLY: No, go to sleep. I'll take some milk. I'll be up right away. The boys in?

LINDA: They're sleeping. Happy took Biff on a date tonight.

WILLY [*interested*]: That so?

LINDA: It was so nice to see them shaving together, one behind the other, in the bathroom. And going out together. You notice? The whole house smells of shaving lotion.

WILLY: Figure it out. Work a lifetime to pay off a house. You finally own it, and there's nobody to live in it.

LINDA: Well, dear, life is a casting off. It's always that way.

WILLY: No, no, some people – some people accomplish something. Did Biff say anything after I went this morning?

LINDA: You shouldn't have criticized him, Willy, especially after he just got off the train. You mustn't lose your temper with him.

WILLY: When the hell did I lose my temper? I simply asked him if he was making any money. Is that a criticism?

LINDA: But, dear, how could he make any money?

WILLY [*worried and angered*]: There's such an undercurrent in him.

He became a moody man. Did he apologize when I left this morning?

LINDA: He was crestfallen, Willy. You know how he admires you. I think if he finds himself, then you'll both be happier and not fight any more.

WILLY: How can he find himself on a farm? Is that a life? A farm-hand? In the beginning, when he was young, I thought, well, a young man, it's good for him to tramp around, take a lot of different jobs. But it's more than ten years now and he has yet to make thirty-five dollars a week!

LINDA: He's finding himself, Willy.

WILLY: Not finding yourself at the age of thirty-four is a disgrace!

LINDA: Shh!

WILLY: The trouble is he's lazy, goddammit!

LINDA: Willy, please!

WILLY: Biff is a lazy bum!

LINDA: They're sleeping. Get something to eat. Go on down.

WILLY: Why did he come home? I would like to know what brought him home.

LINDA: I don't know. I think he's still lost, Willy. I think he's very lost.

WILLY: Biff Loman is lost. In the greatest country in the world a young man with such – personal attractiveness, gets lost. And such a hard worker. There's one thing about Biff – he's not lazy.

LINDA: Never.

WILLY [*with pity and resolve*]: I'll see him in the morning; I'll have a nice talk with him. I'll get him a job selling. He could be big in no time. My God! Remember how they used to follow him around in high school? When he smiled at one of them their faces lit up. When he walked down the street . . . [*He loses himself in reminiscences.*]

LINDA [*trying to bring him out of it*]: Willy, dear, I got a new kind of American-type cheese today. It's whipped.

WILLY: Why do you get American when I like Swiss?

LINDA: I just thought you'd like a change –

WILLY: I don't want a change! I want Swiss cheese. Why am I always being contradicted?

LINDA [*with a covering laugh*]: I thought it would be a surprise.

WILLY: Why don't you open a window in here, for God's sake?

LINDA [*with infinite patience*]: They're all open, dear.

WILLY: The way they boxed us in here. Bricks and windows, windows and bricks.

LINDA: We should've bought the land next door.

WILLY: The street is lined with cars. There's not a breath of fresh air in the neighbourhood. The grass don't grow any more, you can't raise a carrot in the backyard. They should've had a law against apartment houses. Remember those two beautiful elm trees out there? When I and Biff hung the swing between them?

LINDA: Yeah, like being a million miles from the city.

WILLY: They should've arrested the builder for cutting those down. They massacred the neighbourhood. [*Lost*] More and more I think of those days, Linda. This time of year it was lilac and wistaria. And then the peonies would come out, and the daffodils. What a fragrance in this room!

LINDA: Well, after all, people had to move somewhere.

WILLY: No, there's more people now.

LINDA: I don't think there's more people, I think –

WILLY: There's more people! That's what's ruining this country! Population is getting out of control. The competition is maddening! Smell the stink from that apartment house! And another one on the other side . . . How can they whip cheese?

[*On* WILLY's *last line,* BIFF *and* HAPPY *raise themselves up in their beds, listening.*]

LINDA: Go down, try it. And be quiet.

WILLY [*turning to* LINDA, *guiltily*]: You're not worried about me, are you, sweetheart?

BIFF: What's the matter?

HAPPY: Listen!

LINDA: You've got too much on the ball to worry about.

WILLY: You're my foundation and my support, Linda.

LINDA: Just try to relax, dear. You make mountains out of molehills.

WILLY: I won't fight with him any more. If he wants to go back to Texas, let him go.

LINDA: He'll find his way.

WILLY: Sure. Certain men just don't get started till later in life. Like Thomas Edison, I think. Or B. F. Goodrich. One of them was deaf. [*He starts for the bedroom doorway.*] I'll put my money on Biff.

LINDA: And Willy – if it's warm Sunday we'll drive in the country. And we'll open the windshield, and take lunch.

WILLY: No, the windshields don't open on the new cars.

LINDA: But you opened it today.

WILLY: Me? I didn't. [*He stops.*] Now isn't that peculiar! Isn't that a remarkable – [*He breaks off in amazement and fright as the flute is heard distantly.*]

LINDA: What, darling?

WILLY: That is the most remarkable thing.

LINDA: What, dear?

WILLY: I was thinking of the Chevvy. [*Slight pause.*] Nineteen twenty-eight . . . when I had that red Chevvy – [*Breaks off.*] That funny? I coulda sworn I was driving that Chevvy today.

LINDA: Well, that's nothing. Something must've reminded you.

WILLY: Remarkable. Ts. Remember those days? The way Biff used to simonize that car? The dealer refused to believe there was eighty thousand miles on it. [*He shakes his head.*] Heh! [*To* LINDA] Close your eyes, I'll be right up. [*He walks out of the bedroom.*]

HAPPY [*to* BIFF]: Jesus, maybe he smashed up the car again!

LINDA [*calling after* WILLY]: Be careful on the stairs, dear! The cheese is on the middle shelf! [*She turns, goes over to the bed, takes his jacket, and goes out of the bedroom.*]

[*Light has risen on the boys' room. Unseen,* WILLY *is heard talking to himself, 'Eighty thousand miles,' and a little laugh.* BIFF *gets out of bed, comes downstage a bit, and stands attentively.* BIFF *is two years older than his brother* HAPPY, *well built, but in these days bears a worn air and seems less self-assured. He has succeeded less, and his dreams are stronger and less acceptable than* HAPPY's. HAPPY *is tall, powerfully made. Sexuality is like a visible colour on him, or a scent that many women have discovered. He, like his brother, is lost, but in a different way, for he has never allowed himself to turn his face toward defeat and is thus more confused and hard-skinned, although seemingly more content.*]

HAPPY [*getting out of bed*]: He's going to get his licence taken away if he keeps that up. I'm getting nervous about him, y'know, Biff?

BIFF: His eyes are going.

HAPPY: No, I've driven with him. He sees all right. He just doesn't keep his mind on it. I drove into the city with him last week. He stops at a green light and then it turns red and he goes. [*He laughs.*]

BIFF: Maybe he's colour-blind.

HAPPY: Pop? Why, he's got the finest eye for colour in the business. You know that.

BIFF [*sitting down on his bed*]: I'm going to sleep.

HAPPY: You're not still sour on Dad, are you, Biff?

BIFF: He's all right, I guess.

WILLY [*underneath them, in the living-room*]: Yes, sir, eighty thousand miles – eighty-two thousand!

BIFF: You smoking?

HAPPY [*holding out a pack of cigarettes*]: Want one?

BIFF [*taking a cigarette*]: I can never sleep when I smell it.

WILLY: What a simonizing job, heh!

HAPPY [*with deep sentiment*]: Funny, Biff, y'know? Us sleeping in here again? The old beds. [*He pats his bed affectionately.*] All the talk that went across those two beds, huh? Our whole lives.

BIFF: Yeah. Lotta dreams and plans.

HAPPY [*with a deep and masculine laugh*]: About five hundred women would like to know what was said in this room.

[*They share a soft laugh.*]

BIFF: Remember that big Betsy something – what the hell was her name – over on Bushwick Avenue?

HAPPY [*combing his hair*]: With the collie dog!

BIFF: That's the one. I got you in there, remember?

HAPPY: Yeah, that was my first time – I think. Boy, there was a pig! [*They laugh, almost crudely.*] You taught me everything I know about women. Don't forget that.

BIFF: I bet you forgot how bashful you used to be. Especially with girls.

HAPPY: Oh, I still am, Biff.

BIFF: Oh, go on.

HAPPY: I just control it, that's all. I think I got less bashful and you got more so. What happened, Biff? Where's the old humour, the old confidence? [*He shakes* BIFF*'s knee.* BIFF *gets up and moves restlessly about the room.*] What's the matter?

BIFF: Why does Dad mock me all the time?

HAPPY: He's not mocking you, he –

BIFF: Everything I say there's a twist of mockery on his face. I can't get near him.

HAPPY: He just wants you to make good, that's all. I wanted to talk to you about Dad for a long time, Biff. Something's – happening to him. He – talks to himself.

BIFF: I noticed that this morning. But he always mumbled.

HAPPY: But not so noticeable. It got so embarrassing I sent him to Florida. And you know something? Most of the time he's talking to you.

BIFF: What's he say about me?

HAPPY: I can't make it out.

BIFF: What's he say about me?

HAPPY: I think the fact that you're not settled, that you're still kind of up in the air . . .

BIFF: There's one or two other things depressing him, Happy.

HAPPY: What do you mean?

BIFF: Never mind. Just don't lay it all to me.

HAPPY: But I think if you got started – I mean – is there any future for you out there?

BIFF: I tell ya, Hap, I don't know what the future is. I don't know –
what I'm supposed to want.

HAPPY: What do you mean?

BIFF: Well, I spent six or seven years after high school trying to work
myself up. Shipping clerk, salesman, business of one kind or
another. And it's a measly manner of existence. To get on that
subway on the hot mornings in summer. To devote your whole
life to keeping stock, or making phone calls, or selling or buying.
To suffer fifty weeks of the year for the sake of a two-week vac-
ation, when all you really desire is to be outdoors, with your shirt
off. And always to have to get ahead of the next fella. And still –
that's how you build a future.

HAPPY: Well, you really enjoy it on a farm? Are you content out
there?

BIFF [*with rising agitation*]: Hap, I've had twenty or thirty different
kinds of job since I left home before the war, and it always turns
out the same. I just realized it lately. In Nebraska when I herded
cattle, and the Dakotas, and Arizona, and now in Texas. It's why
I came home now, I guess, because I realized it. This farm I work
on, it's spring there now, see? And they've got about fifteen new
colts. There's nothing more inspiring or – beautiful than the sight
of a mare and a new colt. And it's cool there now, see? Texas is
cool now, and it's spring. And whenever spring comes to where I
am, I suddenly get the feeling, my God, I'm not gettin' anywhere.
What the hell am I doing, playing around with horses,
twenty-eight dollars a week! I'm thirty-four years old, I oughta be
makin' my future. That's when I come running home. And now,
I get here, and I don't know what to do with myself. [*After a pause*]
I've always made a point of not wasting my life, and everytime I
come back here I know that all I've done is to waste my life.

HAPPY: You're a poet, you know that, Biff? You're a – you're an
idealist!

BIFF: No, I'm mixed up very bad. Maybe I oughta get married. Maybe
I oughta get stuck into something. Maybe that's my trouble. I'm
like a boy. I'm not married, I'm not in business, I just – I'm like a

boy. Are you content, Hap? You're a success, aren't you? Are you content?

HAPPY: Hell, no!

BIFF: Why? You're making money, aren't you?

HAPPY [*moving about with energy, expressiveness*]: All I can do now is wait for the merchandise manager to die. And suppose I get to be merchandise manager? He's a good friend of mine, and he just built a terrific estate on Long Island. And he lived there about two months and sold it, and now he's building another one. He can't enjoy it once it's finished. And I know that's just what I would do. I don't know what the hell I'm workin' for. Sometimes I sit in my apartment – all alone. And I think of the rent I'm paying. And it's crazy. But then, it's what I always wanted. My own apartment, a car, and plenty of women. And still, goddammit, I'm lonely.

BIFF [*with enthusiasm*]: Listen, why don't you come out West with me?

HAPPY: You and I, heh?

BIFF: Sure, maybe we could buy a ranch. Raise cattle, use our muscles. Men built like we are should be working out in the open.

HAPPY [*avidly*]: The Loman Brothers, heh?

BIFF [*with vast affection*]: Sure, we'd be known all over the counties!

HAPPY [*enthralled*]: That's what I dream about, Biff. Sometimes I want to just rip my clothes off in the middle of the store and outbox that goddam merchandise manager. I mean I can outbox, outrun, and outlift anybody in that store, and I have to take orders from those common, petty sons-of-bitches till I can't stand it any more.

BIFF: I'm tellin' you, kid, if you were with me I'd be happy out there.

HAPPY [*enthused*]: See, Biff, everybody around me is so false that I'm constantly lowering my ideals . . .

BIFF: Baby, together we'd stand up for one another, we'd have someone to trust.

HAPPY: If I were around you –

BIFF: Hap, the trouble is we weren't brought up to grub for money. I don't know how to do it

HAPPY: Neither can I!

BIFF: Then let's go!

HAPPY: The only thing is – what can you make out there?

BIFF: But look at your friend. Builds an estate and then hasn't the peace of mind to live in it.

HAPPY: Yeah, but when he walks into the store the waves part in front of him. That's fifty-two thousand dollars a year coming through the revolving door, and I got more in my pinky finger than he's got in his head.

BIFF: Yeah, but you just said –

HAPPY: I gotta show some of those pompous, self-important executives over there that Hap Loman can make the grade. I want to walk into the store the way he walks in. Then I'll go with you, Biff. We'll be together yet, I swear. But take those two we had tonight. Now weren't they gorgeous creatures?

BIFF: Yeah, yeah, most gorgeous I've had in years.

HAPPY: I get that any time I want, Biff. Whenever I feel disgusted. The only trouble is, it gets like bowling or something. I just keep knockin' them over and it doesn't mean anything. You still run around a lot?

BIFF: Naa. I'd like to find a girl – steady, somebody with substance.

HAPPY: That's what I long for.

BIFF: Go on! You'd never come home.

HAPPY: I would! Somebody with character, with resistance! Like Mom, y'know? You're gonna call me a bastard when I tell you this. That girl Charlotte I was with tonight is engaged to be married in five weeks. [*He tries on his new hat.*]

BIFF: No kiddin'!

HAPPY: Sure, the guy's in line for the vice-presidency of the store. I don't know what gets into me, maybe I just have an over-developed sense of competition or something, but I went and ruined her, and furthermore I can't get rid of her. And he's the third executive I've done that to. Isn't that a crummy characteristic? And to top it all, I go to their weddings! [*Indignantly, but laughing*] Like I'm not supposed to take bribes. Manufacturers offer me a hundred-dollar bill now and then to throw an order their way. You know how honest I am, but it's like this girl, see. I hate myself for it. Because I don't want the girl, and, still, I take it and – I love it!

BIFF: Let's go to sleep.

HAPPY: I guess we didn't settle anything, heh?

BIFF: I just got one idea that I think I'm going to try.

HAPPY: What's that?

BIFF: Remember Bill Oliver?

HAPPY: Sure, Oliver is very big now. You want to work for him again?

BIFF: No, but when I quit he said something to me. He put his arm on my shoulder, and he said, 'Biff, if you ever need anything, come to me.'

HAPPY: I remember that. That sounds good.

BIFF: I think I'll go to see him. If I could get ten thousand or even seven or eight thousand dollars I could buy a beautiful ranch.

HAPPY: I bet he'd back you. 'Cause he thought highly of you, Biff. I mean, they all do. You're well liked, Biff. That's why I say to come back here, and we both have the apartment. And I'm tellin' you, Biff, any babe you want . . .

BIFF: No, with a ranch I could do the work I like and still be something. I just wonder though. I wonder if Oliver still thinks I stole that carton of basketballs.

HAPPY: Oh, he probably forgot that long ago. It's almost ten years. You're too sensitive. Anyway, he didn't really fire you.

BIFF: Well, I think he was going to. I think that's why I quit. I was never sure whether he knew or not. I know he thought the world of me, though. I was the only one he'd let lock up the place.

WILLY [*below*]: You gonna wash the engine, Biff?

HAPPY: Shh!

[BIFF *looks at* HAPPY, *who is gazing down, listening.* WILLY *is mumbling in the parlour.*]

HAPPY: You hear that?

[*They listen.* WILLY *laughs warmly.*]

BIFF [*growing angry*]: Doesn't he know Mom can hear that?
WILLY: Don't get your sweater dirty, Biff!

[*A look of pain crosses* BIFF's *face.*]

HAPPY: Isn't that terrible? Don't leave again, will you? You'll find a job here. You gotta stick around. I don't know what to do about him, it's getting embarrassing.
WILLY: What a simonizing job!
BIFF: Mom's hearing that!
WILLY: No kiddin', Biff, you got a date? Wonderful!
HAPPY: Go on to sleep. But talk to him in the morning, will you?
BIFF [*reluctantly getting into bed*]: With her in the house. Brother!
HAPPY [*getting into bed*]: I wish you'd have a good talk with him.

[*The light on their room begins to fade.*]

BIFF [*to himself in bed*]: That selfish, stupid . . .
HAPPY: Sh . . . Sleep, Biff.

[*Their light is out. Well before they have finished speaking,* WILLY's *form is dimly seen below in the darkened kitchen. He opens the refrigerator, searches in there, and takes out a bottle of milk. The apartment houses are fading out, and the entire house and surroundings become covered with leaves. Music insinuates itself as the leaves appear.*]

WILLY: Just wanna be careful with those girls, Biff, that's all. Don't make any promises. No promises of any kind. Because a girl, y'know, they always believe what you tell 'em, and you're very young, Biff, you're too young to be talking seriously to girls.

[*Light rises on the kitchen.* WILLY, *talking, shuts the refrigerator door and comes downstage to the kitchen table. He pours milk into a glass. He is totally immersed in himself, smiling faintly.*]

WILLY: Too young entirely, Biff. You want to watch your schooling first. Then when you're all set, there'll be plenty of girls for a boy like you. [*He smiles broadly at a kitchen chair.*] That so? The girls pay for you? [*He laughs.*] Boy, you must really be makin' a hit.

[WILLY *is gradually addressing – physically – a point off-stage, speaking through the wall of the kitchen, and his voice has been rising in volume to that of a normal conversation.*]

WILLY: I been wondering why you polish the car so careful. Ha! Don't leave the hubcaps, boys. Get the chamois to the hubcaps. Happy, use newspaper on the windows, it's the easiest thing. Show him how to do it, Biff! You see, Happy? Pad it up, use it like a pad. That's it, that's it, good work. You're doin' all right, Hap. [*He pauses, then nods in approbation for a few seconds, then looks upward.*] Biff, first thing we gotta do when we get time is clip that big branch over the house. Afraid it's gonna fall in a storm and hit the roof. Tell you what. We get a rope and sling her around, and then we climb up there with a couple of saws and take her down. Soon as you finish the car, boys, I wanna see ya. I got a surprise for you, boys.
BIFF [*offstage*]: Whatta ya got, Dad?
WILLY: No, you finish first. Never leave a job till you're finished – remember that. [*Looking toward the 'big trees'*] Biff, up in Albany I saw a beautiful hammock. I think I'll buy it next trip, and we'll hang it right between those two elms. Wouldn't that be something? Just swingin' there under those branches. Boy, that would be . . .

[YOUNG BIFF *and* YOUNG HAPPY *appear from the direction* WILLY *was addressing.* HAPPY *carries rags and a pail of water.* BIFF, *wearing a sweater with a block 'S', carries a football.*]

BIFF [*pointing in the direction of the car offstage*]: How's that, Pop, professional?

WILLY: Terrific. Terrific job, boys. Good work, Biff.

HAPPY: Where's the surprise, Pop?

WILLY: In the back seat of the car.

HAPPY: Boy! [*He runs off.*]

BIFF: What is it, Dad? Tell me, what'd you buy?

WILLY [*laughing, cuffs him*]: Never mind, something I want you to have.

BIFF [*turns and starts off*]: What is it, Hap?

HAPPY [*offstage*]: It's a punching bag!

BIFF: Oh, Pop!

WILLY: It's got Gene Tunney's signature on it!

[*HAPPY runs onstage with a punching bag.*]

BIFF: Gee, how'd you know we wanted a punching bag?

WILLY: Well, it's the finest thing for the timing.

HAPPY [*lies down on his back and pedals with his feet*]: I'm losing weight, you notice, Pop?

WILLY [*to* HAPPY]: Jumping rope is good too.

BIFF: Did you see the new football I got?

WILLY [*examining the ball*]: Where'd you get a new ball?

BIFF: The coach told me to practise my passing.

WILLY: That so? And he gave you the ball, heh?

BIFF: Well, I borrowed it from the locker room. [*He laughs confidentially.*]

WILLY [*laughing with him at the theft*]: I want you to return that.

HAPPY: I told you he wouldn't like it!

BIFF [*angrily*]: Well, I'm bringing it back!

WILLY [*stopping the incipient argument, to* HAPPY]: Sure, he's gotta practise with a regulation ball, doesn't he? [*To* BIFF] Coach'll probably congratulate you on your initiative!

BIFF: Oh, he keeps congratulating my initiative all the time, Pop.

WILLY: That's because he likes you. If somebody else took that ball there'd be an uproar. So what's the report, boys, what's the report?

BIFF: Where'd you go this time, Dad? Gee, we were lonesome for you.

WILLY [*pleased, puts an arm around each boy and they come down to the apron*]: Lonesome, heh?

BIFF: Missed you every minute.

WILLY: Don't say? Tell you a secret, boys. Don't breathe it to a soul. Someday I'll have my own business, and I'll never have to leave home any more.

HAPPY: Like Uncle Charley, heh?

WILLY: Bigger than Uncle Charley! Because Charley is not – liked. He's liked, but he's not – well liked.

BIFF: Where'd you go this time, Dad?

WILLY: Well, I got on the road, and I went north to Providence. Met the Mayor.

BIFF: The Mayor of Providence!

WILLY: He was sitting in the hotel lobby.

BIFF: What'd he say?

WILLY: He said, 'Morning!' And I said, 'You got a fine city here, Mayor.' And then he had coffee with me. And then I went to Waterbury. Waterbury is a fine city. Big clock city, the famous Waterbury clock. Sold a nice bill there. And then Boston – Boston is the cradle of the Revolution. A fine city. And a couple of other towns in Mass., and on to Portland and Bangor and straight home!

BIFF: Gee, I'd love to go with you sometime, Dad.

WILLY: Soon as summer comes.

HAPPY: Promise?

WILLY: You and Hap and I, and I'll show you all the towns. America is full of beautiful towns and fine, upstanding people. And they know me, boys, they know me up and down New England. The finest people. And when I bring you fellas up, there'll be open sesame for all of us, 'cause one thing, boys: I have friends. I can park my car in any street in New England, and the cops protect it like their own. This summer, heh?

BIFF *and* HAPPY [*together*]: Yeah! You bet!

WILLY: We'll take our bathing-suits.

HAPPY: We'll carry your bags, Pop!

WILLY: Oh, won't that be something! Me comin' into the Boston stores with you boys carryin' my bags. What a sensation!

[BIFF *is prancing around, practising passing the ball.*]

WILLY: You nervous, Biff, about the game?

BIFF: Not if you're gonna be there.

WILLY: What do they say about you in school, now that they made you captain?

HAPPY: There's a crowd of girls behind him every time the classes change.

BIFF [*taking* WILLY's *hand*]: This Saturday, Pop, this Saturday – just for you, I'm going to break through for a touchdown.

HAPPY: You're supposed to pass.

BIFF: I'm takin' one play for Pop. You watch me, Pop, and when I take off my helmet, that means I'm breakin' out. Then watch me crash through that line!

WILLY [*kisses* BIFF]: Oh, wait'll I tell this in Boston!

[BERNARD *enters in knickers. He is younger than* BIFF, *earnest and loyal, a worried boy.*]

BERNARD: Biff, where are you? You're supposed to study with me today.

WILLY: Hey, looka Bernard. What're you lookin' so anaemic about, Bernard?

BERNARD: He's gotta study, Uncle Willy. He's got Regents next week.

HAPPY [*tauntingly, spinning* BERNARD *around*]: Let's box, Bernard!

BERNARD: Biff! [*He gets away from* HAPPY.] Listen, Biff, I heard Mr Birnbaum say that if you don't start studyin' math he's gonna flunk you, and you won't graduate. I heard him!

WILLY: You better study with him, Biff. Go ahead now.

BERNARD: I heard him!

BIFF: Oh, Pop, you didn't see my sneakers! [*He holds up a foot for* WILLY *to look at.*]

WILLY: Hey, that's a beautiful job of printing!

BERNARD [*wiping his glasses*]: Just because he printed University of Virginia on his sneakers doesn't mean they've got to graduate him, Uncle Willy!

WILLY [*angrily*]: What're you talking about? With scholarships to three universities they're gonna flunk him?

BERNARD: But I heard Mr Birnbaum say –

WILLY: Don't be a pest, Bernard! [*To his boys*] What an anaemic!

BERNARD: Okay, I'm waiting for you in my house, Biff.

[BERNARD *goes off. The* LOMANS *laugh.*]

WILLY: Bernard is not well liked, is he?

BIFF: He's liked, but he's not well liked.

HAPPY: That's right, Pop.

WILLY: That's just what I mean. Bernard can get the best marks in school, y'understand, but when he gets out in the business world, y'understand, you are going to be five times ahead of him. That's why I thank Almighty God you're both built like Adonises. Because the man who makes an appearance in the business world, the man who creates personal interest, is the man who gets ahead. Be liked and you will never want. You take me, for instance. I never have to wait in line to see a buyer. 'Willy Loman is here!' That's all they have to know, and I go right through.

BIFF: Did you knock them dead, Pop?

WILLY: Knocked 'em cold in Providence, slaughtered 'em in Boston.

HAPPY [*on his back, pedalling again*]: I'm losing weight, you notice, Pop?

[LINDA *enters, as of old, a ribbon in her hair, carrying a basket of washing.*]

LINDA [*with youthful energy*]: Hello, dear!

WILLY: Sweetheart!

LINDA: How'd the Chevvy run?

WILLY: Chevrolet, Linda, is the greatest car ever built. [*To the boys*] Since when do you let your mother carry wash up the stairs?

BIFF: Grab hold there, boy!

HAPPY: Where to, Mom?

LINDA: Hang them up on the line. And you better go down to your friends, Biff. The cellar is full of boys. They don't know what to do with themselves.

BIFF: Ah, when Pop comes home they can wait!

WILLY [*laughs appreciatively*]: You better go down and tell them what to do, Biff.

BIFF: I think I'll have them sweep out the furnace room.

WILLY: Good work, Biff.

BIFF [*goes through wall-line of kitchen to doorway at back and calls down*]: Fellas! Everybody sweep out the furnace room! I'll be right down!

VOICES: All right! Okay, Biff.

BIFF: George and Sam and Frank, come out back! We're hangin' up the wash! Come on, Hap, on the double! [*He and* HAPPY *carry out the basket.*]

LINDA: The way they obey him!

WILLY: Well, that's training, the training. I'm tellin' you, I was sellin' thousands and thousands, but I had to come home.

LINDA: Oh, the whole block'll be at that game. Did you sell anything?

WILLY: I did five hundred gross in Providence and seven hundred gross in Boston.

LINDA: No! Wait a minute, I've got a pencil. [*She pulls pencil and paper out of her apron pocket.*] That makes your commission . . . Two hundred – my God! Two hundred and twelve dollars!

WILLY: Well, I didn't figure it yet, but . . .

LINDA: How much did you do?

WILLY: Well, I – I did – about a hundred and eighty gross in Providence. Well, no – it came to – roughly two hundred gross on the whole trip.

LINDA [*without hesitation*]: Two hundred gross. That's . . . [*She figures.*]

WILLY: The trouble was that three of the stores were half-closed for inventory in Boston. Otherwise I woulda broke records.

LINDA: Well, it makes seventy dollars and some pennies. That's very good.

WILLY: What do we owe?

LINDA: Well, on the first there's sixteen dollars on the refrigerator –

WILLY: Why sixteen?

LINDA: Well, the fan belt broke, so it was a dollar eighty.

WILLY: But it's brand new.

LINDA: Well, the man said that's the way it is. Till they work themselves in, y'know.

[*They move through the wall-line into the kitchen.*]

WILLY: I hope we didn't get stuck on that machine.

LINDA: They got the biggest ads of any of them!

WILLY: I know, it's a fine machine. What else?

LINDA: Well, there's nine-sixty for the washing-machine. And for the vacuum cleaner there's three and a half due on the fifteenth. Then the roof, you got twenty-one dollars remaining.

WILLY: It don't leak, does it?

LINDA: No, they did a wonderful job. Then you owe Frank for the carburettor.

WILLY: I'm not going to pay that man! That goddam Chevrolet, they ought to prohibit the manufacture of that car!

LINDA: Well, you owe him three and a half. And odds and ends, comes to around a hundred and twenty dollars by the fifteenth.

WILLY: A hundred and twenty dollars! My God, if business don't pick up I don't know what I'm gonna do!

LINDA: Well, next week you'll do better.

WILLY: Oh, I'll knock 'em dead next week. I'll go to Hartford. I'm very well liked in Hartford. You know, the trouble is, Linda, people don't seem to take to me.

[*They move on to the forestage.*]

LINDA: Oh, don't be foolish.

WILLY: I know it when I walk in. They seem to laugh at me.

LINDA: Why? Why would they laugh at you? Don't talk that way, Willy.

[WILLY *moves to the edge of the stage.* LINDA *goes into the kitchen and starts to darn stockings.*]

WILLY: I don't know the reason for it, but they just pass me by. I'm not noticed.

LINDA: But you're doing wonderful, dear. You're making seventy to a hundred dollars a week.

WILLY: But I gotta be at it ten, twelve hours a day. Other men – I don't know – they do it easier. I don't know why – I can't stop myself – I talk too much. A man oughta come in with a few words. One thing about Charley. He's a man of few words, and they respect him.

LINDA: You don't talk too much, you're just lively.

WILLY [*smiling*]: Well, I figure, what the hell, life is short, a couple of jokes. [*To himself*] I joke too much! [*The smile goes.*]

LINDA: Why? You're –

WILLY: I'm fat. I'm very – foolish to look at, Linda. I didn't tell you, but Christmas-time I happened to be calling on F. H. Stewarts, and a salesman I know, as I was going in to see the buyer I heard him say something about – walrus. And I – I cracked him right across the face. I won't take that. I simply will not take that. But they do laugh at me. I know that.

LINDA: Darling . . .

WILLY: I gotta overcome it. I know I gotta overcome it. I'm not dressing to advantage, maybe.

LINDA: Willy, darling, you're the handsomest man in the world –

WILLY: Oh, no, Linda.

LINDA: To me you are. [*Slight pause.*] The handsomest.

[*From the darkness is heard the laughter of a woman.* WILLY *doesn't turn to it, but it continues through* LINDA'*s lines.*]

LINDA: And the boys, Willy. Few men are idolized by their children the way you are.

[*Music is heard as behind a scrim, to the left of the house, the* WOMAN, *dimly seen, is dressing.*]

WILLY [*with great feeling*]: You're the best there is, Linda, you're a pal, you know that? On the road – on the road I want to grab you sometimes and just kiss the life outa you.

[*The laughter is loud now, and he moves into a brightening area at the left, where the* WOMAN *has come from behind the scrim and is standing, putting on her hat, looking into a 'mirror', and laughing.*]

WILLY: 'Cause I get so lonely – especially when business is bad and there's nobody to talk to. I get the feeling that I'll never sell anything again, that I won't make a living for you, or a business, a business for the boys. [*He talks through the* WOMAN'*s subsiding laughter; the* WOMAN *primps at the 'mirror'.*] There's so much I want to make for –

THE WOMAN: Me? You didn't make me, Willy. I picked you.

WILLY [*pleased*]: You picked me?

THE WOMAN [*who is quite proper-looking,* WILLY'*s age*]: I did. I've been sitting at that desk watching all the salesmen go by, day in, day out. But you've got such a sense of humour, and we do have such a good time together, don't we?

WILLY: Sure, sure. [*He takes her in his arms.*] Why do you have to go now?

THE WOMAN: It's two o'clock . . .

WILLY: No, come on in! [*He pulls her.*]

THE WOMAN: . . . my sisters'll be scandalized. When'll you be back?

WILLY: Oh, two weeks about. Will you come up again?

THE WOMAN: Sure thing. You do make me laugh. It's good for me. [*She squeezes his arm, kisses him.*] And I think you're a wonderful man.

WILLY: You picked me, heh?

THE WOMAN: Sure. Because you're so sweet. And such a kidder.

WILLY: Well, I'll see you next time I'm in Boston.

THE WOMAN: I'll put you right through to the buyers.

WILLY [*slapping her bottom*]: Right. Well, bottoms up!

THE WOMAN [*slaps him gently and laughs*]: You just kill me, Willy. [*He suddenly grabs her and kisses her roughly.*] You kill me. And thanks for the stockings. I love a lot of stockings. Well, good night.

WILLY: Good night. And keep your pores open!

THE WOMAN: Oh, Willy!

[*The* WOMAN *bursts out laughing, and* LINDA*'s laughter blends in. The* WOMAN *disappears into the dark. Now the area at the kitchen table brightens.* LINDA *is sitting where she was at the kitchen table, but now is mending a pair of her silk stockings.*]

LINDA: You are, Willy. The handsomest man. You've got no reason to feel that –

WILLY [*coming out of the* WOMAN*'s dimming area and going over to* LINDA]: I'll make it all up to you, Linda, I'll –

LINDA: There's nothing to make up, dear. You're doing fine, better than –

WILLY [*noticing her mending*]: What's that?

LINDA: Just mending my stockings. They're so expensive –

WILLY [*angrily, taking them from her*]: I won't have you mending stockings in this house! Now throw them out!

[LINDA *puts the stockings in her pocket.*]

BERNARD [*entering on the run*]: Where is he? If he doesn't study!

WILLY [*moving to the forestage, with great agitation*]: You'll give him the answers!

BERNARD: I do, but I can't on a Regents! That's a state exam! They're liable to arrest me!

WILLY: Where is he? I'll whip him, I'll whip him!

LINDA: And he'd better give back that football, Willy, it's not nice.

WILLY: Biff! Where is he? Why is he taking everything?

LINDA: He's too rough with the girls, Willy. All the mothers are afraid of him!

WILLY: I'll whip him!

BERNARD: He's driving the car without a licence!

[*The* WOMAN*'s laugh is heard.*]

WILLY: Shut up!

LINDA: All the mothers –

WILLY: Shut up!

BERNARD [*backing quietly away and out*]: Mr Birnbaum says he's stuck up.

WILLY: Get outa here!

BERNARD: If he doesn't buckle down he'll flunk math! [*He goes off.*]

LINDA: He's right, Willy, you've gotta –

WILLY [*exploding at her*]: There's nothing the matter with him! You want him to be a worm like Bernard? He's got spirit, personality . . .

[*As he speaks,* LINDA, *almost in tears, exits into the living-room.* WILLY *is alone in the kitchen, wilting and staring. The leaves are gone. It is night again, and the apartment houses look down from behind.*]

WILLY: Loaded with it. Loaded! What is he stealing? He's giving it back, isn't he? Why is he stealing? What did I tell him? I never in my life told him anything but decent things.

[HAPPY *in pyjamas has come down the stairs;* WILLY *suddenly becomes aware of* HAPPY*'s presence.*]

HAPPY: Let's go now, come on.

WILLY [*sitting down at the kitchen table*]: Huh! Why did she have to wax the floors herself? Every time she waxes the floors she keels over. She knows that!

HAPPY: Shh! Take it easy. What brought you back tonight?

WILLY: I got an awful scare. Nearly hit a kid in Yonkers. God! Why didn't I go to Alaska with my brother Ben that time! Ben! That man was a genius, that man was success incarnate! What a mistake! He begged me to go.

HAPPY: Well, there's no use in –

WILLY: You guys! There was a man started with the clothes on his back and ended up with diamond mines!

HAPPY: Boy, someday I'd like to know how he did it.

WILLY: What's the mystery? The man knew what he wanted and went out and got it! Walked into a jungle, and comes out, the age of twenty-one, and he's rich! The world is an oyster, but you don't crack it open on a mattress!

HAPPY: Pop, I told you I'm gonna retire you for life.

WILLY: You'll retire me for life on seventy goddam dollars a week? And your women and your car and your apartment, and you'll retire me for life! Christ's sake, I couldn't get past Yonkers today! Where are you guys, where are you? The woods are burning! I can't drive a car!

[CHARLEY *has appeared in the doorway. He is a large man, slow of speech, laconic, immovable. In all he says, despite what he says, there is pity, and now, trepidation. He has a robe over pyjamas, slippers on his feet. He enters the kitchen.*]

CHARLEY: Everything all right?

HAPPY: Yeah, Charley, everything's . . .

WILLY: What's the matter?

CHARLEY: I heard some noise. I thought something happened. Can't we do something about the walls? You sneeze in here, and in my house hats blow off.

HAPPY: Let's go to bed, Dad. Come on.

[CHARLEY *signals to* HAPPY *to go.*]

WILLY: You go ahead, I'm not tired at the moment.

HAPPY [*to* WILLY]: Take it easy, huh? [*He exits.*]

WILLY: What're you doin' up?

CHARLEY [*sitting down at the kitchen table opposite* WILLY]: Couldn't sleep good. I had a heartburn.

WILLY: Well, you don't know how to eat.

CHARLEY: I eat with my mouth.

WILLY: No, you're ignorant. You gotta know about vitamins and things like that.

CHARLEY: Come on, let's shoot. Tire you out a little.

WILLY [*hesitantly*]: All right. You got cards?

CHARLEY [*taking a deck from his pocket*]: Yeah, I got them. Someplace. What is it with those vitamins?

WILLY [*dealing*]: They build up your bones. Chemistry.

CHARLEY: Yeah, but there's no bones in a heartburn.

WILLY: What are you talkin' about? Do you know the first thing about it?

CHARLEY: Don't get insulted.

WILLY: Don't talk about something you don't know anything about.

[*They are playing. Pause.*]

CHARLEY: What're you doin' home?

WILLY: A little trouble with the car.

CHARLEY: Oh. [*Pause.*] I'd like to take a trip to California.

WILLY: Don't say.

CHARLEY: You want a job?

WILLY: I got a job, I told you that. [*After a slight pause*] What the hell are you offering me a job for?

CHARLEY: Don't get insulted.

WILLY: Don't insult me.

CHARLEY: I don't see no sense in it. You don't have to go on this way.

WILLY: I got a good job. [*Slight pause.*] What do you keep comin' in here for?

CHARLEY: You want me to go?

WILLY [*after a pause, withering*]: I can't understand it. He's going back to Texas again. What the hell is that?

CHARLEY: Let him go.

WILLY: I got nothin' to give him, Charley, I'm clean, I'm clean.

CHARLEY: He won't starve. None of them starve. Forget about him.

WILLY: Then what have I got to remember?

CHARLEY: You take it too hard. To hell with it. When a deposit bottle is broken you don't get your nickel back.

WILLY: That's easy enough for you to say.

CHARLEY: That ain't easy for me to say.

WILLY: Did you see the ceiling I put up in the living-room?

CHARLEY: Yeah, that's a piece of work. To put up a ceiling is a mystery to me. How do you do it?

WILLY: What's the difference?

CHARLEY: Well, talk about it.

WILLY: You gonna put up a ceiling?

CHARLEY: How could I put up a ceiling?

WILLY: Then what the hell are you bothering me for?

CHARLEY: You're insulted again.

WILLY: A man who can't handle tools is not a man. You're disgusting.

CHARLEY: Don't call me disgusting, Willy.

[UNCLE BEN, *carrying a valise and an umbrella, enters the forestage from around the right corner of the house. He is a stolid man, in his sixties, with a moustache and an authoritative air. He is utterly certain of his destiny, and there is an aura of far places about him. He enters exactly as* WILLY *speaks.*]

WILLY: I'm getting awfully tired, Ben.

[BEN's *music is heard.* BEN *looks around at everything.*]

CHARLEY: Good, keep playing; you'll sleep better. Did you call me Ben?

[BEN *looks at his watch.*]

WILLY: That's funny. For a second there you reminded me of my brother Ben.

BEN: I only have a few minutes. [*He strolls, inspecting the place.* WILLY *and* CHARLEY *continue playing.*]

CHARLEY: You never heard from him again, heh? Since that time?

WILLY: Didn't Linda tell you? Couple of weeks ago we got a letter from his wife in Africa. He died.

CHARLEY: That so.

BEN [*chuckling*]: So this is Brooklyn, eh?

CHARLEY: Maybe you're in for some of his money.

WILLY: Naa, he had seven sons. There's just one opportunity I had with that man . . .

BEN: I must make a train, William. There are several properties I'm looking at in Alaska.

WILLY: Sure, sure! If I'd gone with him to Alaska that time, everything would've been totally different.

CHARLEY: Go on, you'd froze to death up there.

WILLY: What're you talking about?

BEN: Opportunity is tremendous in Alaska, William. Surprised you're not up there.

WILLY: Sure, tremendous.

CHARLEY: Heh?

WILLY: There was the only man I ever met who knew the answers.

CHARLEY: Who?

BEN: How are you all?

WILLY [*taking a pot, smiling*]: Fine, fine.

CHARLEY: Pretty sharp tonight.

BEN: Is Mother living with you?

WILLY: No, she died a long time ago.

CHARLEY: Who?

BEN: That's too bad. Fine specimen of a lady, Mother.

WILLY [*to* CHARLEY]: Heh?

BEN: I'd hoped to see the old girl.

CHARLEY: Who died?

BEN: Heard anything from Father, have you?

WILLY [*unnerved*]: What do you mean, who died?

CHARLEY [*taking a pot*]: What're you talkin' about?

BEN [*looking at his watch*]: William, it's half past eight!

WILLY [*as though to dispel his confusion he angrily stops* CHARLEY's *hand*]: That's my build!

CHARLEY: I put the ace –

WILLY: If you don't know how to play the game I'm not gonna throw my money away on you!

CHARLEY [*rising*]: It was my ace, for God's sake!

WILLY: I'm through, I'm through!

BEN: When did Mother die?

WILLY: Long ago. Since the beginning you never knew how to play cards.

CHARLEY [*picks up the cards and goes to the door*]: All right! Next time I'll bring a deck with five aces.

WILLY: I don't play that kind of game!

CHARLEY [*turning to him*]: You ought to be ashamed of yourself!

WILLY: Yeah?

CHARLEY: Yeah! [*He goes out.*]

WILLY [*slamming the door after him*]: Ignoramus!

BEN [*as* WILLY *comes toward him through the wall-line of the kitchen*]: So you're William.

WILLY [*shaking* BEN's *hand*]: Ben! I've been waiting for you so long! What's the answer? How did you do it?

BEN: Oh, there's a story in that.

[LINDA *enters the forestage, as of old, carrying the wash basket.*]

LINDA: Is this Ben?

BEN [*gallantly*]: How do you do, my dear?

LINDA: Where've you been all these years? Willy's always wondered why you –

WILLY [*pulling* BEN *away from her impatiently*]: Where is Dad? Didn't you follow him? How did you get started?

BEN: Well, I don't know how much you remember.

WILLY: Well, I was just a baby, of course, only three or four years old –

BEN: Three years and eleven months.

WILLY: What a memory, Ben!

BEN: I have many enterprises, William, and I have never kept books.

WILLY: I remember I was sitting under the wagon in – was it Nebraska?

BEN: It was South Dakota, and I gave you a bunch of wild flowers.

WILLY: I remember you walking away down some open road.

BEN [*laughing*]: I was going to find Father in Alaska.

WILLY: Where is he?

BEN: At that age I had a very faulty view of geography, William. I discovered after a few days that I was heading due south, so instead of Alaska, I ended up in Africa.

LINDA: Africa!

WILLY: The Gold Coast!

BEN: Principally diamond mines.

LINDA: Diamond mines!

BEN: Yes, my dear. But I've only a few minutes –

WILLY: No! Boys! Boys! [YOUNG BIFF *and* HAPPY *appear.*] Listen to this. This is your Uncle Ben, a great man! Tell my boys, Ben!

BEN: Why boys, when I was seventeen I walked into the jungle, and when I was twenty-one I walked out. [*He laughs.*] And by God I was rich.

WILLY [*to the boys*]: You see what I been talking about? The greatest things can happen!

BEN [*glancing at his watch*]: I have an appointment in Ketchikan Tuesday week.

WILLY: No, Ben! Please tell about Dad. I want my boys to hear. I want them to know the kind of stock they spring from. All I remember is a man with a big beard, and I was in Mamma's lap, sitting around a fire, and some kind of high music.

BEN: His flute. He played the flute.

WILLY: Sure, the flute, that's right!

[*New music is heard, a high, rollicking tune.*]

BEN: Father was a very great and a very wild-hearted man. We would start in Boston, and he'd toss the whole family into the wagon, and then he'd drive the team right across the country; through Ohio, and Indiana, Michigan, Illinois, and all the Western states. And we'd stop in the towns and sell the flutes that he'd made on the way. Great inventor, Father. With one gadget he made more in a week than a man like you could make in a lifetime.

WILLY: That's just the way I'm bringing them up, Ben – rugged, well liked, all-around.

BEN: Yeah? [*To* BIFF] Hit that, boy – hard as you can. [*He pounds his stomach.*]

BIFF: Oh, no, sir!

BEN [*taking boxing stance*]: Come on, get to me! [*He laughs.*]

WILLY: Go to it, Biff! Go ahead, show him!

BIFF: Okay! [*He cocks his fists and starts in.*]

LINDA [*to* WILLY]: Why must he fight, dear?

BEN [*sparring with* BIFF]: Good boy! Good boy!

WILLY: How's that, Ben, heh?

HAPPY: Give him the left, Biff!

LINDA: Why are you fighting?

BEN: Good boy! [*Suddenly comes in, trips* BIFF, *and stands over him, the point of his umbrella poised over* BIFF's *eye.*]

LINDA: Look out, Biff!

BIFF: Gee!

BEN [*patting* BIFF's *knee*]: Never fight fair with a stranger, boy. You'll never get out of the jungle that way. [*Taking* LINDA's *hand and bowing*] It was an honour and a pleasure to meet you, Linda.

LINDA [*withdrawing her hand coldly, frightened*]: Have a nice – trip.

BEN [*to* WILLY]: And good luck with your – what do you do?

WILLY: Selling.

BEN: Yes. Well . . . [*He raises his hand in farewell to all.*]

WILLY: No, Ben, I don't want you to think . . . [*He takes* BEN's *arm to show him.*] It's Brooklyn, I know, but we hunt too.

BEN: Really, now.

WILLY: Oh, sure, there's snakes and rabbits and – that's why I moved out here. Why, Biff can fell any one of these trees in no time! Boys! Go right over to where they're building the apartment house and get some sand. We're gonna rebuild the entire front stoop right now! Watch this, Ben!

BIFF: Yes, sir! On the double, Hap!

HAPPY [*as he and* BIFF *run off*]: I lost weight, Pop, you notice?

[CHARLEY *enters in knickers, even before the boys are gone.*]

CHARLEY: Listen, if they steal any more from that building the watchman'll put the cops on them!

LINDA [*to* WILLY]: Don't let Biff . . .

[BEN *laughs lustily.*]

WILLY: You shoulda seen the lumber they brought home last week. At least a dozen six-by-tens worth all kinds a money.

CHARLEY: Listen, if that watchman –

WILLY: I gave them hell, understand. But I got a couple of fearless characters there.

CHARLEY: Willy, the jails are full of fearless characters.

BEN [*clapping* WILLY *on the back, with a laugh at* CHARLEY]: And the stock exchange, friend!

WILLY [*joining in* BEN*'s laughter*]: Where are the rest of your pants?

CHARLEY: My wife bought them.

WILLY: Now all you need is a golf club and you can go upstairs and go to sleep. [*To* BEN] Great athlete! Between him and his son Bernard they can't hammer a nail!

BERNARD [*rushing in*]: The watchman's chasing Biff!

WILLY [*angrily*]: Shut up! He's not stealing anything!

LINDA [*alarmed, hurrying off left*]: Where is he? Biff, dear! [*She exits.*]

WILLY [*moving toward the left, away from* BEN]: There's nothing wrong. What's the matter with you?

BEN: Nervy boy. Good!

WILLY [*laughing*]: Oh, nerves of iron, that Biff!

CHARLEY: Don't know what it is. My New England man comes back and he's bleedin', they murdered him up there.

WILLY: It's contacts, Charley, I got important contacts!

CHARLEY [*sarcastically*]: Glad to hear it, Willy. Come in later, we'll shoot a little casino. I'll take some of your Portland money. [*He laughs at* WILLY *and exits.*]

WILLY [*turning to* BEN]: Business is bad, it's murderous. But not for me, of course.

BEN: I'll stop by on my way back to Africa.

WILLY [*longingly*]: Can't you stay a few days? You're just what I need, Ben, because I – I have a fine position here, but I – well, Dad left when I was such a baby and I never had a chance to talk to him and I still feel – kind of temporary about myself.

BEN: I'll be late for my train.

[*They are at opposite ends of the stage.*]

WILLY: Ben, my boys – can't we talk? They'd go into the jaws of hell for me, see, but I –

BEN: William, you're being first-rate with your boys. Outstanding, manly chaps!

WILLY [*hanging on to his words*]: Oh, Ben, that's good to hear! Because sometimes I'm afraid that I'm not teaching them the right kind of – Ben, how should I teach them?

BEN [*giving great weight to each word, and with a certain vicious audacity*]: William, when I walked into the jungle, I was seventeen. When I walked out I was twenty-one. And, by God, I was rich! [*He goes off into darkness around the right corner of the house.*]

WILLY: . . . was rich! That's just the spirit I want to imbue them with! To walk into a jungle! I was right! I was right! I was right!

[BEN *is gone, but* WILLY *is still speaking to him as* LINDA, *in night-gown and robe, enters the kitchen, glances around for* WILLY, *then goes to the door of the house, looks out and sees him. Comes down to his left. He looks at her.*]

LINDA: Willy, dear? Willy?

WILLY: I was right!

LINDA: Did you have some cheese? [*He can't answer.*] It's very late, darling. Come to bed, heh?

WILLY [*looking straight up*]: Gotta break your neck to see a star in this yard.

LINDA: You coming in?

WILLY: Whatever happened to that diamond watch fob? Remember?

When Ben came from Africa that time? Didn't he give me a watch fob with a diamond in it?

LINDA: You pawned it, dear. Twelve, thirteen years ago. For Biff's radio correspondence course.

WILLY: Gee, that was a beautiful thing. I'll take a walk.

LINDA: But you're in your slippers.

WILLY [*starting to go around the house at the left*]: I was right! I was! [*Half to* LINDA, *as he goes, shaking his head*] What a man! There was a man worth talking to. I was right!

LINDA [*calling after* WILLY]: But in your slippers, Willy!

[WILLY *is almost gone when* BIFF, *in his pyjamas, comes down the stairs and enters the kitchen.*]

BIFF: What is he doing out there?

LINDA: Sh!

BIFF: God Almighty, Mom, how long has he been doing this?

LINDA: Don't, he'll hear you.

BIFF: What the hell is the matter with him?

LINDA: It'll pass by morning.

BIFF: Shouldn't we do anything?

LINDA: Oh, my dear, you should do a lot of things, but there's nothing to do, so go to sleep.

[HAPPY *comes down the stairs and sits on the steps.*]

HAPPY: I never heard him so loud, Mom.

LINDA: Well, come around more often; you'll hear him.

[*She sits down at the table and mends the lining of* WILLY'*s jacket.*]

BIFF: Why didn't you ever write me about this, Mom?

LINDA: How would I write to you? For over three months you had no address.

BIFF: I was on the move. But you know I thought of you all the time. You know that, don't you, pal?

LINDA: I know, dear, I know. But he likes to have a letter. Just to know that there's still a possibility for better things.

BIFF: He's not like this all the time, is he?

LINDA: It's when you come home he's always the worst.

BIFF: When I come home?

LINDA: When you write you're coming, he's all smiles, and talks about the future, and – he's just wonderful. And then the closer you seem to come, the more shaky he gets, and then, by the time you get here, he's arguing, and he seems angry at you. I think it's just that maybe he can't bring himself to – to open up to you. Why are you so hateful to each other? Why is that?

BIFF [*evasively*]: I'm not hateful, Mom.

LINDA: But you no sooner come in the door than you're fighting!

BIFF: I don't know why, I mean to change. I'm tryin', Mom; you understand?

LINDA: Are you home to stay now?

BIFF: I don't know. I want to look around, see what's doin'.

LINDA: Biff, you can't look around all your life, can you?

BIFF: I just can't take hold, Mom. I can't take hold of some kind of a life.

LINDA: Biff, a man is not a bird, to come and go with the springtime.

BIFF: Your hair . . . [*He touches her hair.*] Your hair got so grey.

LINDA: Oh, it's been grey since you were in high school. I just stopped dyeing it, that's all.

BIFF: Dye it again, will ya? I don't want my pal looking old. [*He smiles.*]

LINDA: You're such a boy! You think you can go away for a year and . . . You've got to get it into your head now that one day you'll knock on this door and there'll be strange people here –

BIFF: What are you talking about? You're not even sixty, Mom.

LINDA: But what about your father?

BIFF [*lamely*]: Well, I meant him too.

HAPPY: He admires Pop.

LINDA: Biff, dear, if you don't have any feeling for him, then you can't have any feeling for me.

BIFF: Sure I can, Mom.

LINDA: No. You can't just come to see me, because I love him. [*With a threat, but only a threat, of tears*] He's the dearest man in the world to me, and I won't have anyone making him feel unwanted and low and blue. You've got to make up your mind now, darling, there's no leeway any more. Either he's your father and you pay him that respect, or else you're not to come here. I know he's not easy to get along with – nobody knows that better than me – but . . .

WILLY [*from the left, with a laugh*]: Hey, hey, Biffo!

BIFF [*starting to go out after* WILLY]: What the hell is the matter with him? [HAPPY *stops him.*]

LINDA: Don't – don't go near him!

BIFF: Stop making excuses for him! He always, always wiped the floor with you. Never had an ounce of respect for you.

HAPPY: He's always had respect for –

BIFF: What the hell do you know about it?

HAPPY [*surlily*]: Just don't call him crazy!

BIFF: He's got no character – Charley wouldn't do this. Not in his own house – spewing out that vomit from his mind.

HAPPY: Charley never had to cope with what he's got to.

BIFF: People are worse off than Willy Loman. Believe me, I've seen them!

LINDA: Then make Charley your father, Biff. You can't do that, can you? I don't say he's a great man. Willy Loman never made a lot of money. His name was never in the paper. He's not the finest character that ever lived. But he's a human being, and a terrible thing is happening to him. So attention must be paid. He's not to be allowed to fall into his grave like an old dog. Attention, attention must be finally paid to such a person. You called him crazy –

BIFF: I didn't mean –

LINDA: No, a lot of people think he's lost his – balance. But you don't have to be very smart to know what his trouble is. The man is exhausted.

HAPPY: Sure!

LINDA: A small man can be just as exhausted as a great man. He works for a company thirty-six years this March, opens up unheard-of territories to their trademark, and now in his old age they take his salary away.

HAPPY [*indignantly*]: I didn't know that, Mom.

LINDA: You never asked, my dear! Now that you get your spending money someplace else you don't trouble your mind with him.

HAPPY: But I gave you money last –

LINDA: Christmas-time, fifty dollars! To fix the hot water it cost ninety-seven fifty! For five weeks he's been on straight commission, like a beginner, an unknown!

BIFF: Those ungrateful bastards!

LINDA: Are they any worse than his sons? When he brought them business, when he was young, they were glad to see him. But now his old friends, the old buyers that loved him so and always found some order to hand him in a pinch – they're all dead, retired. He used to be able to make six, seven calls a day in Boston. Now he takes his valises out of the car and puts them back and takes them out again and he's exhausted. Instead of walking he talks now. He drives seven hundred miles, and when he gets there no one knows him any more, no one welcomes him. And what goes through a man's mind, driving seven hundred miles home without having earned a cent? Why shouldn't he talk to himself? Why? When he has to go to Charley and borrow fifty dollars a week and pretend to me that it's his pay? How long can that go on? How long? You see what I'm sitting here and waiting for? And you tell me he has no character? The man who never worked a day but for your benefit? When does he get the medal for that? Is this his reward – to turn around at the age of sixty-three and find his sons, who he loved better than his life, one a philandering bum –

HAPPY: Mom!

LINDA: That's all you are, my baby! [*To* BIFF] And you! What happened to the love you had for him? You were such pals! How you used to talk to him on the phone every night! How lonely he was till he could come home to you!

BIFF: All right, Mom. I'll live here in my room, and I'll get a job. I'll keep away from him, that's all.

LINDA: No, Biff. You can't stay here and fight all the time.

BIFF: He threw me out of this house, remember that.

LINDA: Why did he do that? I never knew why.

BIFF: Because I know he's a fake and he doesn't like anybody around who knows!

LINDA: Why a fake? In what way? What do you mean?

BIFF: Just don't lay it all at my feet. It's between me and him – that's all I have to say. I'll chip in from now on. He'll settle for half my pay cheque. He'll be all right. I'm going to bed. [*He starts for the stairs.*]

LINDA: He won't be all right.

BIFF [*turning on the stairs, furiously*]: I hate this city and I'll stay here. Now what do you want?

LINDA: He's dying, Biff.

[*HAPPY turns quickly to her, shocked.*]

BIFF [*after a pause*]: Why is he dying?

LINDA: He's been trying to kill himself.

BIFF [*with great horror*]: How?

LINDA: I live from day to day.

BIFF: What're you talking about?

LINDA: Remember I wrote you that he smashed up the car again? In February?

BIFF: Well?

LINDA: The insurance inspector came. He said that they have evidence. That all these accidents in the last year – weren't – weren't – accidents.

HAPPY: How can they tell that? That's a lie.

LINDA: It seems there's a woman . . . [*She takes a breath as*]

BIFF [*sharply but contained*]: What woman? ⎫

LINDA [*simultaneously*]: . . . and this woman . . . ⎭

LINDA: What?

BIFF: Nothing. Go ahead.

LINDA: What did you say?

BIFF: Nothing. I just said what woman?

HAPPY: What about her?

LINDA: Well, it seems she was walking down the road and saw his car. She says that he wasn't driving fast at all, and that he didn't skid. She says he came to that little bridge, and then deliberately smashed into the railing, and it was only the shallowness of the water that saved him.

BIFF: Oh, no, he probably just fell asleep again.

LINDA: I don't think he fell asleep.

BIFF: Why not?

LINDA: Last month . . . [*With great difficulty*] Oh, boys, it's so hard to say a thing like this! He's just a big stupid man to you, but I tell you there's more good in him than in many other people. [*She chokes, wipes her eyes.*] I was looking for a fuse. The lights blew out, and I went down the cellar. And behind the fuse-box – it happened to fall out – was a length of rubber pipe – just short.

HAPPY: No kidding?

LINDA: There's a little attachment on the end of it. I knew right away. And sure enough, on the bottom of the water heater there's a new little nipple on the gas pipe.

HAPPY [*angrily*]: That – jerk.

BIFF: Did you have it taken off?

LINDA: I'm – I'm ashamed to. How can I mention it to him? Every day I go down and take away that little rubber pipe. But, when he comes home, I put it back where it was. How can I insult him that way? I don't know what to do. I live from day to day, boys. I tell you, I know every thought in his mind. It sounds so old-fashioned and silly, but I tell you he put his whole life into you and you've turned your backs on him. [*She is bent over in the chair, weeping, her face in her hands.*] Biff, I swear to God! Biff, his life is in your hands!

HAPPY [*to* BIFF]: How do you like that damned fool!

BIFF [*kissing her*]: All right, pal, all right. It's all settled now. I've been remiss. I know that, Mom. But now I'll stay, and I swear to you,

I'll apply myself. [*Kneeling in front of her, in a fever of self-reproach*] It's just – you see, Mom, I don't fit in business. Not that I won't try. I'll try, and I'll make good.

HAPPY: Sure you will. The trouble with you in business was you never tried to please people.

BIFF: I know, I –

HAPPY: Like when you worked for Harrison's. Bob Harrison said you were tops, and then you go and do some damn fool thing like whistling whole songs in the elevator like a comedian.

BIFF [*against* HAPPY]: So what? I like to whistle sometimes.

HAPPY: You don't raise a guy to a responsible job who whistles in the elevator!

LINDA: Well, don't argue about it now.

HAPPY: Like when you'd go off and swim in the middle of the day instead of taking the line around.

BIFF [*his resentment rising*]: Well, don't you run off? You take off sometimes, don't you? On a nice summer day?

HAPPY: Yeah, but I cover myself!

LINDA: Boys!

HAPPY: If I'm going to take a fade the boss can call any number where I'm supposed to be and they'll swear to him that I just left. I'll tell you something that I hate to say, Biff, but in the business world some of them think you're crazy.

BIFF [*angered*]: Screw the business world!

HAPPY: All right, screw it! Great, but cover yourself!

LINDA: Hap, Hap!

BIFF: I don't care what they think! They've laughed at Dad for years, and you know why? Because we don't belong in this nuthouse of a city! We should be mixing cement on some open plain, or – or carpenters. A carpenter is allowed to whistle!

[WILLY *walks in from the entrance of the house, at left.*]

WILLY: Even your grandfather was better than a carpenter. [*Pause. They watch him.*] You never grew up. Bernard does not whistle in the elevator, I assure you.

BIFF [*as though to laugh* WILLY *out of it*]: Yeah, but you do, Pop.

WILLY: I never in my life whistled in an elevator! And who in the business world thinks I'm crazy?

BIFF: I didn't mean it like that, Pop. Now don't make a whole thing out of it, will ya?

WILLY: Go back to the West? Be a carpenter, a cowboy, enjoy yourself!

LINDA: Willy, he was just saying –

WILLY: I heard what he said!

HAPPY [*trying to quiet* WILLY]: Hey, Pop, come on now . . .

WILLY [*continuing over* HAPPY's *line*]: They laugh at me, heh? Go to Filene's, go to the Hub, go to Slattery's, Boston. Call out the name Willy Loman and see what happens! Big shot!

BIFF: All right, Pop.

WILLY: Big!

BIFF: All right!

WILLY: Why do you always insult me?

BIFF: I didn't say a word. [*To* LINDA] Did I say a word?

LINDA: He didn't say anything, Willy.

WILLY [*going to the doorway of the living-room*]: All right, good night, good night.

LINDA: Willy, dear, he just decided . . .

WILLY [*to* BIFF]: If you get tired hanging around tomorrow, paint the ceiling I put up in the living-room.

BIFF: I'm leaving early tomorrow.

HAPPY: He's going to see Bill Oliver, Pop.

WILLY [*interestedly*]: Oliver? For what?

BIFF [*with reserve, but trying, trying*]: He always said he'd stake me. I'd like to go into business, so maybe I can take him up on it.

LINDA: Isn't that wonderful?

WILLY: Don't interrupt. What's wonderful about it? There's fifty men in the City of New York who'd stake him. [*To* BIFF] Sporting goods?

BIFF: I guess so. I know something about it and –

WILLY: He knows something about it! You know sporting goods better than Spalding, for God's sake! How much is he giving you?

BIFF: I don't know, I didn't even see him yet, but –

WILLY: Then what're you talkin' about?

BIFF [*getting angry*]: Well, all I said was I'm gonna see him, that's all!

WILLY [*turning away*]: Ah, you're counting your chickens again.

BIFF [*starting left for the stairs*]: Oh, Jesus, I'm going to sleep!

WILLY [*calling after him*]: Don't curse in this house!

BIFF [*turning*]: Since when did you get so clean?

HAPPY [*trying to stop them*]: Wait a . . .

WILLY: Don't use that language to me! I won't have it!

HAPPY [*grabbing* BIFF, *shouts*]: Wait a minute! I got an idea. I got a feasible idea. Come here, Biff, let's talk this over now, let's talk some sense here. When I was down in Florida last time, I thought of a great idea to sell sporting goods. It just came back to me. You and I, Biff – we have a line, the Loman Line. We train a couple of weeks, and put on a couple of exhibitions, see?

WILLY: That's an idea!

HAPPY: Wait! We form two basketball teams, see? Two water-polo teams. We play each other. It's a million dollars' worth of publicity. Two brothers, see? The Loman Brothers. Displays in the Royal Palms – all the hotels. And banners over the ring and the basketball court: 'Loman Brothers'. Baby, we could sell sporting goods!

WILLY: That is a one-million-dollar idea!

LINDA: Marvellous!

BIFF: I'm in great shape as far as that's concerned.

HAPPY: And the beauty of it is, Biff, it wouldn't be like a business. We'd be out playin' ball again . . .

BIFF [*enthused*]: Yeah, that's . . .

WILLY: Million-dollar . . .

HAPPY: And you wouldn't get fed up with it, Biff. It'd be the family again. There'd be the old honour, and comradeship, and if you wanted to go off for a swim or somethin' – well you'd do it! Without some smart cooky gettin' up ahead of you!

WILLY: Lick the world! You guys together could absolutely lick the civilized world.

BIFF: I'll see Oliver tomorrow. Hap, if we could work that out . . .

LINDA: Maybe things are beginning to –

WILLY [*wildly enthused, to* LINDA]: Stop interrupting! [*To* BIFF] But don't wear sport jacket and slacks when you see Oliver.

BIFF: No, I'll –

WILLY: A business suit, and talk as little as possible, and don't crack any jokes.

BIFF: He did like me. Always liked me.

LINDA: He loved you!

WILLY [*to* LINDA]: Will you stop! [*To* BIFF] Walk in very serious. You are not applying for a boy's job. Money is to pass. Be quiet, fine, and serious. Everybody likes a kidder, but nobody lends him money.

HAPPY: I'll try to get some myself, Biff. I'm sure I can.

WILLY: I see great things for you kids, I think your troubles are over. But remember, start big and you'll end big. Ask for fifteen. How much you gonna ask for?

BIFF: Gee, I don't know –

WILLY: And don't say 'Gee'. 'Gee' is a boy's word. A man walking in for fifteen thousand dollars does not say 'Gee'!

BIFF: Ten, I think, would be top though.

WILLY: Don't be so modest. You always started too low. Walk in with a big laugh. Don't look worried. Start off with a couple of your good stories to lighten things up. It's not what you say, it's how you say it – because personality always wins the day.

LINDA: Oliver always thought the highest of him –

WILLY: Will you let me talk?

BIFF: Don't yell at her, Pop, will ya?

WILLY [*angrily*]: I was talking, wasn't I?

BIFF: I don't like you yelling at her all the time, and I'm tellin' you, that's all.

WILLY: What're you, takin' over this house?

LINDA: Willy –

WILLY [*turning on her*]: Don't take his side all the time, goddammit!

BIFF [*furiously*]: Stop yelling at her!

WILLY [*suddenly pulling on his cheek, beaten down, guilt ridden*]: Give my best to Bill Oliver – he may remember me. [*He exits through the living-room doorway.*]

LINDA [*her voice subdued*]: What'd you have to start that for? [BIFF *turns away.*] You see how sweet he was as soon as you talked hopefully? [*She goes over to* BIFF.] Come up and say good night to him. Don't let him go to bed that way.

HAPPY: Come on, Biff, let's buck him up.

LINDA: Please, dear. Just say good night. It takes so little to make him happy. Come. [*She goes through the living-room doorway, calling upstairs from within the living-room*] Your pyjamas are hanging in the bathroom, Willy!

HAPPY [*looking toward where* LINDA *went out*]: What a woman! They broke the mould when they made her. You know that, Biff?

BIFF: He's off salary. My God, working on commission!

HAPPY: Well, let's face it: he's no hot-shot selling man. Except that sometimes, you have to admit, he's a sweet personality.

BIFF [*deciding*]: Lend me ten bucks, will ya? I want to buy some new ties.

HAPPY: I'll take you to a place I know. Beautiful stuff. Wear one of my striped shirts tomorrow.

BIFF: She got grey. Mom got awful old. Gee. I'm gonna go in to Oliver tomorrow and knock him for a –

HAPPY: Come on up. Tell that to Dad. Let's give him a whirl. Come on.

BIFF [*steamed up*]: You know, with ten thousand bucks, boy!

HAPPY [*as they go into the living-room*]: That's the talk, Biff, that's the first time I've heard the old confidence out of you! [*From within the living-room, fading off*] You're gonna live with me, kid, and any babe you want just say the word . . . [*The last lines are hardly heard. They are mounting the stairs to their parents' bedroom.*]

LINDA [*entering her bedroom and addressing* WILLY, *who is in the bathroom. She is straightening the bed for him.*] Can you do anything about the shower? It drips.

WILLY [*from the bathroom*]: All of a sudden everything falls to pieces! Goddam plumbing, oughta be sued, those people. I hardly finished putting it in and the thing . . . [*His words rumble off.*]

LINDA: I'm just wondering if Oliver will remember him. You think he might?

WILLY [*coming out of the bathroom in his pyjamas*]: Remember him? What's the matter with you, you crazy? If he'd've stayed with Oliver he'd be on top by now! Wait'll Oliver gets a look at him. You don't know the average calibre any more. The average young man today – [*he is getting into bed*] – is got a calibre of zero. Greatest thing in the world for him was to bum around.

[BIFF *and* HAPPY *enter the bedroom. Slight pause.*]

WILLY [*stops short, looking at* BIFF]: Glad to hear it, boy.

HAPPY: He wanted to say good night to you, sport.

WILLY [*to* BIFF]: Yeah. Knock him dead, boy. What'd you want to tell me?

BIFF: Just take it easy, Pop. Good night. [*He turns to go.*]

WILLY [*unable to resist*]: And if anything falls off the desk while you're talking to him – like a package or something – don't you pick it up. They have office boys for that.

LINDA: I'll make a big breakfast –

WILLY: Will you let me finish? [*To* BIFF] Tell him you were in the business in the West. Not farm work.

BIFF: All right, Dad.

LINDA: I think everything –

WILLY [*going right through her speech*]: And don't undersell yourself. No less than fifteen thousand dollars.

BIFF [*unable to bear him*]: Okay. Good night, Mom. [*He starts moving.*]

WILLY: Because you got a greatness in you, Biff, remember that. You got all kinds a greatness . . . [*He lies back, exhausted.* BIFF *walks out.*]

LINDA [*calling after* BIFF]: Sleep well, darling!

HAPPY: I'm gonna get married, Mom. I wanted to tell you.

LINDA: Go to sleep, dear.

HAPPY [*going*]: I just wanted to tell you.

WILLY: Keep up the good work. [HAPPY *exits.*] God . . . remember that Ebbets Field game? The championship of the city?

LINDA: Just rest. Should I sing to you?

WILLY: Yeah. Sing to me. [LINDA *hums a soft lullaby.*] When that team came out – he was the tallest, remember?

LINDA: Oh, yes. And in gold.

[BIFF *enters the darkened kitchen, takes a cigarette, and leaves the house. He comes downstage into a golden pool of light. He smokes, staring at the night.*]

WILLY: Like a young god. Hercules – something like that. And the sun, the sun all around him. Remember how he waved to me? Right up from the field, with the representatives of three colleges standing by? And the buyers I brought, and the cheers when he came out – Loman, Loman, Loman! God Almighty, he'll be great yet. A star like that, magnificent, can never really fade away!

[*The light on* WILLY *is fading. The gas heater begins to glow through the kitchen wall, near the stairs, a blue flame beneath red coils.*]

LINDA [*timidly*]: Willy dear, what has he got against you?

WILLY: I'm so tired. Don't talk any more.

[BIFF *slowly returns to the kitchen. He stops, stares toward the heater.*]

LINDA: Will you ask Howard to let you work in New York?

WILLY: First thing in the morning. Everything'll be all right.

[BIFF *reaches behind the heater and draws out a length of rubber tubing. He is horrified and turns his head toward* WILLY'S *room, still dimly lit, from which the strains of* LINDA'S *desperate but monotonous humming rise.*]

WILLY [*staring through the window into the moonlight*]: Gee, look at the moon moving between the buildings!

[BIFF *wraps the tubing around his hand and quickly goes up the stairs.*]

CURTAIN

Act Two

Music is heard, gay and bright. The curtain rises as the music fades away.

WILLY, in shirt sleeves, is sitting at the kitchen table, sipping coffee, his hat in his lap. LINDA is filling his cup when she can.

WILLY: Wonderful coffee. Meal in itself.

LINDA: Can I make you some eggs?

WILLY: No. Take a breath.

LINDA: You look so rested, dear.

WILLY: I slept like a dead one. First time in months. Imagine, sleeping till ten on a Tuesday morning. Boys left nice and early, heh?

LINDA: They were out of here by eight o'clock.

WILLY: Good work!

LINDA: It was so thrilling to see them leaving together. I can't get over the shaving lotion in this house!

WILLY [*smiling*]: Mmm –

LINDA: Biff was very changed this morning. His whole attitude seemed to be hopeful. He couldn't wait to get downtown to see Oliver.

WILLY: He's heading for a change. There's no question, there simply are certain men that take longer to get – solidified. How did he dress?

LINDA: His blue suit. He's so handsome in that suit. He could be a – anything in that suit!

[WILLY *gets up from the table.* LINDA *holds his jacket for him.*]

WILLY: There's no question, no question at all. Gee, on the way home tonight I'd like to buy some seeds.

LINDA [*laughing*]: That'd be wonderful. But not enough sun gets back there. Nothing'll grow any more.

WILLY: You wait, kid, before it's all over we're gonna get a little place out in the country, and I'll raise some vegetables, a couple of chickens . . .

LINDA: You'll do it yet, dear.

[WILLY *walks out of his jacket.* LINDA *follows him.*]

WILLY: And they'll get married, and come for a weekend. I'd build a little guest house. 'Cause I got so many fine tools, all I'd need would be a little lumber and some peace of mind.

LINDA [*joyfully*]: I sewed the lining . . .

WILLY: I could build two guest houses, so they'd both come. Did he decide how much he's going to ask Oliver for?

LINDA [*getting him into the jacket*]: He didn't mention it, but I imagine ten or fifteen thousand. You going to talk to Howard today?

WILLY: Yeah. I'll put it to him straight and simple. He'll just have to take me off the road.

LINDA: And Willy, don't forget to ask for a little advance, because we've got the insurance premium. It's the grace period now.

WILLY: That's hundred . . . ?

LINDA: A hundred and eight, sixty-eight. Because we're a little short again.

WILLY: Why are we short?

LINDA: Well, you had the motor job on the car . . .

WILLY: That goddam Studebaker!

LINDA: And you got one more payment on the refrigerator . . .

WILLY: But it just broke again!

LINDA: Well, it's old, dear.

WILLY: I told you we should've bought a well-advertised machine. Charley bought a General Electric and it's twenty years old and it's still good, that son-of-a-bitch.

LINDA: But, Willy –

WILLY: Whoever heard of a Hastings refrigerator? Once in my life I would like to own something outright before it's broken! I'm always in a race with the junkyard! I just finished paying for the car and it's on its last legs. The refrigerator consumes belts like a goddam maniac. They time those things. They time them so when you finally paid for them, they're used up.

LINDA [*buttoning up his jacket as he unbuttons it*]: All told, about two hundred dollars would carry us, dear. But that includes the last payment on the mortgage. After this payment, Willy, the house belongs to us.

WILLY: It's twenty-five years!

LINDA: Biff was nine years old when we bought it.

WILLY: Well, that's a great thing. To weather a twenty-five-year mortgage is –

LINDA: It's an accomplishment.

WILLY: All the cement, the lumber, the reconstruction I put in this house! There ain't a crack to be found in it any more.

LINDA: Well, it served its purpose.

WILLY: What purpose? Some stranger'll come along, move in, and that's that. If only Biff would take this house, and raise a family . . . [*He starts to go.*] Good-bye, I'm late.

LINDA [*suddenly remembering*]: Oh, I forgot! You're supposed to meet them for dinner.

WILLY: Me?

LINDA: At Frank's Chop House on Forty-eighth near Sixth Avenue.

WILLY: Is that so! How about you?

LINDA: No, just the three of you. They're gonna blow you to a big meal!

WILLY: Don't say! Who thought of that?

LINDA: Biff came to me this morning, Willy, and he said, 'Tell Dad, we want to blow him to a big meal.' Be there six o'clock. You and your two boys are going to have dinner.

WILLY: Gee whiz! That's really somethin'. I'm gonna knock Howard for a loop, kid. I'll get an advance, and I'll come home with a New York job. Goddammit, now I'm gonna do it!

LINDA: Oh, that's the spirit, Willy!

WILLY: I will never get behind a wheel the rest of my life!

LINDA: It's changing, Willy, I can feel it changing!

WILLY: Beyond a question. G'bye, I'm late. [*He starts to go again.*]

LINDA [*calling after him as she runs to the kitchen table for a handkerchief*]: You got your glasses?

WILLY [*feels for them, then comes back in*]: Yeah, yeah, got my glasses.

LINDA [*giving him the handkerchief*]: And a handkerchief.

WILLY: Yeah, handkerchief.

LINDA: And your saccharine?

WILLY: Yeah, my saccharine.

LINDA: Be careful on the subway stairs.

[*She kisses him, and a silk stocking is seen hanging from her hand. WILLY notices it.*]

WILLY: Will you stop mending stockings? At least while I'm in the house. It gets me nervous. I can't tell you. Please.

[LINDA *hides the stocking in her hand as she follows* WILLY *across the forestage in front of the house.*]

LINDA: Remember, Frank's Chop House.

WILLY [*passing the apron*]: Maybe beets would grow out there.

LINDA [*laughing*]: But you tried so many times.

WILLY: Yeah. Well, don't work hard today. [*He disappears around the right corner of the house.*]

LINDA: Be careful!

[*As* WILLY *vanishes,* LINDA *waves to him. Suddenly the phone rings. She runs across the stage and into the kitchen and lifts it.*]

LINDA: Hello? Oh, Biff! I'm so glad you called, I just . . . Yes, sure, I just told him. Yes, he'll be there for dinner at six o'clock, I didn't forget. Listen, I was just dying to tell you. You know that little rubber pipe I told you about? That he connected to the gas heater? I finally decided to go down the cellar this morning and take it away and destroy it. But it's gone! Imagine! He took it away himself, it isn't there! [*She listens.*] When? Oh, then you took it. Oh – nothing, it's just that I'd hoped he'd taken it away himself.

Oh, I'm not worried, darling, because this morning he left in such high spirits, it was like the old days! I'm not afraid any more. Did Mr Oliver see you? . . . Well, you wait there then. And make a nice impression on him, darling. Just don't perspire too much before you see him. And have a nice time with Dad. He may have big news too! . . . That's right, a New York job. And be sweet to him tonight, dear. Be loving to him. Because he's only a little boat looking for a harbour. [*She is trembling with sorrow and joy.*] Oh, that's wonderful, Biff, you'll save his life. Thanks, darling. Just put your arms around him when he comes into the restaurant. Give him a smile. That's the boy . . . Good-bye, dear . . . You got your comb? . . . That's fine. Good-bye, Biff dear.

[*In the middle of her speech,* HOWARD WAGNER, *thirty-six, wheels on a small typewriter table on which is a wire-recording machine and proceeds to plug it in. This is on the left forestage. Light slowly fades on* LINDA *as it rises on* HOWARD. HOWARD *is intent on threading the machine and only glances over his shoulder as* WILLY *appears.*]

WILLY: Pst! Pst!

HOWARD: Hello, Willy, come in.

WILLY: Like to have a little talk with you, Howard.

HOWARD: Sorry to keep you waiting. I'll be with you in a minute.

WILLY: What's that, Howard?

HOWARD: Didn't you ever see one of these? Wire recorder.

WILLY: Oh. Can we talk a minute?

HOWARD: Records things. Just got delivery yesterday. Been driving me crazy, the most terrific machine I ever saw in my life. I was up all night with it.

WILLY: What do you do with it?

HOWARD: I bought it for dictation, but you can do anything with it. Listen to this. I had it home last night. Listen to what I picked up. The first one is my daughter. Get this. [*He flicks the switch and 'Roll out the Barrel' is heard being whistled.*] Listen to that kid whistle.

WILLY: That is lifelike, isn't it?

HOWARD: Seven years old. Get that tone.

WILLY: Ts, ts. Like to ask a little favour if you . . .

[*The whistling breaks off, and the voice of* HOWARD's *daughter is heard.*]

HIS DAUGHTER: 'Now you, Daddy.'

HOWARD: She's crazy for me! [*Again the same song is whistled.*] That's me! Ha! [*He winks.*]

WILLY: You're very good!

[*The whistling breaks off again. The machine runs silent for a moment.*]

HOWARD: Sh! Get this now, this is my son.

HIS SON: 'The capital of Alabama is Montgomery; the capital of Arizona is Phoenix; the capital of Arkansas is Little Rock; the capital of California is Sacramento . . .' [*and on, and on.*]

HOWARD [*holding up five fingers*]: Five years old, Willy!

WILLY: He'll make an announcer some day!

HIS SON [*continuing*]: 'The capital . . .'

HOWARD: Get that – alphabetical order! [*The machine breaks off suddenly.*] Wait a minute. The maid kicked the plug out.

WILLY: It certainly is a –

HOWARD: Sh, for God's sake!

HIS SON: 'It's nine o'clock, Bulova watch time. So I have to go to sleep.'

WILLY: That really is –

HOWARD: Wait a minute! The next is my wife.

[*They wait.*]

HOWARD'S VOICE: 'Go on, say something.' [*Pause.*] 'Well, you gonna talk?'

HIS WIFE: 'I can't think of anything.'

HOWARD'S VOICE: 'Well, talk – it's turning.'

HIS WIFE [*shyly, beaten*]: 'Hello.' [*Silence.*] 'Oh, Howard, I can't talk into this . . .'

HOWARD [*snapping the machine off*]: That was my wife.

WILLY: That is a wonderful machine. Can we –

HOWARD: I tell you, Willy, I'm gonna take my camera, and my band-saw, and all my hobbies, and out they go. This is the most fascinating relaxation I ever found.

WILLY: I think I'll get one myself.

HOWARD: Sure, they're only a hundred and a half. You can't do without it. Supposing you wanna hear Jack Benny, see? But you can't be at home at that hour. So you tell the maid to turn the radio on when Jack Benny comes on, and this automatically goes on with the radio . . .

WILLY: And when you come home you . . .

HOWARD: You can come home twelve o'clock, one o'clock, any time you like, and you get yourself a Coke and sit yourself down, throw the switch, and there's Jack Benny's programme in the middle of the night!

WILLY: I'm definitely going to get one. Because lots of time I'm on the road, and I think to myself, what I must be missing on the radio!

HOWARD: Don't you have a radio in the car?

WILLY: Well, yeah, but who ever thinks of turning it on?

HOWARD: Say, aren't you supposed to be in Boston?

WILLY: That's what I want to talk to you about, Howard. You got a minute? [*He draws a chair in from the wing.*]

HOWARD: What happened? What're you doing here?

WILLY: Well . . .

HOWARD: You didn't crack up again, did you?

WILLY: Oh, no. No . . .

HOWARD: Geez, you had me worried there for a minute. What's the trouble?

WILLY: Well, tell you the truth, Howard. I've come to the decision that I'd rather not travel any more.

HOWARD: Not travel! Well, what'll you do?

WILLY: Remember, Christmas-time, when you had the party here? You said you'd try to think of some spot for me here in town.

HOWARD: With us?

WILLY: Well, sure.

HOWARD: Oh, yeah, yeah. I remember. Well, I couldn't think of anything for you, Willy.

WILLY: I tell ya, Howard. The kids are all grown up, y'know. I don't need much any more. If I could take home – well, sixty-five dollars a week, I could swing it.

HOWARD: Yeah, but Willy, see I –

WILLY: I tell ya why, Howard. Speaking frankly and between the two of us, y'know – I'm just a little tired.

HOWARD: Oh, I could understand that, Willy. But you're a road man, Willy, and we do a road business. We've only got a half-dozen salesmen on the floor here.

WILLY: God knows, Howard, I never asked a favour of any man. But I was with the firm when your father used to carry you in here in his arms.

HOWARD: I know that, Willy, but –

WILLY: Your father came to me the day you were born and asked me what I thought of the name of Howard, may he rest in peace.

HOWARD: I appreciate that, Willy, but there just is no spot here for you. If I had a spot I'd slam you right in, but I just don't have a single solitary spot.

[*He looks for his lighter,* WILLY *has picked it up and gives it to him. Pause.*]

WILLY [*with increasing anger*]: Howard, all I need to set my table is fifty dollars a week.

HOWARD: But where am I going to put you, kid?

WILLY: Look, it isn't a question of whether I can sell merchandise, is it?

HOWARD: No, but it's a business, kid, and everybody's gotta pull his own weight.

WILLY [*desperately*]: Just let me tell you a story, Howard –

HOWARD: 'Cause you gotta admit, business is business.

WILLY [*angrily*]: Business is definitely business, but just listen for a minute. You don't understand this. When I was a boy – eighteen, nineteen – I was already on the road. And there was a question in my mind as to whether selling had a future for me. Because in those days I had a yearning to go to Alaska. See, there were three gold strikes in one month in Alaska, and I felt like going out. Just for the ride, you might say.

HOWARD [*barely interested*]: Don't say.

WILLY: Oh, yeah, my father lived many years in Alaska. He was an adventurous man. We've got quite a little streak of self-reliance in our family. I thought I'd go out with my older brother and try to locate him, and maybe settle in the North with the old man. And I was almost decided to go, when I met a salesman in the Parker House. His name was Dave Singleman. And he was eighty-four years old, and he'd drummed merchandise in thirty-one states. And old Dave, he'd go up to his room, y'understand, put on his green velvet slippers – I'll never forget – and pick up his phone and call the buyers, and without ever leaving his room, at the age of eighty-four, he made his living. And when I saw that, I realized that selling was the greatest career a man could want. 'Cause what could be more satisfying than to be able to go, at the age of eighty-four, into twenty or thirty different cities, and pick up a phone, and be remembered and loved and helped by so many different people? Do you know? when he died – and by the way he died the death of a salesman, in his green velvet slippers in the smoker of the New York, New Haven, and Hartford, going into Boston – when he died, hundreds of salesmen and buyers were at his funeral. Things were sad on a lotta trains for months after that. [*He stands up.* HOWARD *has not looked at him.*] In those days there was personality in it, Howard. There was respect, and comradeship, and gratitude in it. Today, it's all cut and dried, and there's no chance for bringing friendship to bear – or personality. You see what I mean? They don't know me any more.

HOWARD [*moving away, toward the right*]: That's just the thing, Willy.

WILLY: If I had forty dollars a week – that's all I'd need. Forty dollars, Howard.

HOWARD: Kid, I can't take blood from a stone, I –

WILLY [*desperation is on him now*]: Howard, the year Al Smith was nominated, your father came to me and –

HOWARD [*starting to go off*]: I've got to see some people, kid.

WILLY [*stopping him*]: I'm talking about your father! There were promises made across this desk! You mustn't tell me you've got people to see – I put thirty-four years into this firm, Howard, and now I can't pay my insurance! You can't eat the orange and throw the peel away – a man is not a piece of fruit! [*After a pause*] Now pay attention. Your father – in 1928 I had a big year. I averaged a hundred and seventy dollars a week in commissions.

HOWARD [*impatiently*]: Now, Willy, you never averaged –

WILLY [*banging his hand on the desk*]: I averaged a hundred and seventy dollars a week in the year of 1928! And your father came to me – or rather, I was in the office here – it was right over this desk – and he put his hand on my shoulder –

HOWARD [*getting up*]: You'll have to excuse me, Willy, I gotta see some people. Pull yourself together. [*Going out*] I'll be back in a little while.

[*On* HOWARD*'s exit, the light on his chair grows very bright and strange.*]

WILLY: Pull myself together! What the hell did I say to him? My God, I was yelling at him! How could I! [WILLY *breaks off, staring at the light, which occupies the chair, animating it. He approaches this chair, standing across the desk from it.*] Frank, Frank, don't you remember what you told me that time? How you put your hand on my shoulder, and Frank . . . [*He leans on the desk and as he speaks the dead man's name he accidentally switches on the recorder, and instantly –*]

HOWARD'S SON: ' . . . of New York is Albany. The capital of Ohio is Cincinnati, the capital of Rhode Island is . . .'

[*The recitation continues.*]

WILLY [*leaping away with fright, shouting*]: Ha! Howard! Howard! Howard!

HOWARD [*rushing in*]: What happened?

WILLY [*pointing at the machine, which continues nasally, childishly, with the capital cities*]: Shut it off! Shut it off!

HOWARD [*pulling the plug out*]: Look, Willy . . .

WILLY [*pressing his hands to his eyes*]: I gotta get myself some coffee. I'll get some coffee . . .

[WILLY *starts to walk out.* HOWARD *stops him.*]

HOWARD [*rolling up the cord*]: Willy, look . . .

WILLY: I'll go to Boston.

HOWARD: Willy, you can't go to Boston for us.

WILLY: Why can't I go?

HOWARD: I don't want you to represent us. I've been meaning to tell you for a long time now.

WILLY: Howard, are you firing me?

HOWARD: I think you need a good long rest, Willy.

WILLY: Howard –

HOWARD: And when you feel better, come back, and we'll see if we can work something out.

WILLY: But I gotta earn money, Howard. I'm in no position to –

HOWARD: Where are your sons? Why don't your sons give you a hand?

WILLY: They're working on a very big deal.

HOWARD: This is no time for false pride, Willy. You go to your sons and you tell them that you're tired. You've got two great boys, haven't you?

WILLY: Oh, no question, no question, but in the meantime . . .

HOWARD: Then that's that, heh?

WILLY: All right, I'll go to Boston tomorrow.

HOWARD: No, no.

WILLY: I can't throw myself on my sons. I'm not a cripple!

HOWARD: Look, kid, I'm busy this morning.

WILLY [*grasping* HOWARD's *arm*]: Howard, you've got to let me go to Boston!

HOWARD [*hard, keeping himself under control*]: I've got a line of people to see this morning. Sit down, take five minutes, and pull yourself together, and then go home, will ya? I need the office, Willy. [*He starts to go, turns, remembering the recorder, starts to push off the table holding the recorder.*] Oh, yeah. Whenever you can this week, stop by and drop off the samples. You'll feel better, Willy, and then come back and we'll talk. Pull yourself together, kid, there's people outside.

[HOWARD *exits, pushing the table off left.* WILLY *stares into space, exhausted. Now the music is heard –* BEN's *music – first distantly, then closer, closer. As* WILLY *speaks,* BEN *enters from the right. He carries valise and umbrella.*]

WILLY: Oh, Ben, how did you do it? What is the answer? Did you wind up the Alaska deal already?
BEN: Doesn't take much time if you know what you're doing. Just a short business trip. Boarding ship in an hour. Wanted to say good-bye.
WILLY: Ben, I've got to talk to you.
BEN [*glancing at his watch*]: Haven't the time, William.
WILLY [*crossing the apron to* BEN]: Ben, nothing's working out. I don't know what to do.
BEN: Now, look here, William. I've bought timberland in Alaska and I need a man to look after things for me.
WILLY: God, timberland! Me and my boys in those grand outdoors!
BEN: You've a new continent at your doorstep, William. Get out of these cities, they're full of talk and time payments and courts of law. Screw on your fists and you can fight for a fortune up there.
WILLY: Yes, yes! Linda, Linda!

[LINDA *enters as of old, with the wash.*]

LINDA: Oh, you're back?
BEN: I haven't much time.

WILLY: No, wait! Linda, he's got a proposition for me in Alaska.

LINDA: But you've got – [*To* BEN] He's got a beautiful job here.

WILLY: But in Alaska, kid, I could –

LINDA: You're doing well enough, Willy!

BEN [*to* LINDA]: Enough for what, my dear?

LINDA [*frightened of* BEN *and angry at him*]: Don't say those things to him! Enough to be happy right here, right now. [*To* WILLY, *while* BEN *laughs*] Why must everybody conquer the world? You're well liked, and the boys love you, and someday – [*to* BEN] – why, old man Wagner told him just the other day that if he keeps it up he'll be a member of the firm, didn't he, Willy?

WILLY: Sure, sure. I am building something with this firm, Ben, and if a man is building something he must be on the right track, mustn't he?

BEN: What are you building? Lay your hand on it. Where is it?

WILLY [*hesitantly*]: That's true, Linda, there's nothing.

LINDA: Why? [*To* BEN] There's a man eighty-four years old –

WILLY: That's right, Ben, that's right. When I look at that man I say, what is there to worry about?

BEN: Bah!

WILLY: It's true, Ben. All he has to do is go into any city, pick up the phone, and he's making his living and you know why?

BEN [*picking up his valise*]: I've got to go.

WILLY [*holding* BEN *back*]: Look at this boy!

[BIFF, *in his high-school sweater, enters carrying suitcase.* HAPPY *carries* BIFF's *shoulder guards, gold helmet, and football pants.*]

WILLY: Without a penny to his name, three great universities are begging for him, and from there the sky's the limit, because it's not what you do, Ben. It's who you know and the smile on your face! It's contacts, Ben, contacts! The whole wealth of Alaska passes over the lunch table at the Commodore Hotel, and that's the wonder, the wonder of this country, that a man can end with diamonds here on the basis of being liked! [*He turns to* BIFF] And that's why when you get out on that field today it's important.

Because thousands of people will be rooting for you and loving you. [*To* BEN, *who has again begun to leave*] And Ben! when he walks into a business office his name will sound out like a bell and all the doors will open to him! I've seen it, Ben, I've seen it a thousand times! You can't feel it with your hand like timber, but it's there!

BEN: Good-bye, William.

WILLY: Ben, am I right? Don't you think I'm right? I value your advice.

BEN: There's a new continent at your doorstep, William. You could walk out rich. Rich! [*He is gone.*]

WILLY: We'll do it here, Ben! You hear me? We're gonna do it here!

[*Young* BERNARD *rushes in. The gay music of the boys is heard.*]

BERNARD: Oh, gee, I was afraid you left already!

WILLY: Why? What time is it?

BERNARD: It's half past one!

WILLY: Well, come on, everybody! Ebbets Field next stop! Where's the pennants? [*He rushes through the wall-line of the kitchen and out into the living-room.*]

LINDA [*to* BIFF]: Did you pack fresh underwear?

BIFF [*who has been limbering up*]: I want to go!

BERNARD: Biff, I'm carrying your helmet, ain't I?

HAPPY: No, I'm carrying the helmet.

BERNARD: Oh, Biff, you promised me.

HAPPY: I'm carrying the helmet.

BERNARD: How am I going to get in the locker room?

LINDA: Let him carry the shoulder guards. [*She puts her coat and hat on in the kitchen.*]

BERNARD: Can I, Biff? 'Cause I told everybody I'm going to be in the locker room.

HAPPY: In Ebbets Field it's the clubhouse.

BERNARD: I meant the clubhouse. Biff!

HAPPY: Biff!

BIFF [*grandly, after a slight pause*]: Let him carry the shoulder guards.

HAPPY [*as he gives* BERNARD *the shoulder guards*]: Stay close to us now.

[WILLY *rushes in with the pennants.*]

WILLY [*handing them out*]: Everybody wave when Biff comes out on the field. [HAPPY *and* BERNARD *run off.*] You set now, boys?

[*The music has died away.*]

BIFF: Ready to go, Pop. Every muscle is ready.

WILLY [*at the edge of the apron*]: You realize what this means?

BIFF: That's right, Pop.

WILLY [*feeling* BIFF's *muscles*]: You're comin' home this afternoon captain of the All-Scholastic Championship Team of the City of New York.

BIFF: I got it, Pop. And remember, pal, when I take off my helmet, that touchdown is for you.

WILLY: Let's go! [*He is starting out, with his arm around* BIFF, *when* CHARLEY *enters, as of old, in knickers.*] I got no room for you, Charley.

CHARLEY: Room? For what?

WILLY: In the car.

CHARLEY: You goin' for a ride? I wanted to shoot some casino.

WILLY [*furiously*]: Casino! [*Incredulously*] Don't you realize what today is?

LINDA: Oh, he knows, Willy. He's just kidding you.

WILLY: That's nothing to kid about!

CHARLEY: No, Linda, what's goin' on?

LINDA: He's playing in Ebbets Field.

CHARLEY: Baseball in this weather?

WILLY: Don't talk to him. Come on, come on! [*He is pushing them out.*]

CHARLEY: Wait a minute, didn't you hear the news?

WILLY: What?

CHARLEY: Don't you listen to the radio? Ebbets Field just blew up.

WILLY: You go to hell! [CHARLEY *laughs. Pushing them out*] Come on, come on! We're late.

CHARLEY [*as they go*]: Knock a homer, Biff, knock a homer!

WILLY [*the last to leave, turning to* CHARLEY]: I don't think that was funny, Charley. This is the greatest day of his life.

CHARLEY: Willy, when are you going to grow up?

WILLY: Yeah, heh? When this game is over, Charley, you'll be laughing out of the other side of your face. They'll be calling him another Red Grange. Twenty-five thousand a year.

CHARLEY [*kidding*]: Is that so?

WILLY: Yeah, that's so.

CHARLEY: Well, then, I'm sorry, Willy. But tell me something.

WILLY: What?

CHARLEY: Who is Red Grange?

WILLY: Put up your hands. Goddam you, put up your hands! [CHARLEY, *chuckling, shakes his head and walks away, around the left corner of the stage.* WILLY *follows him. The music rises to a mocking frenzy.*]

WILLY: Who the hell do you think you are, better than everybody else? You don't know everything, you big, ignorant, stupid . . . Put up your hands!

[*Light rises, on the right side of the forestage, on a small table in the reception room of* CHARLEY's *office. Traffic sounds are heard.* BERNARD, *now mature, sits whistling to himself. A pair of tennis rackets and an overnight bag are on the floor beside him.*]

WILLY [*offstage*]: What are you walking away for? Don't walk away! If you're going to say something say it to my face! I know you laugh at me behind my back. You'll laugh out of the other side of your goddam face after this game. Touchdown! Touchdown! Eighty thousand people! Touchdown! Right between the goal posts.

[BERNARD *is a quiet, earnest, but self-assured young man.* WILLY's *voice is coming from right upstage now.* BERNARD *lowers his feet off the table and listens.* JENNY, *his father's secretary, enters.*]

JENNY [*distressed*]: Say, Bernard, will you go out in the hall?

BERNARD: What is that noise? Who is it?

JENNY: Mr Loman. He just got off the elevator.

BERNARD [*getting up*]: Who's he arguing with?

JENNY: Nobody. There's nobody with him. I can't deal with him any more, and your father gets all upset everytime he comes. I've got a lot of typing to do, and your father's waiting to sign it. Will you see him?

WILLY [*entering*]: Touchdown! Touch – [*He sees* JENNY] Jenny, Jenny, good to see you. How're ya? Workin'? Or still honest?

JENNY: Fine. How've you been feeling?

WILLY: Not much any more, Jenny. Ha, ha! [*He is surprised to see the rackets.*]

BERNARD: Hello, Uncle Willy.

WILLY [*almost shocked*]: Bernard! Well, look who's here! [*He comes quickly, guiltily, to* BERNARD *and warmly shakes his hand.*]

BERNARD: How are you? Good to see you.

WILLY: What are you doing here?

BERNARD: Oh, just stopped by to see Pop. Get off my feet till my train leaves. I'm going to Washington in a few minutes.

WILLY: Is he in?

BERNARD: Yes, he's in his office with the accountant. Sit down.

WILLY [*sitting down*]: What're you going to do in Washington?

BERNARD: Oh, just a case I've got there, Willy.

WILLY: That so? [*Indicating the rackets*] You going to play tennis there?

BERNARD: I'm staying with a friend who's got a court.

WILLY: Don't say. His own tennis court. Must be fine people, I bet.

BERNARD: They are, very nice. Dad tells me Biff's in town.

WILLY [*with a big smile*]: Yeah, Biff's in. Working on a very big deal, Bernard.

BERNARD: What's Biff doing?

WILLY: Well, he's been doing very big things in the West. But he decided to establish himself here. Very big. We're having dinner. Did I hear your wife had a boy?

BERNARD: That's right. Our second.

WILLY: Two boys! What do you know!

BERNARD: What kind of a deal has Biff got?

WILLY: Well, Bill Oliver – very big sporting-goods man – he wants Biff very badly. Called him in from the West. Long distance, *carte blanche*, special deliveries. Your friends have their own private tennis court?

BERNARD: You still with the old firm, Willy?

WILLY [*after a pause*]: I'm – I'm overjoyed to see how you made the grade, Bernard, overjoyed. It's an encouraging thing to see a young man really – really – Looks very good for Biff – very – [*He breaks off, then*] Bernard – [*He is so full of emotion, he breaks off again.*]

BERNARD: What is it, Willy?

WILLY [*small and alone*]: What – what's the secret?

BERNARD: What secret?

WILLY: How – how did you? Why didn't he ever catch on?

BERNARD: I wouldn't know that, Willy.

WILLY [*confidentially, desperately*]: You were his friend, his boyhood friend. There's something I don't understand about it. His life ended after that Ebbets Field game. From the age of seventeen nothing good ever happened to him.

BERNARD: He never trained himself for anything.

WILLY: But he did, he did. After high school he took so many correspondence courses. Radio mechanics; television; God knows what, and never made the slightest mark.

BERNARD [*taking off his glasses*]: Willy, do you want to talk candidly?

WILLY [*rising, faces* BERNARD]: I regard you as a very brilliant man, Bernard. I value your advice.

BERNARD: Oh, the hell with the advice, Willy. I couldn't advise you. There's just one thing I've always wanted to ask you. When he was supposed to graduate, and the math teacher flunked him –

WILLY: Oh, that son-of-a-bitch ruined his life.

BERNARD: Yeah, but, Willy, all he had to do was to go to summer school and make up that subject.

WILLY: That's right, that's right.

BERNARD: Did you tell him not to go to summer school?

WILLY: Me? I begged him to go. I ordered him to go!

BERNARD: Then why wouldn't he go?

WILLY: Why? Why? Bernard, that question has been trailing me like a ghost for the last fifteen years. He flunked the subject, and laid down and died like a hammer hit him!

BERNARD: Take it easy, kid.

WILLY: Let me talk to you – I got nobody to talk to. Bernard, Bernard, was it my fault? Y'see? It keeps going around in my mind, maybe I did something to him. I got nothing to give him.

BERNARD: Don't take it so hard.

WILLY: Why did he lay down? What is the story there? You were his friend!

BERNARD: Willy, I remember, it was June, and our grades came out. And he'd flunked math.

WILLY: That son-of-a-bitch!

BERNARD: No, it wasn't right then. Biff just got very angry, I remember, and he was ready to enrol in summer school.

WILLY [*surprised*]: He was?

BERNARD: He wasn't beaten by it at all. But then, Willy, he disappeared from the block for almost a month. And I got the idea that he'd gone up to New England to see you. Did he have a talk with you then?

[WILLY *stares in silence.*]

BERNARD: Willy?

WILLY [*with a strong edge of resentment in his voice*]: Yeah, he came to Boston. What about it?

BERNARD: Well, just that when he came back – I'll never forget this, it always mystifies me. Because I'd thought so well of Biff, even though he'd always taken advantage of me. I loved him, Willy, y'know? And he came back after that month and took his sneakers – remember those sneakers with 'University of Virginia' printed on them? He was so proud of those, wore them every day. And he took them down in the cellar, and burned them up in the furnace. We had a fist fight. It lasted at least half an hour. Just the two of us, punching each other down the cellar, and crying right through it. I've often thought of how strange it was that I knew he'd given up his life. What happened in Boston, Willy?

[WILLY *looks at him as at an intruder.*]

BERNARD: I just bring it up because you asked me.

WILLY [*angrily*]: Nothing. What do you mean, 'What happened?' What's that got to do with anything?

BERNARD: Well, don't get sore.

WILLY: What are you trying to do, blame it on me? If a boy lays down is that my fault?

BERNARD: Now, Willy, don't get –

WILLY: Well, don't – don't talk to me that way! What does that mean, 'What happened?'

[CHARLEY *enters. He is in his vest, and he carries a bottle of bourbon.*]

CHARLEY: Hey, you're going to miss that train. [*He waves the bottle.*]

BERNARD: Yeah, I'm going. [*He takes the bottle.*] Thanks, Pop. [*He picks up his rackets and bag.*] Good-bye, Willy, and don't worry about it. You know, 'If at first you don't succeed . . .'

WILLY: Yes, I believe in that.

BERNARD: But sometimes, Willy, it's better for a man just to walk away.

WILLY: Walk away?

BERNARD: That's right.

WILLY: But if you can't walk away?

BERNARD [*after a slight pause*]: I guess that's when it's tough. [*Extending his hand*] Good-bye, Willy.

WILLY [*shaking* BERNARD's *hand*]: Good-bye, boy.

CHARLEY [*an arm on* BERNARD's *shoulder*]: How do you like this kid? Gonna argue a case in front of the Supreme Court.

BERNARD [*protesting*]: Pop!

WILLY [*genuinely shocked, pained, and happy*]: No! The Supreme Court!

BERNARD: I gotta run. 'Bye, Dad!

CHARLEY: Knock 'em dead, Bernard!

[BERNARD *goes off.*]

WILLY [*as* CHARLEY *takes out his wallet*]: The Supreme Court! And he didn't even mention it!

CHARLEY [*counting out money on the desk*]: He don't have to – he's gonna do it.

WILLY: And you never told him what to do, did you? You never took any interest in him.

CHARLEY: My salvation is that I never took any interest in anything. There's some money – fifty dollars. I got an accountant inside.

WILLY: Charley, look . . . [*With difficulty*] I got my insurance to pay. If you can manage it – I need a hundred and ten dollars.

[CHARLEY *doesn't reply for a moment, merely stops moving.*]

WILLY: I'd draw it from my bank but Linda would know, and I . . .

CHARLEY: Sit down, Willy.

WILLY [*moving toward the chair*]: I'm keeping an account of everything, remember. I'll pay every penny back. [*He sits.*]

CHARLEY: Now listen to me, Willy.

WILLY: I want you to know I appreciate . . .

CHARLEY [*sitting down on the table*]: Willy, what're you doin'? What the hell is goin' on in your head?

WILLY: Why? I'm simply . . .

CHARLEY: I offered you a job. You can make fifty dollars a week. And I won't send you on the road.

WILLY: I've got a job.

CHARLEY: Without pay? What kind of a job is a job without pay? [*He rises.*] Now, look, kid, enough is enough. I'm no genius but I know when I'm being insulted.

WILLY: Insulted!

CHARLEY: Why don't you want to work for me?

WILLY: What's the matter with you? I've got a job.

CHARLEY: Then what're you walkin' in here every week for?

WILLY [*getting up*]: Well, if you don't want me to walk in here –

CHARLEY: I am offering you a job.

WILLY: I don't want your goddam job!

CHARLEY: When the hell are you going to grow up?

WILLY [*furiously*]: You big ignoramus, if you say that to me again I'll rap you one! I don't care how big you are! [*He's ready to fight.*]

[*Pause.*]

CHARLEY [*kindly, going to him*]: How much do you need, Willy?

WILLY: Charley, I'm strapped, I'm strapped. I don't know what to do. I was just fired.

CHARLEY: Howard fired you?

WILLY: That snotnose. Imagine that? I named him. I named him Howard.

CHARLEY: Willy, when're you gonna realize that them things don't mean anything? You named him Howard, but you can't sell that. The only thing you got in this world is what you can sell. And the funny thing is that you're a salesman, and you don't know that.

WILLY: I've always tried to think otherwise, I guess. I always felt that if a man was impressive, and well liked, that nothing –

CHARLEY: Why must everybody like you? Who liked J. P. Morgan? Was he impressive? In a Turkish bath he'd look like a butcher. But with his pockets on he was very well liked. Now listen, Willy, I know you don't like me, and nobody can say I'm in love with you, but I'll give you a job because – just for the hell of it, put it that way. Now what do you say?

WILLY: I – I just can't work for you, Charley.

CHARLEY: What're you, jealous of me?

WILLY: I can't work for you, that's all, don't ask me why.

CHARLEY [*angered, takes out more bills*]: You been jealous of me all your life, you damned fool! Here, pay your insurance. [*He puts the money in* WILLY's *hand.*]

WILLY: I'm keeping strict accounts.

CHARLEY: I've got some work to do. Take care of yourself. And pay your insurance.

WILLY [*moving to the right*]: Funny, y'know? After all the highways, and the trains, and the appointments, and the years, you end up worth more dead than alive.

CHARLEY: Willy, nobody's worth nothin' dead. [*After a slight pause*] Did you hear what I said?

[WILLY *stands still, dreaming.*]

CHARLEY: Willy!

WILLY: Apologize to Bernard for me when you see him. I didn't mean to argue with him. He's a fine boy. They're all fine boys, and they'll end up big – all of them. Someday they'll all play tennis together. Wish me luck, Charley. He saw Bill Oliver today.

CHARLEY: Good luck.

WILLY [*on the verge of tears*]: Charley, you're the only friend I got. Isn't that a remarkable thing? [*He goes out.*]

CHARLEY: Jesus!

[CHARLEY *stares after him a moment and follows. All light blacks out. Suddenly raucous music is heard, and a red glow rises behind the screen at right.* STANLEY, *a young waiter, appears, carrying a table, followed by* HAPPY, *who is carrying two chairs.*]

STANLEY [*putting the table down*]: That's all right, Mr Loman, I can handle it myself. [*He turns and takes the chairs from* HAPPY *and places them at the table.*]

HAPPY [*glancing around*]: Oh, this is better.

STANLEY: Sure, in the front there you're in the middle of all kinds a noise. Whenever you got a party, Mr Loman, you just tell me and I'll put you back here. Y'know, there's a lotta people they don't like it private, because when they go out they like to see a lotta action around them because they're sick and tired to stay in the house by theirself. But I know you, you ain't from Hackensack. You know what I mean?

HAPPY [*sitting down*]: So how's it coming, Stanley?

STANLEY: Ah, it's a dog's life. I only wish during the war they'd a took me in the Army. I coulda been dead by now.

HAPPY: My brother's back, Stanley.

STANLEY: Oh, he come back, heh? From the Far West.

HAPPY: Yeah, big cattle man, my brother, so treat him right. And my father's coming too.

STANLEY: Oh, your father too!

HAPPY: You got a couple of nice lobsters?

STANLEY: Hundred per cent, big.

HAPPY: I want them with the claws.

STANLEY: Don't worry, I don't give you no mice. [HAPPY *laughs*.] How about some wine? It'll put a head on the meal.

HAPPY: No. You remember, Stanley, that recipe I brought you from overseas? With the champagne in it?

STANLEY: Oh, yeah, sure. I still got it tacked up yet in the kitchen. But that'll have to cost a buck apiece anyways.

HAPPY: That's all right.

STANLEY: What'd you, hit a number or somethin'?

HAPPY: No, it's a little celebration. My brother is – I think he pulled off a big deal today. I think we're going into business together.

STANLEY: Great! That's the best for you. Because a family business, you know what I mean? – that's the best.

HAPPY: That's what I think.

STANLEY: 'Cause what's the difference? Somebody steals? It's in the family. Know what I mean? [*Sotto voce*] Like this bartender here. The boss is goin' crazy what kinda leak he's got in the cash register. You put it in but it don't come out.

HAPPY [*raising his head*]: Sh!

STANLEY: What?

HAPPY: You notice I wasn't lookin' right or left, was I?

STANLEY: No.

HAPPY: And my eyes are closed.

STANLEY: So what's the – ?

HAPPY: Strudel's comin'.

STANLEY [*catching on, looks around*]: Ah, no, there's no –

[*He breaks off as a furred, lavishly dressed girl enters and sits at the next table. Both follow her with their eyes.*]

STANLEY: Geez, how'd ya know?

HAPPY: I got radar or something. [*Staring directly at her profile*] Oooooooo . . . Stanley.

STANLEY: I think that's for you, Mr Loman.

HAPPY: Look at that mouth. Oh, God. And the binoculars.

STANLEY: Geez, you got a life, Mr Loman.

HAPPY: Wait on her.

STANLEY [*going to the girl's table*]: Would you like a menu, ma'am?

GIRL: I'm expecting someone, but I'd like a –

HAPPY: Why don't you bring her – excuse me, miss, do you mind? I sell champagne, and I'd like you to try my brand. Bring her a champagne, Stanley.

GIRL: That's awfully nice of you.

HAPPY: Don't mention it. It's all company money. [*He laughs.*]

GIRL: That's a charming product to be selling, isn't it?

HAPPY: Oh, gets to be like everything else. Selling is selling, y'know.

GIRL: I suppose.

HAPPY: You don't happen to sell, do you?

GIRL: No, I don't sell.

HAPPY: Would you object to a compliment from a stranger? You ought to be on a magazine cover.

GIRL [*looking at him a little archly*]: I have been.

[STANLEY *comes in with a glass of champagne.*]

HAPPY: What'd I say before, Stanley? You see? She's a cover girl.

STANLEY: Oh, I could see, I could see.

HAPPY [*to the* GIRL]: What magazine?

GIRL: Oh, a lot of them. [*She takes the drink.*] Thank you.

HAPPY: You know what they say in France, don't you? 'Champagne is the drink of the complexion' – Hya, Biff!

[BIFF *has entered and sits with* HAPPY.]

BIFF: Hello, kid. Sorry I'm late.

HAPPY: I just got here. Uh, Miss – ?

GIRL: Forsythe.

HAPPY: Miss Forsythe, this is my brother.

BIFF: Is Dad here?

HAPPY: His name is Biff. You might've heard of him. Great football player.

GIRL: Really? What team?

HAPPY: Are you familiar with football?

GIRL: No, I'm afraid I'm not.

HAPPY: Biff is quarterback with the New York Giants.

GIRL: Well, that is nice, isn't it? [*She drinks.*]

HAPPY: Good health.

GIRL: I'm happy to meet you.

HAPPY: That's my name. Hap. It's really Harold, but at West Point they called me Happy.

GIRL [*now really impressed*]: Oh, I see. How do you do? [*She turns her profile.*]

BIFF: Isn't Dad coming?

HAPPY: You want her?

BIFF: Oh, I could never make that.

HAPPY: I remember the time that idea would never come into your head. Where's the old confidence, Biff?

BIFF: I just saw Oliver –

HAPPY: Wait a minute. I've got to see that old confidence again. Do you want her? She's on call.

BIFF: Oh, no. [*He turns to look at the* GIRL.]

HAPPY: I'm telling you. Watch this. [*Turning to the* GIRL] Honey? [*She turns to him.*] Are you busy?

GIRL: Well, I am . . . but I could make a phone call.

HAPPY: Do that, will you, honey? And see if you can get a friend. We'll be here for a while. Biff is one of the greatest football players in the country.

GIRL [*standing up*]: Well, I'm certainly happy to meet you.

HAPPY: Come back soon.

GIRL: I'll try.

HAPPY: Don't try, honey, try hard.

[*The* GIRL *exits.* STANLEY *follows, shaking his head in bewildered admiration.*]

HAPPY: Isn't that a shame now? A beautiful girl like that? That's why I can't get married. There's not a good woman in a thousand. New York is loaded with them, kid!

BIFF: Hap, look –

HAPPY: I told you she was on call!

BIFF [*strangely unnerved*]: Cut it out, will ya? I want to say something to you.

HAPPY: Did you see Oliver?

BIFF: I saw him all right. Now look, I want to tell Dad a couple of things and I want you to help me.

HAPPY: What? Is he going to back you?

BIFF: Are you crazy? You're out of your goddam head, you know that?

HAPPY: Why? What happened?

BIFF [*breathlessly*]: I did a terrible thing today, Hap. It's been the strangest day I ever went through. I'm all numb, I swear.

HAPPY: You mean he wouldn't see you?

BIFF: Well, I waited six hours for him, see? All day. Kept sending my name in. Even tried to date his secretary so she'd get me to him, but no soap.

HAPPY: Because you're not showin' the old confidence, Biff. He remembered you, didn't he?

BIFF [*stopping* HAPPY *with a gesture*]: Finally, about five o'clock, he comes out. Didn't remember who I was or anything. I felt like such an idiot, Hap.

HAPPY: Did you tell him my Florida idea?

BIFF: He walked away. I saw him for one minute. I got so mad I could've torn the walls down! How the hell did I ever get the idea I was a salesman there? I even believed myself that I'd been a salesman for him! And then he gave me one look and – I realized what a ridiculous lie my whole life has been. We've been talking in a dream for fifteen years. I was a shipping clerk.

HAPPY: What'd you do?

BIFF [*with great tension and wonder*]: Well, he left, see. And the secretary went out. I was all alone in the waiting-room. I don't know what came over me, Hap. The next thing I know I'm in his office – panelled walls, everything. I can't explain it. I – Hap, I took his fountain pen.

HAPPY: Geez, did he catch you?

BIFF: I ran out. I ran down all eleven flights. I ran and ran and ran.

HAPPY: That was an awful dumb – what'd you do that for?

BIFF [*agonized*]: I don't know, I just – wanted to take something, I don't know. You gotta help me, Hap, I'm gonna tell Pop.

HAPPY: You crazy? What for?

BIFF: Hap, he's got to understand that I'm not the man somebody lends that kind of money to. He thinks I've been spiting him all these years and it's eating him up.

HAPPY: That's just it. You tell him something nice.

BIFF: I can't.

HAPPY: Say you got a lunch date with Oliver tomorrow.

BIFF: So what do I do tomorrow?

HAPPY: You leave the house tomorrow and come back at night and say Oliver is thinking it over. And he thinks it over for a couple of weeks, and gradually it fades away and nobody's the worse.

BIFF: But it'll go on for ever!

HAPPY: Dad is never so happy as when he's looking forward to something!

[WILLY *enters.*]

HAPPY: Hello, scout!

WILLY: Gee, I haven't been here in years!

[STANLEY *has followed* WILLY *in and sets a chair for him.* STANLEY *starts off but* HAPPY *stops him.*]

HAPPY: Stanley!

[STANLEY *stands by, waiting for an order.*]

BIFF [*going to* WILLY *with guilt, as to an invalid*]: Sit down, Pop. You
   want a drink?

WILLY: Sure, I don't mind.

BIFF: Let's get a load on.

WILLY: You look worried.

BIFF: N-no. [*To* STANLEY] Scotch all around. Make it doubles.

STANLEY: Doubles, right. [*He goes.*]

WILLY: You had a couple already, didn't you?

BIFF: Just a couple, yeah.

WILLY: Well, what happened, boy? [*Nodding affirmatively, with a
   smile*] Everything go all right?

BIFF [*takes a breath, then reaches out and grasps* WILLY'*s hand*]: Pal . . .
   [*He is smiling bravely, and* WILLY *is smiling too.*] I had an experience
   today.

HAPPY: Terrific, Pop.

WILLY: That so? What happened?

BIFF [*high, slightly alcoholic, above the earth*]: I'm going to tell you
   everything from first to last. It's been a strange day. [*Silence. He looks
   around, composes himself as best he can, but his breath keeps breaking
   the rhythm of his voice.*] I had to wait quite a while for him, and –

WILLY: Oliver?

BIFF: Yeah, Oliver. All day, as a matter of cold fact. And a lot of –
   instances – facts, Pop, facts about my life came back to me.
   Who was it, Pop? Who ever said I was a salesman with Oliver?

WILLY: Well, you were.

BIFF: No, Dad, I was a shipping clerk.

WILLY: But you were practically –

BIFF [*with determination*]: Dad, I don't know who said it first, but I
   was never a salesman for Bill Oliver.

WILLY: What're you talking about?

BIFF: Let's hold on to the facts tonight, Pop. We're not going to get
   anywhere bullin' around. I was a shipping clerk.

WILLY [*angrily*]: All right, now listen to me –

BIFF: Why don't you let me finish?

WILLY: I'm not interested in stories about the past or any crap of that kind because the woods are burning, boys, you understand? There's a big blaze going on all around. I was fired today.

BIFF [*shocked*]: How could you be?

WILLY: I was fired, and I'm looking for a little good news to tell your mother, because the woman has waited and the woman has suffered. The gist of it is that I haven't got a story left in my head, Biff. So don't give me a lecture about facts and aspects. I am not interested. Now what've you got to say to me?

[STANLEY *enters with three drinks. They wait until he leaves.*]

WILLY: Did you see Oliver?

BIFF: Jesus, Dad!

WILLY: You mean you didn't go up there?

HAPPY: Sure he went up there.

BIFF: I did. I – saw him. How could they fire you?

WILLY [*on the edge of his chair*]: What kind of a welcome did he give you?

BIFF: He won't even let you work on commission?

WILLY: I'm out! [*Driving*] So tell me, he gave you a warm welcome?

HAPPY: Sure, Pop, sure!

BIFF [*driven*]: Well, it was kind of –

WILLY: I was wondering if he'd remember you. [*To* HAPPY] Imagine, man doesn't see him for ten, twelve years and gives him that kind of a welcome!

HAPPY: Damn right!

BIFF [*trying to return to the offensive*]: Pop, look –

WILLY: You know why he remembered you, don't you? Because you impressed him in those days.

BIFF: Let's talk quietly and get this down to the facts, huh?

WILLY [*as though* BIFF *had been interrupting*]: Well, what happened? It's great news, Biff. Did he take you into his office or'd you talk in the waiting-room?

BIFF: Well, he came in, see, and –

WILLY [*with a big smile*]: What'd he say? Betcha he threw his arm around you.

BIFF: Well, he kinda –

WILLY: He's a fine man. [*To* HAPPY] Very hard man to see, y'know.

HAPPY [*agreeing*]: Oh, I know.

WILLY [*to* BIFF]: Is that where you had the drinks?

BIFF: Yeah, he gave me a couple of – no, no!

HAPPY [*cutting in*]: He told him my Florida idea.

WILLY: Don't interrupt. [*To* BIFF] How'd he react to the Florida idea?

BIFF: Dad, will you give me a minute to explain?

WILLY: I've been waiting for you to explain since I sat down here! What happened? He took you into his office and what?

BIFF: Well – I talked. And – and he listened, see.

WILLY: Famous for the way he listens, y'know. What was his answer?

BIFF: His answer was – [*He breaks off, suddenly angry.*] Dad, you're not letting me tell you what I want to tell you!

WILLY [*accusing, angered*]: You didn't see him, did you?

BIFF: I did see him!

WILLY: What'd you insult him or something? You insulted him, didn't you?

BIFF: Listen, will you let me out of it, will you just let me out of it!

HAPPY: What the hell!

WILLY: Tell me what happened!

BIFF [*to* HAPPY]: I can't talk to him!

[*A single trumpet note jars the ear. The light of green leaves stains the house, which holds the air of night and a dream.* YOUNG BERNARD *enters and knocks on the door of the house.*]

YOUNG BERNARD [*frantically*]: Mrs Loman, Mrs Loman!

HAPPY: Tell him what happened!

BIFF [*to* HAPPY]: Shut up and leave me alone!

WILLY: No, no! You had to go and flunk math!

BIFF: What math? What're you talking about?

YOUNG BERNARD: Mrs Loman, Mrs Loman!

[LINDA *appears in the house, as of old.*]

WILLY [*wildly*]: Math, math, math!

BIFF: Take it easy, Pop!

YOUNG BERNARD: Mrs Loman!

WILLY [*furiously*]: If you hadn't flunked you'd've been set by now!

BIFF: Now, look, I'm gonna tell you what happened, and you're going to listen to me.

YOUNG BERNARD: Mrs Loman!

BIFF: I waited six hours –

HAPPY: What the hell are you saying?

BIFF: I kept sending in my name but he wouldn't see me. So finally he . . . [*He continues unheard as light fades low on the restaurant.*]

YOUNG BERNARD: Biff flunked math!

LINDA: No!

YOUNG BERNARD: Birnbaum flunked him! They won't graduate him!

LINDA: But they have to. He's gotta go to the university. Where is he? Biff! Biff!

YOUNG BERNARD: No, he left. He went to Grand Central.

LINDA: Grand – You mean he went to Boston!

YOUNG BERNARD: Is Uncle Willy in Boston?

LINDA: Oh, maybe Willy can talk to the teacher. Oh, the poor, poor boy!

[*Light on house area snaps out.*]

BIFF [*at the table, now audible, holding up a gold fountain pen*]: . . . so I'm washed up with Oliver, you understand? Are you listening to me?

WILLY [*at a loss*]: Yeah, sure. If you hadn't flunked –

BIFF: Flunked what? What're you talking about?

WILLY: Don't blame everything on me! I didn't flunk math – you did! What pen?

HAPPY: That was awful dumb, Biff, a pen like that is worth –

WILLY [*seeing the pen for the first time*]: You took Oliver's pen?

BIFF [*weakening*]: Dad, I just explained it to you.

WILLY: You stole Bill Oliver's fountain pen!

BIFF: I didn't exactly steal it! That's just what I've been explaining to you!

HAPPY: He had it in his hand and just then Oliver walked in, so he got nervous and stuck it in his pocket!

WILLY: My God, Biff!

BIFF: I never intended to do it, Dad!

OPERATOR'S VOICE: Standish Arms, good evening!

WILLY [*shouting*]: I'm not in my room!

BIFF [*frightened*]: Dad, what's the matter? [*He and* HAPPY *stand up.*]

OPERATOR: Ringing Mr Loman for you!

WILLY: I'm not there, stop it!

BIFF [*horrified, gets down on one knee before* WILLY]: Dad, I'll make good, I'll make good. [WILLY *tries to get to his feet.* BIFF *holds him down.*] Sit down now.

WILLY: No, you're no good, you're no good for anything.

BIFF: I am, Dad, I'll find something else, you understand? Now don't worry about anything. [*He holds up* WILLY's *face.*] Talk to me, Dad.

OPERATOR: Mr Loman does not answer. Shall I page him?

WILLY [*attempting to stand, as though to rush and silence the* OPERATOR]: No, no, no!

HAPPY: He'll strike something, Pop.

WILLY: No, no . . .

BIFF [*desperately, standing over* WILLY]: Pop, listen! Listen to me! I'm telling you something good. Oliver talked to his partner about the Florida idea. You listening? He – he talked to his partner, and he came to me . . . I'm going to be all right, you hear? Dad, listen to me, he said it was just a question of the amount!

WILLY: Then you . . . got it?

HAPPY: He's gonna be terrific, Pop!

WILLY [*trying to stand*]: Then you got it, haven't you? You got it! You got it!

BIFF [*agonized, holds* WILLY *down*]: No, no. Look, Pop. I'm supposed to have lunch with them tomorrow. I'm just telling you this so you'll know that I can still make an impression, Pop. And I'll make good somewhere, but I can't go tomorrow, see?

WILLY: Why not? You simply –

BIFF: But the pen, Pop!

WILLY: You give it to him and tell him it was an oversight!

HAPPY: Sure, have lunch tomorrow!

BIFF: I can't say that –

WILLY: You were doing a crossword puzzle and accidentally used his pen!

BIFF: Listen, kid, I took those balls years ago, now I walk in with his fountain pen? That clinches it, don't you see? I can't face him like that! I'll try elsewhere.

PAGE'S VOICE: Paging Mr Loman!

WILLY: Don't you want to be anything?

BIFF: Pop, how can I go back?

WILLY: You don't want to be anything, is that what's behind it?

BIFF [*now angry at* WILLY *for not crediting his sympathy*]: Don't take it that way! You think it was easy walking into that office after what I'd done to him? A team of horses couldn't have dragged me back to Bill Oliver!

WILLY: Then why'd you go?

BIFF: Why did I go? Why did I go? Look at you! Look at what's become of you!

[*Off left, the* WOMAN *laughs.*]

WILLY: Biff, you're going to go to that lunch tomorrow, or –

BIFF: I can't go. I've got no appointment!

HAPPY: Biff, for . . . !

WILLY: Are you spiting me?

BIFF: Don't take it that way! Goddammit!

WILLY [*strikes* BIFF *and falters away from the table*]: You rotten little louse! Are you spiting me?

THE WOMAN: Someone's at the door, Willy!

BIFF: I'm no good, can't you see what I am?

HAPPY [*separating them*]: Hey, you're in a restaurant! Now cut it out, both of you! [*The girls enter.*] Hello, girls, sit down.

[*The* WOMAN *laughs, off left.*]

MISS FORSYTHE: I guess we might as well. This is Letta.

THE WOMAN: Willy, are you going to wake up?

BIFF [*ignoring* WILLY]: How're ya, miss, sit down. What do you drink?

MISS FORSYTHE: Letta might not be able to stay long.

LETTA: I gotta get up very early tomorrow. I got jury duty. I'm so excited! Were you fellows ever on a jury?

BIFF: No, but I been in front of them! [*The girls laugh.*] This is my father.

LETTA: Isn't he cute? Sit down with us, Pop.

HAPPY: Sit him down, Biff!

BIFF [*going to him*]: Come on, slugger, drink us under the table. To hell with it! Come on, sit down, pal.

[*On* BIFF's *last insistence,* WILLY *is about to sit.*]

THE WOMAN [*now urgently*]: Willy, are you going to answer the door!

[*The* WOMAN's *call pulls* WILLY *back. He starts right, befuddled.*]

BIFF: Hey, where are you going?

WILLY: Open the door.

BIFF: The door?

WILLY: The washroom . . . the door . . . where's the door?

BIFF [*leading* WILLY *to the left*]: Just go straight down.

[WILLY *moves left.*]

THE WOMAN: Willy, Willy, are you going to get up, get up, get up, get up?

[WILLY *exits left.*]

LETTA: I think it's sweet you bring your daddy along.

MISS FORSYTHE: Oh, he isn't really your father!

BIFF [*at left, turning to her resentfully*]: Miss Forsythe, you've just seen a prince walk by. A fine, troubled prince. A hardworking, unappreciated prince. A pal, you understand? A good companion. Always for his boys.

LETTA: That's so sweet.

HAPPY: Well, girls, what's the programme? We're wasting time. Come on, Biff. Gather round. Where would you like to go?

BIFF: Why don't you do something for him?

HAPPY: Me!

BIFF: Don't you give a damn for him, Hap?

HAPPY: What're you talking about? I'm the one who –

BIFF: I sense it, you don't give a good goddam about him. [*He takes the rolled-up hose from his pocket and puts it on the table in front of* HAPPY.] Look what I found in the cellar, for Christ's sake. How can you bear to let it go on?

HAPPY: Me? Who goes away? Who runs off and –

BIFF: Yeah, but he doesn't mean anything to you. You could help him – I can't. Don't you understand what I'm talking about? He's going to kill himself, don't you know that?

HAPPY: Don't I know it! Me!

BIFF: Hap, help him! Jesus . . . help him . . . Help me, help me, I can't bear to look at his face! [*Ready to weep, he hurries out, up right.*]

HAPPY [*starting after him*]: Where are you going?

MISS FORSYTHE: What's he so mad about?

HAPPY: Come on, girls, we'll catch up with him.

MISS FORSYTHE [*as* HAPPY *pushes her out*]: Say, I don't like that temper of his!

HAPPY: He's just a little overstrung, he'll be all right!

WILLY [*off left, as the* WOMAN *laughs*]: Don't answer! Don't answer!

LETTA: Don't you want to tell your father –

HAPPY: No, that's not my father. He's just a guy. Come on, we'll catch Biff, and, honey, we're going to paint this town! Stanley, where's the check! Hey, Stanley!

[*They exit.* STANLEY *looks toward left.*]

STANLEY [*calling to* HAPPY *indignantly*]: Mr Loman! Mr Loman!

[STANLEY *picks up a chair and follows them off. Knocking is heard off left. The* WOMAN *enters, laughing.* WILLY *follows her. She is in a black slip; he is buttoning his shirt. Raw, sensuous music accompanies their speech.*]

WILLY: Will you stop laughing? Will you stop?

THE WOMAN: Aren't you going to answer the door? He'll wake the whole hotel.

WILLY: I'm not expecting anybody.

THE WOMAN: Whyn't you have another drink, honey, and stop being so damn self-centred?

WILLY: I'm so lonely.

THE WOMAN: You know you ruined me, Willy? From now on, whenever you come to the office, I'll see that you go right through to the buyers. No waiting at my desk any more, Willy. You ruined me.

WILLY: That's nice of you to say that.

THE WOMAN: Gee, you are self-centred! Why so sad? You are the saddest, self-centredest soul I ever did see-saw. [*She laughs. He kisses her.*] Come on inside, drummer boy. It's silly to be dressing in the middle of the night. [*As knocking is heard*] Aren't you going to answer the door?

WILLY: They're knocking on the wrong door.

THE WOMAN: But I felt the knocking. And he heard us talking in here. Maybe the hotel's on fire!

WILLY [*his terror rising*]: It's a mistake.

THE WOMAN: Then tell him to go away!

WILLY: There's nobody there.

THE WOMAN: It's getting on my nerves, Willy. There's somebody standing out there and it's getting on my nerves!

WILLY [*pushing her away from him*]: All right, stay in the bathroom here, and don't come out. I think there's a law in Massachusetts about it, so don't come out. It may be that new room clerk. He looked very mean. So don't come out. It's a mistake, there's no fire.

[*The knocking is heard again. He takes a few steps away from her, and she vanishes into the wing. The light follows him, and now he is facing* YOUNG BIFF, *who carries a suitcase.* BIFF *steps toward him. The music is gone.*]

BIFF: Why didn't you answer?

WILLY: Biff! What are you doing in Boston?

BIFF: Why didn't you answer! I've been knocking for five minutes, I called you on the phone –

WILLY: I just heard you. I was in the bathroom and had the door shut. Did anything happen home?

BIFF: Dad – I let you down.

WILLY: What do you mean?

BIFF: Dad . . .

WILLY: Biffo, what's this about? [*Putting his arm around* BIFF] Come on, let's go downstairs and get you a malted.

BIFF: Dad, I flunked math.

WILLY: Not for the term?

BIFF: The term. I haven't got enough credits to graduate.

WILLY: You mean to say Bernard wouldn't give you the answers?

BIFF: He did, he tried, but I only got a sixty-one.

WILLY: And they wouldn't give you four points?

BIFF: Birnbaum refused absolutely. I begged him, Pop, but he won't give me those points. You gotta talk to him before they close the school. Because if he saw the kind of man you are, and you just talked to him in your way, I'm sure he'd come through for me. The class came right before practice, see, and I didn't go enough. Would you talk to him? He'd like you, Pop. You know the way you could talk.

WILLY: You're on. We'll drive right back.

BIFF: Oh, Dad, good work! I'm sure he'll change it for you!

WILLY: Go downstairs and tell the clerk I'm checkin' out. Go right down.

BIFF: Yes, sir! See, the reason he hates me, Pop – one day he was late for class so I got up at the blackboard and imitated him. I crossed my eyes and talked with a lithp.

WILLY [*laughing*]: You did? The kids like it?

BIFF: They nearly died laughing!

WILLY: Yeah? What'd you do?

BIFF: The thquare root of thixthy-twee is . . . [WILLY *bursts out laughing;* BIFF *joins him.*] And in the middle of it he walked in!

[WILLY *laughs and the* WOMAN *joins in offstage.*]

WILLY [*without hesitation*]: Hurry downstairs and –

BIFF: Somebody in there?

WILLY: No, that was next door.

[*The* WOMAN *laughs offstage.*]

BIFF: Somebody got in your bathroom!

WILLY: No, it's the next room, there's a party –

THE WOMAN [*enters, laughing. She lisps this*]: Can I come in? There's something in the bathtub, Willy, and it's moving!

[WILLY *looks at* BIFF, *who is staring open-mouthed and horrified at the* WOMAN.]

WILLY: Ah – you better go back to your room. They must be finished painting by now. They're painting her room so I let her take a shower here. Go back, go back . . . [*He pushes her.*]

THE WOMAN [*resisting*]: But I've got to get dressed, Willy, I can't –

WILLY: Get out of here! Go back, go back . . . [*Suddenly striving for the ordinary*] This is Miss Francis, Biff, she's a buyer. They're painting her room. Go back, Miss Francis, go back . . .

THE WOMAN: But my clothes, I can't go out naked in the hall!

WILLY [*pushing her offstage*]: Get outa here! Go back, go back!

[BIFF *slowly sits down on his suitcase as the argument continues offstage.*]

THE WOMAN: Where's my stockings? You promised me stockings, Willy!

WILLY: I have no stockings here!

THE WOMAN: You had two boxes of size nine sheers for me, and I want them!

WILLY: Here, for God's sake, will you get outa here!

THE WOMAN [*enters holding a box of stockings*]: I just hope there's nobody in the hall. That's all I hope. [*To* BIFF] Are you football or baseball?

BIFF: Football.

THE WOMAN [*angry, humiliated*]: That's me too. G'night. [*She snatches her clothes from* WILLY, *and walks out.*]

WILLY [*after a pause*]: Well, better get going. I want to get to the school first thing in the morning. Get my suits out of the closet. I'll get my valise. [BIFF *doesn't move.*] What's the matter? [BIFF *remains motionless, tears falling.*] She's a buyer. Buys for J. H. Simmons. She lives down the hall – they're painting. You don't imagine – [*He breaks off. After a pause*] Now listen, pal, she's just a buyer. She sees merchandise in her room and they have to keep it looking just so . . . [*Pause. Assuming command*] All right, get my suits. [BIFF *doesn't move.*] Now stop crying and do as I say. I gave you an order. Biff, I gave you an order! Is that what you do when I give you an order? How dare you cry? [*Putting his arm around* BIFF] Now look, Biff, when you grow up you'll understand about these things. You mustn't – you mustn't over-emphasize a thing like this. I'll see Birnbaum first thing in the morning.

BIFF: Never mind.

WILLY [*getting down beside* BIFF]: Never mind! He's going to give you those points. I'll see to it.

BIFF: He wouldn't listen to you.

WILLY: He certainly will listen to me. You need those points for the U. of Virginia.

BIFF: I'm not going there.

WILLY: Heh? If I can't get him to change that mark you'll make it up in summer school. You've got all summer to –

BIFF [*his weeping breaking from him*]: Dad . . .

WILLY [*infected by it*]: Oh, my boy . . .

BIFF: Dad . . .

WILLY: She's nothing to me, Biff. I was lonely, I was terribly lonely.

BIFF: You – you gave her Mama's stockings! [*His tears break through and he rises to go.*]

WILLY [*grabbing for* BIFF]: I gave you an order!

BIFF: Don't touch me, you – liar!

WILLY: Apologize for that!

BIFF: You fake! You phony little fake! You fake! [*Overcome, he turns quickly and weeping fully goes out with his suitcase.* WILLY *is left on the floor on his knees.*]

WILLY: I gave you an order! Biff, come back here or I'll beat you! Come back here! I'll whip you!

[STANLEY *comes quickly in from the right and stands in front of* WILLY.]

WILLY [*shouts at* STANLEY]: I gave you an order . . .

STANLEY: Hey, let's pick it up, pick it up, Mr Loman. [*He helps* WILLY *to his feet.*] Your boys left with the chippies. They said they'll see you home.

[*A second waiter watches some distance away.*]

WILLY: But we were supposed to have dinner together.

[*Music is heard,* WILLY'*s theme.*]

STANLEY: Can you make it?

WILLY: I'll – sure, I can make it. [*Suddenly concerned about his clothes.*] Do I – I look all right?

STANLEY: Sure, you look all right. [*He flicks a speck off* WILLY'*s lapel.*]

WILLY: Here – here's a dollar.

STANLEY: Oh, your son paid me. It's all right.

WILLY [*putting it in* STANLEY'*s hand*]: No, take it. You're a good boy.

STANLEY: Oh, no, you don't have to . . .

WILLY: Here – here's some more. I don't need it any more. [*After a slight pause*] Tell me – is there a seed store in the neighbourhood?

STANLEY: Seeds? You mean like to plant?

[*As* WILLY *turns,* STANLEY *slips the money back into his jacket pocket.*]

WILLY: Yes. Carrots, peas . . .

STANLEY: Well, there's hardware stores on Sixth Avenue, but it may be too late now.

WILLY [*anxiously*]: Oh, I'd better hurry. I've got to get some seeds. [*He starts off to the right.*] I've got to get some seeds, right away. Nothing's planted. I don't have a thing in the ground.

[WILLY *hurries out as the light goes down.* STANLEY *moves over to the right after him, watches him off. The other waiter has been staring at* WILLY.]

STANLEY [*to the waiter*]: Well, whatta you looking at?

[*The waiter picks up the chairs and moves off right.* STANLEY *takes the table and follows him. The light fades on this area. There is a long pause, the sound of the flute coming over. The light gradually rises on the kitchen, which is empty.* HAPPY *appears at the door of the house, followed by* BIFF. HAPPY *is carrying a large bunch of long-stemmed roses. He enters the kitchen, looks around for* LINDA. *Not seeing her, he turns to* BIFF, *who is just outside the house door, and makes a gesture with his hands, indicating 'Not here, I guess'. He looks into the living-room and freezes. Inside,* LINDA, *unseen, is seated,* WILLY's *coat on her lap. She rises ominously and quietly and moves toward* HAPPY, *who backs up into the kitchen, afraid.*]

HAPPY: Hey, what're you doing up? [LINDA *says nothing but moves toward him implacably.*] Where's Pop? [*He keeps backing to the right, and now* LINDA *is in full view in the doorway to the living-room.*] Is he sleeping?

LINDA: Where were you?

HAPPY [*trying to laugh it off*]: We met two girls, Mom, very fine types.

Here, we brought you some flowers. [*Offering them to her*] Put them in your room, Ma.

[*She knocks them to the floor at* BIFF's *feet. He has now come inside and closed the door behind him. She stares at* BIFF, *silent.*]

HAPPY: Now what'd you do that for? Mom, I want you to have some flowers –

LINDA [*cutting* HAPPY *off, violently to* BIFF]: Don't you care whether he lives or dies?

HAPPY [*going to the stairs*]: Come upstairs, Biff.

BIFF [*with a flare of disgust, to* HAPPY]: Go away from me! [*To* LINDA] What do you mean, lives or dies? Nobody's dying around here, pal.

LINDA: Get out of my sight! Get out of here!

BIFF: I wanna see the boss.

LINDA: You're not going near him!

BIFF: Where is he? [*He moves into the living-room and* LINDA *follows.*]

LINDA [*shouting after* BIFF]: You invite him to dinner. He looks forward to it all day – [BIFF *appears in his parents' bedroom, looks around, and exits*] – and then you desert him there. There's no stranger you'd do that to!

HAPPY: Why? He had a swell time with us. Listen, when I – [LINDA *comes back into the kitchen*] – desert him I hope I don't outlive the day!

LINDA: Get out of here!

HAPPY: Now look, Mom . . .

LINDA: Did you have to go to women tonight? You and your lousy rotten whores!

[BIFF *re-enters the kitchen.*]

HAPPY: Mom, all we did was follow Biff around trying to cheer him up! [*To* BIFF] Boy, what a night you gave me!

LINDA: Get out of here, both of you, and don't come back! I don't want you tormenting him any more. Go on now, get your things together! [*To* BIFF] You can sleep in his apartment. [*She starts to pick up the flowers and stops herself.*] Pick up this stuff, I'm not your maid any more. Pick it up, you bum, you!

[HAPPY *turns his back to her in refusal.* BIFF *slowly moves over and gets down on his knees, picking up the flowers.*]

LINDA: You're a pair of animals! Not one, not another living soul would have had the cruelty to walk out on that man in a restaurant!

BIFF [*not looking at her*]: Is that what he said?

LINDA: He didn't have to say anything. He was so humiliated he nearly limped when he came in.

HAPPY: But, Mom, he had a great time with us —

BIFF [*cutting him off violently*]: Shut up!

[*Without another word,* HAPPY *goes upstairs.*]

LINDA: You! You didn't even go in to see if he was all right!

BIFF [*still on the floor in front of* LINDA, *the flowers in his hand; with self-loathing*]: No. Didn't. Didn't do a damned thing. How do you like that, heh? Left him babbling in a toilet.

LINDA: You louse. You . . .

BIFF: Now you hit it on the nose! [*He gets up, throws the flowers in the wastebasket.*] The scum of the earth, and you're looking at him!

LINDA: Get out of here!

BIFF: I gotta talk to the boss, Mom. Where is he?

LINDA: You're not going near him. Get out of this house!

BIFF [*with absolute assurance, determination*]: No. We're gonna have an abrupt conversation, him and me.

LINDA: You're not talking to him!

[*Hammering is heard from outside the house, off right.* BIFF *turns toward the noise.*]

LINDA [*suddenly pleading*]: Will you please leave him alone?

BIFF: What's he doing out there?

LINDA: He's planting the garden!

BIFF [*quietly*]: Now? Oh, my God!

186

[BIFF *moves outside,* LINDA *following. The light dies down on them and comes up on the centre of the apron as* WILLY *walks into it. He is carrying a flashlight, a hoe, and a handful of seed packets. He raps the top of the hoe sharply to fix it firmly, and then moves to the left, measuring off the distance with his foot. He holds the flashlight to look at the seed packets, reading off the instructions. He is in the blue of night.*]

WILLY: Carrots . . . quarter-inch apart. Rows . . . one-foot rows. [*He measures it off.*] One foot. [*He puts down a package and measures off.*] Beets. [*He puts down another package and measures again.*] Lettuce. [*He reads the package, puts it down.*] One foot – [*He breaks off as* BEN *appears at the right and moves slowly down to him.*] What a proposition, ts, ts. Terrific, terrific. 'Cause she's suffered, Ben, the woman has suffered. You understand me? A man can't go out the way he came in, Ben, a man has got to add up to something. You can't, you can't – [BEN *moves toward him as though to interrupt.*] You gotta consider, now. Don't answer so quick. Remember, it's a guaranteed twenty-thousand-dollar proposition. Now look, Ben, I want you to go through the ins and outs of this thing with me. I've got nobody to talk to, Ben, and the woman has suffered, you hear me?

BEN [*standing still, considering*]: What's the proposition?

WILLY: It's twenty thousand dollars on the barrelhead. Guaranteed, gilt-edged, you understand?

BEN: You don't want to make a fool of yourself. They might not honour the policy.

WILLY: How can they dare refuse? Didn't I work like a coolie to meet every premium on the nose? And now they don't pay off! Impossible!

BEN: It's called a cowardly thing, William.

WILLY: Why? Does it take more guts to stand here the rest of my life ringing up a zero?

BEN [*yielding*]: That's a point, William. [*He moves, thinking, turns.*] And twenty thousand – that *is* something one can feel with the hand, it is there.

WILLY [*now assured, with rising power*]: Oh, Ben, that's the whole beauty of it! I see it like a diamond, shining in the dark, hard and rough, that I can pick up and touch in my hand. Not like – like an appointment! This would not be another damned-fool appointment, Ben, and it changes all the aspects. Because he thinks I'm nothing, see, and so he spites me. But the funeral – [*Straightening up*] Ben, that funeral will be massive! They'll come from Maine, Massachusetts, Vermont, New Hampshire! All the old-timers with the strange licence plates – that boy will be thunderstruck, Ben, because he never realized – I am known! Rhode Island, New York, New Jersey – I am known, Ben, and he'll see it with his eyes once and for all. He'll see what I am, Ben! He's in for a shock, that boy!

BEN [*coming down to the edge of the garden*]: He'll call you a coward.

WILLY [*suddenly fearful*]: No, that would be terrible.

BEN: Yes. And a damned fool.

WILLY: No, no, he mustn't, I won't have that! [*He is broken and desperate.*]

BEN: He'll hate you, William.

[*The gay music of the boys is heard.*]

WILLY: Oh, Ben, how do we get back to all the great times? Used to be so full of light, and comradeship, the sleigh-riding in winter, and the ruddiness on his cheeks. And always some kind of good news coming up, always something nice coming up ahead. And never even let me carry the valises in the house, and simonizing, simonizing that little red car! Why, why can't I give him something and not have him hate me?

BEN: Let me think about it. [*He glances at his watch.*] I still have a little time. Remarkable proposition, but you've got to be sure you're not making a fool of yourself.

[BEN *drifts off upstage and goes out of sight.* BIFF *comes down from the left.*]

WILLY [*suddenly conscious of* BIFF *turns and looks up at him, then begins picking up the packages of seeds in confusion*]: Where the hell is that seed? [*Indignantly*] You can't see nothing out here! They boxed in the whole goddam neighbourhood!

BIFF: There are people all around here. Don't you realize that?

WILLY: I'm busy. Don't bother me.

BIFF [*taking the hoe from* WILLY]: I'm saying good-bye to you, Pop. [WILLY *looks at him, silent, unable to move.*] I'm not coming back any more.

WILLY: You're not going to see Oliver tomorrow?

BIFF: I've got no appointment, Dad.

WILLY: He put his arm around you, and you've got no appointment?

BIFF: Pop, get this now, will you? Every time I've left it's been a fight that sent me out of here. Today I realized something about myself and I tried to explain it to you and I – I think I'm just not smart enough to make any sense out of it for you. To hell with whose fault it is or anything like that. [*He takes* WILLY's *arm.*] Let's just wrap it up, heh? Come on in, we'll tell Mom. [*He gently tries to pull* WILLY *to left.*]

WILLY [*frozen, immobile, with guilt in his voice*]: No, I don't want to see her.

BIFF: Come on! [*He pulls again, and* WILLY *tries to pull away.*]

WILLY [*highly nervous*]: No, no, I don't want to see her.

BIFF [*tries to look into* WILLY's *face, as if to find the answer there*]: Why don't you want to see her?

WILLY [*more harshly now*]: Don't bother me, will you?

BIFF: What do you mean, you don't want to see her? You don't want them calling you yellow, do you? This isn't your fault; it's me, I'm a bum. Now come inside! [WILLY *strains to get away.*] Did you hear what I said to you?

[WILLY *pulls away and quickly goes by himself into the house.* BIFF *follows.*]

LINDA [*to* WILLY]: Did you plant, dear?

BIFF [*at the door, to* LINDA]: All right, we had it out. I'm going and I'm not writing any more.

LINDA [*going to* WILLY *in the kitchen*]: I think that's the best way, dear. 'Cause there's no use drawing it out, you'll just never get along.

[WILLY *doesn't respond.*]

BIFF: People ask where I am and what I'm doing, you don't know, and you don't care. That way it'll be off your mind and you can start brightening up again. All right? That clears it, doesn't it? [WILLY *is silent, and* BIFF *goes to him.*] You gonna wish me luck, scout! [*He extends his hand*] What do you say?

LINDA: Shake his hand, Willy.

WILLY [*turning to her, seething with hurt*]: There's no necessity to mention the pen at all, y'know.

BIFF [*gently*]: I've got no appointment, Dad.

WILLY [*erupting fiercely*]: He put his arm around . . . ?

BIFF: Dad, you're never going to see what I am, so what's the use of arguing? If I strike oil I'll send you a cheque. Meantime forget I'm alive.

WILLY [*to* LINDA]: Spite, see?

BIFF: Shake hands, Dad.

WILLY: Not my hand.

BIFF: I was hoping not to go this way.

WILLY: Well, this is the way you're going. Good-bye.

[BIFF *looks at him a moment, then turns sharply and goes to the stairs.*]

WILLY [*stops him with*]: May you rot in hell if you leave this house!

BIFF [*turning*]: Exactly what is it that you want from me?

WILLY: I want you to know, on the train, in the mountains, in the valleys, wherever you go, that you cut down your life for spite!

BIFF: No, no.

WILLY: Spite, spite, is the word of your undoing! And when you're down and out, remember what did it. When you're rotting somewhere beside the railroad tracks, remember, and don't you dare blame it on me!

BIFF: I'm not blaming it on you!

WILLY: I won't take the rap for this, you hear?

[HAPPY *comes down the stairs and stands on the bottom step, watching.*]

BIFF: That's just what I'm telling you!

WILLY [*sinking into a chair at the table, with full accusation*]: You're trying to put a knife in me – don't think I don't know what you're doing!

BIFF: All right, phony! Then let's lay it on the line. [*He whips the rubber tube out of his pocket and puts it on the table.*]

HAPPY: You crazy –

LINDA: Biff! [*She moves to grab the hose, but* BIFF *holds it down with his hand.*]

BIFF: Leave it there! Don't move it!

WILLY [*not looking at it*]: What is that?

BIFF: You know goddam well what that is.

WILLY [*caged, wanting to escape*]: I never saw that.

BIFF: You saw it. The mice didn't bring it into the cellar! What is this supposed to do, make a hero out of you? This supposed to make me sorry for you?

WILLY: Never heard of it.

BIFF: There'll be no pity for you, you hear it? No pity!

WILLY [*to* LINDA]: You hear the spite!

BIFF: No, you're going to hear the truth – what you are and what I am!

LINDA: Stop it!

WILLY: Spite!

HAPPY [*coming down toward* BIFF]: You cut it now!

BIFF [*to* HAPPY]: The man don't know who we are! The man is gonna know! [*To* WILLY] We never told the truth for ten minutes in this house!

HAPPY: We always told the truth!

BIFF [*turning on him*]: You big blow, are you the assistant buyer? You're one of the two assistants to the assistant, aren't you?

HAPPY: Well, I'm practically –

BIFF: You're practically full of it! We all are! And I'm through with it. [*To* WILLY] Now hear this, Willy, this is me.

WILLY: I know you!

BIFF: You know why I had no address for three months? I stole a suit in Kansas City and I was in jail. [*To* LINDA, *who is sobbing*] Stop crying. I'm through with it.

[LINDA *turns away from them, her hands covering her face.*]

WILLY: I suppose that's my fault!

BIFF: I stole myself out of every good job since high school!

WILLY: And whose fault is that?

BIFF: And I never got anywhere because you blew me so full of hot air I could never stand taking orders from anybody! That's whose fault it is!

WILLY: I hear that!

LINDA: Don't, Biff!

BIFF: It's goddam time you heard that! I had to be boss big shot in two weeks, and I'm through with it!

WILLY: Then hang yourself! For spite, hang yourself!

BIFF: No! Nobody's hanging himself, Willy! I ran down eleven flights with a pen in my hand today. And suddenly I stopped, you hear me? And in the middle of that office building, do you hear this? I stopped in the middle of that building and I saw – the sky. I saw the things that I love in this world. The work and the food and time to sit and smoke. And I looked at the pen and said to myself, what the hell am I grabbing this for? Why am I trying to become what I don't want to be? What am I doing in an office, making a contemptuous, begging fool of myself, when all I want is out there, waiting for me the minute I say I know who I am! Why can't I say that, Willy? [*He tries to make* WILLY *face him, but* WILLY *pulls away and moves to the left.*]

WILLY [*with hatred, threateningly*]: The door of your life is wide open!

BIFF: Pop! I'm a dime a dozen, and so are you!

WILLY [*turning on him now in an uncontrolled outburst*]: I am not a dime a dozen! I am Willy Loman, and you are Biff Loman!

[BIFF *starts for* WILLY, *but is blocked by* HAPPY. *In his fury,* BIFF *seems on the verge of attacking his father.*]

BIFF: I am not a leader of men, Willy, and neither are you. You were never anything but a hard-working drummer who landed in the ash-can like all the rest of them! I'm one dollar an hour, Willy! I tried seven states and couldn't raise it. A buck an hour! Do you gather my meaning? I'm not bringing home any prizes any more, and you're going to stop waiting for me to bring them home!

WILLY [*directly to* BIFF]: You vengeful, spiteful mut!

[BIFF *breaks from* HAPPY. WILLY, *in fright, starts up the stairs.* BIFF *grabs him.*]

BIFF [*at the peak of his fury*]: Pop, I'm nothing! I'm nothing, Pop. Can't you understand that? There's no spite in it any more. I'm just what I am, that's all.

[BIFF*'s fury has spent itself, and he breaks down, sobbing, holding on to* WILLY, *who dumbly fumbles for* BIFF*'s face.*]

WILLY [*astonished*]: What're you doing? What're you doing? [*To* LINDA] Why is he crying?

BIFF [*crying, broken*]: Will you let me go, for Christ's sake? Will you take that phony dream and burn it before something happens? [*Struggling to contain himself, he pulls away and moves to the stairs.*] I'll go in the morning. Put him – put him to bed. [*Exhausted,* BIFF *moves up the stairs to his room.*]

WILLY [*after a long pause, astonished, elevated*]: Isn't that – isn't that remarkable? Biff – he likes me!

LINDA: He loves you, Willy!

HAPPY [*deeply moved*]: Always did, Pop.

WILLY: Oh, Biff! [*Staring wildly*] He cried! Cried to me. [*He is chocking with his love, and now cries out his promise*] That boy – that boy is going to be magnificent!

[BEN *appears in the light just outside the kitchen.*]

BEN: Yes, outstanding, with twenty thousand behind him.

LINDA [*sensing the racing of his mind, fearfully, carefully*]: Now come to bed, Willy. It's all settled now.

WILLY [*finding it difficult not to rush out of the house*]: Yes, we'll sleep. Come on. Go to sleep, Hap.

BEN: And it does take a great kind of a man to crack the jungle.

[*In accents of dread,* BEN's *idyllic music starts up.*]

HAPPY [*his arm around* LINDA]: I'm getting married, Pop, don't forget it. I'm changing everything. I'm gonna run that department before the year is up. You'll see, Mom. [*He kisses her.*]

BEN: The jungle is dark but full of diamonds, Willy.

[WILLY *turns, moves, listening to* BEN.]

LINDA: Be good. You're both good boys, just act that way, that's all.

HAPPY: 'Night, Pop. [*He goes upstairs.*]

LINDA [*to* WILLY]: Come, dear.

BEN [*with greater force*]: One must go in to fetch a diamond out.

WILLY [*to* LINDA, *as he moves slowly along the edge of the kitchen, toward the door*]: I just want to get settled down, Linda. Let me sit alone for a little.

LINDA [*almost uttering her fear*]: I want you upstairs.

WILLY [*taking her in his arms*]: In a few minutes, Linda. I couldn't sleep right now. Go on, you look awful tired. [*He kisses her.*]

BEN: Not like an appointment at all. A diamond is rough and hard to the touch.

WILLY: Go on now. I'll be right up.

LINDA: I think this is the only way, Willy.

WILLY: Sure, it's the best thing.

BEN: Best thing!

WILLY: The only way. Everything is gonna be – go on, kid, get to bed. You look so tired.

LINDA: Come right up.

WILLY: Two minutes.

[LINDA *goes into the living-room, then reappears in her bedroom.* WILLY *moves just outside the kitchen door.*]

WILLY: Loves me. [*Wonderingly*] Always loved me. Isn't that a remarkable thing? Ben, he'll worship me for it!

BEN [*with promise*]: It's dark there, but full of diamonds.

WILLY: Can you imagine that magnificence with twenty thousand dollars in his pocket?

LINDA [*calling from her room*]: Willy! Come up!

WILLY [*calling into the kitchen*]: Yes! Yes. Coming! It's very smart, you realize that, don't you, sweetheart? Even Ben sees it. I gotta go, baby. 'Bye! 'Bye! [*Going over to* BEN, *almost dancing*] Imagine? When the mail comes he'll be ahead of Bernard again!

BEN: A perfect proposition all around.

WILLY: Did you see how he cried to me? Oh, if I could kiss him, Ben!

BEN: Time, William, time!

WILLY: Oh, Ben, I always knew one way or another we were gonna make it, Biff and I!

BEN [*looking at his watch*]: The boat. We'll be late. [*He moves slowly off into the darkness.*]

WILLY [*elegiacally, turning to the house*]: Now when you kick off, boy, I want a seventy-yard boot, and get right down the field under the ball, and when you hit, hit low and hit hard, because it's important, boy. [*He swings around and faces the audience.*] There's all kinds of important people in the stands, and the first thing you know . . . [*Suddenly realizing he is alone*] Ben! Ben, where do I . . . ? [*He makes a sudden movement of search.*] Ben, how do I . . . ?

LINDA [*calling*]: Willy, you coming up?

WILLY [*uttering a gasp of fear, whirling about as if to quiet her*]: Sh! [*He turns around as if to find his way; sounds, faces, voices, seem to be swarming in upon him and he flicks at them, crying*] Sh! Sh! [*Suddenly music, faint and high, stops him. It rises in intensity, almost to an unbearable scream. He goes up and down on his toes, and rushes off around the house.*] Shhh!

LINDA: Willy?

[*There is no answer.* LINDA *waits.* BIFF *gets up off his bed. He is still in his clothes.* HAPPY *sits up.* BIFF *stands listening.*]

LINDA [*with real fear*]: Willy, answer me! Willy!

[*There is the sound of a car starting and moving away at full speed.*]

LINDA: No!
BIFF [*rushing down the stairs*]: Pop!

[*As the car speeds off, the music crashes down in a frenzy of sound, which becomes the soft pulsation of a single 'cello string.* BIFF *slowly returns to his bedroom. He and* HAPPY *gravely don their jackets.* LINDA *slowly walks out of her room. The music has developed into a dead march. The leaves of day are appearing over everything.* CHARLEY *and* BERNARD, *sombrely dressed, appear and knock on the kitchen door.* BIFF *and* HAPPY *slowly descend the stairs to the kitchen as* CHARLEY *and* BERNARD *enter. All stop a moment when* LINDA, *in clothes of mourning, bearing a little bunch of roses, comes through the draped doorway into the kitchen. She goes to* CHARLEY *and takes his arm. Now all move toward the audience, through the wall-line of the kitchen. At the limit of the apron,* LINDA *lays down the flowers, kneels, and sits back on her heels. All stare down at the grave.*]

Requiem

CHARLEY: It's getting dark, Linda.

[LINDA *doesn't react. She stares at the grave.*]

BIFF: How about it, Mom? Better get some rest, heh? They'll be closing the gate soon.

[LINDA *makes no move. Pause.*]

HAPPY [*deeply angered*]: He had no right to do that. There was no necessity for it. We would've helped him.

CHARLEY [*grunting*]: Hmmm.

BIFF: Come along, Mom.

LINDA: Why didn't anybody come?

CHARLEY: It was a very nice funeral.

LINDA: But where are all the people he knew? Maybe they blame him.

CHARLEY: Naa. It's a rough world, Linda. They wouldn't blame him.

LINDA: I can't understand it. At this time especially. First time in thirty-five years we were just about free and clear. He only needed a little salary. He was even finished with the dentist.

CHARLEY: No man only needs a little salary.

LINDA: I can't understand it.

BIFF: There were a lot of nice days. When he'd come home from a trip; or on Sundays, making the stoop; finishing the cellar; putting on the new porch; when he built the extra bathroom; and put up the garage. You know something, Charley, there's more of him in that front stoop than in all the sales he ever made.

CHARLEY: Yeah. He was a happy man with a batch of cement.

LINDA: He was so wonderful with his hands.

BIFF: He had the wrong dreams. All, all, wrong.

HAPPY [*almost ready to fight* BIFF]: Don't say that!

BIFF: He never knew who he was.

CHARLEY [*stopping* HAPPY'*s movement and reply. To* BIFF]: Nobody dast blame this man. You don't understand; Willy was a salesman. And for a salesman, there is no rock bottom to the life. He don't put a bolt to a nut, he don't tell you the law or give you medicine. He's a man way out there in the blue, riding on a smile and a shoeshine. And when they start not smiling back – that's an earthquake. And then you get yourself a couple of spots on your hat, and you're finished. Nobody dast blame this man. A salesman is got to dream, boy. It comes with the territory.

BIFF: Charley, the man didn't know who he was.

HAPPY [*infuriated*]: Don't say that!

BIFF: Why don't you come with me, Happy?

HAPPY: I'm not licked that easily. I'm staying right in this city, and I'm gonna beat this racket! [*He looks at* BIFF, *his chin set*] The Loman Brothers!

BIFF: I know who I am, kid.

HAPPY: All right, boy. I'm gonna show you and everybody else that Willy Loman did not die in vain. He had a good dream. It's the only dream you can have – to come out number-one man. He fought it out here, and this is where I'm gonna win it for him.

BIFF [*with a hopeless glance at* HAPPY, *bends toward his mother*]: Let's go, Mom.

LINDA: I'll be with you in a minute. Go on, Charley. [*He hesitates.*] I want to, just for a minute. I never had a chance to say good-bye.

[CHARLEY *moves away, followed by* HAPPY. BIFF *remains a slight distance up and left of* LINDA. *She sits there, summoning herself. The flute begins, not far away, playing behind her speech.*]

LINDA: Forgive me, dear. I can't cry. I don't know what it is, but I can't cry. I don't understand it. Why did you ever do that? Help me, Willy, I can't cry. It seems to me that you're just on another trip. I keep expecting you. Willy, dear, I can't cry. Why did you do it? I search and search and I search, and I can't understand it, Willy. I made the last payment on the house today. Today, dear.

And there'll be nobody home. [*A sob rises in her throat.*] We're free and clear. [*Sobbing more fully, released*] We're free. [BIFF *comes slowly toward her.*] We're free . . . We're free . . .

[BIFF *lifts her to her feet and moves out up right with her in his arms.* LINDA *sobs quietly.* BERNARD *and* CHARLEY *come together and follow them, followed by* HAPPY. *Only the music of the flute is left on the darkening stage as over the house the hard towers of the apartment buildings rise into sharp focus.*]

CURTAIN

1. Director Elia Kazan and Arthur Miller sitting on the Broadway set of *Death of a Salesman* at the Morosco Theatre, 1949. Photograph by W. Eugene Smith.

2. (*top*) The original production design sketch by Jo Mielziner: the innovative skeletal framework allowed separate times and places to be shown simultaneously.

3. (*bottom*) Lee J. Cobb (*left*) with the original cast, in the play's first production at the Locust Street Theatre in Philadelphia, 1949. Photographs 3 and 4 by Eileen Darby.

4. Lee J. Cobb (*seated*) with Arthur Kennedy (*left*) and Cameron Mitchell.

5. Playbill featuring the iconic figure of Fredric March as Willy Loman from the original Broadway production, 1949.

death of a Salesman

The PLAYBILL for the Morosco Theatre

6. (*above*) Paul Muni (*seated*) and cast in the play's first London production, at the Phoenix Theatre, 1949.

7. (*right*) Fredric March (*right*) and Kevin McCarthy in the first film adaptation, 1951. Photograph by John Swope.

8. (*left*) Miller on stage reading *Death of a Salesman* in the 1960s. Photograph by Daniel Bernstein.

9. (*below*) Dustin Hoffman with Lee J. Cobb, who had originated the role of Willy Loman, at an audio recording of the play in 1965. Hoffman (here as Bernard) would take on the role nearly twenty years later. Photograph by Inge Morath.

10. (*top*) George C. Scott directed and starred in *Death of a Salesman* in New York, 1975, alongside a cast that included Harvey Keitel. Photographs 10-13 by Inge Morath.

11. (*bottom*) Miller directing Ying Ruocheng and the cast of the Beijing production, 1983.

12. (*left*) Dustin Hoffman with Miller, 1983.

13. (*below*) John Malkovich, Kate Reid, Dustin Hoffman and Stephen Lang in rehearsals for a critically acclaimed Broadway revival in 1984.

14. (*top*) Philip Seymour Hoffman in Mike Nichols' 2012 Broadway revival. Nichols had first seen the play as a teenager some sixty years earlier. Photograph by Brigitte Lacombe.

15. (*bottom*) Antony Sher and Harriet Walter in the Royal Shakespeare Company's 2015 production directed by Gregory Doran. Photograph by Robbie Jack.

The Crucible

FOR MARY

First presented in England at The Bristol Old Vic on 9 November 1954 with the following cast:

BETTY PARRIS	*Annette Crosbie*
REVEREND SAMUEL PARRIS	*John Cairney*
TITUBA	*Barbara Assoon*
ABIGAIL WILLIAMS	*Pat Sandys*
SUSANNA WALLCOT	*Patricia Healey*
MRS ANN PUTNAM	*Phyllida Law*
THOMAS PUTNAM	*Ronald Hines*
MERCY LEWIS	*Gillian Lewis*
MARY WARREN	*Perlita Neilson*
JOHN PROCTOR	*Edgar Wreford*
REBECCA NURSE	*Mary Savidge*
GILES COREY	*Paul Lee*
REVEREND JOHN HALE	*Michael Allinson*
MRS ELIZABETH PROCTOR	*Rosemary Harris*
FRANCIS NURSE	*Antony Tuckey*
EZEKIEL CHEEVER	*Bruce Sharman*
JOHN WILLARD	*Edward Hardwicke*
JUDGE HATHORNE	*Peter Wylde*
DEPUTY-GOVERNOR DANFORTH	*John Kidd*
SARAH GOOD	*Phyllida Law*

Produced by WARREN JENKINS
Settings designed by PATRICK ROBERTSON

CHARACTERS

REVEREND PARRIS

BETTY PARRIS

TITUBA

ABIGAIL WILLIAMS

SUSANNA WALCOTT

ANN PUTNAM

THOMAS PUTNAM

MERCY LEWIS

MARY WARREN

JOHN PROCTOR

REBECCA NURSE

GILES COREY

REVEREND JOHN HALE

ELIZABETH PROCTOR

FRANCIS NURSE

EZEKIEL CHEEVER

MARSHAL HERRICK

JUDGE HATHORNE

DEPUTY-GOVERNOR

DANFORTH

SARAH GOOD

HOPKINS

A Note on the Historical Accuracy of this Play

This play is not history in the sense in which the word is used by the academic historian. Dramatic purposes have sometimes required many characters to be fused into one; the number of girls involved in the 'crying-out' has been reduced; Abigail's age has been raised; while there were several judges of almost equal authority, I have symbolized them all in Hathorne and Danforth. However, I believe that the reader will discover here the essential nature of one of the strangest and most awful chapters in human history. The fate of each character is exactly that of his historical model, and there is no one in the drama who did not play a similar – and in some cases exactly the same – role in history.

As for the characters of the persons, little is known about most of them excepting what may be surmised from a few letters, the trial record, certain broadsides written at the time, and references to their conduct in sources of varying reliability. They may therefore be taken as creations of my own, drawn to the best of my ability in conformity with their known behaviour, except as indicated in the commentary I have written for this text.

Act One

A small upper bedroom in the home of REVEREND SAMUEL PARRIS, *Salem, Massachusetts, in the spring of the year 1692.*

There is a narrow window at the left. Through its leaded panes the morning sunlight streams. A candle still burns near the bed, which is at the right. A chest, a chair, and a small table are the other furnishings. At the back a door opens on the landing of the stairway to the ground floor. The room gives off an air of clean spareness. The roof rafters are exposed, and the wood colours are raw and unmellowed.

As the curtain rises, REVEREND PARRIS *is discovered kneeling beside the bed, evidently in prayer. His daughter,* BETTY PARRIS, *aged ten, is lying on the bed, inert.*

At the time of these events Parris was in his middle forties. In history he cut a villainous path, and there is very little good to be said for him. He believed he was being persecuted wherever he went, despite his best efforts to win people and God to his side. In meeting, he felt insulted if someone rose to shut the door without first asking his permission. He was a widower with no interest in children, or talent with them. He regarded them as young adults, and until this strange crisis he, like the rest of Salem, never conceived that the children were anything but thankful for being permitted to walk straight, eyes slightly lowered, arms at the sides, and mouths shut until bidden to speak.

His house stood in the 'town' – but we today would hardly call it a village. The meeting house was near by, and from this point outward – toward the bay or inland – there were a few small-windowed, dark houses snuggling against the raw Massachusetts winter. Salem had been established hardly forty years before. To the European world the whole province was a barbaric frontier inhabited by a sect of fanatics who, nevertheless, were shipping out products of slowly increasing quantity and value.

No one can really know what their lives were like. They had no novelists – and would not have permitted anyone to read a novel if one were handy. Their creed forbade anything resembling a theatre or 'vain enjoyment'. They did not celebrate Christmas, and a holiday from work meant only that they must concentrate even more upon prayer.

Which is not to say that nothing broke into this strict and sombre way of life. When a new farmhouse was built, friends assembled to 'raise the roof', and there would be special foods cooked and probably some potent cider passed around. There was a good supply of ne'er-do-wells in Salem, who dallied at the shovelboard in Bridget Bishop's tavern. Probably more than the creed, hard work kept the morals of the place from spoiling, for the people were forced to fight the land like heroes for every grain of corn, and no man had very much time for fooling around.

That there were some jokers, however, is indicated by the practice of appointing a two-man patrol whose duty was to 'walk forth in the time of God's worship to take notice of such as either lye about the meeting house, without attending to the word and ordinances, or that lye at home or in the fields without giving good account thereof, and to take the names of such persons, and to present them to the magistrates, whereby they may be accordingly proceeded against'. This predilection for minding other people's business was time-honoured among the people of Salem, and it undoubtedly created many of the suspicions which were to feed the coming madness. It was also, in my opinion, one of the things that a John Proctor would rebel against, for the time of the armed camp had almost passed, and since the country was reasonably – although not wholly – safe, the old disciplines were beginning to rankle. But, as in all such matters, the issue was not clear-cut, for danger was still a possibility, and in unity still lay the best promise of safety.

The edge of the wilderness was close by. The American continent stretched endlessly west, and it was full of mystery for them. It stood, dark and threatening, over their shoulders night and day, for out of it Indian tribes marauded from time to time, and Reverend Parris had parishioners who had lost relatives to these heathen.

The parochial snobbery of these people was partly responsible for their failure to convert the Indians. Probably they also preferred to take land from heathens rather than from fellow Christians. At any rate, very few Indians were converted, and the Salem folk believed that the virgin forest was the Devil's last preserve, his home base and the citadel of his final stand. To the best of their knowledge the American forest was the last place on earth that was not paying homage to God.

For these reasons, among others, they carried about an air of innate resistance, even of persecution. Their fathers had, of course, been persecuted in England. So now they and their church found it necessary to deny any other sect its freedom, lest their New Jerusalem be defiled and corrupted by wrong ways and deceitful ideas.

They believed, in short, that they held in their steady hands the candle that would light the world. We have inherited this belief, and it has helped and hurt us. It helped them with the discipline it gave them. They were a dedicated folk, by and large, and they had to be to survive the life they had chosen or been born into in this country.

The proof of their belief's value to them may be taken from the opposite character of the first Jamestown settlement, farther south, in Virginia. The Englishmen who landed there were motivated mainly by a hunt for profit. They had thought to pick off the wealth of the new country and then return rich to England. They were a band of individualists, and a much more ingratiating group than the Massachusetts men. But Virginia destroyed them. Massachusetts tried to kill off the Puritans, but they combined; they set up a communal society which, in the beginning, was little more than an armed camp with an autocratic and very devoted leadership. It was, however, an autocracy by consent, for they were united from top to bottom by a commonly held ideology whose perpetuation was the reason and justification for all their sufferings. So their self-denial, their purposefulness, their suspicion of all vain pursuits, their hard-handed justice, were altogether perfect instruments for the conquest of this space so antagonistic to man.

But the people of Salem in 1692 were not quite the dedicated folk that arrived on the *Mayflower*. A vast differentiation had taken place, and in their own time a revolution had unseated the royal government and substituted a junta which was at this moment in power. The times, to their eyes, must have been out of joint, and to the common folk must have seemed as insoluble and complicated as do ours today. It is not hard to see how easily many could have been led to believe that the time of confusion had been brought upon them by deep and darkling forces. No hint of such speculation appears on the court record, but social disorder in any age breeds such mystical suspicions, and when, as in Salem, wonders are brought forth from below the social surface, it is too much to expect people to hold back very long from laying on the victims with all the force of their frustrations.

The Salem tragedy, which is about to begin in these pages, developed from a paradox. It is a paradox in whose grip we still live, and there is no prospect yet that we will discover its resolution. Simply, it was this: for good purposes, even high purposes, the people of Salem developed a theocracy, a combine of state and religious power whose function was to keep the community together, and to prevent any kind of disunity that might open it to destruction by material or ideological enemies. It was forged for a necessary purpose and accomplished that purpose. But all organization is and must be grounded on the idea of exclusion and prohibition, just as two objects cannot occupy the same space. Evidently the time came in New England when the repressions of order were heavier than seemed warranted by the dangers against which the order was organized. The witch-hunt was a perverse manifestation of the panic which set in among all classes when the balance began to turn toward greater individual freedom.

When one rises above the individual villainy displayed, one can only pity them all, just as we shall be pitied some day. It is still impossible for man to organize his social life without repressions, and the balance has yet to be struck between order and freedom.

The witch-hunt was not, however, a mere repression. It was also, and as importantly, a long overdue opportunity for everyone so inclined to express publicly his guilt and sins, under the cover of accusations against the victims. It suddenly became possible – and patriotic and holy – for a man to say that Martha Corey had come into his bedroom at night, and that, while his wife was sleeping at his side, Martha laid herself down on his chest and 'nearly suffocated him'. Of course it was her spirit only, but his satisfaction at confessing himself was no lighter than if it had been Martha herself. One could not ordinarily speak such things in public.

Long-held hatreds of neighbours could now be openly expressed, and vengeance taken, despite the Bible's charitable injunctions. Land-lust which had been expressed before by constant bickering over boundaries and deeds, could now be elevated to the arena of morality; one could cry witch against one's neighbour and feel perfectly justified in the bargain. Old scores could be settled on a plane of heavenly combat between Lucifer and the Lord; suspicions and the envy of the miserable toward the happy could and did burst out in the general revenge.

REVEREND PARRIS *is praying now, and, though we cannot hear his words, a sense of his confusion hangs about him. He mumbles, then seems about to weep; then he weeps, then prays again; but his daughter does not stir on the bed.*

The door opens, and his Negro slave enters. TITUBA *is in her forties.* PARRIS *brought her with him from Barbados, where he spent some years as a merchant before entering the ministry. She enters as one does who can no longer bear to be barred from the sight of her beloved, but she is also very frightened because her slave sense has warned her that, as always, trouble in this house eventually lands on her back.*

TITUBA [*already taking a step backward*]: My Betty be hearty soon?
PARRIS: Out of here!
TITUBA [*backing to the door*]: My Betty not goin' die . . .

PARRIS [*scrambling to his feet in a fury*]: Out of my sight! [*She is gone.*] Out of my – [*He is overcome with sobs. He clamps his teeth against them and closes the door and leans against it, exhausted.*] Oh, my God! God help me! [*Quaking with fear, mumbling to himself through his sobs, he goes to the bed and gently takes* BETTY's *hand.*] Betty. Child. Dear child. Will you wake, will you open up your eyes! Betty, little one . . .

[*He is bending to kneel again when his niece,* ABIGAIL WILLIAMS, *seventeen, enters – a strikingly beautiful girl, an orphan, with an endless capacity for dissembling. Now she is all worry and apprehension and propriety.*]

ABIGAIL: Uncle? [*He looks to her.*] Susanna Walcott's here from Doctor Griggs.

PARRIS: Oh? Let her come, let her come.

ABIGAIL [*leaning out the door to call to* SUSANNA, *who is down the hall a few steps*]: Come in, Susanna.

[SUSANNA WALCOTT, *a little younger than* ABIGAIL, *a nervous, hurried girl, enters.*]

PARRIS [*eagerly*]: What does the doctor say, child?

SUSANNA [*craning around* PARRIS *to get a look at* BETTY]: He bid me come and tell you, reverend sir, that he cannot discover no medicine for it in his books.

PARRIS: Then he must search on.

SUSANNA: Aye, sir, he have been searchin' his books since he left you, sir. But he bid me tell you, that you might look to unnatural things for the cause of it.

PARRIS [*his eyes going wide*]: No – no. There be no unnatural cause here. Tell him I have sent for Reverend Hale of Beverly, and Mr Hale will surely confirm that. Let him look to medicine and put out all thought of unnatural causes here. There be none.

SUSANNA: Aye, sir. He bid me tell you. [*She turns to go.*]

ABIGAIL: Speak nothin' of it in the village, Susanna.

PARRIS: Go directly home and speak nothing of unnatural causes.

SUSANNA: Aye, sir. I pray for her. [*She goes out.*]

ABIGAIL: Uncle, the rumour of witchcraft is all about; I think you'd best go down and deny it yourself. The parlour's packed with people, sir. I'll sit with her.

PARRIS [*pressed, turns on her*]: And what shall I say to them? That my daughter and my niece I discovered dancing like heathen in the forest?

ABIGAIL: Uncle, we did dance; let you tell them I confessed it – and I'll be whipped if I must be. But they're speakin' of witchcraft. Betty's not witched.

PARRIS: Abigail, I cannot go before the congregation when I know you have not opened with me. What did you do with her in the forest?

ABIGAIL: We did dance, uncle, and when you leaped out of the bush so suddenly, Betty was frightened and then she fainted. And there's the whole of it.

PARRIS: Child. Sit you down.

ABIGAIL [*quavering, as she sits*]: I would never hurt Betty. I love her dearly.

PARRIS: Now look you, child, your punishment will come in its time. But if you trafficked with spirits in the forest I must know it now, for surely my enemies will, and they will ruin me with it.

ABIGAIL: But we never conjured spirits.

PARRIS: Then why can she not move herself since midnight? This child is desperate! [ABIGAIL *lowers her eyes.*] It must come out – my enemies will bring it out. Let me know what you done there. Abigail, do you understand that I have many enemies?

ABIGAIL: I have heard of it, uncle.

PARRIS: There is a faction that is sworn to drive me from my pulpit. Do you understand that?

ABIGAIL: I think so, sir.

PARRIS: Now then, in the midst of such disruption, my own household is discovered to be the very centre of some obscene practice. Abominations are done in the forest –

ABIGAIL: It were sport, uncle!

PARRIS [*pointing at* BETTY]: You call this sport? [*She lowers her eyes. He pleads*] Abigail, if you know something that may help the doctor, for God's sake tell it to me. [*She is silent.*] I saw Tituba waving her arms over the fire when I came on you. Why was she doing that? And I heard a screeching and gibberish coming from her mouth. She were swaying like a dumb beast over that fire!

ABIGAIL: She always sings her Barbados songs, and we dance.

PARRIS: I cannot blink what I saw, Abigail, for my enemies will not blink it. I saw a dress lying on the grass.

ABIGAIL [*innocently*]: A dress?

PARRIS [*it is very hard to say*]: Aye, a dress. And I thought I saw – someone naked running through the trees!

ABIGAIL [*in terror*]: No one was naked! You mistake yourself, uncle!

PARRIS [*with anger*]: I saw it! [*He moves from her. Then, resolved*] Now tell me true, Abigail. And I pray you feel the weight of truth upon you, for now my ministry's at stake, my ministry and perhaps your cousin's life. Whatever abomination you have done, give me all of it now, for I dare not be taken unaware when I go before them down there.

ABIGAIL: There is nothin' more. I swear it, uncle.

PARRIS [*studies her, then nods, half convinced*]: Abigail, I have fought here three long years to bend these stiff-necked people to me, and now, just now when some good respect is rising for me in the parish, you compromise my very character. I have given you a home, child, I have put clothes upon your back – now give me upright answer. Your name in the town – it is entirely white, is it not?

ABIGAIL [*with an edge of resentment*]: Why, I am sure it is, sir. There be no blush about my name.

PARRIS [*to the point*]: Abigail, is there any other cause than you have told me, for your being discharged from Goody Proctor's service? I have heard it said, and I tell you as I heard it, that she comes so rarely to the church this year for she will not sit so close to some-thing soiled. What signified that remark?

ABIGAIL: She hates me, uncle, she must, for I would not be her slave. It's a bitter woman, a lying, cold, snivelling woman, and I will not work for such a woman!

PARRIS: She may be. And yet it has troubled me that you are now seven month out of their house, and in all this time no other family has ever called for your service.

ABIGAIL: They want slaves, not such as I. Let them send to Barbados for that. I will not black my face for any of them! [*With ill-concealed resentment at him*] Do you begrudge my bed, uncle?

PARRIS: No – no.

ABIGAIL [*in a temper*]: My name is good in the village! I will not have it said my name is soiled! Goody Proctor is a gossiping liar!

[*Enter* MRS ANN PUTNAM. *She is a twisted soul of forty-five, a death-ridden woman, haunted by dreams.*]

PARRIS [*as soon as the door begins to open*]: No – no, I cannot have any-one. [*He sees her, and a certain deference springs into him, although his worry remains.*] Why, Goody Putnam, come in.

MRS PUTNAM [*full of breath, shiny-eyed*]: It is a marvel. It is surely a stroke of hell upon you.

PARRIS: No, Goody Putnam, it is –

MRS PUTNAM [*glancing at* BETTY]: How high did she fly, how high?

PARRIS: No, no, she never flew –

MRS PUTNAM [*very pleased with it*]: Why, it's sure she did. Mr Collins saw her goin' over Ingersoll's barn, and come down light as bird, he says!

PARRIS: Now, look you, Goody Putnam, she never – [*Enter* THOMAS PUTNAM, *a well-to-do, hard-handed landowner, near fifty.*] Oh, good morning, Mr Putnam.

PUTNAM: It is a providence the thing is out now! It is a providence. [*He goes directly to the bed.*]

PARRIS: What's out, sir, what's – ?

[MRS PUTNAM *goes to the bed.*]

PUTNAM [*looking down at* BETTY]: Why, *her* eyes is closed! Look you, Ann.

MRS PUTNAM: Why, that's strange. [*To* PARRIS] Ours is open.

PARRIS [*shocked*]: Your Ruth is sick?

MRS PUTNAM [*with vicious certainty*]: I'd not call it sick; the Devil's touch is heavier than sick. It's death, y'know, it's death drivin' into them, forked and hoofed.

PARRIS: Oh, pray not! Why, how does Ruth ail?

MRS PUTNAM: She ails as she must – she never waked this morning, but her eyes open and she walks, and hears naught, sees naught, and cannot eat. Her soul is taken, surely.

[PARRIS *is struck.*]

PUTNAM [*as though for further details*]: They say you've sent for Reverend Hale of Beverly?

PARRIS [*with dwindling conviction now*]: A precaution only. He has much experience in all demonic arts, and I –

MRS PUTNAM: He has indeed; and found a witch in Beverly last year, and let you remember that.

PARRIS: Now, Goody Ann, they only thought that were a witch, and I am certain there be no element of witchcraft here.

PUTNAM: No witchcraft! Now look you, Mr Parris –

PARRIS: Thomas, Thomas, I pray you, leap not to witchcraft. I know that you – you least of all, Thomas, would ever wish so disastrous a charge laid upon me. We cannot leap to witchcraft. They will howl me out of Salem for such corruption in my house.

A word about Thomas Putnam. He was a man with many grievances, at least one of which appears justified. Some time before, his wife's brother-in-law, James Bayley, had been turned down as minister of Salem. Bayley had all the qualifications, and a two-thirds vote into the bargain, but a faction stopped his acceptance, for reasons that are not clear.

Thomas Putnam was the eldest son of the richest man in the village. He had fought the Indians at Narragansett, and was deeply interested in parish affairs. He undoubtedly felt it poor payment that the village should so blatantly disregard his candidate for one of its more important offices, especially since he regarded himself as the intellectual superior of most of the people around him.

His vindictive nature was demonstrated long before the witchcraft began. Another former Salem minister, George Burroughs, had had to borrow money to pay for his wife's funeral, and, since the parish was remiss in his salary, he was soon bankrupt. Thomas and his brother John had Burroughs jailed for debts the man did not owe. The incident is important only in that Burroughs succeeded in becoming minister where Bayley, Thomas Putnam's brother-in-law, had been rejected; the motif of resentment is clear here. Thomas Putnam felt that his own name and the honour of his family had been smirched by the village, and he meant to right matters however he could.

Another reason to believe him a deeply embittered man was his attempt to break his father's will, which left a disproportionate amount to a stepbrother. As with every other public cause in which he tried to force his way, he failed in this.

So it is not surprising to find that so many accusations against people are in the handwriting of Thomas Putnam, or that his name is so often found as a witness corroborating the supernatural testimony, or that his daughter led the crying-out at the most opportune junctures of the trials, especially when – But we'll speak of that when we come to it.

PUTNAM [*at the moment he is intent upon getting* PARRIS, *for whom he has only contempt, to move toward the abyss*]: Mr Parris, I have taken your part in all contention here, and I would continue; but I cannot if you hold back in this. There are hurtful, vengeful spirits layin' hands on these children.

PARRIS: But, Thomas, you cannot –

PUTNAM: Ann! Tell Mr Parris what you have done.

MRS PUTNAM: Reverend Parris, I have laid seven babies unbaptized in the earth. Believe me, sir, you never saw more hearty babies born. And yet, each would wither in my arms the very night of their birth. I have spoke nothin', but my heart has clamoured intimations. And now, this year, my Ruth, my only – I see her turning strange. A secret child she has become this year, and shrivels like a sucking mouth were pullin' on her life too. And so I thought to send her to your Tituba –

PARRIS: To Tituba! What may Tituba – ?

MRS PUTNAM: Tituba knows how to speak to the dead, Mr Parris.

PARRIS: Goody Ann, it is a formidable sin to conjure up the dead!

MRS PUTNAM: I take it on my soul, but who else may surely tell us what person murdered my babies?

PARRIS [*horrified*]: Woman!

MRS PUTNAM: They were murdered, Mr Parris! And mark this proof! Mark it! Last night my Ruth were ever so close to their little spirits; I know it, sir. For how else is she struck dumb now except some power of darkness would stop her mouth? It is a marvellous sign, Mr Parris!

PUTNAM: Don't you understand it, sir? There is a murdering witch among us, bound to keep herself in the dark. [PARRIS *turns to* BETTY, *a frantic terror rising in him.*] Let your enemies make of it what they will, you cannot blink it more.

PARRIS [*to* ABIGAIL]: Then you were conjuring spirits last night.

ABIGAIL [*whispering*]: Not I, sir – Tituba and Ruth.

PARRIS [*turns now, with new fear, and goes to* BETTY, *looks down at her, and then, gazing off*]: Oh, Abigail, what proper payment for my charity! Now I am undone.

PUTNAM: You are not undone! Let you take hold here. Wait for no one to charge you – declare it yourself. You have discovered witchcraft –

PARRIS: In my house? In my house, Thomas? They will topple me with this! They will make of it a –

[*Enter* MERCY LEWIS, *the Putnams' servant, a fat, sly, merciless girl of eighteen.*]

MERCY: Your pardons. I only thought to see how Betty is.

PUTNAM: Why aren't you home? Who's with Ruth?

MERCY: Her grandma come. She's improved a little, I think – she give a powerful sneeze before.

MRS PUTNAM: Ah, there's a sign of life!

MERCY: I'd fear no more, Goody Putnam. It were a grand sneeze; another like it will shake her wits together, I'm sure. [*She goes to the bed to look.*]

PARRIS: Will you leave me now, Thomas? I would pray a while alone.

ABIGAIL: Uncle, you've prayed since midnight. Why do you not go down and –

PARRIS: No – no. [*To* PUTNAM] I have no answer for that crowd. I'll wait till Mr Hale arrives. [*To get* MRS PUTNAM *to leave*] If you will, Goody Ann . . .

PUTNAM: Now look you, sir. Let you strike out against the Devil, and the village will bless you for it! Come down, speak to them – pray with them. They're thirsting for your word, Mister! Surely you'll pray with them.

PARRIS [*swayed*]: I'll lead them in a psalm, but let you say nothing of witchcraft yet. I will not discuss it. The cause is yet unknown. I have had enough contention since I came; I want no more.

MRS PUTNAM: Mercy, you go home to Ruth, d'y'hear?

MERCY: Aye, mum.

[MRS PUTNAM *goes out.*]

PARRIS [*to* ABIGAIL]: If she starts for the window, cry for me at once.

ABIGAIL: I will, uncle.

PARRIS [*to* PUTNAM]: There is a terrible power in her arms today. [*He goes out with* PUTNAM.]

ABIGAIL [*with hushed trepidation*]: How is Ruth sick?

MERCY: It's weirdish, I know not – she seems to walk like a dead one since last night.

ABIGAIL [*turns at once and goes to* BETTY, *and now, with fear in her voice*]: Betty? [BETTY *doesn't move. She shakes her.*] Now stop this! Betty! Sit up now!

[BETTY *doesn't stir.* MERCY *comes over.*]

MERCY: Have you tried beatin' her? I gave Ruth a good one and it waked her for a minute. Here, let me have her.

ABIGAIL [*holding* MERCY *back*]: No, he'll be comin' up. Listen, now; if they be questioning us, tell them we danced – I told him as much already.

MERCY: Aye. And what more?

ABIGAIL: He knows Tituba conjured Ruth's sisters to come out of the grave.

MERCY: And what more?

ABIGAIL: He saw you naked.

MERCY [*clapping her hands together with a frightened laugh*]: Oh, Jesus!

[*Enter* MARY WARREN, *breathless. She is seventeen, a subservient, naïve, lonely girl.*]

MARY WARREN: What'll we do? The village is out! I just come from the farm; the whole country's talkin' witchcraft! They'll be callin' us witches, Abby!

MERCY [*pointing and looking at* MARY WARREN]: She means to tell, I know it.

MARY WARREN: Abby, we've got to tell. Witchery's a hangin' error, a hangin' like they done in Boston two year ago! We must tell the truth, Abby! You'll only be whipped for *dancin'*, and the other things!

ABIGAIL: Oh, *we'll* be whipped!

MARY WARREN: I never done none of it, Abby. I only looked!

MERCY [*moving menacingly toward* MARY]: Oh, you're a great one for lookin', aren't you, Mary Warren? What a grand peeping courage you have!

[BETTY, *on the bed, whimpers.* ABIGAIL *turns to her at once.*]

ABIGAIL: Betty? [*She goes to* BETTY.] Now, Betty, dear, wake up now. It's Abigail. [*She sits* BETTY *up and furiously shakes her.*] I'll beat you, Betty! [BETTY *whimpers.*] My, you seem improving. I talked to your papa and I told him everything. So there's nothing to –

BETTY [*darts off the bed, frightened of* ABIGAIL, *and flattens herself against the wall*]: I want my mama!

ABIGAIL [*with alarm, as she cautiously approaches* BETTY]: What ails you, Betty? Your mama's dead and buried.

BETTY: I'll fly to Mama. Let me fly! [*She raises her arms as though to fly, and streaks for the window, gets one leg out.*]

ABIGAIL [*pulling her away from the window*]: I told him everything; he knows now, he knows everything we –

BETTY: You drank blood, Abby! You didn't tell him that!

ABIGAIL: Betty, you never say that again! You will never –

BETTY: You did, you did! You drank a charm to kill John Proctor's wife! You drank a charm to kill Goody Proctor!

ABIGAIL [*smashes her across the face*]: Shut it! Now shut it!

BETTY [*collapsing on the bed*]: Mama, Mama! [*She dissolves into sobs.*]

ABIGAIL: Now look you. All of you. We danced. And Tituba conjured Ruth Putnam's dead sisters. And that is all. And mark this. Let either of you breathe a word, or the edge of a word, about the other things, and I will come to you in the black of some terrible night and I will bring a pointy reckoning that will shudder you. And you know I can do it; I saw Indians smash my dear parents' heads on the pillow next to mine, and I have seen some reddish work done at night, and I can make you wish you had never seen the sun go down! [*She goes to* BETTY *and roughly sits her up.*] Now, you – sit up and stop this!

[*But* BETTY *collapses in her hands and lies inert on the bed.*]

MARY WARREN [*with hysterical fright*]: What's got her? [ABIGAIL *stares in fright at* BETTY.] Abby, she's going to die! It's a sin to conjure, and we –

ABIGAIL [*starting for* MARY]: I say shut it, Mary Warren!

[*Enter* JOHN PROCTOR. *On seeing him,* MARY WARREN *leaps in fright.*]

Proctor was a farmer in his middle thirties. He need not have been a partisan of any faction in the town, but there is evidence to suggest that he had a sharp and biting way with hypocrites. He was the kind of man – powerful of body, even-tempered, and not easily led – who cannot refuse support to partisans without drawing their deepest resentment. In Proctor's presence a fool felt his foolishness instantly – and a Proctor is always marked for calumny therefore.

But as we shall see, the steady manner he displays does not spring from an untroubled soul. He is a sinner, a sinner not only against the moral fashion of the time, but against his own vision of decent conduct. These people had no ritual for the washing away of sins. It is another trait we inherited from them, and it has helped to discipline us as well as to breed hypocrisy among us. Proctor, respected and even feared in Salem, has come to regard himself as a kind of fraud. But no hint of this has yet appeared on the surface, and as he enters from the crowded parlour below it is a man in his prime we see, with a quiet confidence and an unexpressed, hidden force. Mary Warren, his servant, can barely speak for embarrassment and fear.

MARY WARREN: Oh! I'm just going home, Mr Proctor.
PROCTOR: Be you foolish, Mary Warren? Be you deaf? I forbid you leave the house, did I not? Why shall I pay you? I am looking for you more often than my cows!
MARY WARREN: I only come to see the great doings in the world.
PROCTOR: I'll show you a great doin' on your arse one of these days. Now get you home; my wife is waitin' with your work!

[*Trying to retain a shred of dignity, she goes slowly out.*]

MERCY LEWIS [*both afraid of him and strangely titillated*]: I'd best be off. I have my Ruth to watch. Good morning, Mr Proctor.

[MERCY *sidles out. Since* PROCTOR'*s entrance,* ABIGAIL *has stood as though on tiptoe, absorbing his presence, wide-eyed. He glances at her, then goes to* BETTY *on the bed.*]

ABIGAIL: Gah! I'd almost forgot how strong you are, John Proctor!

PROCTOR [*looking at* ABIGAIL *now, the faintest suggestion of a knowing smile on his face*]: What's this mischief here?

ABIGAIL [*with a nervous laugh*]: Oh, she's only gone silly somehow.

PROCTOR: The road past my house is a pilgrimage to Salem all morning. The town's mumbling witchcraft.

ABIGAIL: Oh, posh! [*Winningly she comes a little closer, with a confidential, wicked air.*] We were dancin' in the woods last night, and my uncle leaped in on us. She took fright, is all.

PROCTOR [*his smile widening*]: Ah, you're wicked yet, aren't y'! [*A trill of expectant laughter escapes her, and she dares come closer, feverishly looking into his eyes.*] You'll be clapped in the stocks before you're twenty.

[*He takes a step to go, and she springs into his path.*]

ABIGAIL: Give me a word, John. A soft word. [*Her concentrated desire destroys his smile.*]

PROCTOR: No, no, Abby. That's done with.

ABIGAIL [*tauntingly*]: You come five mile to see a silly girl fly? I know you better.

PROCTOR [*setting her firmly out of his path*]: I come to see what mischief your uncle's brewin' now. [*With final emphasis*] Put it out of mind, Abby.

ABIGAIL [*grasping his hand before he can release her*]: John – I am waitin' for you every night.

PROCTOR: Abby, I never give you hope to wait for me.

ABIGAIL [*now beginning to anger – she can't believe it*]: I have something better than hope, I think!

PROCTOR: Abby, you'll put it out of mind. I'll not be comin' for you more.

ABIGAIL: You're surely sportin' with me.

PROCTOR: You know me better.

ABIGAIL: I know how you clutched my back behind your house and sweated like a stallion whenever I come near! Or did I dream that? It's she put me out, you cannot pretend it were you. I saw your face when she put me out, and you loved me then and you do now!

PROCTOR: Abby, that's a wild thing to say –

ABIGAIL: A wild thing may say wild things. But not so wild, I think. I have seen you since she put me out; I have seen you nights.

PROCTOR: I have hardly stepped off my farm this seven-month.

ABIGAIL: I have a sense for heat, John, and yours has drawn me to my window, and I have seen you looking up, burning in your loneliness. Do you tell me you've never looked up at my window?

PROCTOR: I may have looked up.

ABIGAIL [*now softening*]. And you must. You are no wintry man. I know you, John. I *know* you. [*She is weeping.*] I cannot sleep for dreamin'; I cannot dream but I wake and walk about the house as though I'd find you comin' through some door. [*She clutches him desperately.*]

PROCTOR [*gently pressing her from him, with great sympathy but firmly*]: Child –

ABIGAIL [*with a flash of anger*]: How do you call me child!

PROCTOR: Abby, I may think of you softly from time to time. But I will cut off my hand before I'll ever reach for you again. Wipe it out of mind. We never touched, Abby.

ABIGAIL: Aye, but we did.

PROCTOR: Aye, but we did not.

ABIGAIL [*with a bitter anger*]: Oh, I marvel how such a strong man may let such a sickly wife be –

PROCTOR [*angered – at himself as well*]: You'll speak nothin' of Elizabeth!

ABIGAIL: She is blackening my name in the village! She is telling lies about me! She is a cold, snivelling woman, and you bend to her! Let her turn you like a –

PROCTOR [*shaking her*]: Do you look for whippin'?

[*A psalm is heard being sung below.*]

ABIGAIL [*in tears*]: I look for John Proctor that took me from my sleep and put knowledge in my heart! I never knew what pretence Salem was, I never knew the lying lessons I was taught by all these Christian women and their covenanted men! And now you bid me tear the light out of my eyes? I will not, I cannot! You loved me, John Proctor, and whatever sin it is, you love me yet! [*He turns abruptly to go out. She rushes to him.*] John, pity me, pity me!

[*The words 'going up to Jesus' are heard in the psalm, and* BETTY *claps her ears suddenly and whines loudly.*]

ABIGAIL: Betty? [*She hurries to* BETTY, *who is now sitting up and screaming.* PROCTOR *goes to* BETTY *as* ABIGAIL *is trying to pull her hands down, calling 'Betty!'*]

PROCTOR [*growing unnerved*]: What's she doing? Girl, what ails you? Stop that wailing!

[*The singing has stopped in the midst of this, and now* PARRIS *rushes in.*]

PARRIS: What happened? What are you doing to her? Betty! [*He rushes to the bed, crying, 'Betty, Betty!'* MRS PUTNAM *enters, feverish with curiosity, and with her* THOMAS PUTNAM *and* MERCY LEWIS. PARRIS, *at the bed, keeps lightly slapping* BETTY'S *face, while she moans and tries to get up.*]

ABIGAIL: She heard you singin' and suddenly she's up and screamin'.

MRS PUTNAM: The psalm! The psalm! She cannot bear to hear the Lord's name!

PARRIS: No, God forbid. Mercy, run to the doctor! Tell him what's happened here! [MERCY LEWIS *rushes out.*]

MRS PUTNAM: Mark it for a sign, mark it!

[REBECCA NURSE, *seventy-two, enters. She is white-haired, leaning upon her walking-stick.*]

PUTNAM [*pointing at the whimpering* BETTY]: That is a notorious sign of witchcraft afoot, Goody Nurse, a prodigious sign!

MRS PUTNAM: My mother told me that! When they cannot bear to hear the name of –

PARRIS [*trembling*]: Rebecca, Rebecca, go to her, we're lost. She suddenly cannot bear to hear the Lord's –

[GILES COREY, *eighty-three, enters. He is knotted with muscle, canny, inquisitive, and still powerful.*]

REBECCA: There is hard sickness here, Giles Corey, so please to keep the quiet.

GILES: I've not said a word. No one here can testify I've said a word. Is she going to fly again? I hear she flies.

PUTNAM: Man, be quiet now!

[*Everything is quiet.* REBECCA *walks across the room to the bed. Gentleness exudes from her.* BETTY *is quietly whimpering, eyes shut.* REBECCA *simply stands over the child, who gradually quiets.*]

And while they are so absorbed, we may put a word in for Rebecca. Rebecca was the wife of Francis Nurse, who, from all accounts, was one of those men for whom both sides of the argument had to have respect. He was called upon to arbitrate disputes as though he were an unofficial judge, and Rebecca also enjoyed the high opinion most people had for him. By the time of the delusion, they had three hundred acres, and their children were settled in separate homesteads within the same estate. However, Francis had originally rented the land, and one theory has it that, as he gradually paid for it and raised his social status, there were those who resented his rise.

Another suggestion to explain the systematic campaign against Rebecca, and inferentially against Francis, is the land war he fought with his neighbours, one of whom was a Putnam. This squabble grew to the proportions of a battle in the woods between partisans of both sides, and it is said to have lasted for two days. As for Rebecca herself, the general opinion of her character was so high that to explain how anyone dared cry her out for a witch – and more, how adults could bring themselves to lay hands on her – we must look to the fields and boundaries of that time.

As we have seen, Thomas Putnam's man for the Salem ministry was Bayley. The Nurse clan had been in the faction that prevented Bayley's taking office. In addition, certain families allied to the Nurses by blood or friendship, and whose farms were contiguous with the Nurse farm or close to it, combined to break away from the Salem town authority and set up Topsfield, a new and independent entity whose existence was resented by old Salemites.

That the guiding hand behind the outcry was Putnam's is indicated by the fact that, as soon as it began, this Topsfield-Nurse faction absented themselves from church in protest and disbelief. It was Edward and Jonathan Putnam who signed the first complaint against Rebecca; and Thomas Putnam's little daughter was the one who fell into a fit at the hearing and pointed to Rebecca as her attacker. To top it all, Mrs Putnam – who is now staring at the bewitched child on the bed – soon accused Rebecca's spirit of 'tempting her to iniquity', a charge that had more truth in it than Mrs Putnam could know.

MRS PUTNAM [*astonished*]: What have you done?

[REBECCA, *in thought, now leaves the bedside and sits.*]

PARRIS [*wondrous and relieved*]: What do you make of it, Rebecca?
PUTNAM [*eagerly*]: Goody Nurse, will you go to my Ruth and see if you can wake her?
REBECCA [*sitting*]: I think she'll wake in time. Pray calm yourselves. I have eleven children, and I am twenty-six times a grandma, and I have seen them all through their silly seasons, and when it come on them they will run the Devil bowlegged keeping up with their mischief. I think she'll wake when she tires of it. A child's spirit is like a child, you can never catch it by running after it; you must stand still, and, for love, it will soon itself come back.

PROCTOR: Aye, that's the truth of it, Rebecca.

MRS PUTNAM: This is no silly season, Rebecca. My Ruth is bewildered, Rebecca; she cannot eat.

REBECCA: Perhaps she is not hungered yet. [*To* PARRIS] I hope you are not decided to go in search of loose spirits, Mr Parris. I've heard promise of that outside.

PARRIS: A wide opinion's running in the parish that the Devil may be among us, and I would satisfy them that they are wrong.

PROCTOR: Then let you come out and call them wrong. Did you consult the wardens before you called this minister to look for devils?

PARRIS: He is not coming to look for devils!

PROCTOR: Then what's he coming for?

PUTNAM: There be children dyin' in the village, Mister!

PROCTOR: I seen none dyin'. This society will not be a bag to swing around your head, Mr Putnam. [*To* PARRIS] Did you call a meeting before you – ?

PUTNAM: I am sick of meetings; cannot the man turn his head without he have a meeting?

PROCTOR: He may turn his head, but not to Hell!

REBECCA: Pray, John, be calm. [*Pause. He defers to her.*] Mr Parris, I think you'd best send Reverend Hale back as soon as he come. This will set us all to arguin' again in the society, and we thought to have peace this year. I think we ought rely on the doctor now, and good prayer.

MRS PUTNAM: Rebecca, the doctor's baffled!

REBECCA: If so he is, then let us go to God for the cause of it. There is prodigious danger in the seeking of loose spirits. I fear it, I fear it. Let us rather blame ourselves and –

PUTNAM: How may we blame ourselves? I am one of nine sons; the Putnam seed have peopled this province. And yet I have but one child left of eight – and now she shrivels!

REBECCA: I cannot fathom that.

MRS PUTNAM [*with a growing edge of sarcasm*]: But I must! You think it God's work you should never lose a child, nor grandchild either, and I bury all but one? There are wheels within wheels in this village, and fires within fires!

PUTNAM [*to* PARRIS]: When Reverend Hale comes, you will proceed to look for signs of witchcraft here.

PROCTOR [*to* PUTNAM]: You cannot command Mr Parris. We vote by name in this society, not by acreage.

PUTNAM: I never heard you worried so on this society, Mr Proctor. I do not think I saw you at Sabbath meeting since snow flew.

PROCTOR: I have trouble enough without I come five mile to hear him preach only hellfire and bloody damnation. Take it to heart, Mr Parris. There are many others who stay away from church these days because you hardly ever mention God any more.

PARRIS [*now aroused*]: Why, that's a drastic charge!

REBECCA: It's somewhat true; there are many that quail to bring their children –

PARRIS: I do not preach for children, Rebecca. It is not the children who are unmindful of their obligations toward this ministry.

REBECCA: Are there really those unmindful?

PARRIS: I should say the better half of Salem village –

PUTNAM: And more than that!

PARRIS: Where is my wood? My contract provides I be supplied with all my firewood. I am waiting since November for a stick, and even in November I had to show my frostbitten hands like some London beggar!

GILES: You are allowed six pound a year to buy your wood, Mr Parris.

PARRIS: I regard that six pound as part of my salary. I am paid little enough without I spend six pound on firewood.

PROCTOR: Sixty, plus six for firewood –

PARRIS: The salary is sixty-six pound, Mr Proctor! I am not some preaching farmer with a book under my arm; I am a graduate of Harvard College.

GILES: Aye, and well instructed in arithmetic!

PARRIS: Mr Corey, you will look far for a man of my kind at sixty pound a year! I am not used to this poverty; I left a thrifty business in the Barbados to serve the Lord. I do not fathom it, why am I persecuted here? I cannot offer one proposition but there be a howling riot of argument. I have often wondered if the Devil be in it somewhere; I cannot understand you people otherwise.

PROCTOR: Mr Parris, you are the first minister ever did demand the deed to this house –

PARRIS: Man! Don't minister deserve a house to live in?

PROCTOR: To live in, yes. But to ask ownership is like you shall own the meeting house itself; the last meeting I were at you spoke so long on deeds and mortgages I thought it were an auction.

PARRIS: I want a mark of confidence, is all! I am your third preacher in seven years. I do not wish to be put out like the cat whenever some majority feels the whim. You people seem not to comprehend that a minister is the Lord's man in the parish; a minister is not to be so lightly crossed and contradicted –

PUTNAM: Aye!

PARRIS: There is either obedience or the church will burn like Hell is burning!

PROCTOR: Can you speak one minute without we land in Hell again? I am sick of Hell!

PARRIS: It is not for you to say what is good for you to hear!

PROCTOR: I may speak my heart, I think!

PARRIS [*in a fury*]: What, are we Quakers? We are not Quakers here yet, Mr Proctor. And you may tell that to your followers!

PROCTOR: My followers!

PARRIS [*now he's out with it*]: There is a party in this church. I am not blind; there is a faction and a party.

PROCTOR: Against you?

PUTNAM: Against him and all authority!

PROCTOR: Why, then I must find it and join it.

[*There is shock among the others.*]

REBECCA: He does not mean that.

PUTNAM: He confessed it now!

PROCTOR: I mean it solemnly, Rebecca; I like not the smell of this 'authority'.

REBECCA: No, you cannot break charity with your minister. You are another kind, John. Clasp his hand, make your peace.

PROCTOR: I have a crop to sow and lumber to drag home. [*He goes angrily to the door and turns to* COREY *with a smile.*] What say you, Giles, let's find the party. He says there's a party.

GILES: I've changed my opinion of this man, John. Mr Parris, I beg your pardon. I never thought you had so much iron in you.

PARRIS [*surprised*]: Why, thank you, Giles!

GILES: It suggests to the mind what the trouble be among us all these years. [*To all*] Think on it. Wherefore is everybody suing everybody else? Think on it now, it's a deep thing, and dark as a pit. I have been six time in court this year –

PROCTOR [*familiarly, with warmth, although he knows he is approaching the edge of* GILES' *tolerance with this*]: Is it the Devil's fault that a man cannot say you good morning without you clap him for defamation? You're old, Giles, and you're not hearin' so well as you did.

GILES [*he cannot be crossed*]: John Proctor, I have only last month collected four pound damages for you publicly sayin' I burned the roof off your house, and I –

PROCTOR [*laughing*]: I never said no such thing, but I've paid you for it, so I hope I can call you deaf without charge. Now come along, Giles, and help me drag my lumber home.

PUTNAM: A moment, Mr Proctor. What lumber is that you're draggin', if I may ask you?

PROCTOR: My lumber. From out my forest by the riverside.

PUTNAM: Why, we are surely gone wild this year. What anarchy is this? That tract is in my bounds, it's in my bounds, Mr Proctor.

PROCTOR: In your bounds! [*Indicating* REBECCA] I bought that tract from Goody Nurse's husband five months ago.

PUTNAM: He had no right to sell it. It stands clear in my grandfather's will that all the land between the river and –

PROCTOR: Your grandfather had a habit of willing land that never belonged to him, if I may say it plain.

GILES: That's God's truth; he nearly willed away my north pasture but he knew I'd break his fingers before he'd set his name to it. Let's get your lumber home, John. I feel a sudden will to work coming on.

PUTNAM: You load one oak of mine and you'll fight to drag it home!

GILES: Aye, and we'll win too, Putnam – this fool and I. Come on!

[*He turns to* PROCTOR *and starts out.*]

PUTNAM: I'll have my men on you, Corey! I'll clap a writ on you!

[*Enter* REVEREND JOHN HALE *of Beverly.*]

Mr Hale is nearing forty, a tight-skinned, eager-eyed intellectual. This is a beloved errand for him; on being called here to ascertain witchcraft he felt the pride of the specialist whose unique knowledge has at last been publicly called for. Like almost all men of learning, he spent a good deal of his time pondering the invisible world, especially since he had himself encountered a witch in his parish not long before. That woman, however, turned into a mere pest under his searching scrutiny, and the child she had allegedly been afflicting recovered her normal behaviour after Hale had given her his kindness and a few days of rest in his own house. However, that experience never raised a doubt in his mind as to the reality of the underworld or the existence of Lucifer's many-faced lieutenants. And his belief is not to his discredit. Better minds than Hale's were – and still are – convinced that there is a society of spirits beyond our ken. One cannot help noting that one of his lines has never yet raised a laugh in any audience that has seen this play; it is his assurance that 'We cannot look to superstition in this. The Devil is precise.' Evidently we are not quite certain even now whether diabolism is holy and not to be scoffed at. And it is no accident that we should be so bemused.

Like Reverend Hale and the others on this stage, we conceive the Devil as a necessary part of a respectable view of cosmology. Ours is a divided empire in which certain ideas and emotions and actions are of God, and their opposites are of Lucifer. It is as impossible for most men to conceive of a morality without sin as of an earth without 'sky'. Since 1692 a great but superficial change has wiped out God's beard and the Devil's horns, but the world is still gripped between two diametrically opposed absolutes. The concept of unity, in which positive and negative are attributes of the same force, in which good and evil are relative, ever-changing, and always joined to the same phenomenon – such a concept is still reserved to the physical sciences and to the few who have grasped the history of ideas. When it is recalled that until the Christian era the underworld was never regarded as a hostile area, that all gods were useful and essentially friendly to man despite occasional lapses; when we see the steady and methodical inculcation into humanity of the idea of man's worthlessness – until redeemed – the necessity of the Devil may become evident as a weapon, a weapon designed and used time and time again in every age to whip men into a surrender to a particular church or church-state.

Our difficulty in believing the – for want of a better word – political inspiration of the Devil is due in great part to the fact that he is called up and damned not only by our social antagonists but by our own side, whatever it may be. The Catholic Church, through its Inquisition, is famous for cultivating Lucifer as the arch-fiend, but the Church's enemies relied no less upon the Old Boy to keep the human mind enthralled. Luther was himself accused of alliance with Hell, and he in turn accused his enemies. To complicate matters further, he believed that he had had contact with the Devil and had argued theology with him. I am not surprised at this, for at my own university a professor of history – a Lutheran, by the way – used to assemble his graduate students, draw the shades, and commune in the classroom with Erasmus. He was never, to my knowledge, officially scoffed at for this, the reason being that the university officials, like most of us, are the children of a history which still sucks at the Devil's teats. At this writing, only England has held back before the temptations of contemporary diabolism.

In the countries of the Communist ideology, all resistance of any import is linked to the totally malign capitalist succubi, and in America any man who is not reactionary in his views is open to the charge of alliance with the Red hell. Political opposition, thereby, is given an inhumane overlay which then justifies the abrogation of all normally applied customs of civilized intercourse. A political policy is equated with moral right, and opposition to it with diabolical malevolence. Once such an equation is effectively made, society becomes a congerie of plots and counterplots, and the main role of government changes from that of the arbiter to that of the scourge of God.

The results of this process are no different now from what they ever were, except sometimes in the degree of cruelty inflicted, and not always even in that department. Normally the actions and deeds of a man were all that society felt comfortable in judging. The secret intent of an action was left to the ministers, priests, and rabbis to deal with. When diabolism rises, however, actions are the least important manifests of the true nature of a man. The Devil, as Reverend Hale said, is a wily one, and, until an hour before he fell, even God thought him beautiful in Heaven.

The analogy, however, seems to falter when one considers that, while there were no witches then, there are Communists and capitalists now, and in each camp there is certain proof that spies of each side are at work undermining the other. But this is a snobbish objection and not at all warranted by the facts. I have no doubt that people *were* communing with, and even worshipping, the Devil in Salem, and if the whole truth could be known in this case, as it is in others, we should discover a regular and conventionalized propitiation of the dark spirit. One certain evidence of this is the confession of Tituba, the slave of Reverend Parris, and another is the behaviour of the children who were known to have indulged in sorceries with her.

There are accounts of similar *klatsches* in Europe, where the daughters of the towns would assemble at night and, sometimes with fetishes, sometimes with a selected young man, give them-

selves to love, with some bastardly results. The Church, sharp-eyed
as it must be when gods long dead are brought to life, condemned
these orgies as witchcraft and interpreted them, rightly, as a resur-
gence of the Dionysiac forces it had crushed long before. Sex, sin,
and the Devil were early linked, and so they continued to be in
Salem, and are today. From all accounts there are no more puritan-
ical mores in the world than those enforced by the Communists in
Russia, where women's fashions, for instance, are as prudent and
all-covering as any American Baptist would desire. The divorce laws
lay a tremendous responsibility on the father for the care of his
children. Even the laxity of divorce regulations in the early years of
the revolution was undoubtedly a revulsion from the nineteenth-
century Victorian immobility of marriage and the consequent
hypocrisy that developed from it. If for no other reasons, a state so
powerful, so jealous of the uniformity of its citizens, cannot long
tolerate the atomization of the family. And yet, in American eyes at
least, there remains the conviction that the Russian attitude toward
women is lascivious. It is the Devil working again, just as he is working within the Slav who is shocked at the very idea of a woman's
disrobing herself in a burlesque show. Our opposites are always
robed in sexual sin, and it is from this unconscious conviction that
demonology gains both its attractive sensuality and its capacity to
infuriate and frighten.

Coming into Salem now, Reverend Hale conceives of himself
much as a young doctor on his first call. His painfully acquired
armoury of symptoms, catchwords, and diagnostic procedures are
now to be put to use at last. The road from Beverly is unusually
busy this morning, and he has passed a hundred rumours that make
him smile at the ignorance of the yeomanry in this most precise sci-
ence. He feels himself allied with the best minds of Europe – kings,
philosophers, scientists, and ecclesiasts of all churches. His goal is
light, goodness and its preservation, and he knows the exaltation of
the blessed whose intelligence, sharpened by minute examinations
of enormous tracts, is finally called upon to face what may be a
bloody fight with the Fiend himself.

[*He appears loaded down with half a dozen heavy books.*]

HALE: Pray you, someone take these!

PARRIS [*delighted*]: Mr Hale! Oh! it's good to see you again! [*Taking some books*] My, they're heavy!

HALE [*setting down his books*]: They must be; they are weighted with authority.

PARRIS [*a little scared*]: Well, you do come prepared!

HALE: We shall need hard study if it comes to tracking down the Old Boy. [*Noticing* REBECCA] You cannot be Rebecca Nurse?

REBECCA: I am, sir. Do you know me?

HALE: It's strange how I knew you, but I suppose you look as such a good soul should. We have all heard of your great charities in Beverly.

PARRIS: Do you know this gentleman? Mr Thomas Putnam. And his good wife Ann.

HALE: Putnam! I had not expected such distinguished company, sir.

PUTNAM [*pleased*]: It does not seem to help us today, Mr Hale. We look to you to come to our house and save our child.

HALE: Your child ails too?

MRS PUTNAM: Her soul, her soul seems flown away. She sleeps and yet she walks . . .

PUTNAM: She cannot eat.

HALE: Cannot eat! [*Thinks on it. Then, to* PROCTOR *and* GILES COREY] Do you men have afflicted children?

PARRIS: No, no, these are farmers. John Proctor –

GILES COREY: He don't believe in witches.

PROCTOR [*to* HALE]: I never spoke on witches one way or the other. Will you come, Giles?

GILES: No – no, John, I think not. I have some few queer questions of my own to ask this fellow.

PROCTOR: I've heard you to be a sensible man, Mr Hale. I hope you'll leave some of it in Salem.

[PROCTOR *goes.* HALE *stands embarrassed for an instant.*]

PARRIS [*quickly*]: Will you look at my daughter, sir? [*Leads* HALE *to the bed.*] She has tried to leap out the window; we discovered her this morning on the highroad, waving her arms as though she'd fly.

HALE [*narrowing his eyes*]: Tries to fly.

PUTNAM: She cannot bear to hear the Lord's name, Mr Hale; that's a sure sign of witchcraft afloat.

HALE [*holding up his hands*]: No, no. Now let me instruct you. We cannot look to superstition in this. The Devil is precise; the marks of his presence are definite as stone, and I must tell you all that I shall not proceed unless you are prepared to believe me if I should find no bruise of hell upon her.

PARRIS: It is agreed, sir – it is agreed – we will abide by your judgement.

HALE: Good then. [*He goes to the bed, looks down at* BETTY. *To* PARRIS] Now, sir, what were your first warning of this strangeness?

PARRIS: Why, sir – I discovered her [*indicating* ABIGAIL] – and my niece and ten or twelve of the other girls, dancing in the forest last night.

HALE [*surprised*]: You permit dancing?

PARRIS: No, no, it were secret –

MRS PUTNAM [*unable to wait*]: Mr Parris's slave has knowledge of conjurin', sir.

PARRIS [*to* MRS PUTNAM]: We cannot be sure of that, Goody Ann –

MRS PUTNAM [*frightened, very softly*]: I know it, sir. I sent my child – she should learn from Tituba who murdered her sisters.

REBECCA [*horrified*]: Goody Ann! You sent a child to conjure up the dead?

MRS PUTNAM: Let God blame me, not you, not you, Rebecca! I'll not have you judging me any more! [*To* HALE] Is it a natural work to lose seven children before they live a day?

PARRIS: Sssh!

[REBECCA, *with great pain, turns her face away. There is a pause.*]

HALE: Seven dead in childbirth.

MRS PUTNAM [*softly*]: Aye. [*Her voice breaks; she looks up at him. Silence.* HALE *is impressed.* PARRIS *looks to him. He goes to his books, opens one, turns pages, then reads. All wait, avidly.*]

PARRIS [*hushed*]: What book is that?

MRS PUTNAM: What's there, sir?

HALE [*with a tasty love of intellectual pursuit*]: Here is all the invisible world, caught, defined, and calculated. In these books the Devil stands stripped of all his brute disguises. Here are all your familiar spirits – your incubi and succubi; your witches that go by land, by air, and by sea; your wizards of the night and of the day. Have no fear now – we shall find him out if he has come among us, and I mean to crush him utterly if he has shown his face! [*He starts for the bed.*]

REBECCA: Will it hurt the child, sir?

HALE: I cannot tell. If she is truly in the Devil's grip we may have to rip and tear to get her free.

REBECCA: I think I'll go, then. I am too old for this. [*She rises.*]

PARRIS [*striving for conviction*]: Why, Rebecca, we may open up the boil of all our troubles today!

REBECCA: Let us hope for that. I go to God for you, sir.

PARRIS [*with trepidation – and resentment*]: I hope you do not mean we go to Satan here!]

[*Slight pause.*

REBECCA: I wish I knew. [*She goes out; they feel resentful of her note of moral superiority.*]

PUTNAM [*abruptly*]: Come, Mr Hale, let's get on. Sit you here.

GILES: Mr Hale, I have always wanted to ask a learned man – what signifies the readin' of strange books?

HALE: What books?

GILES: I cannot tell; she hides them.

HALE: Who does this?

GILES: Martha, my wife. I have waked at night many a time and found her in a corner, readin' of a book. Now what do you make of that?

HALE: Why, that's not necessarily –

GILES: It discomforts me! Last night – mark this – I tried and tried and could not say my prayers. And then she close her book and walks out of the house, and suddenly – mark this – I could pray again!

Old Giles must be spoken for, if only because his fate was to be so remarkable and so different from that of all the others. He was in his early eighties at this time, and was the most comical hero in the history. No man has ever been blamed for so much. If a cow was missed, the first thought was to look for her around Corey's house; a fire blazing up at night brought suspicion of arson to his door. He didn't give a hoot for public opinion, and only in his last years – after he had married Martha – did he bother much with the church. That she stopped his prayer is very probable, but he forgot to say that he'd only recently learned any prayers and it didn't take much to make him stumble over them. He was a crank and a nuisance, but withal a deeply innocent and brave man. In court, once, he was asked if it were true that he had been frightened by the strange behaviour of a hog and had then said he knew it to be the Devil in an animal's shape. 'What frighted you?' he was asked. He forgot everything but the word 'frighted', and instantly replied, 'I do not know that I ever spoke that word in my life.'

HALE: Ah! The stoppage of prayer – that is strange. I'll speak further on that with you.

GILES: I'm not sayin' she's touched the Devil, now, but I'd admire to know what books she reads and why she hides them. She'll not answer me, y'see.

HALE: Aye, we'll discuss it. [*To all*] Now mark me, if the Devil is in her you will witness some frightful wonders in this room, so please to keep your wits about you. Mr Putnam, stand close in case she flies. Now, Betty, dear, will you sit up? [PUTNAM *comes in closer, ready-handed.* HALE *sits* BETTY *up, but she hangs limp in his hands.*] Hmmm. [*He observes her carefully. The others watch breathlessly.*] Can you hear me? I am John Hale, minister of Beverly. I have come to help you, dear. Do you remember my two little girls in Beverly?

[*She does not stir in his hands.*]

PARRIS [*in fright*]: How can it be the Devil? Why would he choose my house to strike? We have all manner of licentious people in the village!

HALE: What victory would the Devil have to win a soul already bad? It is the best the Devil wants, and who is better than the minister?

GILES: That's deep, Mr Parris, deep, deep!

PARRIS [*with resolution now*]: Betty! Answer Mr Hale! Betty!

HALE: Does someone afflict you, child? It need not be a woman, mind you, or a man. Perhaps some bird invisible to others comes to you – perhaps a pig, a mouse, or any beast at all. Is there some figure bids you fly? [*The child remains limp in his hands. In silence he lays her back on the pillow. Now, holding out his hands toward her, he intones*] In nomine Domini Sabaoth sui filiique ite ad infernos. [*She does not stir. He turns to* ABIGAIL, *his eyes narrowing.*] Abigail, what sort of dancing were you doing with her in the forest?

ABIGAIL: Why – common dancing is all.

PARRIS: I think I ought to say that I – I saw a kettle in the grass where they were dancing.

ABIGAIL: That were only soup.

HALE: What sort of soup were in this kettle, Abigail?

ABIGAIL: Why, it were beans – and lentils, I think, and –

HALE: Mr Parris, you did not notice, did you, any living thing in the kettle? A mouse, perhaps, a spider, a frog – ?

PARRIS [*fearfully*]: I – do believe there were some movement – in the soup.

ABIGAIL: That jumped in, we never put it in!

HALE [*quickly*]: What jumped in?

ABIGAIL: Why, a very little frog jumped –

PARRIS: A frog, Abby!

HALE [*grasping* ABIGAIL]: Abigail, it may be your cousin is dying. Did you call the Devil last night?

ABIGAIL: I never called him! Tituba, Tituba . . .

PARRIS [*blanched*]: She called the Devil?

HALE: I should like to speak with Tituba.

PARRIS: Goody Ann, will you bring her up? [MRS PUTNAM *exits*.]

HALE: How did she call him?

ABIGAIL: I know not – she spoke Barbados.

HALE: Did you feel any strangeness when she called him? A sudden cold wind, perhaps? A trembling below the ground?

ABIGAIL: I didn't see no Devil! [*Shaking* BETTY] Betty, wake up. Betty! Betty!

HALE: You cannot evade me, Abigail. Did your cousin drink any of the brew in that kettle?

ABIGAIL: She never drank it!

HALE: Did you drink it?

ABIGAIL: No, sir!

HALE: Did Tituba ask you to drink it?

ABIGAIL: She tried, but I refused.

HALE: Why are you concealing? Have you sold yourself to Lucifer?

ABIGAIL: I never sold myself! I'm a good girl! I'm a proper girl!

[MRS PUTNAM *enters with* TITUBA, *and instantly* ABIGAIL *points at* TITUBA.]

ABIGAIL: She made me do it! She made Betty do it!

TITUBA [*shocked and angry*]: Abby!

ABIGAIL: She makes me drink blood!

PARRIS: Blood!!

MRS PUTNAM: My baby's blood?

TITUBA: No, no, chicken blood. I give she chicken blood!

HALE: Woman, have you enlisted these children for the Devil?

TITUBA: No, no, sir, I don't truck with no Devil!

HALE: Why can she not wake? Are you silencing this child?

TITUBA: I love me Betty!

HALE: You have sent your spirit out upon this child, have you not? Are you gathering souls for the Devil?

ABIGAIL: She sends her spirit on me in church; she makes me laugh at prayer!

PARRIS: She have often laughed at prayer!

ABIGAIL: She comes to me every night to go and drink blood!

TITUBA: You beg *me* to conjure! She beg *me* make charm –

ABIGAIL: Don't lie! [*To* HALE] She comes to me while I sleep; she's always making me dream corruptions!

TITUBA: Why you say that, Abby?

ABIGAIL: Sometimes I wake and find myself standing in the open doorway and not a stitch on my body! I always hear her laughing in my sleep. I hear her singing her Barbados songs and tempting me with –

TITUBA: Mister Reverend, I never –

HALE [*resolved now*]: Tituba, I want you to wake this child.

TITUBA: I have no power on this child, sir.

HALE: You most certainly do, and you will free her from it now! When did you compact with the Devil?

TITUBA: I don't compact with no Devil!

PARRIS: You will confess yourself or I will take you out and whip you to your death, Tituba!

PUTNAM: This woman must be hanged! She must be taken and hanged!

TITUBA [*terrified, falls to her knees*]: No, no, don't hang Tituba! I tell him I don't desire to work for him, sir.

PARRIS: The Devil?

HALE: Then you saw him! [TITUBA *weeps.*] Now Tituba, I know that when we bind ourselves to Hell it is very hard to break with it. We are going to help you tear yourself free –

TITUBA [*frightened by the coming process*]: Mister Reverend, I do believe somebody else be witchin' these children.

HALE: Who?

TITUBA: I don't know, sir, but the Devil got him numerous witches.

HALE: Does he! [*It is a clue.*] Tituba, look into my eyes. Come, look into me. [*She raises her eyes to his fearfully.*] You would be a good Christian woman, would you not, Tituba?

TITUBA: Aye, sir, a good Christian woman.

HALE: And you love these little children?

TITUBA: Oh, yes, sir, I don't desire to hurt little children.

HALE: And you love God, Tituba?

TITUBA: I love God with all my bein'.

HALE: Now, in God's holy name –

TITUBA: Bless Him. Bless Him. [*She is rocking on her knees, sobbing in terror.*]

HALE: And to His glory –

TITUBA: Eternal glory. Bless Him – bless God . . .

HALE: Open yourself, Tituba – open yourself and let God's holy light shine on you.

TITUBA: Oh, bless the Lord.

HALE: When the Devil comes to you does he ever come – with another person? [*She stares up into his face.*] Perhaps another person in the village? Someone you know.

PARRIS: Who came with him?

PUTNAM: Sarah Good? Did you ever see Sarah Good with him? Or Osburn?

PARRIS: Was it man or woman came with him?

TITUBA: Man or woman. Was – was woman.

PARRIS: What woman? A woman, you said. What woman?

TITUBA: It was black dark, and I –

PARRIS: You could see him, why could you not see her?

TITUBA: Well, they was always talking; they was always runnin' round and carryin' on –

PARRIS: You mean out of Salem? Salem witches?

TITUBA: I believe so, yes, sir.

[*Now* HALE *takes her hand. She is surprised.*]

HALE: Tituba. You must have no fear to tell us who they are, do you understand? We will protect you. The Devil can never overcome a minister. You know that, do you not?

TITUBA [*kisses* HALE's *hand*]: Aye, sir, oh, I do.

HALE: You have confessed yourself to witchcraft, and that speaks a wish to come to Heaven's side. And we will bless you, Tituba.

TITUBA [*deeply relieved*]: Oh, God bless you, Mr Hale!

HALE [*with rising exaltation*]: You are God's instrument put in our hands to discover the Devil's agents among us. You are selected, Tituba, you are chosen to help us cleanse our village. So speak utterly, Tituba, turn your back on him and face God – face God, Tituba, and God will protect you.

TITUBA [*joining with him*]: Oh, God, protect Tituba!

HALE [*kindly*]: Who came to you with the Devil? Two? Three? Four? How many?

[TITUBA *pants, and begins rocking back and forth again, staring ahead.*]

TITUBA: There was four. There was four.

PARRIS [*pressing in on her*]: Who? Who? Their names, their names!

TITUBA [*suddenly bursting out*]: Oh, how many times he bid me kill you, Mr Parris!

PARRIS: Kill me!

TITUBA [*in a fury*]: He say Mr Parris must be kill! Mr Parris no goodly man, Mr Parris mean man and no gentle man, and he bid me rise out of my bed and cut your throat! [*They gasp.*] But I tell him 'No! I don't hate that man. I don't want kill that man.' But he say, 'You work for me, Tituba, and I make you free! I give you pretty dress to wear, and put you way high up in the air, and you gone fly back to Barbados!' And I say, 'You lie, Devil, you lie!' And then he come one stormy night to me, and he say, 'Look! I have *white* people belong to me.' And I look – and there was Goody Good.

PARRIS: Sarah Good!

TITUBA [*rocking and weeping*]: Aye, sir, and Goody Osburn.

MRS PUTNAM: I knew it! Goody Osburn were midwife to me three

times. I begged you, Thomas, did I not? I begged him not to call
Osburn because I feared her. My babies always shrivelled in her
hands!

HALE: Take courage, you must give us all their names. How can you
bear to see this child suffering? Look at her, Tituba. [*He is indicating* BETTY *on the bed.*] Look at her God-given innocence; her soul
is so tender; we must protect her, Tituba; the Devil is out and
preying on her like a beast upon the flesh of the pure lamb. God
will bless you for your help.

[ABIGAIL *rises, staring as though inspired, and cries out.*]

ABIGAIL: I want to open myself! [*They turn to her, startled. She is
enraptured, as though in a pearly light.*] I want the light of God, I
want the sweet love of Jesus! I danced for the Devil; I saw him; I
wrote in his book; I go back to Jesus; I kiss His hand. I saw Sarah
Good with the Devil! I saw Goody Osburn with the Devil! I saw
Bridget Bishop with the Devil!
[*As she is speaking,* BETTY *is rising from the bed, a fever in her eyes, and
picks up the chant.*]

BETTY [*staring too*]: I saw George Jacobs with the Devil! I saw Goody
Howe with the Devil!

PARRIS: She speaks! [*He rushes to embrace* BETTY.] She speaks!

HALE: Glory to God! It is broken, they are free!

BETTY [*calling out hysterically and with great relief*]: I saw Martha
Bellows with the Devil!

ABIGAIL: I saw Goody Sibber with the Devil! [*It is rising to a great
glee.*]

PUTNAM: The marshal, I'll call the marshal!

[PARRIS *is shouting a prayer of thanksgiving.*]

BETTY: I saw Alice Barrow with the Devil!

[*The curtain begins to fall.*]

HALE [*as* PUTNAM *goes out*]: Let the marshal bring irons!

ABIGAIL: I saw Goody Hawkins with the Devil!
BETTY: I saw Goody Bibber with the Devil!
ABIGAIL: I saw Goody Booth with the Devil!
  [*On their ecstatic cries*]

THE CURTAIN FALLS

Act Two

The common room of PROCTOR's *house, eight days later.*

At the right is a door opening on the fields outside. A fireplace is at the left, and behind it a stairway leading upstairs. It is the low, dark, and rather long living-room of the time. As the curtain rises, the room is empty. From above, ELIZABETH *is heard softly singing to the children. Presently the door opens and* JOHN PROCTOR *enters, carrying his gun. He glances about the room as he comes toward the fireplace, then halts for an instant as he hears her singing. He continues on to the fireplace, leans the gun against the wall as he swings a pot out of the fire and smells it. Then he lifts out the ladle and tastes. He is not quite pleased. He reaches to a cupboard, takes a pinch of salt, and drops it into the pot. As he is tasting again, her footsteps are heard on the stair. He swings the pot into the fireplace and goes to a basin and washes his hands and face.* ELIZABETH *enters.*

ELIZABETH: What keeps you so late? It's almost dark.

PROCTOR: I were planting far out to the forest edge.

ELIZABETH: Oh, you're done then.

PROCTOR: Aye, the farm is seeded. The boys asleep?

ELIZABETH: They will be soon. [*And she goes to the fireplace, proceeds to ladle up stew in a dish.*]

PROCTOR: Pray now for a fair summer.

ELIZABETH: Aye.

PROCTOR: Are you well today?

ELIZABETH: I am. [*She brings the plate to the table, and, indicating the food*] It is a rabbit.

PROCTOR [*going to the table*]: Oh, is it! In Jonathan's trap?

ELIZABETH: No, she walked into the house this afternoon; I found her sittin' in the corner like she come to visit.

PROCTOR: Oh, that's a good sign walkin' in.

ELIZABETH: Pray God. It hurt my heart to strip her, poor rabbit. [*She sits and watches him taste it.*]

PROCTOR: It's well seasoned.

ELIZABETH [*blushing with pleasure*]: I took great care. She's tender?

PROCTOR: Aye. [*He eats. She watches him.*] I think we'll see green fields soon. It's warm as blood beneath the clods.

ELIZABETH: That's well.

[PROCTOR *eats, then looks up.*]

PROCTOR: If the crop is good I'll buy George Jacob's heifer. How would that please you?

ELIZABETH: Aye, it would.

PROCTOR [*with a grin*]: I mean to please you, Elizabeth.

ELIZABETH [*it is hard to say*]: I know it, John.

[*He gets up, goes to her, kisses her. She receives it. With a certain disappointment, he returns to the table.*]

PROCTOR [*as gently as he can*]: Cider?

ELIZABETH [*with a sense of reprimanding herself for having forgot*]: Aye! [*She gets up and goes and pours a glass for him. He now arches his back.*]

PROCTOR: This farm's a continent when you go foot by foot droppin' seeds in it.

ELIZABETH [*coming with the cider*]: It must be.

PROCTOR [*drinks a long draught, then, putting the glass down*]: You ought to bring some flowers in the house.

ELIZABETH: Oh, I forgot! I will tomorrow.

PROCTOR: It's winter in here yet. On Sunday let you come with me, and we'll walk the farm together; I never see such a load of flowers on the earth. [*With good feeling he goes and looks up at the sky through the open doorway.*] Lilacs have a purple smell. Lilac is the smell of nightfall, I think. Massachusetts is a beauty in the spring!

ELIZABETH: Aye, it is.

[*There is a pause. She is watching him from the table as he stands there absorbing the night. It is as though she would speak but cannot. Instead, now, she takes up his plate and glass and fork and goes with them to the basin. Her back is turned to him. He turns to her and watches her. A sense of their separation rises.*]

PROCTOR: I think you're sad again. Are you?

ELIZABETH [*she doesn't want friction, and yet she must*]: You come so late I thought you'd gone to Salem this afternoon.

PROCTOR: Why? I have no business in Salem.

ELIZABETH: You did speak of going, earlier this week.

PROCTOR [*he knows what she means*]: I thought better of it since.

ELIZABETH: Mary Warren's there today.

PROCTOR: Why'd you let her? You heard me forbid her go to Salem any more!

ELIZABETH: I couldn't stop her.

PROCTOR [*holding back a full condemnation of her*]: It is a fault, it is a fault, Elizabeth – you're the mistress here, not Mary Warren.

ELIZABETH: She frightened all my strength away.

PROCTOR: How may that mouse frighten you, Elizabeth? You –

ELIZABETH: It is a mouse no more. I forbid her go, and she raises up her chin like the daughter of a prince and says to me, 'I must go to Salem, Goody Proctor; I am an official of the court!'

PROCTOR: Court! What court?

ELIZABETH: Aye, it is a proper court they have now. They've sent four judges out of Boston, she says, weighty magistrates of the General Court, and at the head sits the Deputy Governor of the Province.

PROCTOR [*astonished*]: Why, she's mad.

ELIZABETH: I would to God she were. There be fourteen people in the jail now, she says. [PROCTOR *simply looks at her, unable to grasp it.*] And they'll be tried, and the court have power to hang them too, she says.

PROCTOR [*scoffing, but without conviction*]: Ah, they'd never hang –

ELIZABETH: The Deputy Governor promise hangin' if they'll not confess, John. The town's gone wild, I think. She speak of Abigail, and I thought she were a saint, to hear her. Abigail brings the other girls into the court, and where she walks the crowd will part like the sea for Israel. And folks are brought before them, and if they scream and howl and fall to the floor – the person's clapped in the jail for bewitchin' them.

PROCTOR [*wide-eyed*]: Oh, it is a black mischief.

ELIZABETH: I think you must go to Salem, John. [*He turns to her.*] I think so. You must tell them it is a fraud.

PROCTOR [*thinking beyond this*]: Aye, it is, it is surely.

ELIZABETH: Let you go to Ezekiel Cheever – he knows you well. And tell him what she said to you last week in her uncle's house. She said it had naught to do with witchcraft, did she not?

PROCTOR [*in thought*]: Aye, she did, she did.

[*Now, a pause.*]

ELIZABETH [*quietly, fearing to anger him by prodding*]: God forbid you keep that from the court, John. I think they must be told.

PROCTOR [*quietly, struggling with his thought*]: Aye, they must, they must. It is a wonder they do believe her.

ELIZABETH: I would go to Salem now, John – let you go tonight.

PROCTOR: I'll think on it.

ELIZABETH [*with her courage now*]: You cannot keep it, John.

PROCTOR [*angering*]: I know I cannot keep it. I say I will think on it!

ELIZABETH [*hurt, and very coldly*]: Good, then, let you think on it. [*She stands and starts to walk out of the room.*]

PROCTOR: I am only wondering how I may prove what she told me, Elizabeth. If the girl's a saint now, I think it is not easy to prove she's fraud, and the town gone so silly. She told it to me in a room alone – I have no proof for it.

ELIZABETH: You were alone with her?

PROCTOR [*stubbornly*]: For a moment alone, aye.

ELIZABETH: Why, then, it is not as you told me.

PROCTOR [*his anger rising*]: For a moment, I say. The others come in soon after.

ELIZABETH [*quietly – she has suddenly lost all faith in him*]: Do as you wish, then. [*She starts to turn.*]

PROCTOR: Woman. [*She turns to him.*] I'll not have your suspicion any more.

ELIZABETH [*a little loftily*]: I have no –

PROCTOR: I'll not have it!

ELIZABETH: Then let you not earn it.

PROCTOR [*with a violent undertone*]: You doubt me yet?

ELIZABETH [*with a smile, to keep her dignity*]: John, if it were not Abigail that you must go to hurt, would you falter now? I think not.

PROCTOR: Now look you –

ELIZABETH: I see what I see, John.

PROCTOR [*with solemn warning*]: You will not judge me more, Elizabeth. I have good reason to think before I charge fraud on Abigail, and I will think on it. Let you look to your own improvement before you go to judge your husband any more. I have forgot Abigail, and –

ELIZABETH: And I.

PROCTOR: Spare me! You forget nothin' and forgive nothin'. Learn charity, woman. I have gone tiptoe in this house all seven month since she is gone. I have not moved from there to there without I think to please you, and still an everlasting funeral marches round your heart. I cannot speak but I am doubted, every moment judged for lies, as though I come into a court when I come into this house!

ELIZABETH: John, you are not open with me. You saw her with a crowd, you said. Now you –

PROCTOR: I'll plead my honesty no more, Elizabeth.

ELIZABETH [*now she would justify herself*]: John, I am only –

PROCTOR: No more! I should have roared you down when first you told me your suspicion. But I wilted, and, like a Christian, I confessed. Confessed! Some dream I had must have mistaken you for

God that day. But you're not, you're not, and let you remember it! Let you look sometimes for the goodness in me, and judge me not.

ELIZABETH: I do not judge you. The magistrate sits in your heart that judges you. I never thought you but a good man, John – [*with a smile*] – only somewhat bewildered.

PROCTOR [*laughing bitterly*]: Oh, Elizabeth, your justice would freeze beer! [*He turns suddenly toward a sound outside. He starts for the door as* MARY WARREN *enters. As soon as he sees her, he goes directly to her and grabs her by her cloak, furious.*] How do you go to Salem when I forbid it? Do you mock me? [*Shaking her.*] I'll whip you if you dare leave this house again!

[*Strangely, she doesn't resist him, but hangs limply by his grip.*]

MARY WARREN: I am sick, I am sick, Mr Proctor. Pray, pray, hurt me not. [*Her strangeness throws him off, and her evident pallor and weakness. He frees her.*] My insides are all shuddery; I am in the proceedings all day, sir.

PROCTOR [*with draining anger – his curiosity is draining it*]: And what of these proceedings here? When will you proceed to keep this house, as you are paid nine pound a year to do – and my wife not wholly well?

[*As though to compensate,* MARY WARREN *goes to* ELIZABETH *with a small rag doll.*]

MARY WARREN: I made a gift for you today, Goody Proctor. I had to sit long hours in a chair, and passed the time with sewing.

ELIZABETH [*perplexed, looking at the doll*]: Why, thank you, it's a fair poppet.

MARY WARREN [*with a trembling, decayed voice*]: We must all love each other now, Goody Proctor.

ELIZABETH [*amazed at her strangeness*]: Aye, indeed we must.

MARY WARREN [*glancing at the room*]: I'll get up early in the morning and clean the house. I must sleep now. [*She turns and starts off.*]

PROCTOR: Mary. [*She halts.*] Is it true? There be fourteen women arrested?

MARY WARREN: No, sir. There be thirty-nine now – [*She suddenly breaks off and sobs and sits down, exhausted.*]

ELIZABETH: Why, she's weepin'! What ails you, child?

MARY WARREN: Goody Osburn – will hang!

[*There is a shocked pause, while she sobs.*]

PROCTOR: Hang! [*He calls into her face*] Hang, y'say?

MARY WARREN [*through her weeping*]: Aye.

PROCTOR: The Deputy Governor will permit it?

MARY WARREN: He sentenced her. He must. [*To ameliorate it*] But not Sarah Good. For Sarah Good confessed, y'see.

PROCTOR: Confessed! To what?

MARY WARREN: That she – [*in horror at the memory*] – she sometimes made a compact with Lucifer, and wrote her name in his black book – with her blood – and bound herself to torment Christians till God's thrown down – and we all must worship Hell forevermore.

[*Pause.*]

PROCTOR: But – surely you know what a jabberer she is. Did you tell them that?

MARY WARREN: Mr Proctor, in open court she near to choked us all to death.

PROCTOR: How, choked you?

MARY WARREN: She sent her spirit out.

ELIZABETH: Oh, Mary, Mary, surely you –

MARY WARREN [*with an indignant edge*]: She tried to kill me many times, Goody Proctor!

ELIZABETH: Why, I never heard you mention that before.

MARY WARREN: I never knew it before. I never knew anything before. When she come into the court I say to myself, I must not accuse this woman, for she sleep in ditches, and so very old and poor. But then – then she sit there, denying and denying, and I feel a misty coldness climbin' up my back, and the skin on my skull begin to creep, and I feel a clamp around my neck and I cannot breathe air; and then – [*entranced*] – I hear a voice, a screamin' voice, and it were my voice – and all at once I remembered everything she done to me!

PROCTOR: Why? What did she do to you?

MARY WARREN [*like one awakened to a marvellous secret insight*]: So many time, Mr Proctor, she come to this very door, beggin' bread and a cup of cider – and mark this: whenever I turned her away empty, she *mumbled*.

ELIZABETH: Mumbled! She may mumble if she's hungry.

MARY WARREN: But *what* does she mumble? You must remember, Goody Proctor. Last month – a Monday, I think – she walked away, and I thought my guts would burst for two days after. Do you remember it?

ELIZABETH: Why – I do, I think, but –

MARY WARREN: And so I told that to Judge Hathorne, and he asks her so. 'Goody Osburn,' says he, 'what curse do you mumble that this girl must fall sick after turning you away?' And then she replies – [*mimicking an old crone*] – 'Why, your excellence, no curse at all. I only say my commandments; I hope I may say my commandments,' says she!

ELIZABETH: And that's an upright answer.

MARY WARREN: Aye, but then Judge Hathorne say, 'Recite for us your commandments!' – [*leaning avidly toward them*] – and of all the ten she could not say a single one. She never knew no commandments, and they had her in a flat lie!

PROCTOR: And so condemned her?

MARY WARREN [*now a little strained, seeing his stubborn doubt*]: Why, they must when she condemned herself.

PROCTOR: But the proof, the proof!

MARY WARREN [*with greater impatience with him*]: I told you the proof. It's hard proof, hard as rock, the judges said.

PROCTOR [*pauses an instant, then*]: You will not go to court again, Mary Warren.

MARY WARREN: I must tell you, sir, I will be gone every day now. I am amazed you do not see what weighty work we do.

PROCTOR: What work you do! It's strange work for a Christian girl to hang old women!

MARY WARREN: But, Mr Proctor, they will not hang them if they confess. Sarah Good will only sit in jail some time – [*recalling*] – and here's wonder for you; think on this. Goody Good is pregnant!

ELIZABETH: Pregnant! Are they mad? The woman's near to sixty!

MARY WARREN: They had Doctor Griggs examine her, and she's full to the brim. And smokin' a pipe all these years, and no husband either! But she's safe, thank God, for they'll not hurt the innocent child. But be that not a marvel? You must see it, sir, it's God's work we do. So I'll be gone every day for some time. I'm – I am an official of the court, they say, and I – [*She has been edging toward offstage.*]

PROCTOR: I'll official you! [*He strides to the mantel, takes down the whip hanging there.*]

MARY WARREN [*terrified, but coming erect, striving for her authority*]: I'll not stand whipping any more!

ELIZABETH [*hurriedly, as PROCTOR approaches*]: Mary, promise now you'll stay at home –

MARY WARREN [*backing from him, but keeping her erect posture, striving, striving for her way*]: The Devil's loose in Salem, Mr Proctor; we must discover where he's hiding!

PROCTOR: I'll whip the Devil out of you! [*With whip raised he reaches out for her, and she streaks away and yells.*]

MARY WARREN [*pointing at ELIZABETH*]: I saved her life today!

[*Silence. His whip comes down.*]

ELIZABETH [*softly*]: I am accused?

MARY WARREN [*quaking*]: Somewhat mentioned. But I said I never see no sign you ever sent your spirit out to hurt no one, and seeing I do live so closely with you, they dismissed it.

ELIZABETH: Who accused me?

MARY WARREN: I am bound by law, I cannot tell it. [*To* PROCTOR] I only hope you'll not be so sarcastical no more. Four judges and the King's deputy sat to dinner with us but an hour ago. I – I would have you speak civilly to me, from this out.

PROCTOR [*in horror, muttering in disgust at her*]: Go to bed.

MARY WARREN [*with a stamp of her foot*]: I'll not be ordered to bed no more, Mr Proctor! I am eighteen and a woman, however single!

PROCTOR: Do you wish to sit up? Then sit up.

MARY WARREN: I wish to go to bed!

PROCTOR [*in anger*]: Good night, then!

MARY WARREN: Good night. [*Dissatisfied, uncertain of herself, she goes out. Wide-eyed, both,* PROCTOR *and* ELIZABETH *stand staring.*]

ELIZABETH [*quietly*]: Oh, the noose, the noose is up!

PROCTOR: There'll be no noose.

ELIZABETH: She wants me dead. I knew all week it would come to this!

PROCTOR [*without conviction*]: They dismissed it. You heard her say –

ELIZABETH: And what of tomorrow? She will cry me out until they take me!

PROCTOR: Sit you down.

ELIZABETH: She wants me dead, John, you know it!

PROCTOR: I say sit down! [*She sits, trembling. He speaks quietly, trying to keep his wits*] Now we must be wise, Elizabeth.

ELIZABETH [*with sarcasm, and a sense of being lost*]: Oh, indeed, indeed!

PROCTOR: Fear nothing. I'll find Ezekiel Cheever. I'll tell him she said it were all sport.

ELIZABETH: John, with so many in the jail, more than Cheever's help is needed now, I think. Would you favour me with this? Go to Abigail.

PROCTOR [*his soul hardening as he senses . . .*]: What have I to say to Abigail?

ELIZABETH [*delicately*]: John – grant me this. You have a faulty understanding of young girls. There is a promise made in any bed –

PROCTOR [*striving against his anger*]: What promise?

ELIZABETH: Spoke or silent, a promise is surely made. And she may dote on it now – I am sure she does – and thinks to kill me, then to take my place.

[PROCTOR's *anger is rising; he cannot speak.*]

ELIZABETH: It is her dearest hope, John, I know it. There be a thousand names; why does she call mine? There be a certain danger in calling such a name – I am no Goody Good that sleeps in ditches, nor Osburn, drunk and half-witted. She'd dare not call out such a farmer's wife but there be monstrous profit in it. She thinks to take my place, John.

PROCTOR: She cannot think it! [*He knows it is true.*]

ELIZABETH [*reasonably*]: John, have you ever shown her somewhat of contempt? She cannot pass you in the church but you will blush –

PROCTOR: I may blush for my sin.

ELIZABETH: I think she sees another meaning in that blush.

PROCTOR: And what see you? What see you, Elizabeth?

ELIZABETH [*conceding*]: I think you be somewhat ashamed, for I am there, and she so close.

PROCTOR: When will you know me, woman? Were I stone I would have cracked for shame this seven month!

ELIZABETH: Then go and tell her she's a whore. Whatever promise she may sense – break it, John, break it.

PROCTOR [*between his teeth*]: Good, then. I'll go. [*He starts for his rifle.*]

ELIZABETH [*trembling, fearfully*]: Oh, how unwillingly!

PROCTOR [*turning on her, rifle in hand*]: I will curse her hotter than the oldest cinder in hell. But pray, begrudge me not my anger!

ELIZABETH: Your anger! I only ask you –

PROCTOR: Woman, am I so base? Do you truly think me base?

ELIZABETH: I never called you base.

PROCTOR: Then how do you charge me with such a promise? The promise that a stallion gives a mare I gave that girl!

ELIZABETH: Then why do you anger with me when I bid you break it?

PROCTOR: Because it speaks deceit, and I am honest! But I'll plead no more! I see now your spirit twists around the single error of my life, and I will never tear it free!

ELIZABETH [*crying out*]: You'll tear it free – when you come to know that I will be your only wife, or no wife at all! She has an arrow in you yet, John Proctor, and you know it well!

[*Quite suddenly, as though from the air, a figure appears in the doorway. They start slightly. It is* MR HALE. *He is different now – drawn a little, and there is a quality of deference, even of guilt, about his manner now.*]

HALE: Good evening.

PROCTOR [*still in his shock*]: Why, Mr Hale! Good evening to you, sir. Come in, come in.

HALE [*to* ELIZABETH]: I hope I do not startle you.

ELIZABETH: No, no, it's only that I heard no horse –

HALE: You are Goodwife Proctor.

PROCTOR: Aye; Elizabeth.

HALE [*nods, then*]: I hope you're not off to bed yet.

PROCTOR [*setting down his gun*]: No, no. [HALE *comes farther into the room. And* PROCTOR, *to explain his nervousness*] We are not used to visitors after dark, but you're welcome here. Will you sit you down, sir?

HALE: I will. [*He sits.*] Let you sit, Goodwife Proctor.

[*She does, never letting him out of her sight. There is a pause as* HALE *looks about the room.*]

PROCTOR [*to break the silence*]: Will you drink cider, Mr Hale?

HALE: No, it rebels my stomach; I have some further travelling yet tonight. Sit you down, sir. [PROCTOR *sits.*] I will not keep you long, but I have some business with you.

PROCTOR: Business of the court?

HALE: No – no, I come of my own, without the court's authority.

Hear me. [*He wets his lips.*] I know not if you are aware, but your wife's name is – mentioned in the court.

PROCTOR: We know it, sir. Our Mary Warren told us. We are entirely amazed.

HALE: I am a stranger here, as you know. And in my ignorance I find it hard to draw a clear opinion of them that come accused before the court. And so this afternoon, and now tonight, I go from house to house – I come now from Rebecca Nurse's house and –

ELIZABETH [*shocked*]: Rebecca's charged!

HALE: God forbid such a one be charged. She is, however – mentioned somewhat.

ELIZABETH [*with an attempt at a laugh*]: You will never believe, I hope, that Rebecca trafficked with the Devil.

HALE: Woman, it is possible.

PROCTOR [*taken aback*]: Surely you cannot think so.

HALE: This is a strange time, Mister. No man may longer doubt the powers of the dark are gathered in monstrous attack upon this village. There is too much evidence now to deny it. You will agree, sir?

PROCTOR [*evading*]: I – have no knowledge in that line. But it's hard to think so pious a woman be secretly a Devil's bitch after seventy year of such good prayer.

HALE: Aye. But the Devil is a wily one, you cannot deny it. However, she is far from accused, and I know she will not be. [*Pause.*] I thought, sir, to put some questions as to the Christian character of this house, if you'll permit me.

PROCTOR [*coldly, resentful*]: Why, we – have no fear of questions, sir.

HALE: Good, then. [*He makes himself more comfortable.*] In the book of record that Mr Parris keeps, I note that you are rarely in the church on Sabbath Day.

PROCTOR: No, sir, you are mistaken.

HALE: Twenty-six time in seventeen month, sir. I must call that rare. Will you tell me why you are so absent?

PROCTOR: Mr Hale, I never knew I must account to that man for I come to church or stay at home. My wife were sick this winter.

HALE: So I am told. But you, Mister, why could you not come alone?

PROCTOR: I surely did come when I could, and when I could not I prayed in this house.

HALE: Mr Proctor, your house is not a church; your theology must tell you that.

PROCTOR: It does, sir, it does; and it tells me that a minister may pray to God without he have golden candlesticks upon the altar.

HALE: What golden candlesticks?

PROCTOR: Since we built the church there were pewter candlesticks upon the altar; Francis Nurse made them, y'know, and a sweeter hand never touched the metal. But Parris came, and for twenty week he preach nothin' but golden candlesticks until he had them. I labour the earth from dawn of day to blink of night, and I tell you true, when I look to heaven and see my money glaring at his elbows – it hurt my prayer, sir, it hurt my prayer. I think, sometimes, the man dreams cathedrals, not clapboard meetin' houses.

HALE [*thinks, then*]: And yet, Mister, a Christian on Sabbath Day must be in church. [*Pause.*] Tell me – you have three children?

PROCTOR: Aye. Boys.

HALE: How comes it that only two are baptized?

PROCTOR [*starts to speak, then stops, then, as though unable to restrain this*]: I like it not that Mr Parris should lay his hand upon my baby. I see no light of God in that man. I'll not conceal it.

HALE: I must say it, Mr Proctor; that is not for you to decide. The man's ordained, therefore the light of God is in him.

PROCTOR [*flushed with resentment but trying to smile*]: What's your suspicion, Mr Hale?

HALE: No, no, I have no –

PROCTOR: I nailed the roof upon the church, I hung the door –

HALE: Oh, did you! That's a good sign, then.

PROCTOR: It may be I have been too quick to bring the man to book, but you cannot think we ever desired the destruction of religion. I think that's in your mind, is it not?

HALE [*not altogether giving way*]: I – have – there is a softness in your record, sir, a softness.

ELIZABETH: I think, maybe, we have been too hard with Mr Parris. I think so. But sure we never loved the Devil here.

HALE: [*nods, deliberating this. Then, with the voice of one administering a secret test*]: Do you know your Commandments, Elizabeth?

ELIZABETH [*without hesitation, even eagerly*]: I surely do. There be no mark of blame upon my life, Mr Hale. I am a covenanted Christian woman.

HALE: And you, Mister?

PROCTOR [*a trifle unsteadily*]: I – am sure I do, sir.

HALE [*glances at her open face, then at* JOHN, *then*]: Let you repeat them, if you will.

PROCTOR: The Commandments.

HALE: Aye.

PROCTOR [*looking off, beginning to sweat*]: Thou shalt not kill.

HALE: Aye.

PROCTOR [*counting on his fingers*]: Thou shalt not steal. Thou shalt not covet thy neighbour's goods, nor make unto thee any graven image. Thou shalt not take the name of the Lord in vain; thou shalt have no other gods before me. [*With some hesitation*] Thou shalt remember the Sabbath Day and keep it holy. [*Pause. Then*] Thou shalt honour thy father and mother. Thou shalt not bear false witness. [*He is stuck. He counts back on his fingers, knowing one is missing.*] Thou shalt not make unto thee any graven image.

HALE: You have said that twice, sir.

PROCTOR [*lost*]: Aye. [*He is flailing for it.*]

ELIZABETH [*delicately*]: Adultery, John.

PROCTOR [*as though a secret arrow had pained his heart*]: Aye. [*Trying to grin it away – to* HALE] You see, sir, between the two of us we do know them all. [HALE *only looks at* PROCTOR, *deep in his attempt to define this man.* PROCTOR *grows more uneasy.*] I think it be a small fault.

HALE: Theology, sir, is a fortress; no crack in a fortress may be accounted small. [*He rises; he seems worried now. He paces a little, in deep thought.*]

PROCTOR: There be no love for Satan in this house, Mister.

HALE: I pray it, I pray it dearly. [*He looks to both of them, an attempt at a smile on his face, but his misgivings are clear.*] Well, then – I'll bid you good night.

ELIZABETH [*unable to restrain herself*]: Mr Hale. [*He turns.*] I do think you are suspecting me somewhat? Are you not?

HALE [*obviously disturbed – and evasive*]: Goody Proctor, I do not judge you. My duty is to add what I may to the godly wisdom of the court. I pray you both good health and good fortune. [*To* JOHN] Good night, sir. [*He starts out.*]

ELIZABETH [*with a note of desperation*]: I think you must tell him, John.

HALE: What's that?

ELIZABETH [*restraining a call*]: Will you tell him?

[*Slight pause.* HALE *looks questioningly at* JOHN.]

PROCTOR [*with difficulty*]: I – I have no witness and cannot prove it, except my word be taken. But I know the children's sickness had naught to do with witchcraft.

HALE [*stopped, struck*]: Naught to do – ?

PROCTOR: Mr Parris discovered them sportin' in the woods. They were startled and took sick.

[*Pause.*]

HALE: Who told you this?

PROCTOR [*hesitates, then*]: Abigail Williams.

HALE: Abigail!

PROCTOR: Aye.

HALE [*his eyes wide*]: Abigail Williams told you it had naught to do with witchcraft!

PROCTOR: She told me the day you came, sir.

HALE [*suspiciously*]: Why – why did you keep this?

PROCTOR: I never knew until tonight that the world is gone daft with this nonsense.

HALE: Nonsense! Mister, I have myself examined Tituba, Sarah

Good, and numerous others that have confessed to dealing with the Devil. They have *confessed* it.

PROCTOR: And why not, if they must hang for denyin' it? There are them that will swear to anything before they'll hang; have you never thought of that?

HALE: I have. I – I have indeed. [*It is his own suspicion, but he resists it. He glances at* ELIZABETH, *then at* JOHN.] And you – would you testify to this in court?

PROCTOR: I – had not reckoned with goin' into court. But if I must I will.

HALE: Do you falter here?

PROCTOR: I falter nothing, but I may wonder if my story will be credited in such a court. I do wonder on it, when such a steady-minded minister as you will suspicion such a woman that never lied, and cannot, and the world knows she cannot! I may falter somewhat, Mister; I am no fool.

HALE [*quietly – it has impressed him*]: Proctor, let you open with me now, for I have a rumour that troubles me. It's said you hold no belief that there may even be witches in the world. Is that true, sir?

PROCTOR [*he knows this is critical, and is striving against his disgust with* HALE *and with himself for even answering*]: I know not what I have said, I may have said it. I have wondered if there be witches in the world – although I cannot believe they come among us now.

HALE: Then you do not believe –

PROCTOR: I have no knowledge of it; the Bible speaks of witches, and I will not deny them.

HALE: And you, woman?

ELIZABETH: I – I cannot believe it.

HALE [*shocked*]: You cannot!

PROCTOR: Elizabeth, you bewilder him!

ELIZABETH [*to* HALE]: I cannot think the Devil may own a woman's soul, Mr Hale, when she keeps an upright way, as I have. I am a good woman, I know it; and if you believe I may do only good

work in the world, and yet be secretly bound to Satan, then I
must tell you, sir, I do not believe it.

HALE: But, woman, you do believe there are witches in –

ELIZABETH: If you think that I am one, then I say there are none.

HALE: You surely do not fly against the Gospel, the Gospel –

PROCTOR: She believe in the Gospel, every word!

ELIZABETH: Question Abigail Williams about the Gospel, not
myself!

[HALE *stares at her.*]

PROCTOR: She do not mean to doubt the Gospel, sir, you cannot
think it. This be a Christian house, sir, a Christian house.

HALE: God keep you both; let the third child be quickly baptized,
and go you without fail each Sunday in to Sabbath prayer; and
keep a solemn, quiet way among you. I think –

[GILES COREY *appears in doorway.*]

GILES: John!

PROCTOR: Giles! What's the matter?

GILES: They take my wife.

[FRANCIS NURSE *enters.*]

GILES: And his Rebecca!

PROCTOR [*to* FRANCIS]: Rebecca's in the *jail*!

FRANCIS: Aye, Cheever come and take her in his wagon. We've
only now come from the jail, and they'll not even let us to see
them.

ELIZABETH: They've surely gone wild now, Mr Hale!

FRANCIS [*going to* HALE]: Reverend Hale! Can you not speak to the
Deputy Governor? I'm sure he mistakes these people –

HALE: Pray calm yourself, Mr Nurse.

FRANCIS: My wife is the very brick and mortar of the church,
Mr Hale – [*indicating* GILES] – and Martha Corey, there cannot be
a woman closer yet to God than Martha.

HALE: How is Rebecca charged, Mr Nurse?

FRANCIS [*with a mocking, half-hearted laugh*]: For murder, she's charged! [*Mockingly quoting the warrant*] 'For the marvellous and supernatural murder of Goody Putnam's babies.' What am I to do, Mr Hale?

HALE [*turns from* FRANCIS, *deeply troubled, then*]: Believe me, Mr Nurse, if Rebecca Nurse be tainted, then nothing's left to stop the whole green world from burning. Let you rest upon the justice of the court; the court will send her home, I know it.

FRANCIS: You cannot mean she will be tried in court!

HALE [*pleading*]: Nurse, though our hearts break, we cannot flinch; these are new times, sir. There is a misty plot afoot so subtle we should be criminal to cling to old respects and ancient friendships. I have seen too many frightful proofs in court – the Devil is alive in Salem, and we dare not quail to follow wherever the accusing finger points!

PROCTOR [*angered*]: How may such a woman murder children?

HALE [*in great pain*]: Man, remember, until an hour before the Devil fell, God thought him beautiful in Heaven.

GILES: I never said my wife were a witch, Mr Hale; I only said she were reading books!

HALE: Mr Corey, exactly what complaint were made on your wife?

GILES: That bloody mongrel Walcott charge her. Y'see, he buy a pig of my wife four or five year ago, and the pig died soon after. So he come dancin' in for his money back. So my Martha, she says to him, 'Walcott, if you haven't the wit to feed a pig properly, you'll not live to own many,' she says. Now he goes to court and claims that from that day to this he cannot keep a pig alive for more than four weeks because my Martha bewitch them with her books!

[*Enter* EZEKIEL CHEEVER. *A shocked silence.*]

CHEEVER: Good evening to you, Proctor.

PROCTOR: Why, Mr Cheever. Good evening.

CHEEVER: Good evening, all. Good evening, Mr Hale.

PROCTOR: I hope you come not on business of the court.

CHEEVER: I do, Proctor, aye. I am clerk of the court now, y'know.

[*Enter* MARSHAL HERRICK, *a man in his early thirties, who is somewhat shamefaced at the moment.*]

GILES: It's a pity, Ezekiel, that an honest tailor might have gone to Heaven must burn in Hell. You'll burn for this, do you know it?

CHEEVER: You know yourself I must do as I'm told. You surely know that, Giles. And I'd as lief you'd not be sending me to Hell. I like not the sound of it, I tell you; I like not the sound of it. [*He fears* PROCTOR, *but starts to reach inside his coat.*] Now believe me, Proctor, how heavy be the law, all its tonnage I do carry on my back tonight. [*He takes out a warrant.*] I have a warrant for your wife.

PROCTOR [*to* HALE]: You said she were not charged!

HALE: I know nothin' of it. [*To* CHEEVER] When were she charged?

CHEEVER: I am given sixteen warrant tonight, sir, and she is one.

PROCTOR: Who charged her?

CHEEVER: Why, Abigail Williams charge her.

PROCTOR: On what proof, what proof?

CHEEVER [*looking about the room*]: Mr Proctor, I have little time. The court bid me search your house, but I like not to search a house. So will you hand me any poppets that your wife may keep here?

PROCTOR: Poppets?

ELIZABETH: I have kept no poppets, not since I were a girl.

CHEEVER [*embarrassed, glancing toward the mantel where sits* MARY WARREN's *poppet*]: I spy a poppet, Goody Proctor.

ELIZABETH: Oh! [*Going for it*] Why, this is Mary's.

CHEEVER [*shyly*]: Would you please to give it to me?

ELIZABETH [*handing it to him, asks* HALE]: Has the court discovered a text in poppets now?

CHEEVER [*carefully holding the poppet*]: Do you keep any others in this house?

PROCTOR: No, nor this one either till tonight. What signifies a poppet?

CHEEVER: Why, a poppet – [*he gingerly turns the poppet over*] – a poppet may signify – Now, woman, will you please to come with me?

PROCTOR: She will not! [*To* ELIZABETH] Fetch Mary here.

CHEEVER [*ineptly reaching toward* ELIZABETH]: No, no, I am forbid to leave her from my sight.

PROCTOR [*pushing his arm away*]: You'll leave her out of sight and out of mind, Mister. Fetch Mary, Elizabeth. [ELIZABETH *goes upstairs.*]

HALE: What signifies a poppet, Mr Cheever?

CHEEVER [*turning the poppet over in his hands*]: Why, they say it may signify that she – [*He has lifted the poppet's skirt, and his eyes widen in astonished fear.*] Why, this, this –

PROCTOR [*reaching for the poppet*]: What's there?

CHEEVER: Why – [*he draws out a long needle from the poppet*] – it is a needle! Herrick, Herrick, it is a needle!

[HERRICK *comes toward him.*]

PROCTOR [*angrily, bewildered*]: And what signifies a needle!

CHEEVER [*his hands shaking*]: Why, this go hard with her, Proctor, this – I had my doubts, Proctor, I had my doubts, but here's calamity. [*To* HALE, *showing the needle*] You see it, sir, it is a needle!

HALE: Why? What meanin' has it?

CHEEVER [*wide-eyed, trembling*]: The girl, the Williams girl, Abigail Williams, sir. She sat to dinner in Reverend Parris's house tonight, and without word nor warnin' she falls to the floor. Like a struck beast, he says, and screamed a scream that a bull would weep to hear. And he goes to save her, and, stuck two inches in the flesh of her belly, he draw a needle out. And demandin' of her how she come to be so stabbed, she – [*to* PROCTOR *now*] – testify it were your wife's familiar spirit pushed it in.

PROCTOR: Why, she done it herself! [*To* HALE] I hope you're not takin' this for proof, Mister!

[HALE, *struck by the proof, is silent.*]

CHEEVER: 'Tis hard proof! [*To* HALE] I find here a poppet Goody Proctor keeps. I have found it, sir. And in the belly of the poppet a needle's stuck. I tell you true, Proctor, I never warranted to see such proof of Hell, and I bid you obstruct me not, for I –

[*Enter* ELIZABETH *with* MARY WARREN. PROCTOR, *seeing* MARY WARREN, *draws her by the arm to* HALE.]

PROCTOR: Here now! Mary, how did this poppet come into my house?

MARY WARREN [*frightened for herself, her voice very small*]: What poppet's that, sir?

PROCTOR [*impatiently, pointing at the doll in* CHEEVER's *hand*]: This poppet, this poppet.

MARY WARREN [*evasively, looking at it*]: Why, I – I think it is mine.

PROCTOR: It is your poppet, is it not?

MARY WARREN [*not understanding the direction of this*]: It – is, sir.

PROCTOR: And how did it come into this house?

MARY WARREN [*glancing about at the avid faces*]: Why – I made it in the court, sir, and – give it to Goody Proctor tonight.

PROCTOR [*to* HALE]: Now, sir – do you have it?

HALE: Mary Warren, a needle have been found inside this poppet.

MARY WARREN [*bewildered*]: Why, I meant no harm by it, sir.

PROCTOR [*quickly*]: You stuck that needle in yourself?

MARY WARREN: I – I believe I did, sir, I –

PROCTOR [*to* HALE]: What say you now?

HALE [*watching* MARY WARREN *closely*]: Child, you are certain this be your natural memory? May it be, perhaps, that someone conjures you even now to say this?

MARY WARREN: Conjures me? Why, no, sir, I am entirely myself, I think. Let you ask Susanna Walcott – she saw me sewin' it in court. [*Or better still*] Ask Abby, Abby sat beside me when I made it.

PROCTOR [*to* HALE, *of* CHEEVER]: Bid him begone. Your mind is surely settled now. Bid him out, Mr Hale.

ELIZABETH: What signifies a needle?

HALE: Mary – you charge a cold and cruel murder on Abigail.

MARY WARREN: Murder! I charge no –

HALE: Abigail were stabbed tonight; a needle were found stuck into her belly –

ELIZABETH: And she charges me?

HALE: Aye.

ELIZABETH [*her breath knocked out*]: Why – ! The girl is murder! She must be ripped out of the world!

CHEEVER [*pointing at* ELIZABETH]: You've heard that, sir! Ripped out of the world! Herrick, you heard it!

PROCTOR [*suddenly snatching the warrant out of* CHEEVER's *hands*]: Out with you.

CHEEVER: Proctor, you dare not touch the warrant.

PROCTOR [*ripping the warrant*]: Out with you!

CHEEVER: You've ripped the Deputy Governor's warrant, man!

PROCTOR: Damn the Deputy Governor! Out of my house!

HALE: Now, Proctor, Proctor!

PROCTOR: Get y'gone with them! You are a broken minister.

HALE: Proctor, if she is innocent, the court –

PROCTOR: If *she* is innocent! Why do you never wonder if Parris be innocent, or Abigail? Is the accuser always holy now? Were they born this morning as clean as God's fingers? I'll tell you what's walking Salem – vengeance is walking Salem. We are what we always were in Salem, but now the little crazy children are jangling the keys of the kingdom, and common vengeance writes the law! This warrant's vengeance! I'll not give my wife to vengeance!

ELIZABETH: I'll go, John –

PROCTOR: You will not go!

HERRICK: I have nine men outside. You cannot keep her. The law binds me, John, I cannot budge.

PROCTOR [*to* HALE, *ready to break him*]: Will you see her taken?

HALE: Proctor, the court is just –

PROCTOR: Pontius Pilate! God will not let you wash your hands of this!

ELIZABETH: John – I think I must go with them. [*He cannot bear to look at her.*] Mary, there is bread enough for the morning; you will bake in the afternoon. Help Mr Proctor as you were his daughter – you owe me that, and much more. [*She is fighting her weeping. To* PROCTOR] When the children wake, speak nothing of witchcraft – it will frighten them. [*She cannot go on.*]

PROCTOR: I will bring you home. I will bring you soon.

ELIZABETH: Oh, John, bring me soon!

PROCTOR: I will fall like an ocean on that court! Fear nothing, Elizabeth.

ELIZABETH [*with great fear*]: I will fear nothing. [*She looks about the room, as though to fix it in her mind.*] Tell the children I have gone to visit someone sick.

[*She walks out the door,* HERRICK *and* CHEEVER *behind her. For a moment,* PROCTOR *watches from the doorway. The clank of chain is heard.*]

PROCTOR: Herrick! Herrick, don't chain her! [*He rushes out the door. From outside*] Damn you, man, you will not chain her! Off with them! I'll not have it! I will not have her chained!

[*There are other men's voices against his.* HALE, *in a fever of guilt and uncertainty, turns from the door to avoid the sight;* MARY WARREN *bursts into tears and sits weeping.* GILES COREY *calls to* HALE.]

GILES: And yet silent, minister? It is fraud, you know it is fraud! What keeps you, man?

[PROCTOR *is half braced, half pushed into the room by two deputies and* HERRICK.]

PROCTOR: I'll pay you, Herrick, I will surely pay you!

HERRICK [*panting*]: In God's name, John, I cannot help myself. I must chain them all. Now let you keep inside this house till I am gone! [*He goes out with his deputies.*]

[PROCTOR *stands there, gulping air. Horses and a wagon creaking are heard.*]

HALE [*in great uncertainty*]: Mr Proctor –

PROCTOR: Out of my sight!

HALE: Charity, Proctor, charity. What I have heard in her favour, I will not fear to testify in court. God help me, I cannot judge her guilty or innocent – I know not. Only this consider: the world goes mad, and it profit nothing you should lay the cause to the vengeance of a little girl.

PROCTOR: You are a coward! Though you be ordained in God's own tears, you are a coward now!

HALE: Proctor, I cannot think God be provoked so grandly by such a petty cause. The jails are packed – our greatest judges sit in Salem now – and hangin's promised. Man, we must look to cause proportionate. Were there murder done, perhaps, and never brought to light? Abomination? Some secret blasphemy that stinks to Heaven? Think on cause, man, and let you help me to discover it. For there's your way, believe it, there is your only way, when such confusion strikes upon the world. [*He goes to* GILES *and* FRANCIS.] Let you counsel among yourselves; think on your village and what may have drawn from heaven such thundering wrath upon you all. I shall pray God open up our eyes.

[HALE *goes out.*]

FRANCIS [*struck by* HALE's *mood*]: I never heard no murder done in Salem.

PROCTOR [*he has been reached by* HALE's *words*]: Leave me, Francis, leave me.

GILES [*shaken*]: John – tell me, are we lost?

PROCTOR: Go home now, Giles. We'll speak on it tomorrow.

GILES: Let you think on it. We'll come early, eh?

PROCTOR: Aye. Go now, Giles.

GILES: Good night, then.

[GILES COREY *goes out. After a moment:*]

MARY WARREN [*in a fearful squeak of a voice*]: Mr Proctor, very likely they'll let her come home once they're given proper evidence.

PROCTOR: You're coming to the court with me, Mary. You will tell it in the court.

MARY WARREN: I cannot charge murder on Abigail.

PROCTOR [*moving menacingly toward her*]: You will tell the court how that poppet come here and who stuck the needle in.

MARY WARREN: She'll kill me for sayin' that! [PROCTOR *continues toward her.*] Abby'll charge lechery on you, Mr Proctor!

PROCTOR [*halting*]: She's told you!

MARY WARREN: I have known it, sir. She'll ruin you with it, I know she will.

PROCTOR [*hesitating, and with deep hatred of himself*]: Good. Then her saintliness is done with. [MARY *backs from him.*] We will slide together into our pit; you will tell the court what you know.

MARY WARREN [*in terror*]: I cannot, they'll turn on me –

[PROCTOR *strides and catches her, and she is repeating, 'I cannot, I cannot!'*]

PROCTOR: My wife will never die for me! I will bring your guts into your mouth but that goodness will not die for me!

MARY WARREN [*struggling to escape him*]: I cannot do it, I cannot!

PROCTOR [*grasping her by the throat as though he would strangle her*]: Make your peace with it! Now Hell and Heaven grapple on our backs, and all our old pretence is ripped away – make your peace! [*He throws her to the floor, where she sobs, 'I cannot, I cannot . . .' And now, half to himself, staring, and turning to the open door*] Peace.

It is a providence, and no great change; we are only what we always were, but naked now. [*He walks as though toward a great horror, facing the open sky.*] Aye, naked! And the wind, God's icy wind, will blow!

[*And she is over and over again sobbing, 'I cannot, I cannot, I cannot', as*]

THE CURTAIN FALLS

Act Three

The vestry room of the Salem meeting house, now serving as the ante-room of the General Court.

As the curtain rises, the room is empty, but for sunlight pouring through two high windows in the back wall. The room is solemn, even forbidding. Heavy beams jut out, boards of random widths make up the walls. At the right are two doors leading into the meeting house proper, where the court is being held. At the left another door leads outside.

There is a plain bench at the left, and another at the right. In the center a rather long meeting table, with stools and a considerable armchair snugged up to it.

Through the partitioning wall at the right we hear a prosecutor's voice, JUDGE HATHORNE's, asking a question; then a woman's voice, MARTHA COREY's, replying.

HATHORNE'S VOICE: Now, Martha Corey, there is abundant evidence in our hands to show that you have given yourself to the reading of fortunes. Do you deny it?

MARTHA COREY'S VOICE: I am innocent to a witch. I know not what a witch is.

HATHORNE'S VOICE: How do you know, then, that you are not a witch?

MARTHA COREY'S VOICE: If I were, I would know it.

HATHORNE'S VOICE: Why do you hurt these children?

MARTHA COREY'S VOICE: I do not hurt them. I scorn it!

GILES' VOICE [roaring]: I have evidence for the court!

[Voices of townspeople rise in excitement.]

DANFORTH'S VOICE: You will keep your seat!

GILES' VOICE: Thomas Putnam is reaching out for land!

DANFORTH'S VOICE: Remove that man, Marshal!

GILES' VOICE: You're hearing lies, lies!

[*A roaring goes up from the people.*]

HATHORNE'S VOICE: Arrest him, Excellency!

GILES' VOICE: I have evidence. Why will you not hear my evidence?

[*The door opens and* GILES *is half carried into the vestry room by* HERRICK.]

GILES: Hands off, damn you, let me go!

HERRICK: Giles, Giles!

GILES: Out of my way, Herrick! I bring evidence –

HERRICK: You cannot go in there, Giles; it's a court!

[*Enter* HALE *from the court.*]

HALE: Pray be calm a moment.

GILES: You, Mr Hale, go in there and demand I speak.

HALE: A moment, sir, a moment.

GILES: They'll be hangin' my wife!

[JUDGE HATHORNE *enters. He is in his sixties, a bitter, remorseless Salem judge.*]

HATHORNE: How do you dare come roarin' into this court! Are you gone daft, Corey?

GILES: You're not a Boston judge yet, Hathorne. You'll not call me daft!

[*Enter* DEPUTY GOVERNOR DANFORTH *and, behind him,* EZEKIEL CHEEVER *and* PARRIS. *On his appearance, silence falls.* DANFORTH *is a grave man in his sixties, of some humour and sophistication that does not, however, interfere with an exact loyalty to his position and his cause. He comes down to* GILES, *who awaits his wrath.*]

DANFORTH [*looking directly at* GILES]: Who is this man?

PARRIS: Giles Corey, sir, and a more contentious –

GILES [*to* PARRIS]: I am asked the question, and I am old enough to answer it! [*To* DANFORTH, *who impresses him and to whom he smiles through his strain.*] My name is Corey, sir, Giles Corey. I have six hundred acres, and timber in addition. It is my wife you be condemning now. [*He indicates the courtroom.*]

DANFORTH: And how do you imagine to help her cause with such contemptuous riot? Now be gone. Your old age alone keeps you out of jail for this.

GILES [*beginning to plead*]: They be tellin' lies about my wife sir, I –

DANFORTH: Do you take it upon yourself to determine what this court shall believe and what it shall set aside?

GILES: Your Excellency, we mean no disrespect for –

DANFORTH: Disrespect indeed! It is disruption, Mister. This is the highest court of the supreme government of this province, do you know it?

GILES [*beginning to weep*]: Your Excellency, I only said she were readin' books, sir, and they come and take her out of my house for –

DANFORTH [*mystified*]: Books! What books?

GILES [*through helpless sobs*]: It is my third wife, sir; I never had no wife that be so taken with books, and I thought to find the cause of it, d'y'see, but it were no witch I blamed her for. [*He is openly weeping.*] I have broke charity with the woman, I have broke charity with her. [*He covers his face, ashamed.* DANFORTH *is respectfully silent.*]

HALE: Excellency, he claims hard evidence for his wife's defence. I think that in all justice you must –

DANFORTH: Then let him submit his evidence in proper affidavit. You are certainly aware of our procedure here, Mr Hale. [*To* HERRICK] Clear this room.

HERRICK: Come now, Giles. [*He gently pushes* COREY *out.*]

FRANCIS: We are desperate, sir; we come here three days now and cannot be heard.

DANFORTH: Who is this man?

FRANCIS: Francis Nurse, Your Excellency.

HALE: His wife's Rebecca that were condemned this morning.

DANFORTH: Indeed! I am amazed to find you in such uproar. I have only good report of your character, Mr Nurse.

HATHORNE: I think they must both be arrested in contempt, sir.

DANFORTH [*to* FRANCIS]: Let you write your plea, and in due time I will –

FRANCIS: Excellency, we have proof for your eyes; God forbid you shut them to it. The girls, sir, the girls are frauds.

DANFORTH: What's that?

FRANCIS: We have proof of it, sir. They are all deceiving you.

[DANFORTH *is shocked, but studying* FRANCIS.]

HATHORNE: This is contempt, sir, contempt!

DANFORTH: Peace, Judge Hathorne. Do you know who I am, Mr Nurse?

FRANCIS: I surely do, sir, and I think you must be a wise judge to be what you are.

DANFORTH: And do you know that near to four hundred are in the jails from Marblehead to Lynn, and upon my signature?

FRANCIS: I –

DANFORTH: And seventy-two condemned to hang by that signature?

FRANCIS: Excellency, I never thought to say it to such a weighty judge, but you are deceived.

[*Enter* GILES COREY *from left. All turn to see as he beckons in* MARY WARREN *with* PROCTOR. MARY *is keeping her eyes to the ground;* PROCTOR *has her elbow as though she were near collapse.*]

PARRIS [*on seeing her, in shock*]: Mary Warren! [*He goes directly to bend close to her face.*] What are you about here?

PROCTOR [*pressing* PARRIS *away from her with a gentle but firm motion of protectiveness*]: She would speak with the Deputy Governor.

DANFORTH [*shocked by this, turns to* HERRICK]: Did you not tell me Mary Warren were sick in bed?

HERRICK: She were, Your Honour. When I go to fetch her to the court last week, she said she were sick.

GILES: She has been strivin' with her soul all week, Your Honour; she comes now to tell the truth of this to you.

DANFORTH: Who is this?

PROCTOR: John Proctor, sir. Elizabeth Proctor is my wife.

PARRIS: Beware this man, Your Excellency, this man is mischief.

HALE [*excitedly*]: I think you must hear the girl, sir, she –

DANFORTH [*who has become very interested in* MARY WARREN *and only raises a hand toward* HALE]: Peace. What would you tell us, Mary Warren?

[PROCTOR *looks at her, but she cannot speak.*]

PROCTOR: She never saw no spirits, sir.

DANFORTH [*with great alarm and surprise, to* MARY]: Never saw no spirits!

GILES [*eagerly*]: Never.

PROCTOR [*reaching into his jacket*]: She has signed a deposition, sir –

DANFORTH [*instantly*]: No, no, I accept no depositions. [*He is rapidly calculating this; he turns from her to* PROCTOR.] Tell me, Mr Proctor, have you given out this story in the village?

PROCTOR: We have not.

PARRIS: They've come to overthrow the court, sir! This man is –

DANFORTH: I pray you, Mr Parris. Do you know, Mr Proctor, that the entire contention of the state in these trials is that the voice of Heaven is speaking through the children?

PROCTOR: I know that, sir.

DANFORTH [*thinks, staring at* PROCTOR, *then turns to* MARY WARREN]: And you, Mary Warren, how came you to cry out people for sending their spirits against you?

MARY WARREN: It were pretence, sir.

DANFORTH: I cannot hear you.

PROCTOR: It were pretence, she says.

DANFORTH: Ah? And the other girls? Susanna Walcott, and – the others? They are also pretending?

MARY WARREN: Aye, sir.

DANFORTH [*wide-eyed*]: Indeed. [*Pause. He is baffled by this. He turns to study* PROCTOR's *face.*]

PARRIS [*in a sweat*]: Excellency, you surely cannot think to let so vile a lie be spread in open court!

DANFORTH: Indeed not, but it strike hard upon me that she will dare come here with such a tale. Now, Mr Proctor, before I decide whether I shall hear you or not, it is my duty to tell you this. We burn a hot fire here; it melts down all concealment.

PROCTOR: I know that, sir.

DANFORTH: Let me continue. I understand well, a husband's tenderness may drive him to extravagance in defence of a wife. Are you certain in your conscience, Mister, that your evidence is the truth?

PROCTOR: It is. And you will surely know it.

DANFORTH: And you thought to declare this revelation in the open court before the public?

PROCTOR: I thought I would, aye – with your permission.

DANFORTH [*his eyes narrowing*]: Now, sir, what is your purpose in so doing?

PROCTOR: Why, I – I would free my wife, sir.

DANFORTH: There lurks nowhere in your heart, nor hidden in your spirit, any desire to undermine this court?

PROCTOR [*with the faintest faltering*]: Why, no, sir.

CHEEVER [*clears his throat, awakening*]: I – Your Excellency.

DANFORTH: Mr Cheever.

CHEEVER: I think it be my duty, sir – [*Kindly, to* PROCTOR] You'll not deny it, John. [*To* DANFORTH] When we come to take his wife, he damned the court and ripped your warrant.

PARRIS: Now you have it!

DANFORTH: He did that, Mr Hale?

HALE [*takes a breath*]: Aye, he did.

PROCTOR: It were a temper, sir. I knew not what I did.

DANFORTH [*studying him*]: Mr Proctor.

PROCTOR: Aye, sir.

DANFORTH [*straight into his eyes*]: Have you ever seen the Devil?

PROCTOR: No, sir.

DANFORTH: You are in all respects a Gospel Christian?

PROCTOR: I am, sir.

PARRIS: Such a Christian that will not come to church but once in a month!

DANFORTH [*restrained – he is curious*]: Not come to church?

PROCTOR: I – I have no love for Mr Parris. It is no secret. But God I surely love.

CHEEVER: He plough on Sunday, sir.

DANFORTH: Plough on Sunday!

CHEEVER [*apologetically*]: I think it be evidence, John. I am an official of the court, I cannot keep it.

PROCTOR: I – I have once or twice ploughed on Sunday. I have three children, sir, and until last year my land give little.

GILES: You'll find other Christians that do plough on Sunday, if the truth be known.

HALE: Your Honour, I cannot think you may judge the man on such evidence.

DANFORTH: I judge nothing. [*Pause. He keeps watching* PROCTOR, *who tries to meet his gaze.*] I tell you straight, Mister – I have seen marvels in this court. I have seen people choked before my eyes by spirits; I have seen them stuck by pins and slashed by daggers. I have until this moment not the slightest reason to suspect that the children may be deceiving me. Do you understand my meaning?

PROCTOR: Excellency, does it not strike upon you that so many of these women have lived so long with such upright reputation, and –

PARRIS: Do you read the Gospel, Mr Proctor?

PROCTOR: I read the Gospel.

PARRIS: I think not, or you should surely know that Cain were an upright man, and yet he did kill Abel.

PROCTOR: Ay, God tells us that. [*To* DANFORTH] But who tells us Rebecca Nurse murdered seven babies by sending out her spirit on them? It is the children only, and this one will swear she lied to you.

[DANFORTH *considers, then beckons* HATHORNE *to him.* HATHORNE *leans in, and he speaks in his ear.* HATHORNE *nods.*]

HATHORNE: Aye, she's the one.

DANFORTH: Mr Proctor, this morning, your wife send me a claim in which she states that she is pregnant now.

PROCTOR: My wife pregnant!

DANFORTH: There be no sign of it – we have examined her body.

PROCTOR: But if she say she is pregnant, then she must be! That woman will never lie, Mr Danforth.

DANFORTH: She will not?

PROCTOR: Never, sir, never.

DANFORTH: We have thought it too convenient to be credited. However, if I should tell you now that I will let her be kept another month; and if she begin to show her natural signs, you shall have her living yet another year until she is delivered – what say you to that? [JOHN PROCTOR *is struck silent.*] Come now. You say your only purpose is to save your wife. Good, then, she is saved at least this year, and a year is long. What say you, sir? It is done now. [*In conflict,* PROCTOR *glances at* FRANCIS *and* GILES.] Will you drop this charge?

PROCTOR: I – I think I cannot.

DANFORTH [*now an almost imperceptible hardness in his voice*]: Then your purpose is somewhat larger.

PARRIS: He's come to overthrow this court, Your Honour!

PROCTOR: These are my friends. Their wives are also accused –

DANFORTH [*with a sudden briskness of manner*]: I judge you not, sir. I am ready to hear your evidence.

PROCTOR: I come not to hurt the court; I only –

DANFORTH [*cutting him off*]: Marshal, go into the court and bid Judge Stoughton and Judge Sewall declare recess for one hour. And let them go to the tavern, if they will. All witnesses and prisoners are to be kept in the building.

HERRICK: Aye, sir. [*Very deferentially*] If I may say it, sir, I know this man all my life. It is a good man, sir.

DANFORTH [*it is the reflection on himself he resents*]: I am sure of it, Marshal. [HERRICK *nods, then goes out.*] Now, what deposition do you have for us, Mr Proctor? And I beg you be clear, open as the sky, and honest.

PROCTOR [*as he takes out several papers*]: I am no lawyer, so I'll –

DANFORTH: The pure in heart need no lawyers. Proceed as you will.

PROCTOR [*handing* DANFORTH *a paper*]: Will you read this first, sir? It's a sort of testament. The people signing it declare their good opinion of Rebecca, and my wife, and Martha Corey.

[DANFORTH *looks down at the paper.*]

PARRIS [*to enlist* DANFORTH's *sarcasm*]: Their good opinion!

[*But* DANFORTH *goes on reading, and* PROCTOR *is heartened.*]

PROCTOR: These are all landholding farmers, members of the church. [*Delicately, trying to point out a paragraph*] If you'll notice, sir – they've known the women many years and never saw no sign they had dealings with the Devil.

[PARRIS *nervously moves over and reads over* DANFORTH's *shoulder.*]

DANFORTH [*glancing down a long list*]: How many names are here?

FRANCIS: Ninety-one, Your Excellency.

PARRIS [*sweating*]: These people should be summoned. [DANFORTH *looks up at him questioningly.*] For questioning.

FRANCIS [*trembling with anger*]: Mr Danforth, I gave them all my word no harm would come to them for signing this.

PARRIS: This is a clear attack upon the court!

HALE [*to* PARRIS, *trying to contain himself*]: Is every defence an attack upon the court? Can no one – ?

PARRIS: All innocent and Christian people are happy for the courts in Salem! These people are gloomy for it. [*To* DANFORTH *directly*] And I think you will want to know, from each and every one of them, what discontents them with you!

HATHORNE: I think they ought to be examined, sir.

DANFORTH: It is not necessarily an attack, I think. Yet –

FRANCIS: These are all covenanted Christians, sir.

DANFORTH: Then I am sure they may have nothing to fear. [*Hands* CHEEVER *the paper.*] Mr Cheever, have warrants drawn for all of these – arrest for examination. [*To* PROCTOR] Now, Mister, what other information do you have for us? [FRANCIS *is still standing, horrified.*] You may sit, Mr Nurse.

FRANCIS: I have brought trouble on these people; I have –

DANFORTH: No, old man, you have not hurt these people if they are of good conscience. But you must understand, sir, that a person is either with this court or he must be counted against it, there be no road between. This is a sharp time, now, a precise time – we live no longer in the dusky afternoon when evil mixed itself with good and befuddled the world. Now, by God's grace, the shining sun is up, and them that fear not light will surely praise it. I hope you will be one of those. [MARY WARREN *suddenly sobs.*] She's not hearty, I see.

PROCTOR: No, she's not, sir. [*To* MARY, *bending to her, holding her hand, quietly*] Now remember what the angel Raphael said to the boy Tobias. Remember it.

MARY WARREN [*hardly audible*]: Aye.

PROCTOR: 'Do that which is good, and no harm shall come to thee.'

MARY WARREN: Aye.

DANFORTH: Come, man, we wait you.

[MARSHAL HERRICK *returns, and takes his post at the door.*]

GILES: John, my deposition, give him mine.

PROCTOR: Aye. [*He hands* DANFORTH *another paper.*] This is Mr Corey's deposition.

DANFORTH: Oh? [*He looks down at it. Now* HATHORNE *comes behind him and reads with him.*]

HATHORNE [*suspiciously*]: What lawyer drew this, Corey?

GILES: You know I never hired a lawyer in my life, Hathorne.

DANFORTH [*finishing the reading*]: It is very well phrased. My compliments. Mr Parris, if Mr Putnam is in the court, will you bring him in? [HATHORNE *takes the deposition, and walks to the window with it.* PARRIS *goes into the court.*] You have no legal training, Mr Corey?

GILES [*very pleased*]: I have the best, sir – I am thirty-three time in court in my life. And always plaintiff, too.

DANFORTH: Oh, then you're much put-upon.

GILES: I am never put-upon; I know my rights, sir, and I will have them. You know, your father tried a case of mine – might be thirty-five year ago, I think.

DANFORTH: Indeed.

GILES: He never spoke to you of it?

DANFORTH: No, I cannot recall it.

GILES: That's strange, he give me nine pound damages. He were a fair judge, your father. Y'see, I had a white mare that time, and this fellow come to borrow the mare – [*Enter* PARRIS *with* THOMAS PUTNAM. *When he sees* PUTNAM, GILES' *ease goes; he is hard.*] Aye, there he is.

DANFORTH: Mr Putnam, I have here an accusation by Mr Corey against you. He states that you coldly prompted your daughter to cry witchery upon George Jacobs that is now in jail.

PUTNAM: It is a lie.

DANFORTH [*turning to* GILES]: Mr Putnam states your charge is a lie. What say you to that?

GILES [*furious, his fists clenched*]: A fart on Thomas Putnam, that is what I say to that!

DANFORTH: What proof do you submit for your charge, sir?

GILES: My proof is there! [*Pointing to the paper.*] If Jacobs hangs for a witch he forfeit up his property – that's law! And there is none but Putnam with the coin to buy so great a piece. This man is killing his neighbours for their land!

DANFORTH: But proof, sir, proof.

GILES [*pointing at his deposition*]: The proof is there! I have it from an honest man who heard Putnam say it! The day his daughter cried out on Jacobs, he said she'd given him a fair gift of land.

HATHORNE: And the name of this man?

GILES [*taken aback*]: What name?

HATHORNE: The man that give you this information.

GILES [*hesitates, then*]: Why, I – I cannot give you his name.

HATHORNE: And why not?

GILES [*hesitates, then bursts out*]: You know well why not! He'll lay in jail if I give his name!

HATHORNE: This is contempt of the court, Mr Danforth!

DANFORTH [*to avoid that*]: You will surely tell us the name.

GILES: I will not give you no name. I mentioned my wife's name once and I'll burn in hell long enough for that. I stand mute.

DANFORTH: In that case, I have no choice but to arrest you for contempt of this court, do you know that?

GILES: This is a hearing; you cannot clap me for contempt of a hearing.

DANFORTH: Oh, it is a proper lawyer! Do you wish me to declare the court in full session here? Or will you give me good reply?

GILES [*faltering*]: I cannot give you no name, sir, I cannot.

DANFORTH: You are a foolish old man. Mr Cheever, begin the record. The court is now in session. I ask you, Mr Corey –

PROCTOR [*breaking in*]: Your Honour – he has the story in confidence, sir, and he –

PARRIS: The Devil lives on such confidences! [*To* DANFORTH] Without confidences there could be no conspiracy, Your Honour!

HATHORNE: I think it must be broken, sir.

DANFORTH [*to* GILES]: Old man, if your informant tells the truth let him come here openly like a decent man. But if he hide in anonymity I must know why. Now sir, the government and central church demand of you the name of him who reported Mr Thomas Putnam a common murderer.

HALE: Excellency –

DANFORTH: Mr Hale.

HALE: We cannot blink it more. There is a prodigious fear of this court in the country –

DANFORTH: Then there is a prodigious guilt in the country. Are *you* afraid to be questioned here?

HALE: I may only fear the Lord, sir, but there is fear in the country nevertheless.

DANFORTH [*angered now*]: Reproach me not with the fear in the country; there is fear in the country because there is a moving plot to topple Christ in the country!

HALE: But it does not follow that everyone accused is part of it.

DANFORTH: No uncorrupted man may fear this court, Mr Hale! None! [*To* GILES] You are under arrest in contempt of this court. Now sit you down and take counsel with yourself, or you will be set in the jail until you decide to answer all questions.

[GILES COREY *makes a rush for* PUTNAM. PROCTOR *lunges and holds him.*]

PROCTOR: No, Giles!

GILES [*over* PROCTOR's *shoulder at* PUTNAM]: I'll cut your throat, Putnam, I'll kill you yet!

PROCTOR [*forcing him into a chair*]: Peace, Giles, peace. [*Releasing him.*] We'll prove ourselves. Now we will. [*He starts to turn to* DANFORTH.]

GILES: Say nothin' more, John. [*Pointing at* DANFORTH] He's only playin' you! He means to hang us all!

[MARY WARREN *bursts into sobs.*]

DANFORTH: This is a court of law, Mister. I'll have no effrontery here!

PROCTOR: Forgive him, sir, for his old age. Peace, Giles, we'll prove it all now. [*He lifts up* MARY's *chin.*] You cannot weep, Mary. Remember the angel, what he say to the boy. Hold to it, now; there is your rock. [MARY *quiets. He takes out a paper, and turns to* DANFORTH.] This is Mary Warren's deposition. I – I would ask you remember, sir, while you read it, that until two week ago she were no different than the other children are today. [*He is speaking reasonably, restraining all his fears, his anger, his anxiety.*] You saw

295

her scream, she howled, she swore familiar spirits choked her; she even testified that Satan, in the form of women now in jail, tried to win her soul away, and then when she refused –

DANFORTH: We know all this.

PROCTOR: Aye, sir. She swears now that she never saw Satan; nor any spirit, vague or clear, that Satan may have sent to hurt her. And she declares her friends are lying now.

[PROCTOR *starts to hand* DANFORTH *the deposition, and* HALE *comes up to* DANFORTH *in a trembling state.*]

HALE: Excellency, a moment. I think this goes to the heart of the matter.

DANFORTH [*with deep misgivings*]: It surely does.

HALE: I cannot say he is an honest man; I know him little. But in all justice, sir, a claim so weighty cannot be argued by a farmer. In God's name, sir, stop here; send him home and let him come again with a lawyer –

DANFORTH [*patiently*]: Now look you, Mr Hale –

HALE: Excellency, I have signed seventy-two death warrants; I am a minister of the Lord, and I dare not take a life without there be a proof so immaculate no slightest qualm of conscience may doubt it.

DANFORTH: Mr Hale, you surely do not doubt my justice.

HALE: I have this morning signed away the soul of Rebecca Nurse, Your Honour. I'll not conceal it, my hand shakes yet as with a wound! I pray you, sir, *this* argument let lawyers present to you.

DANFORTH: Mr Hale, believe me; for a man of such terrible learning you are most bewildered – I hope you will forgive me. I have been thirty-two year at the bar, sir, and I should be confounded were I called upon to defend these people. Let you consider, now – [*To* PROCTOR *and the others*] And I bid you all do likewise. In an ordinary crime, how does one defend the accused? One calls up witnesses to prove his innocence. But witchcraft is *ipso facto*, on its face and by its nature, an invisible crime, is it not? Therefore, who may possibly be witness to it? The witch and the victim. None other. Now we cannot hope the witch will accuse herself; granted? Therefore, we must rely upon her victims – and they do testify, the children certainly do testify. As for the witches, none will deny that we are most eager for all their confessions. Therefore, what is left for a lawyer to bring out? I think I have made my point. Have I not?

HALE: But this child claims the girls are not truthful, and if they are not –

DANFORTH: That is precisely what I am about to consider, sir. What more may you ask of me? Unless you doubt my probity?

HALE [*defeated*]: I surely do not, sir. Let you consider it, then.

DANFORTH: And let you put your heart to rest. Her deposition, Mr Proctor.

[PROCTOR *hands it to him.* HATHORNE *rises, goes beside* DANFORTH, *and starts reading.* PARRIS *comes to his other side.* DANFORTH *looks at* JOHN PROCTOR, *then proceeds to read.* HALE *gets up, finds position near the judge, reads too,* PROCTOR *glances at* GILES. FRANCIS *prays silently, hands pressed together.* CHEEVER *waits placidly, the sublime official, dutiful.* MARY WARREN *sobs once.* JOHN PROCTOR *touches her head reassuringly. Presently* DANFORTH *lifts his eyes, stands up, takes out a kerchief and blows his nose. The others stand aside as he moves in thought toward the window.*]

PARRIS [*hardly able to contain his anger and fear*]: I should like to question –

DANFORTH [*his first real outburst, in which his contempt for* PARRIS *is clear*]: Mr Parris, I bid you be silent! [*He stands in silence, looking out the window. Now, having established that he will set the gait*] Mr Cheever, will you go into the court and bring the children here? [CHEEVER *gets up and goes out upstage.* DANFORTH *now turns to* MARY.] Mary Warren, how came you to this turnabout? Has Mr Proctor threatened you for this deposition?

MARY WARREN: No, sir.

DANFORTH: Has he ever threatened you?

MARY WARREN [*weaker*]: No, sir.

DANFORTH [*sensing a weakening*]: Has he threatened you?

MARY WARREN: No, sir.

DANFORTH: Then you tell me that you sat in my court, callously lying, when you knew that people would hang by your evidence? [*She does not answer.*] Answer me!

MARY WARREN [*almost inaudibly*]: I did, sir.

DANFORTH: How were you instructed in your life? Do you not know that God damns all liars? [*She cannot speak.*] Or is it now that you lie?

MARY WARREN: No, sir – I am with God now.

DANFORTH: You are with God now.

MARY WARREN: Aye, sir.

DANFORTH [*containing himself*]: I will tell you this – you are either lying now, or you were lying in the court, and in either case you have committed perjury and you will go to jail for it. You cannot lightly say you lied, Mary. Do you know that?

MARY WARREN: I cannot lie no more. I am with God, I am with God.

[*But she breaks into sobs at the thought of it, and the right door opens, and enter* SUSANNA WALCOTT, MERCY LEWIS, BETTY PARRIS, *and finally* ABIGAIL. CHEEVER *comes to* DANFORTH.]

CHEEVER: Ruth Putnam's not in the court, sir, nor the other children.

DANFORTH: These will be sufficient. Sit you down, children. [*Silently they sit.*] Your friend, Mary Warren, has given us a deposition. In which she swears that she never saw familiar spirits, apparitions, nor any manifest of the Devil. She claims as well that none of you have seen these things either. [*Slight pause.*] Now, children, this is a court of law. The law, based upon the Bible, and the Bible, writ by Almighty God, forbid the practice of witchcraft, and describe death as the penalty thereof. But likewise, children, the law and Bible damn all bearers of false witness. [*Slight pause.*] Now then. It does not escape me that this deposition may be devised to blind us; it may well be that Mary Warren has been conquered by Satan, who sends her here to distract our sacred purpose. If so, her neck will break for it. But if she speak true, I bid you now drop your guile and confess your pretence, for a quick confession will go easier with you. [*Pause.*] Abigail Williams, rise. [ABIGAIL *slowly rises.*] Is there any truth in this?

ABIGAIL: No, sir.

DANFORTH [*thinks, glances at* MARY, *then back to* ABIGAIL]: Children, a very augur bit will now be turned into your souls until your honesty is proved. Will either of you change your positions now, or do you force me to hard questioning?

ABIGAIL: I have naught to change, sir. She lies.

DANFORTH [*to* MARY]: You would still go on with this?

MARY WARREN [*faintly*]: Aye, sir.

DANFORTH [*turning to* ABIGAIL]: A poppet were discovered in Mr Proctor's house, stabbed by a needle. Mary Warren claims that you sat beside her in the court when she made it, and that you saw her make it and witnessed how she herself stuck her needle into it for safe-keeping. What say you to that?

ABIGAIL [*with a slight note of indignation*]: It is a lie, sir.

DANFORTH [*after a slight pause*]: While you worked for Mr Proctor, did you see poppets in that house?

ABIGAIL: Goody Proctor always kept poppets.

PROCTOR: Your Honour, my wife never kept no poppets. Mary Warren confesses it was her poppet.

CHEEVER: Your Excellency.

DANFORTH: Mr Cheever.

CHEEVER: When I spoke with Goody Proctor in that house, she said she never kept no poppets. But she said she did keep poppets when she were a girl.

PROCTOR: She has not been a girl these fifteen years, Your Honour.

HATHORNE: But a poppet will keep fifteen years, will it not?

PROCTOR: It will keep if it is kept, but Mary Warren swears she never saw no poppets in my house, nor anyone else.

PARRIS: Why could there not have been poppets hid where no one ever saw them?

PROCTOR [*furious*]: There might also be a dragon with five legs in my house, but no one has ever seen it.

PARRIS: We are here, Your Honour, precisely to discover what no one has ever seen.

PROCTOR: Mr Danforth, what profit this girl to turn herself about? What may Mary Warren gain but hard questioning and worse?

DANFORTH: You are charging Abigail Williams with a marvellous cool plot to murder, do you understand that?

PROCTOR: I do, sir. I believe she means to murder.

DANFORTH [*pointing at* ABIGAIL, *incredulously*]: This child would murder your wife?

PROCTOR: It is not a child. Now hear me, sir. In the sight of the congregation she were twice this year put out of this meetin' house for laughter during prayer.

DANFORTH [*shocked, turning to* ABIGAIL]: What's this? Laughter during – !

PARRIS: Excellency, she were under Tituba's power at that time, but she is solemn now.

GILES: Aye, now she is solemn and goes to hang people!

DANFORTH: Quiet, man.

HATHORNE: Surely it have no bearing on the question, sir. He charges contemplation of murder.

DANFORTH: Aye. [*He studies* ABIGAIL *for a moment, then*] Continue, Mr Proctor.

PROCTOR: Mary. Now tell the Governor how you danced in the woods.

PARRIS [*instantly*]: Excellency, since I come to Salem this man is blackening my name. He –

DANFORTH: In a moment, sir. [*To* MARY WARREN, *sternly, and surprised*] What is this dancing?

MARY WARREN: I – [*She glances at* ABIGAIL, *who is staring down at her remorselessly. Then, appealing to* PROCTOR] Mr Proctor –

PROCTOR [*taking it right up*]: Abigail leads the girls to the woods, Your Honour, and they have danced there naked –

PARRIS: Your Honour, this –

PROCTOR [*at once*]: Mr Parris discovered them himself in the dead of night! There's the 'child' she is!

DANFORTH [*it is growing into a nightmare, and he turns, astonished, to* PARRIS]: Mr Parris –

PARRIS: I can only say, sir, that I never found any of them naked, and this man is –

DANFORTH: But you discovered them dancing in the woods? [*Eyes on* PARRIS, *he points at* ABIGAIL] Abigail?

HALE: Excellency, when I first arrived from Beverly, Mr Parris told me that.

DANFORTH: Do you deny it, Mr Parris?

PARRIS: I do not, sir, but I never saw any of them naked.

DANFORTH: But she have *danced*?

PARRIS [*unwillingly*]: Aye, sir.

[DANFORTH, *as though with new eyes, looks at* ABIGAIL.]

HATHORNE: Excellency, will you permit me? [*He points at* MARY WARREN.]

DANFORTH [*with great worry*]: Pray, proceed.

HATHORNE: You say you never saw no spirits, Mary, were never threatened or afflicted by any manifest of the Devil or the Devil's agents.

MARY WARREN [*very faintly*]: No, sir.

HATHORNE [*with a gleam of victory*]: And yet, when people accused of witchery confronted you in court, you would faint, saying their spirits came out of their bodies and choked you –

MARY WARREN: That were pretence, sir.

DANFORTH: I cannot hear you.

MARY WARREN: Pretence, sir.

PARRIS: But you did turn cold, did you not? I myself picked you up many times, and your skin were icy. Mr Danforth, you –

DANFORTH: I saw that many times.

PROCTOR: She only pretended to faint, Your Excellency. They're all marvellous pretenders.

HATHORNE: Then can she pretend to faint now?

PROCTOR: Now?

PARRIS: Why not? Now there are no spirits attacking her, for none in this room is accused of witchcraft. So let her turn herself cold now, let her pretend she is attacked now, let her faint. [*He turns to* MARY WARREN] Faint!

MARY WARREN: Faint?

PARRIS: Aye, faint. Prove to us how you pretended in the court so many times.

MARY WARREN [*looking to* PROCTOR]: I – cannot faint now, sir.

PROCTOR [*alarmed, quietly*]: Can you not pretend it?

MARY WARREN: I – [*She looks about as though searching for the passion to faint.*] I – have no *sense* of it now, I –

DANFORTH: Why? What is lacking now?

MARY WARREN: I – cannot tell, sir, I –

DANFORTH: Might it be that here we have no afflicting spirit loose, but in the court there were some?

MARY WARREN: I never saw no spirits.

PARRIS: Then see no spirits now, and prove to us that you can faint by your own will, as you claim.

MARY WARREN [*stares, searching for the emotion of it, and then shakes her head*]: I – cannot do it.

PARRIS: Then you will confess, will you not? It were attacking spirits made you faint!

MARY WARREN: No, sir, I –

PARRIS: Your Excellency, this is a trick to blind the court!

MARY WARREN: It's not a trick! [*She stands.*] I – I used to faint because I – I thought I saw spirits.

DANFORTH: *Thought* you saw them!

MARY WARREN: But I did not, Your Honour.

HATHORNE: How could you think you saw them unless you saw them?

MARY WARREN: I – I cannot tell how, but I did. I – I heard the other girls screaming, and you, Your Honour, you seemed to believe them, and I – It were only sport in the beginning, sir, but then the whole world cried spirits, spirits, and I – I promise you, Mr Danforth, I only thought I saw them but I did not.

[DANFORTH *peers at her.*]

PARRIS [*smiling, but nervous because* DANFORTH *seems to be struck by* MARY WARREN's *story*]: Surely Your Excellency is not taken by this simple lie.

DANFORTH [*turning worriedly to* ABIGAIL]: Abigail. I bid you now search your heart and tell me this – and beware of it, child, to God every soul is precious and His vengeance is terrible on them that take life without cause. Is it possible, child, that the spirits you have seen are illusion only, some deception that may cross your mind when –

ABIGAIL: Why, this – this – is a base question, sir.

DANFORTH: Child, I would have you consider it –

ABIGAIL: I have been hurt, Mr Danforth; I have seen my blood runnin' out! I have been near to murdered every day because I done my duty pointing out the Devil's people – and this is my reward? To be mistrusted, denied, questioned like a –

DANFORTH [*weakening*]: Child, I do not mistrust you –

ABIGAIL [*in an open threat*]: Let you beware, Mr Danforth. Think you to be so mighty that the power of Hell may not turn your wits? Beware of it! There is – [*Suddenly, from an accusatory attitude, her face turns, looking into the air above – it is truly frightened.*]

DANFORTH [*apprehensively*]: What is it, child?

ABIGAIL [*looking about in the air, clasping her arms about her as though cold*]: I – I know not. A wind, a cold wind, has come. [*Her eyes fall on* MARY WARREN.]

MARY WARREN [*terrified, pleading*]: Abby!

MERCY LEWIS [*shivering*]: Your Honour, I freeze!

PROCTOR: They're pretending!

HATHORNE [*touching* ABIGAIL's *hand*]: She is cold, Your Honour, touch her!

MERCY LEWIS [*through chattering teeth*]: Mary, do you send this shadow on me?

MARY WARREN: Lord, save me!

SUSANNA WALCOTT: I freeze, I freeze!

ABIGAIL [*shivering visibly*]: It is a wind, a wind!

MARY WARREN: Abby, don't do that!

DANFORTH [*himself engaged and entered by* ABIGAIL]: Mary Warren, do you witch her? I say to you, do you send your spirit out?

[*With a hysterical cry* MARY WARREN *starts to run.* PROCTOR *catches her.*]

MARY WARREN [*almost collapsing*]: Let me go, Mr Proctor. I cannot, I cannot –

ABIGAIL [*crying to Heaven*]: Oh, Heavenly Father, take away this shadow!

[*Without warning or hesitation,* PROCTOR *leaps at* ABIGAIL *and, grabbing her by the hair, pulls her to her feet. She screams in pain.* DANFORTH, *astonished, cries, 'What are you about?' and* HATHORNE *and* PARRIS *call, 'Take your hands off her!' and out of it all comes* PROCTOR's *roaring voice.*]

PROCTOR: How do you call Heaven! Whore! Whore!

[HERRICK *breaks* PROCTOR *from her.*]

HERRICK: John!

DANFORTH: Man! Man, what do you –

PROCTOR [*breathless and in agony*]: It is a whore!

DANFORTH [*dumbfounded*]: You charge – ?

ABIGAIL: Mr Danforth, he is lying!

PROCTOR: Mark her! Now she'll suck a scream to stab me with but –

DANFORTH: You will prove this! This will not pass!

PROCTOR [*trembling, his life collapsing about him*]: I have known her, sir. I have known her.

DANFORTH: You – you are a lecher?

FRANCIS [*horrified*]: John, you cannot say such a –

PROCTOR: Oh, Francis, I wish you had some evil in you that you might know me! [*To* DANFORTH] A man will not cast away his good name. You surely know that.

DANFORTH [*dumbfounded*]: In – in what time? In what place?

PROCTOR [*his voice about to break, and his shame great*]: In the proper place – where my beasts are bedded. On the last night of my joy, some eight months past. She used to serve me in my house, sir. [*He has to clamp his jaw to keep from weeping.*] A man may think God sleeps, but God sees everything, I know it now. I beg you, sir, I beg you – see her what she is. My wife, my dear good wife, took this girl soon after, sir, and put her out on the highroad. And being what she is, a lump of vanity, sir – [*He is being overcome.*] Excellency, forgive me, forgive me. [*Angrily against himself, he turns away from the Governor for a moment. Then, as though to cry out is his only means of speech left*] She thinks to dance with me on my wife's grave! And well she might, for I thought of her softly. God help me, I lusted, and there *is* a promise in such sweat. But it is a whore's vengeance, and you must see it; I set myself entirely in your hands. I know you must see it now.

DANFORTH [*blanched, in horror, turning to* ABIGAIL]: You deny every scrap and tittle of this?

ABIGAIL: If I must answer that, I will leave and I will not come back again!

[DANFORTH *seems unsteady.*]

PROCTOR: I have made a bell of my honour! I have rung the doom of my good name – you will believe me, Mr Danforth! My wife is innocent, except she knew a whore when she saw one!

ABIGAIL [*stepping up to* DANFORTH]: What look do you give me? [DANFORTH *cannot speak.*] I'll not have such looks! [*She turns and starts for the door.*]

DANFORTH: You will remain where you are! [HERRICK *steps into her path. She comes up short, fire in her eyes.*] Mr Parris, go into the court and bring Goodwife Proctor out.

PARRIS [*objecting*]: Your Honour, this is all a –

DANFORTH [*sharply to* PARRIS]: Bring her out! And tell her not one word of what's been spoken here. And let you knock before you enter. [PARRIS *goes out.*] Now we shall touch the bottom of this swamp. [*To* PROCTOR] Your wife, you say, is an honest woman.

PROCTOR: In her life, sir, she have never lied. There are them that cannot sing, and them that cannot weep – my wife cannot lie. I have paid much to learn it, sir.

DANFORTH: And when she put this girl out of your house, she put her out for a harlot?

PROCTOR: Aye, sir.

DANFORTH: And knew her for a harlot?

PROCTOR: Aye, sir, she knew her for a harlot.

DANFORTH: Good, then. [*To* ABIGAIL] And if she tell me, child, it were for harlotry, may God spread His mercy on you! [*There is a knock. He calls to the door*] Hold! [*To* ABIGAIL] Turn your back. Turn your back. [*To* PROCTOR] Do likewise. [*Both turn their backs –* ABIGAIL *with indignant slowness.*] Now let neither of you turn to face Goody Proctor. No one in this room is to speak one word, or raise a gesture aye or nay. [*He turns toward the door, calls*] Enter! [*The door opens.* ELIZABETH *enters with* PARRIS. PARRIS *leaves her. She stands alone, her eyes looking for* PROCTOR.] Mr Cheever, report this testimony in all exactness. Are you ready?

CHEEVER: Ready, sir.

DANFORTH: Come here, woman. [ELIZABETH *comes to him, glancing at* PROCTOR'S *back.*] Look at me only, not at your husband. In my eyes only.

ELIZABETH [*faintly*]: Good, sir.

DANFORTH: We are given to understand that at one time you dismissed your servant, Abigail Williams.

ELIZABETH: That is true, sir.

DANFORTH: For what cause did you dismiss her? [*Slight pause. Then* ELIZABETH *tries to glance at* PROCTOR.] You will look in my eyes only and not at your husband. The answer is in your memory and you need no help to give it to me. Why did you dismiss Abigail Williams?

ELIZABETH [*not knowing what to say, sensing a situation, wetting her lips to stall for time*]: She – dissatisfied me. [*Pause.*] And my husband.

DANFORTH: In what way dissatisfied you?

ELIZABETH: She were – [*She glances at* PROCTOR *for a cue.*]

DANFORTH: Woman, look at me! [ELIZABETH *does.*] Were she slovenly? Lazy? What disturbance did she cause?

ELIZABETH: Your Honour, I – in that time I were sick. And I – My husband is a good and righteous man. He is never drunk as some are, nor wastin' his time at the shovelboard, but always at his work. But in my sickness – you see, sir, I were a long time sick after my last baby, and I thought I saw my husband somewhat turning from me. And this girl – [*She turns to* ABIGAIL.]

DANFORTH: Look at me.

ELIZABETH: Aye, sir. Abigail Williams – [*She breaks off.*]

DANFORTH: What of Abigail Williams?

ELIZABETH: I came to think he fancied her. And so one night I lost my wits, I think, and put her out on the highroad.

DANFORTH: Your husband – did he indeed turn from you?

ELIZABETH [*in agony*]: My husband – is a goodly man, sir.

DANFORTH: Then he did not turn from you.

ELIZABETH [*starting to glance at* PROCTOR]: He –

DANFORTH [*reaches out and holds her face, then*]: Look at me! To your own knowledge, has John Proctor even committed the crime of lechery? [*In a crisis of indecision she cannot speak.*] Answer my question! Is your husband a lecher!

ELIZABETH [*faintly*]: No, sir.

DANFORTH: Remove her, Marshal.

PROCTOR: Elizabeth, tell the truth!

DANFORTH: She has spoken. Remove her!

PROCTOR [*crying out*]: Elizabeth, I have confessed it!

ELIZABETH: Oh, God! [*The door closes behind her.*]

PROCTOR: She only thought to save my name!

HALE: Excellency, it is a natural lie to tell; I beg you, stop now before another is condemned! I may shut my conscience to it no more – private vengeance is working through this testimony! From the beginning this man has struck me true. By my oath to

Heaven, I believe him now, and I pray you call back his wife before we –

DANFORTH: She spoke nothing of lechery, and this man has lied!

HALE: I believe him! [*Pointing at* ABIGAIL] This girl has always struck me false! She has –

[ABIGAIL, *with a weird, wild, chilling cry, screams up to the ceiling.*]

ABIGAIL: You will not! Begone! Begone, I say!

DANFORTH: What is it, child? [*But* ABIGAIL, *pointing with fear, is now raising up her frightened eyes, her awed face, toward the ceiling – the girls are doing the same – and now* HATHORNE, HALE, PUTNAM, CHEEVER, HERRICK, *and* DANFORTH *do the same.*] What's there? [*He lowers his eyes from the ceiling, and now he is frightened; there is real tension in his voice.*] Child! [*She is transfixed – with all the girls, she is whimpering open-mouthed, agape at the ceiling.*] Girls! Why do you – ?

MERCY LEWIS [*pointing*]: It's on the beam! Behind the rafter!

DANFORTH [*looking up*]: Where!

ABIGAIL: Why – ? [*She gulps.*] Why do you come, yellow bird?

PROCTOR: Where's a bird? I see no bird!

ABIGAIL [*to the ceiling*]: My face? My face?

PROCTOR: Mr Hale –

DANFORTH: Be quiet!

PROCTOR [*to* HALE]: Do you see a bird?

DANFORTH: Be quiet!!

ABIGAIL [*to the ceiling, in a genuine conversation with the 'bird', as though trying to talk it out of attacking her*]: But God made my face; you cannot want to tear my face. Envy is a deadly sin, Mary.

MARY WARREN [*on her feet with a spring, and horrified, pleading*]: Abby!

ABIGAIL [*unperturbed, continuing to the 'bird'*]: Oh, Mary, this is a black art to change your shape. No, I cannot, I cannot stop my mouth; it's God's work I do.

MARY WARREN: Abby, I'm *here*!

PROCTOR [*frantically*]: They're pretending, Mr Danforth!

ABIGAIL [*now she takes a backward step, as though in fear the bird will swoop down momentarily*]: Oh, please, Mary! Don't come down.

SUSANNA WALCOTT: Her claws, she's stretching her claws!

PROCTOR: Lies, lies.

ABIGAIL [*backing farther, eyes still fixed above*]: Mary, please don't hurt me!

MARY WARREN [*to* DANFORTH]: I'm not hurting her!

DANFORTH [*to* MARY WARREN]: Why does she see this vision?

MARY WARREN: She sees nothin'!

ABIGAIL [*now staring full front as though hypnotized, and mimicking the exact tone of* MARY WARREN's *cry*]: She sees nothin'!

MARY WARREN [*pleading*]: Abby, you mustn't!

ABIGAIL AND ALL THE GIRLS [*all transfixed*]: Abby, you mustn't!

MARY WARREN [*to all the girls*]: I'm here, I'm here!

GIRLS: I'm here, I'm here!

DANFORTH [*horrified*]: Mary Warren! Draw back your spirit out of them!

MARY WARREN: Mr Danforth!

GIRLS [*cutting her off*]: Mr Danforth!

DANFORTH: Have you compacted with the Devil? Have you?

MARY WARREN: Never, never!

GIRLS: Never, never!

DANFORTH [*growing hysterical*]: Why can they only repeat you?

PROCTOR: Give me a whip – I'll stop it!

MARY WARREN: They're sporting. They – !

GIRLS: They're sporting!

MARY WARREN [*turning on them all hysterically and stamping her feet*]: Abby, stop it!

GIRLS [*stamping their feet*]: Abby, stop it!

MARY WARREN: Stop it!

GIRLS: Stop it!

MARY WARREN [*screaming it out at the top of her lungs, and raising her fists*]: Stop it!!

GIRLS [*raising their fists*]: Stop it!!

[MARY WARREN, *utterly confounded, and becoming overwhelmed by* ABIGAIL*'s – and the girls' – utter conviction, starts to whimper, hands half raised, powerless, and all the girls begin whimpering exactly as she does.*]

DANFORTH: A little while ago you were afflicted. Now it seems you afflict others; where did you find this power?

MARY WARREN [*staring at* ABIGAIL]: I – have no power.

GIRLS: I have no power.

PROCTOR: They're gulling you, Mister!

DANFORTH: Why did you turn about this past two weeks? You have seen the Devil, have you not?

HALE [*indicating* ABIGAIL *and the girls*]: You cannot believe them!

MARY WARREN: I –

PROCTOR [*sensing her weakening*]: Mary, God damns all liars!

DANFORTH [*pounding it into her*]: You have seen the Devil, you have made compact with Lucifer, have you not?

PROCTOR: God damns liars, Mary!

[MARY *utters something unintelligible, staring at* ABIGAIL, *who keeps watching the 'bird' above.*]

DANFORTH: I cannot hear you. What do you say? [MARY *utters again unintelligibly.*] You will confess yourself or you will hang! [*He turns her roughly to face him.*] Do you know who I am? I say you will hang if you do not open with me!

PROCTOR: Mary, remember the angel Raphael – do that which is good and –

ABIGAIL [*pointing upward*]: The wings! Her wings are spreading! Mary, please, don't, don't – !

HALE: I see nothing, Your Honour!

DANFORTH: Do you confess this power! [*He is an inch from her face.*] Speak!

ABIGAIL: She's going to come down! She's walking the beam!

DANFORTH: Will you speak!

MARY WARREN [*staring in horror*]: I cannot!

GIRLS: I cannot!

PARRIS: Cast the Devil out! Look him in the face! Trample him! We'll save you, Mary, only stand fast against him and –

ABIGAIL [*looking up*]: Look out! She's coming down!

[*She and all the girls run to one wall, shielding their eyes. And now, as though cornered, they let out a gigantic scream, and* MARY, *as though infected, opens her mouth and screams with them. Gradually* ABIGAIL *and the girls leave off, until only* MARY *is left there, staring up at the 'bird', screaming madly. All watch her, horrified by this evident fit.* PROCTOR *strides to her.*]

PROCTOR: Mary, tell the Governor what they – [*He has hardly got a word out, when, seeing him coming for her, she rushes out of his reach, screaming in horror.*]

MARY WARREN: Don't touch me – don't touch me! [*At which the girls halt at the door.*]

PROCTOR [*astonished*]: Mary!

MARY WARREN [*pointing at* PROCTOR]: You're the Devil's man!

[*He is stopped in his tracks.*]

PARRIS: Praise God!

GIRLS: Praise God!

PROCTOR [*numbed*]: Mary, how – ?

MARY WARREN: I'll not hang with you! I love God, I love God.

DANFORTH [*to* MARY]: He bid you do the Devil's work?

MARY WARREN [*hysterically, indicating* PROCTOR]: He come at me by night and every day to sign, to sign, to –

DANFORTH: Sign what?

PARRIS: The Devil's book? He come with a book?

MARY WARREN [*hysterically, pointing at* PROCTOR, *fearful of him*]: My name, he want my name. 'I'll murder you', he says, 'if my wife hangs! We must go and overthrow the court,' he says!

[DANFORTH's *head jerks toward* PROCTOR, *shock and horror in his face.*]

PROCTOR [*turning, appealing to* HALE]: Mr Hale!

MARY WARREN [*her sobs beginning*]: He wake me every night, his eyes were like coals and his fingers claw my neck, and I sign, I sign . . .

HALE: Excellency, this child's gone wild!

PROCTOR [*as* DANFORTH's *wide eyes pour on him*]: Mary, Mary!

MARY WARREN [*screaming at him*]: No, I love God; I go your way no more. I love God, I bless God. [*Sobbing, she rushes to* ABIGAIL.] Abby, Abby, I'll never hurt you more!

[*They all watch, as* ABIGAIL, *out of her infinite charity, reaches out and draws the sobbing* MARY *to her, and then looks up to* DANFORTH.]

DANFORTH [*to* PROCTOR]: What are you? [PROCTOR *is beyond speech in his anger.*] You are combined with anti-Christ, are you not? I have seen your power; you will not deny it! What say you, Mister?

HALE: Excellency –

DANFORTH: I will have nothing from you, Mr Hale! [*To* PROCTOR] Will you confess yourself befouled with Hell, or do you keep that black allegiance yet? What say you?

PROCTOR [*his mind wild, breathless*]: I say – I say – God is dead!

PARRIS: Hear it, hear it!

PROCTOR [*laughs insanely, then*]: A fire, a fire is burning! I hear the boot of Lucifer, I see his filthy face! And it is my face, and yours, Danforth! For them that quail to bring men out of ignorance, as I have quailed, and as you quail now when you know in all your black hearts that this be fraud – God damns our kind especially, and we will burn, we will burn together!

DANFORTH: Marshal! Take him and Corey with him to the jail!

HALE [*starting across to the door*]: I denounce these proceedings!

PROCTOR: You are pulling Heaven down and raising up a whore!

HALE: I denounce these proceedings, I quit this court! [*He slams the door to the outside behind him.*]

DANFORTH [*calling to him in a fury*]: Mr Hale! Mr Hale!

THE CURTAIN FALLS

Act Four

A cell in Salem jail, that fall.

   At the back is a high barred window; near it, a great, heavy door.
Along the walls are two benches.

   The place is in darkness but for the moonlight seeping through the
bars. It appears empty. Presently footsteps are heard coming down a corridor beyond the wall, keys rattle, and the door swings open. MARSHAL
HERRICK enters with a lantern.

   He is nearly drunk, and heavy-footed. He goes to a bench and nudges
a bundle of rags lying on it.

HERRICK: Sarah, wake up! Sarah Good! [He then crosses to the other
   bench.]
SARAH GOOD [rising in her rags]: Oh, Majesty! Comin', comin'!
   Tituba, he's here, His Majesty's come!
HERRICK: Go to the north cell; this place is wanted now. [He hangs
   his lantern on the wall. TITUBA sits up.]
TITUBA: That don't look to me like His Majesty; look to me like the
   marshal.
HERRICK [taking out a flask]: Get along with you now, clear this
   place. [He drinks, and SARAH GOOD comes and peers up into his face.]
SARAH GOOD: Oh, is it you, Marshal! I thought sure you be the Devil
   comin' for us. Could I have a sip of cider for me goin'-away?
HERRICK [handing her the flask]: And where are you off to, Sarah?
TITUBA [as SARAH drinks]: We goin' to Barbados, soon the Devil gits
   here with the feathers and the wings.
HERRICK: Oh? A happy voyage to you.
SARAH GOOD: A pair of bluebirds wingin' southerly, the two of us!
   Oh, it be a grand transformation, Marshal! [She raises the flask to
   drink again.]

HERRICK [*taking the flask from her lips*]: You'd best give me that or you'll never rise off the ground. Come along now.

TITUBA: I'll speak to him for you, if you desires to come along, Marshal.

HERRICK: I'd not refuse it, Tituba; it's the proper morning to fly into Hell.

TITUBA: Oh, it be no Hell in Barbados. Devil, him be pleasure-man in Barbados, him be singin' and dancin' in Barbados. It's you folks – you riles him up 'round here; it be too cold 'round here for that Old Boy. He freeze his soul in Massachusetts, but in Barbados he just as sweet and – [*A bellowing cow is heard, and* TITUBA *leaps us and calls to the window*] Aye, sir! That's him, Sarah!

SARAH GOOD: I'm here, Majesty! [*They hurriedly pick up their rags as* HOPKINS, *a guard, enters.*]

HOPKINS: The Deputy Governor's arrived.

HERRICK [*grabbing* TITUBA]: Come along, come along.

TITUBA [*resisting him*]: No, he comin' for me. I goin' home!

HERRICK [*pulling her to the door*]: That's not Satan, just a poor old cow with a hatful of milk. Come along now, out with you!

TITUBA [*calling to the window*]: Take me home, Devil! Take me home!

SARAH GOOD [*following the shouting* TITUBA *out*]: Tell him I'm goin', Tituba! Now you tell him Sarah Good is goin' too!

[*In the corridor outside* TITUBA *calls on –* 'Take me home, Devil; Devil take me home!' *and* HOPKINS's *voice orders her to move on.* HERRICK *returns and begins to push old rags and straw into a corner. Hearing footsteps, he turns, and enter* DANFORTH *and* JUDGE HATHORNE. *They are in greatcoats and wear hats against the bitter cold. They are followed in by* CHEEVER, *who carries a dispatch case and a flat wooden box containing his writing materials.*]

HERRICK: Good morning, Excellency.

DANFORTH: Where is Mr Parris?

HERRICK: I'll fetch him. [*He starts for the door.*]

DANFORTH: Marshal. [*Herrick stops.*] When did Reverend Hale arrive?

HERRICK: It were toward midnight, I think.

DANFORTH [*suspiciously*]: What is he about here?

HERRICK: He goes among them that will hang, sir. And he prays with them. He sits with Goody Nurse now. And Mr Parris with him.

DANFORTH: Indeed. That man have no authority to enter here, Marshal. Why have you let him in?

HERRICK: Why, Mr Parris command me, sir. I cannot deny him.

DANFORTH: Are you drunk, Marshal?

HERRICK: No, sir; it is a bitter night, and I have no fire here.

DANFORTH [*containing his anger*]: Fetch Mr Parris.

HERRICK: Aye, sir.

DANFORTH: There is a prodigious stench in this place.

HERRICK: I have only now cleared the people out for you.

DANFORTH: Beware hard drink, Marshal.

HERRICK: Aye, sir. [*He waits an instant for further orders. But* DANFORTH, *in dissatisfaction, turns his back on him, and* HERRICK *goes out. There is a pause.* DANFORTH *stands in thought.*]

HATHORNE: Let you question Hale, Excellency; I should not be surprised he have been preaching in Andover lately.

DANFORTH: We'll come to that; speak nothing of Andover. Parris prays with him. That's strange. [*He blows on his hands, moves toward the window, and looks out.*]

HATHORNE: Excellency, I wonder if it be wise to let Mr Parris so continuously with the prisoners. [DANFORTH *turns to him, interested.*] I think, sometimes, the man has a mad look these days.

DANFORTH: Mad?

HATHORNE: I met him yesterday coming out of his house, and I bid him good morning – and he wept and went his way. I think it is not well the village sees him so unsteady.

DANFORTH: Perhaps he have some sorrow.

CHEEVER [*stamping his feet against the cold*]: I think it be the cows, sir.

DANFORTH: Cows?

CHEEVER: There be so many cows wanderin' the highroads, now their masters are in the jails, and much disagreement who they will belong to now. I know Mr Parris be arguin' with farmers all yesterday – there is great contention, sir, about the cows. Contention make him weep, sir; it were always a man that weep for contention. [*He turns, as do* HATHORNE *and* DANFORTH, *hearing someone coming up the corridor.* DANFORTH *raises his head as* PARRIS *enters. He is gaunt, frightened, and sweating in his greatcoat.*]

PARRIS [*to* DANFORTH, *instantly*]: Oh, good morning, sir, thank you for coming, I beg your pardon wakin' you so early. Good morning, Judge Hathorne.

DANFORTH: Reverend Hale have no right to enter this –

PARRIS: Excellency, a moment. [*He hurries back and shuts the door.*]

HATHORNE: Do you leave him alone with the prisoners?

DANFORTH: What's his business here?

PARRIS [*prayerfully holding up his hands*]: Excellency, hear me. It is a providence. Reverend Hale has returned to bring Rebecca Nurse to God.

DANFORTH [*surprised*]: He bids her confess?

PARRIS [*sitting*]: Hear me. Rebecca have not given me a word this three month since she came. Now she sits with him, and her sister and Martha Corey and two or three others, and he pleads with them, confess their crimes and save their lives.

DANFORTH: Why – this is indeed a providence. And they soften, they soften?

PARRIS: Not yet, not yet. But I thought to summon you, sir, that we might think on whether it be not wise, to – [*He dares not say it.*] I had thought to put a question, sir, and I hope you will not –

DANFORTH: Mr Parris, be plain, what troubles you?

PARRIS: There is news, sir, that the court – the court must reckon with. My niece, sir, my niece – I believe she has vanished.

DANFORTH: Vanished!

PARRIS: I had thought to advise you of it earlier in the week, but –

DANFORTH: Why? How long is she gone?

PARRIS: This be the third night. You see, sir, she told me she would stay a night with Mercy Lewis. And next day, when she does not return, I send to Mr Lewis to inquire. Mercy told him she would sleep in *my* house for a night.

DANFORTH: They are both gone?!

PARRIS [*in fear of him*]: They are, sir.

DANFORTH [*alarmed*]: I will send a party for them. Where may they be?

PARRIS: Excellency, I think they be aboard a ship. [DANFORTH *stands agape.*] My daughter tells me how she heard them speaking of ships last week, and tonight I discover my – my strongbox is broke into. [*He presses his fingers against his eyes to keep back tears.*]

HATHORNE [*astonished*]: She have robbed you?

PARRIS: Thirty-one pound is gone. I am penniless. [*He covers his face and sobs.*]

DANFORTH: Mr Parris, you are a brainless man! [*He walks in thought, deeply worried.*]

PARRIS: Excellency, it profit nothing you should blame me. I cannot think they would run off except they fear to keep in Salem any more. [*He is pleading.*] Mark it, sir, Abigail had close knowledge of the town, and since the news of Andover has broken here –

DANFORTH: Andover is remedied. The court returns there on Friday, and will resume examinations.

PARRIS: I am sure of it, sir. But the rumour here speaks rebellion in Andover, and it –

DANFORTH: There is no rebellion in Andover!

PARRIS: I tell you what is said here, sir. Andover have thrown out the court, they say, and will have no part of witchcraft. There be a faction here, feeding on that news, and I tell you true, sir, I fear there will be riot here.

HATHORNE: Riot! Why at every execution I have seen naught but high satisfaction in the town.

PARRIS: Judge Hathorne – it were another sort that hanged till now. Rebecca Nurse is no Bridget that lived three year with Bishop before she married him. John Proctor is not Isaac Ward that drank his family to ruin. [*To* DANFORTH] I would to God it were not so, Excellency, but these people have great weight yet in the town. Let Rebecca stand upon the gibbet and send up some right-eous prayer, and I fear she'll wake a vengeance on you.

HATHORNE: Excellency, she is condemned a witch. The court have –

DANFORTH [*in deep concern, raising a hand to* HATHORNE]: Pray you. [*To* PARRIS] How do you propose, then?

PARRIS: Excellency, I would postpone these hangin's for a time.

DANFORTH: There will be no postponement.

PARRIS: Now Mr Hale's returned, there is hope, I think – for if he bring even one of these to God, that confession surely damns the others in the public eye, and none may doubt more that they are all linked to Hell. This way, unconfessed and claiming inno-cence, doubts are multiplied, many honest people will weep for them, and our good purpose is lost in their tears.

DANFORTH [*after thinking a moment, then going to* CHEEVER]: Give me the list.

[CHEEVER *opens the dispatch case, searches.*]

PARRIS: It cannot be forgot, sir, that when I summoned the congre-gation for John Proctor's excommunication there were hardly thirty people come to hear it. That speak a discontent, I think, and –

DANFORTH [*studying the list*]: There will be no postponement.

PARRIS: Excellency –

DANFORTH: Now, sir – which of these in your opinion may be brought to God? I will myself strive with him till dawn. [*He hands the list to* PARRIS, *who merely glances at it.*]

PARRIS: There is not sufficient time till dawn.

DANFORTH: I shall do my utmost. Which of them do you have hope for?

PARRIS [*not even glancing at the list now, and in a quavering voice, quietly*]: Excellency – a dagger – [*He chokes up.*]

DANFORTH: What do you say?

PARRIS: Tonight, when I open my door to leave my house – a dagger clattered to the ground. [*Silence.* DANFORTH *absorbs this. Now* PARRIS *cries out.*] You cannot hang this sort. There is danger for me. I dare not step outside at night!

[REVEREND HALE *enters. They look at him for an instant in silence. He is steeped in sorrow, exhausted, and more direct than he ever was.*]

DANFORTH: Accept my congratulations, Reverend Hale; we are gladdened to see you returned to your good work.

HALE [*coming to* DANFORTH *now*]: You must pardon them. They will not budge.

[HERRICK *enters, waits.*]

DANFORTH [*conciliatory*]: You misunderstand, sir; I cannot pardon these when twelve are already hanged for the same crime. It is not just.

PARRIS [*with failing heart*]: Rebecca will not confess?

HALE: The sun will rise in a few minutes. Excellency, I must have more time.

DANFORTH: Now hear me, and beguile yourselves no more. I will not receive a single plea for pardon or postponement. Them that will not confess will hang. Twelve are already executed; the names of these seven are given out, and the village expects to see them die this morning. Postponement now speaks a floundering on my part; reprieve or pardon must cast doubt upon the guilt of them that died till now. While I speak God's law, I will not crack its voice with whimpering. If retaliation is your fear, know this – I should hang ten thousand that dared to rise against the law, and an ocean of salt tears could not melt the resolution of the statutes. Now draw yourselves up like men and help me, as you are bound by Heaven to do. Have you spoken with them all, Mr Hale?

HALE: All but Proctor. He is in the dungeon.

DANFORTH [*to* HERRICK]: What's Proctor's way now?

HERRICK: He sits like some great bird; you'd not know he lived except he will take food from time to time.

DANFORTH [*after thinking a moment*]: His wife – his wife must be well on with child now.

HERRICK: She is, sir.

DANFORTH: What think you, Mr Parris? You have closer knowledge of this man; might her presence soften him?

PARRIS: It is possible, sir. He have not laid eyes on her these three months. I should summon her.

DANFORTH [*to* HERRICK]: Is he yet adamant? Has he struck at you again?

HERRICK: He cannot, sir, he is chained to the wall now.

DANFORTH [*after thinking on it*]: Fetch Goody Proctor to me. Then let you bring him up.

HERRICK: Aye, sir. [HERRICK *goes. There is silence.*]

HALE: Excellency, if you postpone a week and publish to the town that you are striving for their confessions, that speak mercy on your part, not faltering.

DANFORTH: Mr Hale, as God have not empowered me like Joshua to stop this sun from rising, so I cannot withhold from them the perfection of their punishment.

HALE [*harder now*]: If you think God wills you to raise rebellion, Mr Danforth, you are mistaken!

DANFORTH [*instantly*]: You have heard rebellion spoken in the town?

HALE: Excellency, there are orphans wandering from house to house; abandoned cattle bellow on the highroads, the stink of rotting crops hangs everywhere, and no man knows when the harlots' cry will end his life – and you wonder yet if rebellion's spoke? Better you should marvel how they do not burn your province!

DANFORTH: Mr Hale, have you preached in Andover this month?

HALE: Thank God they have no need of me in Andover.

DANFORTH: You baffle me, sir. Why have you returned here?

HALE: Why, it is all simple. I come to do the Devil's work. I come to counsel Christians they should belie themselves. [*His sarcasm collapses.*] There is blood on my head! Can you not see the blood on my head!!

PARRIS: Hush! [*For he has heard footsteps. They all face the door.* HER-RICK *enters with* ELIZABETH. *Her wrists are linked by heavy chain, which* HERRICK *now removes. Her clothes are dirty; her face is pale and gaunt.* HERRICK *goes out.*]

DANFORTH [*very politely*]: Goody Proctor. [*She is silent.*] I hope you are hearty?

ELIZABETH [*as a warning reminder*]: I am yet six month before my time.

DANFORTH: Pray be at your ease, we come not for your life. We – [*uncertain how to plead, for he is not accustomed to it.*] Mr Hale, will you speak with the woman?

HALE: Goody Proctor, your husband is marked to hang this morning.

[*Pause.*]

ELIZABETH [*quietly*]: I have heard it.

HALE: You know, do you not, that I have no connection with the court? [*She seems to doubt it.*] I come of my own, Goody Proctor. I would save your husband's life, for if he is taken I count myself his murderer. Do you understand me?

ELIZABETH: What do you want of me?

HALE: Goody Proctor, I have gone this three month like our Lord into the wilderness. I have sought a Christian way, for damnation's doubled on a minister who counsels men to lie.

HATHORNE: It is no lie, you cannot speak of lies.

HALE: It is a lie! They are innocent!

DANFORTH: I'll hear no more of that!

HALE [*continuing to* ELIZABETH]: Let you not mistake your duty as I mistook my own. I came into this village like a bridegroom to his beloved, bearing gifts of high religion; the very crowns of holy law I brought, and what I touched with my bright confidence, it died; and where I turned the eye of my great faith, blood flowed up. Beware, Goody Proctor – cleave to no faith when faith brings blood. It is mistaken law that leads you to sacrifice. Life, woman, life is God's most precious gift; no principle, however glorious, may justify the taking of it. I beg you, woman, prevail upon your husband to confess. Let him give his lie. Quail not before God's judgement in this, for it may well be God damns a liar less than he that throws his life away for pride. Will you plead with him? I cannot think he will listen to another.

ELIZABETH [*quietly*]: I think that be the Devil's argument.

HALE [*with a climactic desperation*]: Woman, before the laws of God we are as swine! We cannot read His will!

ELIZABETH: I cannot dispute with you, sir; I lack learning for it.

DANFORTH [*going to her*]: Goody Proctor, you are not summoned her for disputation. Be there no wifely tenderness within you? He will die with the sunrise. Your husband. Do you understand it? [*She only looks at him.*] What say you? Will you contend with him? [*She is silent.*] Are you stone? I tell you true, woman, had I no other proof of your unnatural life, your dry eyes now would be sufficient evidence that you delivered up your soul to Hell! A very ape would weep at such calamity! Have the Devil dried up any tear of pity in you? [*She is silent.*] Take her out. It profit nothing she should speak to him!

ELIZABETH [*quietly*]: Let me speak with him, Excellency.

PARRIS [*with hope*]: You'll strive with him? [*She hesitates.*]

DANFORTH: Will you plead for his confession or will you not?

ELIZABETH: I promise nothing. Let me speak with him.

[*A sound – the sibilance of dragging feet on stone. They turn. A pause. HERRICK enters with JOHN PROCTOR. His wrists are chained. He is another man, bearded, filthy, his eyes misty as though webs had over-grown them. He halts inside the doorway, his eye caught by the sight of ELIZABETH. The emotion flowing between them prevents anyone from speaking for an instant. Now HALE, visibly affected, goes to DANFORTH and speaks quietly.*]

HALE: Pray, leave them, Excellency.

DANFORTH [*pressing HALE impatiently aside*]: Mr Proctor, you have been notified, have you not? [PROCTOR *is silent, staring at ELIZA-BETH.*] I see light in the sky, Mister; let you counsel with your wife, and may God help you turn your back on Hell. [PROCTOR *is silent, staring at* ELIZABETH.]

HALE [*quietly*]: Excellency, let –

[DANFORTH *brushes past* HALE *and walks out.* HALE *follows.* CHEEVER *stands and follows,* HATHORNE *behind.* HERRICK *goes.* PARRIS, *from a safe distance, offers:*]

PARRIS: If you desire a cup of cider, Mr Proctor, I am sure I – [PROCTOR *turns an icy stare at him, and he breaks off.* PARRIS *raises his palms toward* PROCTOR.] God lead you now. [PARRIS *goes out.*]

[*Alone.* PROCTOR *walks to her, halts. It is as though they stood in a spinning world. It is beyond sorrow, above it. He reaches out his hand as though toward an embodiment not quite real, and as he touches her, a strange soft sound, half laughter, half amazement, comes from his throat. He pats her hand. She covers his hand with hers. And then, weak, he sits. Then she sits, facing him.*]

PROCTOR: The child?

ELIZABETH: It grows.

PROCTOR: There is no word of the boys?

ELIZABETH: They're well. Rebecca's Samuel keeps them.

PROCTOR: You have not seen them?

ELIZABETH: I have not. [*She catches a weakening in herself and downs it.*]

PROCTOR: You are a – marvel, Elizabeth.

ELIZABETH: You – have been tortured?

PROCTOR: Aye. [*Pause. She will not let herself be drowned in the sea that threatens her.*] They come for my life now.

ELIZABETH: I know it.

[*Pause.*]

PROCTOR: None – have yet confessed?

ELIZABETH: There be many confessed.

PROCTOR: Who are they?

ELIZABETH: There be a hundred or more, they say. Goody Ballard is one; Isaiah Goodkind is one. There be many.

PROCTOR: Rebecca?

ELIZABETH: Not Rebecca. She is one foot in Heaven now; naught may hurt her more.

PROCTOR: And Giles?

ELIZABETH: You have not heard of it?

PROCTOR: I hear nothin', where I am kept.

ELIZABETH: Giles is dead.

[*He looks at her incredulously.*]

PROCTOR: When were he hanged?

ELIZABETH [*quietly, factually*]: He were not hanged. He would not answer aye or nay to his indictment; for if he denied the charge they'd hang him surely, and auction out his property. So he stand mute, and died Christian under the law. And so his sons will have his farm. It is the law, for he could not be condemned a wizard without he answer the indictment, aye or nay.

PROCTOR: Then how does he die?

ELIZABETH [*gently*]: They press him, John.

PROCTOR: Press?

ELIZABETH: Great stones they lay upon his chest until he plead aye or nay. [*With a tender smile for the old man*] They say he give them but two words. 'More weight,' he says. And died.

PROCTOR [*numbed – a thread to weave into his agony*]: 'More weight.'

ELIZABETH: Aye. It were a fearsome man, Giles Corey.

[*Pause.*]

PROCTOR [*with great force of will, but not quite looking at her*]: I have been thinking I would confess to them, Elizabeth. [*She shows nothing.*] What say you? If I give them that?

ELIZABETH: I cannot judge you, John.

[*Pause.*]

PROCTOR [*simply – a pure question*]: What would you have me do?

ELIZABETH: As you will, I would have it. [*Slight pause.*] I want you living, John. That's sure.

PROCTOR [*pauses, then with a flailing of hope*]: Giles' wife? Have she confessed?

ELIZABETH: She will not.

[*Pause.*]

PROCTOR: It is a pretence, Elizabeth.

ELIZABETH: What is?

PROCTOR: I cannot mount the gibbet like a saint. It is a fraud. I am not that man. [*She is silent.*] My honesty is broke, Elizabeth; I am no good man. Nothing's spoiled by giving them this lie that were not rotten long before.

ELIZABETH: And yet you've not confessed till now. That speak goodness in you.

PROCTOR: Spite only keeps me silent. It is hard to give a lie to dogs. [*Pause, for the first time he turns directly to her*] I would have your forgiveness, Elizabeth.

ELIZABETH: It is not for me to give, John, I am –

PROCTOR: I'd have you see some honesty in it. Let them that never lied die now to keep their souls. It is pretence for me, a vanity that will not blind God nor keep my children out of the wind. [*Pause.*] What say you?

ELIZABETH [*upon a heaving sob that always threatens*]: John, it come to naught that I should forgive you, if you'll not forgive yourself. [*Now he turns away a little, in great agony.*] It is not my soul, John, it is yours. [*He stands, as though in physical pain, slowly rising to his feet with a great immortal longing to find his answer. It is difficult to say, and she is on the verge of tears.*] Only be sure of this, for I know it now: Whatever you will do, it is a good man does it. [*He turns his doubting, searching gaze upon her.*] I have read my heart this three month, John. [*Pause.*] I have sins of my own to count. It needs a cold wife to prompt lechery.

PROCTOR [*in great pain*]: Enough, enough –

ELIZABETH [*now pouring out her heart*]: Better you should know me!

PROCTOR: I will not hear it! I know you!

ELIZABETH: You take my sins upon you, John –

PROCTOR [*in agony*]: No, I take my own, my own!

ELIZABETH: John, I counted myself so plain, so poorly made, no honest love could come to me! Suspicion kissed you when I did; I never knew how I should say my love. It were a cold house I kept! [*In fright, she swerves, as* HATHORNE *enters.*]

HATHORNE: What say you, Proctor? The sun is soon up.

[PROCTOR, *his chest heaving, stares, turns to* ELIZABETH. *She comes to him as though to plead, her voice quaking.*]

ELIZABETH: Do what you will. But let none be your judge. There be no higher judge under Heaven than Proctor is! Forgive me, forgive me, John – I never knew such goodness in the world! [*She covers her face, weeping.*]

[PROCTOR *turns from her to* HATHORNE; *he is off the earth, his voice hollow.*]

PROCTOR: I want my life.

HATHORNE [*electrified, surprised*]: You'll confess yourself?

PROCTOR: I will have my life.

HATHORNE [*with a mystical tone*]: God be praised! It is a providence! [*He rushes out the door, and his voice is heard calling down the corridor*] He will confess! Proctor will confess!

PROCTOR [*with a cry, as he strides to the door*]: Why do you cry it? [*In great pain he turns back to her*] It is evil, is it not? It is evil.

ELIZABETH [*in terror, weeping*]: I cannot judge you, John, I cannot!

PROCTOR: Then who will judge me? [*Suddenly clasping his hands*] God in Heaven, what is John Proctor, what is John Proctor? [*He moves as an animal, and a fury is riding in him, a tantalized search.*] I think it is honest, I think so; I am no saint. [*As though she had denied this he calls angrily at her*] Let Rebecca go like a saint; for me it is fraud!

[*Voices are heard in the hall, speaking together in suppressed excitement.*]

ELIZABETH: I am not your judge, I cannot be. [*As though giving him release*] Do as you will, do as you will!

PROCTOR: Would you give them such a lie? Say it. Would you ever give them this? [*She cannot answer.*] You would not; if tongs of fire were singeing you you would not! It is evil. Good, then – it is evil, and I do it!

[HATHORNE *enters with* DANFORTH, *and, with them,* CHEEVER, PARRIS, *and* HALE. *It is a businesslike, rapid entrance, as though the ice had been broken.*]

DANFORTH [*with great relief and gratitude*]: Praise to God, man, praise to God; you shall be blessed in Heaven for this. [CHEEVER *has hurried to the bench with pen, ink, and paper.* PROCTOR *watches him.*] Now then, let us have it. Are you ready, Mr Cheever?

PROCTOR [*with a cold, cold horror at their efficiency*]: Why must it be written?

DANFORTH: Why, for the good instruction of the village, Mister; this we shall post upon the church door! [*To* PARRIS, *urgently*] Where is the marshal?

PARRIS [*runs to the door and calls down the corridor*]: Marshal! Hurry!

DANFORTH: Now, then, Mister, will you speak slowly, and directly to the point, for Mr Cheever's sake. [*He is on record now, and is really dictating to* CHEEVER, *who writes.*] Mr Proctor, have you seen the Devil in your life? [PROCTOR's *jaws lock.*] Come, man, there is light in the sky; the town waits at the scaffold; I would give out this news. Did you see the Devil?

PROCTOR: I did.

PARRIS: Praise God!

DANFORTH: And when he come to you, what were his demand? [PROCTOR *is silent.* DANFORTH *helps.*] Did he bid you to do his work upon the earth?

PROCTOR: He did.

DANFORTH: And you bound yourself to his service? [DANFORTH *turns, as* REBECCA NURSE *enters, with* HERRICK *helping to support her. She is barely able to walk.*] Come in, come in, woman!

REBECCA [*brightening as she sees* PROCTOR]: Ah, John! You are well, then, eh?

[PROCTOR *turns his face to the wall.*]

DANFORTH: Courage, man, courage – let her witness your good example that she may come to God herself. Now hear it, Goody Nurse! Say on, Mr Proctor. Did you bind yourself to the Devil's service?

REBECCA [*astonished*]: Why, John!

PROCTOR [*through his teeth, his face turned from* REBECCA]: I did.

DANFORTH: Now, woman, you surely see it profit nothin' to keep this conspiracy any further. Will you confess yourself with him?

REBECCA: Oh, John – God send His mercy on you!

DANFORTH: I say, will you confess yourself, Goody Nurse?

REBECCA: Why, it is a lie, it is a lie; how may I damn myself? I cannot, I cannot.

DANFORTH: Mr Proctor. When the Devil came to you did you see Rebecca Nurse in his company? [PROCTOR *is silent.*] Come, man, take courage – did you ever see her with the Devil?

PROCTOR [*almost inaudibly*]: No.

[DANFORTH, *now sensing trouble, glances at* JOHN *and goes to the table, and picks up a sheet – the list of condemned.*]

DANFORTH: Did you ever see her sister, Mary Easty, with the Devil?

PROCTOR: No, I did not.

DANFORTH [*his eyes narrow on* PROCTOR]: Did you ever see Martha Corey with the Devil?

PROCTOR: I did not.

DANFORTH [*realizing, slowly putting the sheet down*]: Did you ever see anyone with the Devil?

PROCTOR: I did not.

DANFORTH: Proctor, you mistake me. I am not empowered to trade your life for a lie. You have most certainly seen some person with the Devil. [PROCTOR *is silent.*] Mr Proctor, a score of people have already testified they saw this woman with the Devil.

PROCTOR: Then it is proved. Why must I say it?

DANFORTH: Why 'must' you say it! Why, you should rejoice to say it if your soul is truly purged of any love for Hell!

PROCTOR: They think to go like saints. I like not to spoil their names.

DANFORTH [*inquiring, incredulous*]: Mr Proctor, do you think they go like saints?

PROCTOR [*evading*]: This woman never thought she done the Devil's work.

DANFORTH: Look you, sir. I think you mistake your duty here. It matters nothing what she thought – she is convicted of the unnatural murder of children, and you for sending your spirit out upon Mary Warren. Your soul alone is the issue here, Mister, and you will prove its whiteness or you cannot live in a Christian country. Will you tell me now what persons conspired with you in the Devil's company? [PROCTOR *is silent.*] To your knowledge was Rebecca Nurse ever –

PROCTOR: I speak my own sins; I cannot judge another. [*Crying out, with hatred*] I have no tongue for it.

HALE [*quickly to* DANFORTH]: Excellency, it is enough he confess himself. Let him sign it, let him sign it.

PARRIS [*feverishly*]: It is a great service, sir. It is a weighty name; it will strike the village that Proctor confess. I beg you, let him sign it. The sun is up, Excellency!

DANFORTH [*considers; then with dissatisfaction*]: Come, then, sign your testimony. [*To* CHEEVER] Give it to him. [CHEEVER *goes to* PROCTOR, *the confession and a pen in hand.* PROCTOR *does not look at it.*] Come, man, sign it.

PROCTOR [*after glancing at the confession*]: You have all witnessed it – it is enough.

DANFORTH: You will not sign it?

PROCTOR: You have all witnessed it; what more is needed?

DANFORTH: Do you sport with me? You will sign your name or it is no confession, Mister! [*His breast heaving with agonized breathing,* PROCTOR *now lays the paper down and signs his name.*]

PARRIS: Praise be to the Lord!

[PROCTOR *has just finished signing when* DANFORTH *reaches for the paper. But* PROCTOR *snatches it up, and now a wild terror is rising in him, and a boundless anger.*]

DANFORTH [*perplexed, but politely extending his hand*]: If you please, sir.

PROCTOR: No.

DANFORTH [*as though* PROCTOR *did not understand*]: Mr Proctor, I must have –

PROCTOR: No, no. I have signed it. You have seen me. It is done! You have no need for this.

PARRIS: Proctor, the village must have proof that –

PROCTOR: Damn the village! I confess to God, and God has seen my name on this! It is enough!

DANFORTH: No, sir, it is –

PROCTOR: You came to save my soul, did you not? Here! I have confessed myself; it is enough!

DANFORTH: You have not con –

PROCTOR: I have confessed myself! Is there no good penitence but it be public? God does not need my name nailed upon the church! God sees my name; God knows how black my sins are! It is enough!

DANFORTH: Mr Proctor –

PROCTOR: You will not use me! I am no Sarah Good or Tituba, I am John Proctor! You will not use me! It is no part of salvation that you should use me!

DANFORTH: I do not wish to –

PROCTOR: I have three children – how may I teach them to walk like men in the world, and I sold my friends?

DANFORTH: You have not sold your friends –

PROCTOR: Beguile me not! I blacken all of them when this is nailed to the church the very day they hang for silence!

DANFORTH: Mr Proctor, I must have good and legal proof that you –

PROCTOR: You are the high court, your word is good enough! Tell them I confessed myself; say Proctor broke his knees and wept like a woman; say what you will, but my name cannot –

DANFORTH [*with suspicion*]: It is the same, is it not? If I report it or you sign to it?

PROCTOR [*he knows it is insane*]: No, it is not the same! What others say and what I sign to is not the same!

DANFORTH: Why? Do you mean to deny this confession when you are free?

PROCTOR: I mean to deny nothing!

DANFORTH: Then explain to me, Mr Proctor, why you will not let –

PROCTOR [*with a cry of his soul*]: Because it is my name! Because I cannot have another in my life! Because I lie and sign myself to lies! Because I am not worth the dust on the feet of them that hang! How may I live without my name? I have given you my soul; leave me my name!

DANFORTH [*pointing at the confession in* PROCTOR's *hand*]: Is that document a lie? If it is a lie I will not accept it! What say you? I will not deal in lies, Mister! [PROCTOR *is motionless.*] You will give me your honest confession in my hand, or I cannot keep you from the rope. [PROCTOR *does not reply.*] Which way do you go, Mister?

[*His breast heaving, his eyes staring,* PROCTOR *tears the paper and crumples it, and he is weeping in fury, but erect.*]

DANFORTH: Marshal!

PARRIS [*hysterically, as though the tearing paper were his life*]: Proctor, Proctor!

HALE: Man, you will hang! You cannot!

PROCTOR [*his eyes full of tears*]: I can. And there's your first marvel, that I can. You have made your magic now, for now I do think I see some shred of goodness in John Proctor. Not enough to weave a banner with, but white enough to keep it from such dogs. [ELIZABETH, *in a burst of terror, rushes to him and weeps against his hand.*] Give them no tear! Tears pleasure them! Show honour now, show a stony heart and sink them with it! [*He has lifted her, and kisses her now with great passion.*]

REBECCA: Let you fear nothing! Another judgement waits us all!

DANFORTH: Hang them high over the town! Who weeps for these, weeps for corruption! [*He sweeps out past them.* HERRICK *starts to lead* REBECCA, *who almost collapses, but* PROCTOR *catches her, and she glances up at him apologetically.*]

REBECCA: I've had no breakfast.

HERRICK: Come, man.

[HERRICK *escorts them out,* HATHORNE *and* CHEEVER *behind them.* ELIZABETH *stands staring at the empty doorway.*]

PARRIS [*in deadly fear, to* ELIZABETH]: Go to him, Goody Proctor! There is yet time!

[*From outside a drumroll strikes the air.* PARRIS *is startled.* ELIZABETH *jerks about toward the window.*]

PARRIS: Go to him! [*He rushes out the door, as though to hold back his fate.*] Proctor! Proctor!

[*Again, a short burst of drums.*]

HALE: Woman, plead with him! [*He starts to rush out the door, and then goes back to her.*] Woman! It is pride, it is vanity. [*She avoids his eyes, and moves to the window. He drops to his knees.*] Be his helper! – What profit him to bleed? Shall the dust praise him? Shall the worms declare his truth? Go to him, take his shame away!

ELIZABETH [*supporting herself against collapse, grips the bars of the window, and with a cry*]: He have his goodness now. God forbid I take it from him!

[*The final drumroll crashes, then heightens violently.* HALE *weeps in frantic prayer, and the new sun is pouring in upon her face, and the drums rattle like bones in the morning air.*]

THE CURTAIN FALLS

Echoes Down the Corridor

Not long after the fever died, Parris was voted from office, walked out on the highroad, and was never heard of again.

The legend has it that Abigail turned up later as a prostitute in Boston.

Twenty years after the last execution, the government awarded compensation to the victims still living, and to the families of the dead. However, it is evident that some people still were unwilling to admit their total guilt, and also that the factionalism was still alive, for some beneficiaries were actually not victims at all, but informers.

Elizabeth Proctor married again, four years after Proctor's death.

In solemn meeting, the congregation rescinded the excommunications – this in March 1712. But they did so upon orders of the government. The jury, however, wrote a statement praying forgiveness of all who had suffered.

Certain farms which had belonged to the victims were left to ruin, and for more than a century no one would buy them or live on them.

To all intents and purposes, the power of theocracy in Massachusetts was broken.

1. Arthur Miller at a reading of *The Crucible*, 1953. Photograph by Eve Arnold.

2. (*right*) The first Broadway production at the Martin Beck Theatre in New York, 1953. Photograph by Gjon Mili.

3. (*below*) Curtain call at the Martin Beck Theatre, 1953. Photograph by Paul Berg.

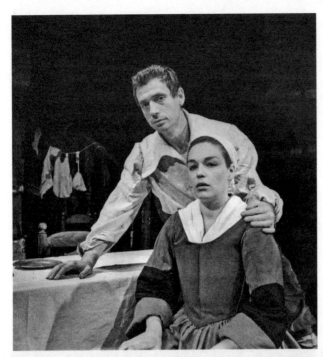

3. (*left*) Simone Signoret and Yves Montand at the Sarah Bernhardt Theatre in Paris, 1954.

4. (*below*) The Royal Court Theatre, London, 1956.

5. (*left*) Miller in the cemetery in Salem, Massachusetts where those involved in the events depicted in *The Crucible* are buried, 1962. Photograph by Inge Morath.

6. (*below*) Miller greeting Sir Laurence Olivier in 1965 at the offices of the National Theatre at the Old Vic in London before the opening of Olivier's production.

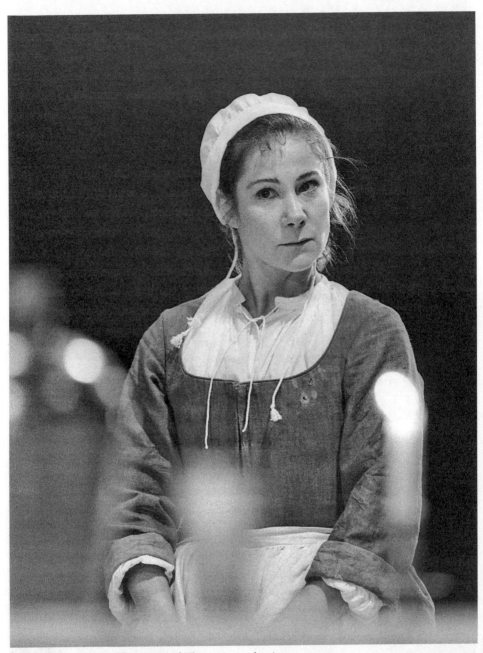

7. Zoë Wanamaker in the National Theatre's production, 1990.
Photograph by Richard Mildenhall.

8. (*top*) Miller and Winona Ryder on set for the film of *The Crucible*, directed by Nicholas Hytner, on Hog's Island, Massachusetts, 1995. Photographs 8-11 by Inge Morath.

9. (*bottom*) Daniel Day-Lewis, who starred as John Proctor, on set.

10. (*top*) Winona Ryder played the role of Abigail Williams in the film.

11. (*bottom*) Miller with Daniel Day-Lewis on set. Miller was nominated for an Academy Award for Best Adapted Screenplay.

12. (*top*) Laura Linney and Liam Neeson in rehearsal for Richard Eyre's Broadway revival, 2002. Photographs 12 and 13 by Inge Morath.

13. (*bottom*) Liam Neeson with Miller during rehearsals.

A View from the Bridge

A *View from the Bridge* was first presented at the New Watergate Theatre Club in London on 11 October 1956, with the following cast:

LOUIS	*Richard Harris*
MIKE	*Norman Mitchell*
ALFIERI	*Michael Gwynn*
EDDIE	*Anthony Quayle*
CATHERINE	*Mary Ure*
BEATRICE	*Megs Jenkins*
MARCO	*Ian Bannen*
TONY	*Ralph Nossek*
RODOLPHO	*Brian Bedford*
FIRST IMMIGRATION OFFICER	*John Stone*
SECOND IMMIGRATION OFFICER	*Colin Rix*
MR LIPARI	*Mervyn Blake*
MRS LIPARI	*Catherine Willmer*
A 'SUBMARINE'	*Peter James*

The production was directed and designed by PETER BROOK

Act One

The street and house front of a tenement building. The front is skeletal entirely. The main acting area is the living room–dining room of EDDIE'S *apartment. It is a worker's flat, clean, sparse, homely. There is a rocker down front; a round dining table at centre, with chairs; and a portable phonograph.*

At back are a bedroom door and an opening to the kitchen; none of these interiors are seen.

At the right, forestage, a desk. This is MR ALFIERI'S *law office.*

There is also a telephone booth. This is not used until the last scenes, so it may be covered or left in view.

A stairway leads up to the apartment, and then farther up to the next storey, which is not seen.

Ramps, representing the street, run upstage and off to right and left.

As the curtain rises, LOUIS *and* MIKE, *longshoremen, are pitching coins against the building at left.*

A distant foghorn blows.

Enter ALFIERI, *a lawyer in his fifties turning grey; he is portly, good-humoured, and thoughtful. The two pitchers nod to him as he passes. He crosses the stage to his desk, removes his hat, runs his fingers through his hair, and grinning, speaks to the audience.*

ALFIERI: You wouldn't have known it, but something amusing has just happened. You see how uneasily they nod to me? That's because I am a lawyer. In this neighbourhood to meet a lawyer or a priest on the street is unlucky. We're only thought of in connection with disasters, and they'd rather not get too close.

I often think that behind that suspicious little nod of theirs lie three thousand years of distrust. A lawyer means the law, and in

Sicily, from where their fathers came, the law has not been a friendly idea since the Greeks were beaten.

I am inclined to notice the ruins in things, perhaps because I was born in Italy . . . I only came here when I was twenty-five. In those days, Al Capone, the greatest Carthaginian of all, was learning his trade on these pavements, and Frankie Yale himself was cut precisely in half by a machine gun on the corner of Union Street, two blocks away. Oh, there were many here who were justly shot by unjust men. Justice is very important here.

But this is Red Hook, not Sicily. This is the slum that faces the bay on the seaward side of Brooklyn Bridge. This is the gullet of New York swallowing the tonnage of the world. And now we are quite civilized, quite American. Now we settle for half, and I like it better. I no longer keep a pistol in my filing cabinet.

And my practice is entirely unromantic.

My wife has warned me, so have my friends; they tell me the people in this neighbourhood lack elegance, glamour. After all, who have I dealt with in my life? Longshoremen and their wives, and fathers and grandfathers, compensation cases, evictions, family squabbles – the petty troubles of the poor – and yet . . . every few years there is still a case, and as the parties tell me what the trouble is, the flat air in my office suddenly washes in with the green scent of the sea, the dust in this air is blown away and the thought comes that in some Caesar's year, in Calabria perhaps or on the cliff at Syracuse, another lawyer, quite differently dressed, heard the same complaint and sat there as powerless as I, and watched it run its bloody course.

[EDDIE *has appeared and has been pitching coins with the men and is highlighted among them. He is forty – a husky, slightly overweight longshoreman.*]

This one's name was Eddie Carbone, a longshoreman working the docks from Brooklyn Bridge to the breakwater where the open sea begins.

[ALFIERI *walks into darkness.*]

EDDIE [*moving up steps into doorway*]: Well, I'll see ya, fellas.

[CATHERINE *enters from kitchen, crosses down to window, looks out.*]

LOUIS: You workin' tomorrow?

EDDIE: Yeah, there's another day yet on that ship. See ya, Louis.

[EDDIE *goes into the house, as light rises in the apartment.*

CATHERINE *is waving to* LOUIS *from the window and turns to him.*]

CATHERINE: Hi, Eddie!

[EDDIE *is pleased and therefore shy about it; he hangs up his cap and jacket.*]

EDDIE: Where you goin' all dressed up?

CATHERINE [*running her hands over her skirt*]: I just got it. You like it?

EDDIE: Yeah, it's nice. And what happened to your hair?

CATHERINE: You like it? I fixed it different. [*Calling to kitchen*] He's here, B.!

EDDIE: Beautiful. Turn around, lemme see in the back. [*She turns for him.*] Oh, if your mother was alive to see you now! She wouldn't believe it.

CATHERINE: You like it, huh?

EDDIE: You look like one of them girls that went to college. Where you goin'?

CATHERINE [*taking his arm*]: Wait'll B. comes in, I'll tell you something. Here, sit down. [*She is walking him to the armchair. Calling offstage*] Hurry up, will you, B.?

EDDIE [*sitting*]: What's goin' on?

CATHERINE: I'll get you a beer, all right?

EDDIE: Well, tell me what happened. Come over here, talk to me.

CATHERINE: I want to wait till B. comes in. [*She sits on her heels beside him.*] Guess how much we paid for the skirt.

EDDIE: I think it's too short, ain't it?

CATHERINE [*standing*]: No! Not when I stand up.

EDDIE: Yeah, but you gotta sit down sometimes.

CATHERINE: Eddie, it's the style now. [*She walks to show him.*] I mean, if you see me walkin' down the street –

EDDIE: Listen, you been givin' me the willies the way you walk down the street, I mean it.

CATHERINE: Why?

EDDIE: Catherine, I don't want to be a pest, but I'm tellin' you you're walkin' wavy.

CATHERINE: I'm walkin' wavy?

EDDIE: Now don't aggravate me, Katie, you are walkin' wavy! I don't like the looks they're givin' you in the candy store. And with them new high heels on the sidewalk – clack, clack, clack. The heads are turnin' like windmills.

CATHERINE: But those guys look at all the girls, you know that.

EDDIE: You ain't 'all the girls'.

CATHERINE [*almost in tears because he disapproves*]: What do you want me to do? You want me to –

EDDIE: Now don't get mad, kid.

CATHERINE: Well, I don't know what you want from me.

EDDIE: Katie, I promised your mother on her deathbed. I'm responsible for you. You're a baby, you don't understand these things. I mean like when you stand here by the window, wavin' outside.

CATHERINE: I was wavin' to Louis!

EDDIE: Listen, I could tell you things about Louis which you wouldn't wave to him no more.

CATHERINE [*trying to joke him out of his warning*]: Eddie, I wish there was one guy you couldn't tell me things about!

EDDIE: Catherine, do me a favour, will you? You're gettin' to be a big girl now, you gotta keep yourself more, you can't be so friendly, kid. [*Calls*] Hey, B., what're you doin' in there? [*To* CATHERINE] Get her in here, will you? I got news for her.

CATHERINE [*starting out*]: What?

EDDIE: Her cousins landed.

CATHERINE [*clapping her hands together*]: No! [*She turns instantly and starts for the kitchen.*] B.! Your cousins!

[BEATRICE *enters, wiping her hands with a towel.*]

BEATRICE [*in the face of* CATHERINE's *shout*]: What?

CATHERINE: Your cousins got in!

BEATRICE [*astounded, turns to* EDDIE]: What are you talkin' about? Where?

EDDIE: I was just knockin' off work before and Tony Bereli come over to me; he says the ship is in the North River.

BEATRICE [*her hands are clasped at her breast; she seems half in fear, half in unutterable joy*]: They're all right?

EDDIE: He didn't see them yet, they're still on board. But as soon as they get off he'll meet them. He figures about ten o'clock they'll be here.

BEATRICE [*sits, almost weak from tension*]: And they'll let them off the ship all right? That's fixed, heh?

EDDIE: Sure, they give them regular seamen papers and they walk off with the crew. Don't worry about it, B., there's nothin' to it. Couple of hours they'll be here.

BEATRICE: What happened? They wasn't supposed to be till next Thursday.

EDDIE: I don't know; they put them on any ship they can get them out on. Maybe the other ship they was supposed to take there was some danger – What you cryin' about?

BEATRICE [*astounded and afraid*]: I'm – I just – I can't believe it! I didn't even buy a new tablecloth; I was gonna wash the walls –

EDDIE: Listen, they'll think it's a millionaire's house compared to the way they live. Don't worry about the walls. They'll be thankful. [*To* CATHERINE] Whyn't you run down buy a tablecloth. Go ahead, here. [*He is reaching into his pocket.*]

CATHERINE: There's no stores open now.

EDDIE *to* [BEATRICE]: You was gonna put a new cover on the chair.

BEATRICE: I know – well, I thought it was gonna be next week! I was gonna clean the walls, I was gonna wax the floors. [*She stands disturbed.*]

CATHERINE [*pointing upward*]: Maybe Mrs Dondero upstairs –

BEATRICE [*of the tablecloth*]: No, hers is worse than this one. [*Suddenly*] My God, I don't even have nothin' to eat for them! [*She starts for the kitchen.*]

EDDIE [*reaching out and grabbing her arm*]: Hey, hey! Take it easy.

BEATRICE: No, I'm just nervous, that's all. [*To* CATHERINE] I'll make the fish.

EDDIE: You're savin' their lives, what're you worryin' about the tablecloth? They probably didn't see a tablecloth in their whole life where they come from.

BEATRICE [*looking into his eyes*]: I'm just worried about you, that's all. I'm worried.

EDDIE: Listen, as long as they know where they're gonna sleep.

BEATRICE: I told them in the letters. They're sleepin' on the floor.

EDDIE: Beatrice, all I'm worried about is you got such a heart that I'll end up on the floor with you, and they'll be in our bed.

BEATRICE: All right, stop it.

EDDIE: Because as soon as you see a tired relative, I end up on the floor.

BEATRICE: When did you end up on the floor?

EDDIE: When your father's house burned down I didn't end up on the floor?

BEATRICE: Well, their house burned down!

EDDIE: Yeah, but it didn't keep burnin' for two weeks!

BEATRICE: All right, look, I'll tell them to go someplace else.

[*She starts into the kitchen.*]

EDDIE: Now wait a minute. Beatrice! [*She halts. He goes to her*]. I just don't want you bein' pushed around, that's all. You got too big a heart. [*He touches her hand*]. What're you so touchy?

BEATRICE: I'm just afraid if it don't turn out good you'll be mad at me.

EDDIE: Listen, if everybody keeps his mouth shut, nothin' can happen. They'll pay for their board.

BEATRICE: Oh, I told them.

EDDIE: Then what the hell. [*Pause. He moves*]. It's an honour, B. I mean it. I was just thinkin' before, comin' home, suppose my father didn't come to this country, and I was starvin' like them over there . . . and I had people in America could keep me a couple of months? The man would be honoured to lend me a place to sleep.

BEATRICE [*there are tears in her eyes. She turns to* CATHERINE]: You see what he is? [*She turns and grabs* EDDIE'*s face in her hands.*] Mmm! You're an angel! God'll bless you. [*He is gratefully smiling.*] You'll see, you'll get a blessing for this!

EDDIE [*laughing*]: I'll settle for my own bed.

BEATRICE: Go, Baby, set the table.

CATHERINE: We didn't tell him about me yet.

BEATRICE: Let him eat first, then we'll tell him. Bring everything in. [*She hurries* CATHERINE *out.*]

EDDIE [*sitting at the table*]: What's all that about? Where's she goin'?

BEATRICE: Noplace. It's very good news, Eddie. I want you to be happy.

EDDIE: What's goin' on?

[CATHERINE *enters with plates, forks.*]

BEATRICE: She's got a job.

[*Pause.* EDDIE *looks at* CATHERINE, *then back to* BEATRICE.]

EDDIE: What job? She's gonna finish school.

CATHERINE: Eddie, you won't believe it –

EDDIE: No – no, you gonna finish school. What kinda job, what do you mean? All of a sudden you –

CATHERINE: Listen a minute, it's wonderful.

EDDIE: It's not wonderful. You'll never get nowheres unless you finish school. You can't take no job. Why didn't you ask me before you take a job?

BEATRICE: She's askin' you now, she didn't take nothin' yet.

CATHERINE: Listen a minute! I came to school this morning and the principal called me out of the class, see? To go to his office.

EDDIE: Yeah?

CATHERINE: So I went in and he says to me he's got my records, y'know? And there's a company wants a girl right away. It ain't exactly a secretary, it's a stenographer first, but pretty soon you get to be secretary. And he says to me that I'm the best student in the whole class –

BEATRICE: You hear that?

EDDIE: Well why not? Sure she's the best.

CATHERINE: I'm the best student, he says, and if I want, I should take the job and the end of the year he'll let me take the examination and he'll give me the certificate. So I'll save practically a year!

EDDIE [*strangely nervous*]: Where's the job? What company?

CATHERINE: It's a big plumbing company over Nostrand Avenue.

EDDIE: Nostrand Avenue and where?

CATHERINE: It's someplace by the Navy Yard.

BEATRICE: Fifty dollars a week, Eddie.

EDDIE [*to* CATHERINE, *surprised*]: Fifty?

CATHERINE: I swear.

[*Pause.*]

EDDIE: What about all the stuff you wouldn't learn this year, though?

CATHERINE: There's nothin' more to learn, Eddie, I just gotta practise from now on. I know all the symbols and I know the keyboard. I'll just get faster, that's all. And when I'm workin' I'll keep gettin' better and better, you see?

BEATRICE: Work is the best practice anyway.

EDDIE: That ain't what I wanted, though.

CATHERINE: Why! It's a great big company –

EDDIE: I don't like that neighbourhood over there.

CATHERINE: It's a block and a half from the subway, he says.

EDDIE: Near the Navy Yard plenty can happen in a block and a half. And a plumbin' company! That's one step over the water front. They're practically longshoremen.

BEATRICE: Yeah, but she'll be in the office, Eddie.

EDDIE: I know she'll be in the office, but that ain't what I had in mind.

BEATRICE: Listen, she's gotta go to work sometime.

EDDIE: Listen, B., she'll be with a lotta plumbers? And sailors up and down the street? So what did she go to school for?

CATHERINE: But it's fifty a week, Eddie.

EDDIE: Look, did I ask you for money? I supported you this long I support you a little more. Please, do me a favour, will ya? I want you to be with different kind of people. I want you to be in a nice office. Maybe a lawyer's office someplace in New York in one of them nice buildings. I mean if you're gonna get outa here then get out; don't go practically in the same kind of neighbourhood.

[*Pause.* CATHERINE *lowers her eyes.*]

BEATRICE: Go, Baby, bring in the supper. [CATHERINE *goes out.*] Think about it a little bit, Eddie. Please. She's crazy to start work. It's not a little shop, it's a big company. Some day she could be a secretary. They picked her out of the whole class. [*He is silent, staring down at the tablecloth, fingering the pattern.*] What are you worried about? She could take care of herself. She'll get out of the subway and be in the office in two minutes.

EDDIE [*somehow sickened*]: I know that neighbourhood, B., I don't like it.

BEATRICE: Listen, if nothin' happened to her in this neighbourhood it ain't gonna happen noplace else. [*She turns his face to her.*] Look, you gotta get used to it, she's no baby no more. Tell her to take it. [*He turns his head away*]. You hear me? [*She is angering.*] I don't understand you; she's seventeen years old, you gonna keep her in the house all her life?

EDDIE [*insulted*]: What kinda remark is that?

BEATRICE [*with sympathy but insistent force*]: Well, I don't understand when it ends. First it was gonna be when she graduated high school, so she graduated high school. Then it was gonna be when she learned stenographer, so she learned stenographer. So what're we gonna wait for now? I mean it, Eddie, sometimes

I don't understand you; they picked her out of the whole class, it's an honour for her.

[CATHERINE *enters with food, which she silently sets on the table. After a moment of watching her face,* EDDIE *breaks into a smile, but it almost seems that tears will form in his eyes.*]

EDDIE: With your hair that way you look like a madonna, you know that? You're the madonna type. [*She doesn't look at him, but continues ladling out food onto the plates.*] You wanna go to work, heh, Madonna?

CATHERINE [*softly*]: Yeah.

EDDIE [*with a sense of her childhood, her babyhood, and the years*]: All right, go to work. [*She looks at him, then rushes and hugs him.*] Hey, hey! Take it easy! [*He holds her face away from him to look at her.*] What're you cryin' about? [*He is affected by her, but smiles his emotion away.*]

CATHERINE [*sitting at her place*]: I just – [*Bursting out*] I'm gonna buy all new dishes with my first pay! [*They laugh warmly*]. I mean it. I'll fix up the whole house! I'll buy a rug!

EDDIE: And then you'll move away.

CATHERINE: No, Eddie!

EDDIE, [*grinning*]: Why not? That's life. And you'll come visit on Sundays, then once a month, then Christmas and New Year's, finally.

CATHERINE [*grasping his arm to reassure him and to erase the accusation*]: No, please!

EDDIE [*smiling but hurt*]: I only ask you one thing – don't trust nobody. You got a good aunt but she's got too big a heart, you learned bad from her. Believe me.

BEATRICE: Be the way you are, Katie, don't listen to him.

EDDIE [*to* BEATRICE – *strangely and quickly resentful*]: You lived in a house all your life, what do you know about it? You never worked in your life.

BEATRICE: She likes people. What's wrong with that?

EDDIE: Because most people ain't people. She's goin' to work; plumbers; they'll chew her to pieces if she don't watch out. [*To*

CATHERINE] Believe me, Katie, the less you trust, the less you be sorry.

[EDDIE *crosses himself and the women do the same, and they eat.*]

CATHERINE: First thing I'll buy is a rug, heh, B.?

BEATRICE: I don't mind. [*To* EDDIE] I smelled coffee all day today. You unloadin' coffee today?

EDDIE: Yeah, a Brazil ship.

CATHERINE: I smelled it too. It smelled all over the neighbourhood.

EDDIE: That's one time, boy, to be a longshoreman is a pleasure. I could work coffee ships twenty hours a day. You go down in the hold, y'know? It's like flowers, that smell. We'll bust a bag tomorrow, I'll bring you some.

BEATRICE: Just be sure there's no spiders in it, will ya? I mean it. [*She directs this to* CATHERINE, *rolling her eyes upward.*] I still remember that spider coming out of that bag he brung home. I nearly died.

EDDIE: You call that a spider? You oughta see what comes outa the bananas sometimes.

BEATRICE: Don't talk about it!

EDDIE: I seen spiders could stop a Buick.

BEATRICE [*clapping her hands over her ears*]: All right, shut up!

EDDIE [*laughing and taking a watch out of his pocket*]: Well, who started with spiders?

BEATRICE: All right, I'm sorry, I didn't mean it. Just don't bring none home again. What time is it?

EDDIE: Quarter nine. [*Puts watch back in his pocket. They continue eating in silence.*]

CATHERINE: He's bringin' them ten o'clock, Tony?

EDDIE: Around, yeah. [*He eats*].

CATHERINE: Eddie, suppose somebody asks if they're livin' here. [*He looks at her as though already she had divulged something publicly. Defensively*] I mean if they ask.

EDDIE: Now look, Baby, I can see we're gettin' mixed up again here.

CATHERINE: No, I just mean . . . people'll see them goin' in and out.

EDDIE: I don't care who sees them goin' in and out as long as you don't see them goin' in and out. And this goes for you too, B. You don't see nothin' and you don't know nothin'.

BEATRICE: What do you mean? I understand.

EDDIE: You don't understand; you still think you can talk about this to somebody just a little bit. Now lemme say it once and for all, because you're makin' me nervous again, both of you. I don't care if somebody comes in the house and sees them sleepin' on the floor, it never comes out of your mouth who they are or what they're doin' here.

BEATRICE: Yeah, but my mother'll know –

EDDIE: Sure she'll know, but just don't you be the one who told her, that's all. This is the United States government you're playin' with now, this is the Immigration Bureau. If you said it you knew it, if you didn't say it you didn't know it.

CATHERINE: Yeah, but Eddie, suppose somebody –

EDDIE: I don't care what question it is. You – don't – know – nothin'. They got stool pigeons all over this neighbourhood they're payin' them every week for information, and you don't know who they are. It could be your best friend. You hear? [*To* BEATRICE] Like Vinny Bolzano, remember Vinny?

BEATRICE: Oh, yeah. God forbid.

EDDIE: Tell her about Vinny. [*To* CATHERINE] You think I'm blowin' steam here? [*To* BEATRICE] Go ahead, tell her. [*To* CATHERINE] You was a baby then. There was a family lived next door to her mother, he was about sixteen –

BEATRICE: No, he was no more than fourteen, 'cause I was to his confirmation in Saint Agnes. But the family had an uncle that they were hidin' in the house, and he snitched to the Immigration.

CATHERINE: The kid snitched?

EDDIE: On his own uncle!

CATHERINE: What, was he crazy?

EDDIE: He was crazy after, I tell you that, boy.

BEATRICE: Oh, it was terrible. He had five brothers and the old father. And they grabbed him in the kitchen and pulled him down the stairs – three flights his head was bouncin' like a coconut. And they spit on him in the street, his own father and his brothers. The whole neighbourhood was cryin'.

CATHERINE: Ts! So what happened to him?

BEATRICE: I think he went away. [*To* EDDIE] I never seen him again, did you?

EDDIE [*rises during this, taking out his watch*]: Him? You'll never see him no more, a guy do a thing like that? How's he gonna show his face? [*To* CATHERINE, *as he gets up uneasily*] Just remember, kid, you can quicker get back a million dollars that was stole than a word that you gave away. [*He is standing now, stretching his back.*]

CATHERINE: Okay, I won't say a word to nobody, I swear.

EDDIE: Gonna rain tomorrow. We'll be slidin' all over the decks. Maybe you oughta put something on for them, they be here soon.

BEATRICE: I only got fish, I hate to spoil it if they ate already. I'll wait, it only takes a few minutes; I could broil it.

CATHERINE: What happens, Eddie, when that ship pulls out and they ain't on it, though? Don't the captain say nothin'?

EDDIE [*slicing an apple with his pocket knife*]: Captain's pieced off, what do you mean?

CATHERINE: Even the captain?

EDDIE: What's the matter, the captain don't have to live? Captain gets a piece, maybe one of the mates, piece for the guy in Italy who fixed the papers for them, Tony here'll get a little bite . . .

BEATRICE: I just hope they get work here, that's all I hope.

EDDIE: Oh, the syndicate'll fix jobs for them; till they pay 'em off they'll get them work every day. It's after the pay-off, then they'll have to scramble like the rest of us.

BEATRICE: Well, it be better than they got there.

EDDIE: Oh sure, well, listen. So you gonna start Monday, heh, Madonna?

CATHERINE [*embarrassed*]: I'm supposed to, yeah.

[EDDIE *is standing facing the two seated women. First* BEATRICE *smiles, then* CATHERINE, *for a powerful emotion is on him, a childish one and a knowing fear, and the tears show in his eyes – and they are shy before the avowal.*]

EDDIE [*sadly smiling, yet somehow proud of her*]: Well . . . I hope you have good luck. I wish you the best. You know that, kid.

CATHERINE [*rising, trying to laugh*]: You sound like I'm goin' a million miles!

EDDIE: I know. I guess I just never figured on one thing.

CATHERINE [*smiling*]: What?

EDDIE: That you would ever grow up. [*He utters a soundless laugh at himself, feeling his breast pocket of his shirt.*] I left a cigar in my other coat, I think. [*He starts for the bedroom.*]

CATHERINE: Stay there! I'll get it for you.

[*She hurries out. There is a slight pause, and* EDDIE *turns to* BEATRICE, *who has been avoiding his gaze.*]

EDDIE: What are you mad at me lately?

BEATRICE: Who's mad? [*She gets up, clearing the dishes.*] I'm not mad. [*She picks up the dishes and turns to him.*] You're the one is mad. [*She turns and goes into the kitchen as* CATHERINE *enters from the bedroom with a cigar and a pack of matches.*]

CATHERINE: Here! I'll light it for you! [*She strikes a match and holds it to his cigar. He puffs. Quietly*]: Don't worry about me, Eddie, heh?

EDDIE: Don't burn yourself. [*Just in time she blows out the match.*] You better go in help her with the dishes.

CATHERINE [*turns quickly to the table, and, seeing the table cleared, she says, almost guiltily*]: Oh! [*She hurries into the kitchen, and as she exits there*] I'll do the dishes, B.!

[*Alone,* EDDIE *stands looking toward the kitchen for a moment. Then he takes out his watch, glances at it, replaces it in his pocket, sits in the armchair, and stares at the smoke flowing out of his mouth.*

The lights go down, then come up on ALFIERI, *who has moved onto the forestage.*]

ALFIERI: He was as good a man as he had to be in a life that was hard and even. He worked on the piers when there was work, he brought home his pay, and he lived. And toward ten o'clock of that night, after they had eaten, the cousins came.

[*The lights fade on* ALFIERI *and rise on the street.*
    Enter TONY, *escorting* MARCO *and* RODOLPHO, *each with a valise.* TONY *halts, indicates the house. They stand for a moment looking at it.*]

MARCO [*he is a square-built peasant of thirty-two, suspicious, tender, and quiet-voiced*]: Thank you.
TONY: You're on your own now. Just be careful, that's all. Ground floor.
MARCO: Thank you.
TONY, [*indicating the house*]: I'll see you on the pier tomorrow. You'll go to work.

[MARCO *nods.* TONY *continues on walking down the street.*]

RODOLPHO: This will be the first house I ever walked into in America! Imagine! She said they were poor!
MARCO: Ssh! Come. [*They go to door.*]

[MARCO *knocks. The lights rise in the room.* EDDIE *goes and opens the door. Enter* MARCO *and* RODOLPHO, *removing their caps.* BEATRICE *and* CATHERINE *enter from the kitchen. The lights fade in the street.*]

EDDIE: You Marco?
MARCO: Marco.
EDDIE: Come on in! [*He shakes* MARCO'*s hand.*]
BEATRICE: Here, take the bags!
MARCO [*nods, looks to the women and fixes on* BEATRICE. *Crosses to* BEATRICE]: Are you my cousin?

[*She nods. He kisses her hand.*]

A View from the Bridge

BEATRICE [*above the table, touching her chest with her hand*]: Beatrice. This is my husband, Eddie. [*All nod.*] Catherine, my sister Nancy's daughter. [*The brothers nod.*]

MARCO [*indicating* RODOLPHO]: My brother. Rodolpho. [RODOLPHO *nods.* MARCO *comes with a certain formal stiffness to* EDDIE] I want to tell you now Eddie – when you say go, we will go.

EDDIE: Oh, no . . . [*Takes* Marco's *bag.*]

MARCO: I see it's a small house, but soon, maybe, we can have our own house.

EDDIE: You're welcome, Marco, we got plenty of room here. Katie, give them supper, heh? [*Exits into bedroom with their bags.*]

CATHERINE: Come here, sit down. I'll get you some soup.

MARCO [*as they go to the table*]: We ate on the ship. Thank you. [*To* EDDIE, *calling off to bedroom*] Thank you.

BEATRICE: Get some coffee. We'll all have coffee. Come sit down.

[RODOLPHO *and* MARCO *sit, at the table.*]

CATHERINE [*wondrously*]: How come he's so dark and you're so light, Rodolpho?

RODOLPHO [*ready to laugh*]: I don't know. A thousand years ago, they say, the Danes invaded Sicily.

[BEATRICE *kisses* RODOLPHO. *They laugh as* EDDIE *enters.*]

CATHERINE [*to* BEATRICE]: He's practically blond!

EDDIE: How's the coffee doin'?

CATHERINE [*brought up*]: I'm gettin' it. [*She hurries out to kitchen.*]

EDDIE [*sits on his rocker*]: Yiz have a nice trip?

MARCO: The ocean is always rough. But we are good sailors.

EDDIE: No trouble gettin' here?

MARCO: No. The man brought us. Very nice man.

RODOLPHO [*to* EDDIE]: He says we start to work tomorrow. Is he honest?

EDDIE [*laughing*]: No. But as long as you owe them money, they'll get you plenty of work. [*To* MARCO] Yiz ever work on the piers in Italy?

MARCO: Piers? Ts! – no.

RODOLPHO [*smiling at the smallness of his town*]: In our town there are no piers, only the beach, and little fishing boats.

BEATRICE: So what kinda work did yiz do?

MARCO [*shrugging shyly, even embarrassed*]: Whatever there is, anything.

RODOLPHO: Sometimes they build a house, or if they fix the bridge – Marco is a mason and I bring him the cement. [*He laughs.*] In harvest time we work in the fields . . . if there is work. Anything.

EDDIE: Still bad there, heh?

MARCO: Bad, yes.

RODOLPHO [*laughing*]: It's terrible! We stand around all day in the piazza listening to the fountain like birds. Everybody waits only for the train.

BEATRICE: What's on the train?

RODOLPHO: Nothing. But if there are many passengers and you're lucky you make a few lire to push the taxi up the hill.

[*Enter* CATHERINE; *she listens.*]

BEATRICE: You gotta push a taxi?

RODOLPHO [*laughing*]: Oh, sure! It's a feature in our town. The horses in our town are skinnier than goats. So if there are too many passengers we help to push the carriages up to the hotel. [*He laughs.*] In our town the horses are only for show.

CATHERINE: Why don't they have automobile taxis?

RODOLPHO: There is one. We push that too. [*They laugh.*] Everything in our town, you gotta push!

BEATRICE [*to* EDDIE]: How do you like that!

EDDIE [*to* MARCO]: So what're you wanna do, you gonna stay here in this country or you wanna go back?

MARCO [*surprised*]: Go back?

EDDIE: Well, you're married, ain't you?

MARCO: Yes. I have three children.

BEATRICE: Three! I thought only one.

MARCO: Oh, no. I have three now. Four years, five years, six years.

BEATRICE: Ah . . . I bet they're cryin' for you already, heh?

MARCO: What can I do? The older one is sick in his chest. My wife – she feeds them from her own mouth. I tell you the truth, if I stay there they will never grow up. They eat the sunshine.

BEATRICE: My God. So how long you want to stay?

MARCO: With your permission, we will stay maybe a –

EDDIE: She don't mean in this house, she means in the country.

MARCO: Oh. Maybe four, five, six years, I think.

RODOLPHO [*smiling*]: He trusts his wife.

BEATRICE: Yeah, but maybe you'll get enough, you'll be able to go back quicker.

MARCO: I hope. I don't know. [*To* EDDIE]: I understand it's not so good here either.

EDDIE: Oh, you guys'll be all right – till you pay them off, anyway. After that, you'll have to scramble, that's all. But you'll make better here than you could there.

RODOLPHO: How much? We hear all kinds of figures. How much can a man make? We work hard, we'll work all day, all night –

[MARCO *raises a hand to hush him.*]

EDDIE [*he is coming more and more to address* MARCO *only*]: On the average a whole year? Maybe – well, it's hard to say, see. Sometimes we lay off, there's no ships three, four weeks.

MARCO: Three, four weeks! – Ts!

EDDIE: But I think you could probably – thirty, forty a week, over the whole twelve months of the year.

MARCO [*rises, crosses to* EDDIE]: Dollars.

EDDIE: Sure dollars.

[MARCO *puts an arm round* RODOLPHO *and they laugh.*]

MARCO: If we can stay here a few months, Beatrice –

BEATRICE: Listen, you're welcome, Marco –

MARCO: Because I could send them a little more if I stay here.

BEATRICE: As long as you want, we got plenty a room.

MARCO [*his eyes are showing tears*]: My wife – [*To* EDDIE] My wife – I want to send right away maybe twenty dollars –

EDDIE: You could send them something next week already.

MARCO [*he is near tears*]: Eduardo . . . [*He goes to* EDDIE, *offering his hand.*

EDDIE: Don't thank me. Listen, what the hell, it's no skin off me. [*To* CATHERINE] What happened to the coffee?

CATHERINE: I got it on. [*To* RODOLPHO] You married too? No.

RODOLPHO [*rises*]: Oh, no . . .

BEATRICE [*to* CATHERINE]: I told you he –

CATHERINE: I know, I just thought maybe he got married recently.

RODOLPHO: I have no money to get married. I have a nice face, but no money. [*He laughs.*]

CATHERINE [*to* BEATRICE]: He's a real blond!

BEATRICE [*to* RODOLPHO]: You want to stay here too, heh? For good?

RODOLPHO: Me? Yes, forever! Me, I want to be an American. And then I want to go back to Italy when I am rich, and I will buy a motorcycle. [*He smiles.* MARCO *shakes him affectionately.*]

CATHERINE: A motorcycle!

RODOLPHO: With a motorcycle in Italy you will never starve any more.

BEATRICE: I'll get you coffee. [*She exits to the kitchen.*]

EDDIE: What you do with a motorcycle?

MARCO: He dreams, he dreams.

RODOLPHO [*to* MARCO]: Why? [*To* EDDIE] Messages! The rich people in the hotel always need someone who will carry a message. But quickly, and with a great noise. With a blue motorcycle I would station myself in the courtyard of the hotel, and in a little while I would have messages.

MARCO: When you have no wife you have dreams.

EDDIE: Why can't you just walk, or take a trolley or sump'm?

[*Enter* BEATRICE *with coffee.*]

RODOLPHO: Oh, no, the machine, the machine is necessary. A man comes into a great hotel and says, I am a messenger. Who is this man? He disappears walking, there is no noise, nothing. Maybe he will never come back, maybe he will never deliver the message. But a man who rides up on a great machine, this man is responsible, this man exists. He will be given messages. [*He helps* BEATRICE *set out the coffee things.*] I am also a singer, though.

EDDIE: You mean a regular – ?

RODOLPHO: Oh, yes. One night last year Andreola got sick. Baritone. And I took his place in the garden of the hotel. Three arias I sang without a mistake! Thousand-lire notes they threw from the tables, money was falling like a storm in the treasury. It was magnificent. We lived six months on that night, eh, Marco?

[MARCO *nods doubtfully.*]

MARCO: Two months.

[EDDIE *laughs.*]

BEATRICE: Can't you get a job in that place?

RODOLPHO: Andreola got better. He's a baritone, very strong.

[BEATRICE *laughs.*]

MARCO [*regretfully, to* BEATRICE]: He sang too loud.

RODOLPHO: Why too loud?

MARCO: Too loud. The guests in that hotel are all Englishmen. They don't like too loud.

RODOLPHO [*to* CATHERINE]: Nobody ever said it was too loud!

MARCO: I say. It was too loud. [*To* BEATRICE] I knew it as soon as he started to sing. Too loud.

RODOLPHO: Then why did they throw so much money?

MARCO: They paid for your courage. The English like courage. But once is enough.

RODOLPHO [*to all but* MARCO]: I never heard anybody say it was too loud.

CATHERINE: Did you ever hear of jazz?

RODOLPHO: Oh, sure! I *sing* jazz.

CATHERINE [*rises*]: You could sing jazz?

RODOLPHO: Oh, I sing Napolidan, jazz, bel canto – I sing 'Paper Doll', you like 'Paper Doll'?

CATHERINE: Oh, sure, I'm crazy for 'Paper Doll'. Go ahead, sing it.

RODOLPHO [*takes his stance after getting a nod of permission from* MARCO, *and with a high tenor voice begins singing*]:

> I'll tell you boys it's tough to be alone,
> And it's tough to love a doll that's not your own.
> I'm through with all of them,
> I'll never fall again,
> Hey, boy, what you gonna do?
> I'm gonna buy a paper doll that I can call my own,
> A doll that other fellows cannot steal.

[EDDIE *rises and moves upstage.*]

> And then those flirty, flirty guys
> With their flirty, flirty eyes
> Will have to flirt with dollies that are real –

EDDIE: Hey, kid – hey, wait a minute –

CATHERINE [*enthralled*]: Leave him finish, it's beautiful! [*To* BEATRICE] He's terrific! It's terrific, Rodolpho.

EDDIE: Look, kid; you don't want to be picked up, do ya?

MARCO: No – no! [*He rises.*]

EDDIE [*indicating the rest of the building*]: Because we never had no singers here . . . and all of a sudden there's a singer in the house, y'know what I mean?

MARCO: Yes, yes. You'll be quiet, Rodolpho.

EDDIE [*he is flushed*]: They got guys all over the place, Marco. I mean.

MARCO: Yes. He'll be quiet. [*To* RODOLPHO]: You'll be quiet.

[RODOLPHO *nods.*

EDDIE *has risen, with iron control, even a smile. He moves to* CATHERINE.]

EDDIE: What's the high heels for, Garbo?

CATHERINE: I figured for tonight –

EDDIE: Do me a favour, will you? Go ahead.

[*Embarrassed now, angered,* CATHERINE *goes out into the bedroom.* BEATRICE *watches her go and gets up; in passing, she gives* EDDIE *a cold look, restrained only by the strangers, and goes to the table to pour coffee.*]

EDDIE [*striving to laugh, and to* MARCO, *but directed as much to* BEATRICE]: All actresses they want to be around here.

RODOLPHO [*happy about it*]: In Italy too! All the girls.

[CATHERINE *emerges from the bedroom in low-heel shoes, comes to the table.* RODOLPHO *is lifting a cup.*]

EDDIE [*he is sizing up* RODOLPHO, *and there is a concealed suspicion*]: Yeah, heh?

RODOLPHO: Yes! [*Laughs, indicating* CATHERINE] Especially when they are so beautiful!

CATHERINE: You like sugar?

RODOLPHO: Sugar? Yes! I like sugar very much!

[EDDIE *is downstage, watching as she pours a spoonful of sugar into his cup, his face puffed with trouble, and the room dies.*
    Lights rise on ALFIERI.]

ALFIERI: Who can ever know what will be discovered? Eddie Carbone had never expected to have a destiny. A man works, raises his family, goes bowling, eats, gets old, and then he dies. Now, as the weeks passed, there was a future, there was a trouble that would not go away.

[*The lights fade on* ALFIERI, *then rise on* EDDIE *standing at the doorway of the house.* BEATRICE *enters on the street. She sees* EDDIE, *smiles at him. He looks away.*
    She starts to enter the house when EDDIE *speaks.*]

EDDIE: It's after eight.

BEATRICE: Well, it's a long show at the Paramount.

EDDIE: They must've seen every picture in Brooklyn by now. He's supposed to stay in the house when he ain't working. He ain't supposed to go advertising himself.

BEATRICE: Well that's his trouble, what do you care? If they pick him up they pick him up, that's all. Come in the house.

EDDIE: What happened to the stenography? I don't see her practise no more.

BEATRICE: She'll get back to it. She's excited, Eddie.

EDDIE: She tell you anything?

BEATRICE [*comes to him, now the subject is opened*]: What's the matter with you? He's a nice kid, what do you want from him?

EDDIE: That's a nice kid? He gives me the heeby-jeebies.

BEATRICE [*smiling*]: Ah, go on, you're just jealous.

EDDIE: Of *him*? Boy, you don't think much of me.

BEATRICE: I don't understand you. What's so terrible about him?

EDDIE: You mean it's all right with you? That's gonna be her husband?

BEATRICE: Why? He's a nice fella, hard workin', he's a good-lookin' fella.

EDDIE: He sings on the ships, didja know that?

BEATRICE: What do you mean, he sings?

EDDIE: Just what I said, he sings. Right on the deck, all of a sudden, a whole song comes out of his mouth – with motions. You know what they're callin' him now? Paper Doll they're callin' him, Canary. He's like a weird. He comes out on the pier, one-two-three, it's a regular free show.

BEATRICE: Well, he's a kid; he don't know how to behave himself yet.

EDDIE: And with that wacky hair; he's like a chorus girl or sump'm.

BEATRICE: So he's blond, so –

EDDIE: I just hope that's his regular hair, that's all I hope.

BEATRICE: You crazy or sump'm? [*She tries to turn him to her.*]

EDDIE [*he keeps his head turned away*]: What's so crazy? I don't like his whole way.

BEATRICE: Listen, you never seen a blond guy in your life? What about Whitey Balso?

EDDIE [*turning to her victoriously*]: Sure, but Whitey don't sing; he don't do like that on the ships.

BEATRICE: Well, maybe that's the way they do in Italy.

EDDIE: Then why don't his brother sing? Marco goes around like a man; nobody kids Marco. [*He moves from her, halts. She realizes there is a campaign solidified in him.*] I tell you the truth I'm surprised I have to tell you all this. I mean I'm surprised, B.

BEATRICE [*she goes to him with purpose now*]: Listen, you ain't gonna start nothin' here.

EDDIE: I ain't startin' nothin', but I ain't gonna stand around lookin' at that. For that character I didn't bring her up. I swear, B., I'm surprised at you; I sit there waitin' for you to wake up but everything is great with you.

BEATRICE: No, everything ain't great with me.

EDDIE: No?

BEATRICE: No. But I got other worries.

EDDIE: Yeah. [*He is already weakening.*]

BEATRICE: Yeah, you want me to tell you?

EDDIE [*in retreat*]: Why? What worries you got?

BEATRICE: When am I gonna be a wife again, Eddie?

EDDIE: I ain't been feelin' good. They bother me since they came.

BEATRICE: It's almost three months you don't feel good; they're only here a couple of weeks. It's three months, Eddie.

EDDIE: I don't know, B. I don't want to talk about it.

BEATRICE: What's the matter, Eddie, you don't like me, heh?

EDDIE: What do you mean, I don't like you? I said I don't feel good, that's all.

BEATRICE: Well, tell me, am I doing something wrong? Talk to me.

EDDIE [*Pause. He can't speak, then*]: I can't. I can't talk about it.

BEATRICE: Well tell me what –

EDDIE: I got nothin' to say about it!

[*She stands for a moment; he is looking off; she turns to go into the house.*]

EDDIE: I'll be all right, B.; just lay off me, will ya? I'm worried about her.

BEATRICE: The girl is gonna be eighteen years old, it's time already.

EDDIE: B., he's taking her for a ride!

BEATRICE: All right, that's her ride. What're you gonna stand over her till she's forty? Eddie, I want you to cut it out now, you hear me? I don't like it! Now come in the house.

EDDIE: I want to take a walk, I'll be in right away.

BEATRICE: They ain't goin' to come any quicker if you stand in the street. It ain't nice, Eddie.

EDDIE: I'll be in right away. Go ahead. [*He walks off.*]

[*She goes into the house.* EDDIE *glances up the street, sees* LOUIS *and* MIKE *coming, and sits on an iron railing.* LOUIS *and* MIKE *enter.*]

LOUIS: Wanna go bowlin' tonight?

EDDIE: I'm too tired. Goin' to sleep.

LOUIS: How's your two submarines?

EDDIE: They're okay.

LOUIS: I see they're gettin' work allatime.

EDDIE: Oh yeah, they're doin' all right.

MIKE: That's what we oughta do. We oughta leave the country and come in under the water. Then we get work.

EDDIE: You ain't kiddin'.

LOUIS: Well, what the hell. Y'know?

EDDIE: Sure.

LOUIS [*sits on railing beside* EDDIE]: Believe me, Eddie, you got a lotta credit comin' to you.

EDDIE: Aah, they don't bother me, don't cost me nutt'n.

MIKE: That older one, boy, he's a regular bull. I seen him the other day liftin' coffee bags over the Matson Line. They leave him alone he woulda load the whole ship by himself.

EDDIE: Yeah, he's a strong guy, that guy. Their father was a regular giant, supposed to be.

LOUIS: Yeah, you could see. He's a regular slave.

MIKE [*grinning*]: That blond one, though – [EDDIE *looks at him.*] He's got a sense of humuor. [LOUIS *snickers.*]

EDDIE [*searchingly*]: Yeah. He's funny –

MIKE [*starting to laugh*]: Well he ain't exackly funny, but he's always like makin' remarks like, y'know? He comes around, everybody's laughin'. [LOUIS *laughs*].

EDDIE, [*uncomfortably, grinning*]: Yeah, well . . . he's got a sense of humour.

MIKE [*laughing*]: Yeah, I mean, he's always makin' like remarks, like, y'know?

EDDIE· Yeah, I know. But he's a kid yet, y'know? He – he's just a kid, that's all.

MIKE [*getting hysterical with* LOUIS]: I know. You take one look at him – everybody's happy. [LOUIS *laughs.*] I worked one day with him last week over the Moore-MacCormack Line, I'm tellin' you they was all hysterical. [LOUIS *and he explode in laughter.*]

EDDIE: Why? What'd he do?

MIKE: I don't know . . . he was just humorous. You never can remember what he says, y'know? But it's the way he says it. I mean he gives you a look sometimes and you start laughin'!

EDDIE: Yeah. [*Troubled*] He's got a sense of humour.

MIKE [*gasping*]: Yeah.

LOUIS [*rising*]: Well, we see ya, Eddie.

EDDIE: Take it easy.

LOUIS: Yeah. See ya.

MIKE: If you wanna come bowlin' later we're goin' Flatbush Avenue.

[*Laughing, they move to exit, meeting* RODOLPHO *and* CATHERINE *entering on the street. Their laughter rises as they see* RODOLPHO, *who does not understand but joins in.* EDDIE *moves to enter the house as* LOUIS *and* MIKE *exit.* CATHERINE *stops him at the door.*]

CATHERINE: Hey, Eddie – what a picture we saw! Did we laugh!

EDDIE [*He can't help smiling at sight of her*]: Where'd you go?

CATHERINE: Paramount. It was with those two guys, y'know? That –

EDDIE: Brooklyn Paramount?

CATHERINE [*with an edge of anger, embarrassed before* RODOLPHO]: Sure, the Brooklyn Paramount. I told you we wasn't goin' to New York.

EDDIE [*retreating before the threat of her anger*]: All right, I only asked you. [*To* RODOLPHO] I just don't want her hangin' around Times Square, see? It's full of tramps over there.

RODOLPHO: I would like to go to Broadway once, Eddie. I would like to walk with her once where the theatres are and the opera. Since I was a boy I see pictures of those lights.

EDDIE [*his little patience waning*]: I want to talk to her a minute, Rodolpho. Go inside, will you?

RODOLPHO: Eddie, we only walk together in the streets. She teaches me.

CATHERINE: You know what he can't get over? That there's no fountains in Brooklyn!

EDDIE [*smiling unwillingly*]: Fountains? [RODOLPHO *smiles at his own naïveté.*]

CATHERINE: In Italy he says, every town's got fountains, and they meet there. And you know what? They got oranges on the trees where he comes from, and lemons. Imagine – on the trees? I mean it's interesting. But he's crazy for New York.

RODOLPHO [*attempting familiarity*]: Eddie, why can't we go once to Broadway – ?

EDDIE: Look, I gotta tell her something –

RODOLPHO: Maybe you can come too. I want to see all those lights. [*He sees no response in* EDDIE's *face. He glances at* CATHERINE.] I'll walk by the river before I go to sleep. [*He walks off down the street.*]

CATHERINE: Why don't you talk to him, Eddie? He blesses you, and you don't talk to him hardly.

EDDIE, [*enveloping her with his eyes*]: I bless you and you don't talk to me. [*He tries to smile.*]

CATHERINE: *I* don't talk to you? [*She hits his arm.*] What do you mean?

EDDIE: I don't see you no more. I come home you're runnin' around someplace –

CATHERINE: Well, he wants to see everything, that's all, so we go . . . You mad at me?

EDDIE: No. [*He moves from her, smiling sadly.*] It's just I used to come home, you was always there. Now, I turn around, you're a big girl. I don't know how to talk to you.

CATHERINE: Why?

EDDIE: I don't know, you're runnin', you're runnin', Katie. I don't think you listening any more to me.

CATHERINE [*going to him*]: Ah, Eddie, sure I am. What's the matter? You don't like him?

[*Slight pause.*]

EDDIE [*turns to her*]: *You* like him, Katie?

CATHERINE, [*with a blush but holding her ground*]: Yeah. I like him.

EDDIE [*his smile goes*]: You like him.

CATHERINE [*looking down*]: Yeah. [*Now she looks at him for the consequences, smiling but tense. He looks at her like a lost boy.*] What're you got against him? I don't understand. He only blesses you.

EDDIE [*turns away*]: He don't bless me, Katie.

CATHERINE: He does! You're like a father to him!

EDDIE [*turns to her*]: Katie.

CATHERINE: What, Eddie?

EDDIE: You gonna marry him?

CATHERINE: I don't know. We just been . . . goin' around, that's all. [*Turns to him*] What're you got against him, Eddie? Please, tell me. What?

EDDIE: He don't respect you.

CATHERINE: Why?

EDDIE: Katie . . . if you wasn't an orphan, wouldn't he ask your father's permission before he run around with you like this?

CATHERINE: Oh, well, he didn't think you'd mind.

EDDIE: He knows I mind, but it don't bother him if I mind, don't you see that?

CATHERINE: No, Eddie, he's got all kinds of respect for me. And you too! We walk across the street he takes my arm – he almost bows to me! You got him all wrong, Eddie; I mean it, you –

EDDIE: Katie, he's only bowin' to his passport.

CATHERINE: His passport!

EDDIE: That's right. He marries you he's got the right to be an American citizen. That's what's goin' on here. [*She is puzzled and surprised.*] You understand what I'm tellin' you? The guy is lookin' for his break, that's all he's lookin' for.

CATHERINE [*pained*]: Oh, no, Eddie, I don't think so.

EDDIE: You don't think so! Katie, you're gonna make me cry here. Is that a workin' man? What does he do with his first money? A snappy new jacket he buys, records, a pointy pair new shoes and his brother's kids are starvin' over there with tuberculosis? That's a hit-and-run guy, Baby; he's got bright lights in his head, Broadway. Them guys don't think of nobody but theirself! You marry him and the next time you see him it'll be for divorce!

CATHERINE [*steps toward him*]: Eddie, he never said a word about his papers or –

EDDIE: You mean he's supposed to tell you that?

CATHERINE: I don't think he's even thinking about it.

EDDIE: What's better for him to think about! He could be picked up any day here and he's back pushin' taxis up the hill!

CATHERINE: No, I don't believe it.

EDDIE: Katie, don't break my heart, listen to me.

CATHERINE: I don't want to hear it.

EDDIE: Katie, listen . . .

CATHERINE: He loves me!

EDDIE [*with deep alarm*]: Don't say that, for God's sake! This is the oldest racket in the country –

CATHERINE [*desperately, as though he had made his imprint*]: I don't believe it! [*She rushes to the house.*]

EDDIE [*following her*]: They been pullin' this since the Immigration Law was put in! They grab a green kid that don't know nothin' and they –

CATHERINE [*sobbing*]: I don't believe it and I wish to hell you'd stop it!

EDDIE: Katie!

[*They enter the apartment. The lights in the living room have risen and* BEATRICE *is there. She looks past the sobbing* CATHERINE *at* EDDIE, *who in the presence of his wife, makes an awkward gesture of eroded command, indicating* CATHERINE.]

EDDIE: Why don't you straighten her out?

BEATRICE [*inwardly angered at his flowing emotion, which in itself alarms her*]: When are you going to leave her alone?

EDDIE: B , the guy is no good!

BEATRICE [*suddenly, with open fright and fury*]: You going to leave her alone? Or you gonna drive me crazy? [*He turns, striving to retain his dignity, but nevertheless in guilt walks out of the house, into the street and away.* CATHERINE *starts into a bedroom.*] Listen, Catherine. [CATHERINE *halts, turns to her sheepishly.*] What are you going to do with yourself?

CATHERINE: I don't know.

BEATRICE: Don't tell me you don't know; you're not a baby any more, what are you going to do with yourself?

CATHERINE: He won't listen to me.

BEATRICE: I don't understand this. He's not your father, Catherine. I don't understand what's going on here.

CATHERINE [*as one who herself is trying to rationalize a buried impulse*]: What am I going to do, just kick him in the face with it?

BEATRICE: Look, honey, you wanna get married, or don't you wanna get married? What are you worried about, Katie?

CATHERINE [*quietly, trembling*]: I don't know B. It just seems wrong if he's against it so much.

BEATRICE [*never losing her aroused alarm*]: Sit down, honey, I want to tell you something. Here, sit down. Was there ever any fella he liked for you? There wasn't, was there?

CATHERINE: But he says Rodolpho's just after his papers.

BEATRICE: Look, he'll say anything. What does he care what he says? If it was a prince came here for you it would be no different. You know that, don't you?

CATHERINE: Yeah, I guess.

BEATRICE: So what does that mean?

CATHERINE [*slowly turns her head to* BEATRICE]: What?

BEATRICE: It means you gotta be your own self more. You still think you're a little girl, honey. But nobody else can make up your mind for you any more, you understand? You gotta give him to understand that he can't give you orders no more.

CATHERINE: Yeah, but how am I going to do that? He thinks I'm a baby.

BEATRICE: Because *you* think you're a baby. I told you fifty times already, you can't act the way you act. You still walk around in front of him in your slip –

CATHERINE: Well I forgot.

BEATRICE: Well you can't do it. Or like you sit on the edge of the bathtub talkin' to him when he's shavin' in his underwear.

CATHERINE: When'd I do that?

BEATRICE: I seen you in there this morning.

CATHERINE: Oh ... well, I wanted to tell him something and I –

BEATRICE: I know, honey. But if you act like a baby and he be treatin' you like a baby. Like when he comes home sometimes you throw yourself at him like when you was twelve years old.

CATHERINE: Well I like to see him and I'm happy so I –

BEATRICE: Look, I'm not tellin' you what to do honey, but –

CATHERINE: No, you could tell me, B.! Gee, I'm all mixed up. See, I – He looks so sad now and it hurts me.

BEATRICE: Well look Katie, if it's goin' to hurt you so much you're gonna end up an old maid here.

CATHERINE: No!

BEATRICE: I'm tellin' you, I'm not makin' a joke. I tried to tell you a couple of times in the last year or so. That's why I was so happy you were going to go out and get work, you wouldn't be here so much, you'd be a little more independent. I mean it. It's wonderful for a whole family to love each other, but you're a grown woman and you're in the same house with a grown man. So you'll act different now, heh?

CATHERINE: Yeah, I will. I'll remember.

BEATRICE: Because it ain't only up to him, Katie, you understand? I told him the same thing already.

CATHERINE [*quickly*]: What?

BEATRICE: That he should let you go. But, you see, if only I tell him, he thinks I'm just bawlin' him out, or maybe I'm jealous or somethin', you know?

CATHERINE [*astonished*]: He said you was jealous?

BEATRICE: No, I'm just sayin' maybe that's what he thinks. [*She reaches over to* CATHERINE's *hand; with a strained smile*] You think I'm jealous of you, honey?

CATHERINE: No! It's the first I thought of it.

BEATRICE [*with a quiet sad laugh*]: Well you should have thought of it before . . . but I'm not. We'll be all right. Just give him to understand; you don't have to fight, you're just – You're a woman, that's all, and you got a nice boy, and now the time came when you said good-bye. All right?

CATHERINE [*strangely moved at the prospect*]: All right . . . If I can.

BEATRICE: Honey . . . you gotta.

[CATHERINE, *sensing now an imperious demand, turns with some fear, with a discovery, to* BEATRICE. *She is at the edge of tears, as though a familiar world had shattered.*]

CATHERINE: Okay.

[*Lights out on them and up on* ALFIERI, *seated behind his desk.*]

ALFIERI: It was at this time that he first came to me. I had represented his father in an accident case some years before, and I was acquainted with the family in a casual way. I remember him now as he walked through my doorway –

[*Enter* EDDIE *down right ramp.*]

His eyes were like tunnels; my first thought was that he had committed a crime. [EDDIE *sits beside the desk, cap in hand, looking out.*]

But soon I saw it was only a passion that had moved into his body, like a stranger. [ALFIERI *pauses, looks down at his desk, then to* EDDIE *as though he were continuing a conversation with him.*] I don't quite understand what I can do for you. Is there a question of law somewhere?

EDDIE: That's what I want to ask you.

ALFIERI: Because there's nothing illegal about a girl falling in love with an immigrant.

EDDIE: Yeah, but what about it if the only reason for it is to get his papers?

ALFIERI: First of all you don't know that.

EDDIE: I see it in his eyes; he's laughin' at her and he's laughin' at me.

ALFIERI: Eddie, I'm a lawyer. I can only deal in what's provable. You understand that, don't you? Can you prove that?

EDDIE: *I know what's in his mind, Mr Alfieri!*

ALFIERI: Eddie, even if you could prove that –

EDDIE: Listen . . . will you listen to me a minute? My father always said you was a smart man. I want you to listen to me.

ALFIERI: I'm only a lawyer, Eddie.

EDDIE: Will you listen a minute? I'm talkin' about the law. Lemme just bring out what I mean. A man, which he comes into the country illegal, don't it stand to reason he's gonna take every penny and put it in the sock? Because they don't know from one day to another, right?

ALFIERI: All right.

EDDIE: He's spendin'. Records he buys now. Shoes. Jackets. Y'understand me? This guy ain't worried. This guy is *here.* So it must be that he's got it all laid out in his mind already – he's stayin'. Right?

ALFIERI: Well? What about it?

EDDIE: All right. [*He glances at* ALFIERI, *then down to the floor.*] I'm talking to you confidential, ain't I?

ALFIERI: Certainly.

EDDIE: I mean it don't go no place but here. Because I don't like to say this about anybody. Even my wife I didn't exactly say this.

ALFIERI: What is it?

EDDIE [*takes a breath and glances briefly over each shoulder*]: The guy ain't right, Mr Alfieri.

ALFIERI: What do you mean?

EDDIE: I mean he ain't right.

ALFIERI: I don't get you.

EDDIE [*shifts to another position in the chair*]: Dja ever get a look at him?

ALFIERI: Not that I know of, no.

EDDIE: He's a blond guy. Like . . . platinum. You know what I mean?

ALFIERI: No.

EDDIE: I mean if you close the paper fast – you could blow him over.

ALFIERI: Well that doesn't mean –

EDDIE: Wait a minute, I'm tellin' you sump'm. He sings, see. Which is – I mean it's all right, but sometimes he hits a note, see. I turn around. I mean – high. You know what I mean?

ALFIERI: Well, that's a tenor.

EDDIE: I know a tenor, Mr Alfieri. This ain't no tenor. I mean if you came in the house and you didn't know who was singin', you wouldn't be lookin' for him you be lookin' for her.

ALFIERI: Yes, but that's not –

EDDIE: I'm tellin' you sump'm, wait a minute. Please, Mr Alfieri. I'm tryin' to bring out my thoughts here. Couple of nights ago my niece brings out a dress which it's too small for her, because she shot up like a light this last year. He takes the dress, lays it on the table, he cuts it up; one-two-three, he makes a new dress. I mean he looked so sweet there, like an angel – you could kiss him he was so sweet.

ALFIERI: Now look, Eddie –

EDDIE: Mr Alfieri, they're laughin' at him on the piers. I'm ashamed. Paper Doll they call him. Blondie now. His brother thinks it's because he's got a sense of humour, see – which he's got – but that ain't what they're laughin'. Which they're not goin' to come out with it because they know he's my relative, which they have to see me if they make a crack, y'know? But I know what they're laughin' at, and when I think of that guy layin' his hands on her I could – I mean it's eatin' me out, Mr Alfieri, because I struggled for that girl. And now he comes in my house and –

ALFIERI: Eddie, look – I have my own children. I understand you. But the law is very specific. The law does not . . .

EDDIE [*with a fuller flow of indignation*]: You mean to tell me that there's no law that a guy which he ain't right can go to work and marry a girl and – ?

ALFIERI: You have no recourse in the law, Eddie.

EDDIE: Yeah, but if he ain't right, Mr Alfieri, you mean to tell me –

ALFIERI: There is nothing you can do, Eddie, believe me.

EDDIE: Nothin'.

ALFIERI: Nothing at all. There's only one legal question here.

EDDIE: What?

ALFIERI: The manner in which they entered the country. But I don't think you want to do anything about that, do you?

EDDIE: You mean – ?

ALFIERI: Well, they entered illegally.

EDDIE: Oh, Jesus, no, I wouldn't do nothin' about that, I mean –

ALFIERI: All right, then, let me talk now, eh?

EDDIE: Mr Alfieri, I can't believe what you tell me. I mean there must be some kinda law which –

ALFIERI: Eddie, I want you to listen to me. [*Pause.*] You know, sometimes God mixes up the people. We all love somebody, the wife, the kids – every man's got somebody that he loves, heh? But sometimes . . . there's too much. You know? There's too much, and it goes where it mustn't. A man works hard, he brings up a child, sometimes it's a niece, sometimes even a daughter, and he never realizes it, but through the years – there is too much love for the daughter, there is too much love for the niece. Do you understand what I'm saying to you?

EDDIE [*sardonically*]: What do you mean, I shouldn't look out for her good?

ALFIERI: Yes, but these things have to end, Eddie, that's all. The child has to grow up and go away, and the man has to learn to forget. Because after all, Eddie – what other way can it end? [*Pause.*] Let her go. That's my advice. You did your job, now it's her life; wish her luck, and let her go. [*Pause.*] Will you do that? Because there's no law, Eddie; make up your mind to it; the law is not interested in this.

EDDIE: You mean to tell me, even if he's a punk? If he's –

ALFIERI: There's nothing you can do.

[EDDIE *stands*]

EDDIE: Well, all right, thanks. Thanks very much.

ALFIERI: What are you going to do?

EDDIE [*with a helpless but ironic gesture*: What can I do? I'm a patsy, what can a patsy do? I worked like a dog twenty years so a punk could have her, so that's what I done. I mean, in the worst times, in the worst, when there wasn't a ship comin' in the harbour, I didn't stand around lookin' for relief – I hustled. When there was empty piers in Brooklyn I went to Hoboken, Staten Island, the West Side, Jersey, all over – because I made a promise. I took out of my own mouth to give to her. I took out of my wife's mouth. I walked hungry plenty days in this city! [*It begins to break through.*] And now I gotta sit in my own house and look at a son-of-a-bitch punk like that – which he came out of nowhere! I give him my house to sleep! I take the blankets off my bed for him, and he takes and puts his dirty filthy hands on her like a god-dam thief!

ALFIERI [*rising*]: But, Eddie, she's a woman now.

EDDIE: He's stealing from me!

ALFIERI: She wants to get married, Eddie. She can't marry you, can she?

EDDIE [*furiously*]: What're you talkin' about, marry me! I don't know what the hell you're talkin' about!

[*Pause.*]

ALFIERI: I gave you my advice, Eddie. That's it.

[EDDIE *gathers himself. A pause.*]

EDDIE: Well, thanks. Thanks very much. It just – it's breakin' my heart, y'know. I –

ALFIERI: I understand. Put it out of your mind. Can you do that?

EDDIE: I'm – [*He feels the threat of sobs, and with a helpless wave*] I'll see you around. [*He goes out up the right ramp.*]

ALFIERI [*sits on desk*]: There are times when you want to spread an alarm, but nothing has happened. I knew, I knew then and there – I could have finished the whole story that afternoon. It wasn't as though there was a mystery to unravel. I could see every step coming, step after step, like a dark figure walking down a hall toward a certain door. I knew where he was heading for, I knew where he was going to end. And I sat here many afternoons asking myself why, being an intelligent man, I was so powerless to stop it. I even went to a certain old lady in the neighbourhood, a very wise old woman, and I told her, and she only nodded, and said, 'Pray for him . . .' And so I – waited here.

[*As lights go out on* ALFIERI, *they rise in the apartment where all are finishing dinner.* BEATRICE *and* CATHERINE *are clearing the table.*]

CATHERINE: You know where they went?
BEATRICE: Where?
CATHERINE: They went to Africa once. On a fishing boat. [EDDIE *glances at her.*] It's true, Eddie.

[BEATRICE *exits into the kitchen with dishes.*]

EDDIE: I didn't say nothin'. [*He goes to his rocker, picks up a newspaper.*]
CATHERINE: And I was never even in Staten Island.

EDDIE [*sitting with the paper*]: You didn't miss nothin'. [*Pause.* CATHERINE *takes dishes out.*] How long that take you, Marco – to get to Africa?

MARCO [*rising*]: Oh . . . two days. We go all over.

RODOLPHO [*rising*]: Once we went to Yugoslavia.

EDDIE [*to* MARCO]: They pay all right on them boats?

[BEATRICE *enters. She and* RODOLPHO *stack the remaining dishes.*]

MARCO: If they catch fish they pay all right. [*Sits on a stool.*]

RODOLPHO: They're family boats, though. And nobody in our family owned one. So we only worked when one of the families was sick.

BEATRICE: Y'know, Marco, what I don't understand – there's an ocean full of fish and yiz are all starvin'.

EDDIE: They gotta have boats, nets, you need money.

[CATHERINE *enters.*]

BEATRICE: Yeah, but couldn't they like fish from the beach? You see them down Coney Island –

MARCO: Sardines.

EDDIE: Sure. [*Laughing*] How you gonna catch sardines on a hook?

BEATRICE: Oh, I didn't know they're sardines. [*To* CATHERINE] They're sardines!

CATHERINE: Yeah, they follow them all over the ocean, Africa, Yugoslavia . . . [*She sits and begins to look through a movie magazine.* RODOLPHO *joins her.*]

BEATRICE [*to* EDDIE]: It's funny, y'know. You never think of it, that sardines are swimming in the ocean! [*She exits to kitchen with dishes.*]

CATHERINE: I know. It's like oranges and lemons on a tree. [*To* EDDIE] I mean you ever think of oranges and lemons on a tree?

EDDIE: Yeah, I know. It's funny. [*To* MARCO] I heard that they paint the oranges to make them look orange.

[BEATRICE *enters.*]

MARCO [*he has been reading a letter*]: Paint?

EDDIE: Yeah, I heard that they grow like green.

MARCO: No, in Italy the oranges are orange.

RODOLPHO: Lemons are green.

EDDIE [*resenting his instruction*]: I know lemons are green, for Christ's sake, you see them in the store they're green sometimes. I said oranges they paint, I didn't say nothin' about lemons.

BEATRICE [*sitting; diverting their attention*]: Your wife is gettin' the money all right, Marco?

MARCO: Oh, yes. She bought medicine for my boy.

BEATRICE: That's wonderful. You feel better, heh?

MARCO: Oh, yes! But I'm lonesome.

BEATRICE: I just hope you ain't gonna do like some of them around here. They're here twenty-five years, some men, and they didn't get enough together to go back twice.

MARCO: Oh, I know. We have many families in our town, the children never saw the father. But I will go home. Three, four years, I think.

BEATRICE: Maybe you should keep more here. Because maybe she thinks it comes so easy you'll never get ahead of yourself.

MARCO: Oh, no, she saves. I send everything. My wife is very lonesome. [*He smiles shyly.*]

BEATRICE: She must be nice. She pretty? I bet, heh?

MARCO [*blushing*]: No, but she understand everything.

RODOLPHO: Oh, he's got a clever wife!

EDDIE: I betcha there's plenty surprises sometimes when those guys get back there, heh?

MARCO: Surprises?

EDDIE, *laughing*: I mean, you know – they count the kids and there's a couple extra than when they left?

MARCO: No – no . . . The women wait, Eddie. Most. Most. Very few surprises.

RODOLPHO: It's more strict in our town. [EDDIE *looks at him now.*] It's not so free.

EDDIE [*rises, paces up and down*]: It ain't so free here either, Rodolpho, like you think. I seen greenhorns sometimes get in trouble that way – they think just because a girl don't go around with a shawl over her head that she ain't strict, y'know? Girl don't have to wear black dress to be strict. Know what I mean?

RODOLPHO: Well, I always have respect –

EDDIE: I know, but in your town you wouldn't just drag off some girl without permission, I mean. [*He turns.*] You know what I mean, Marco? It ain't that much different here.

MARCO [*cautiously*]: Yes.

BEATRICE: Well, he didn't exactly drag her off though, Eddie.

EDDIE: I know, but I seen some of them get the wrong idea some-times. [*To* RODOLPHO] I mean it might be a little more free here but it's just as strict.

RODOLPHO: I have respect for her, Eddie. I do anything wrong?

EDDIE: Look, kid, I ain't her father, I'm only her uncle –

BEATRICE: Well then, be an uncle then. [EDDIE *looks at her, aware of her criticizing force.*] I mean.

MARCO: No, Beatrice, if he does wrong you must tell him. [*To* EDDIE] What does he do wrong?

EDDIE: Well, Marco, till he came here she was never out on the street twelve o'clock at night.

MARCO [*to* RODOLPHO]: You come home early now.

BEATRICE [*to* CATHERINE]: Well, you said the movie ended late, didn't you?

CATHERINE: Yeah.

BEATRICE: Well, tell him, honey. [*To* EDDIE] The movie ended late.

EDDIE: Look, B., I'm just sayin' – he thinks she always stayed out like that.

MARCO: You come home early now, Rodolpho.

RODOLPHO [*embarrassed*]: All right, sure. But I can't stay in the house all the time, Eddie.

EDDIE: Look, kid, I'm not only talkin' about her. The more you run around like that the more chance you're takin'. [*To* BEATRICE] I mean suppose he gets hit by a car or something. [*To* MARCO] Where's his papers, who is he? Know what I mean?

BEATRICE: Yeah, but who is he in the daytime, though? It's the same chance in the daytime.

EDDIE [*holding back a voice full of anger*]: Yeah, but he don't have to go lookin' for it, Beatrice. If he's here to work, then he should work; if he's here for a good time then he could fool around! [*To* MARCO] But I understood, Marco, that you was both comin' to make a livin' for your family. You understand me, don't you, Marco? [*He goes to his rocker.*]

MARCO: I beg your pardon, Eddie.

EDDIE: I mean, that's what I understood in the first place, see.

MARCO: Yes. That's why we came.

EDDIE [*sits on his rocker*]: Well, that's all I'm askin'.

[EDDIE *reads his paper. There is a pause, an awkwardness. Now* CATHERINE *gets up and puts a record on the phonograph – 'Paper Doll.'*]

CATHERINE [*flushed with revolt*]: You wanna dance, Rodolpho?

[EDDIE *freezes.*]

RODOLPHO [*in deference to* EDDIE]: No, I – I'm tired.

BEATRICE: Go ahead, dance, Rodolpho.

CATHERINE: Ah, come on. They got a beautiful quartet, these guys. Come.

[*She has taken his hand and he stiffly rises, feeling* EDDIE*'s eyes on his back, and they dance.*]

EDDIE [*to* CATHERINE]: What's that, a new record?

CATHERINE: It's the same one. We bought it the other day.

BEATRICE [*to* EDDIE]: They only bought three records. [*She watches them dance;* EDDIE *turns his head away.* MARCO *just sits there, waiting. Now* BEATRICE *turns to* EDDIE] Must be nice to go all over in one of them fishin' boats. I would like that myself. See all them other countries?

EDDIE: Yeah.

BEATRICE [*to* MARCO]: But the women don't go along, I bet.

MARCO: No, not on the boats. Hard work.

BEATRICE: What're you got, a regular kitchen and everything?

MARCO: Yes, we eat very good on the boats – especially when Rodolpho comes along; everybody gets fat.

BEATRICE: Oh, he cooks?

MARCO: Sure, very good cook. Rice, pasta, fish, everything.

[EDDIE *lowers his paper.*]

EDDIE: He's a cook, too! [*Looking at* RODOLPHO] He sings, he cooks . . .

[RODOLPHO *smiles thankfully.*]

BEATRICE: Well it's good, he could always make a living.

EDDIE: It's wonderful. He sings, he cooks, he could make dresses . . .

CATHERINE: They get some high pay, them guys. The head chefs in all the big hotels are men. You read about them.

EDDIE: That's what I'm sayin'.

[CATHERINE *and* RODOLPHO *continue dancing.*]

CATHERINE: Yeah, well, I mean.

EDDIE [*to* BEATRICE]: He's lucky, believe me. [*Slight pause. He looks away, then back to* BEATRICE.] That's why the water front is no place for him. [*They stop dancing.* RODOLPHO *turns off phonograph.*] I mean like me – I can't cook, I can't sing, I can't make dresses, so I'm on the water front. But if I could cook, if I could sing, if I could make dresses, I wouldn't be on the water front. [*He has been unconsciously twisting the newspaper into a tight roll. They are all regarding him now; he senses he is exposing the issue and he is driven on.*] I would be someplace else. I would be like in a dress store. [*He has bent the rolled paper and it suddenly tears in two. He suddenly gets up and pulls his pants up over his belly and goes to* MARCO.] What do you say, Marco, we go to the bouts next Saturday night. You never seen a fight, did you?

MARCO [*uneasily*]: Only in the moving pictures.

EDDIE [*going to* RODOLPHO]: I'll treat yiz. What do you say, Danish? You wanna come along? I'll buy the tickets.

RODOLPHO: Sure. I like to go.

CATHERINE [*goes to* EDDIE; *nervously happy now*]: I'll make some coffee, all right?

EDDIE: Go ahead, make some! Make it nice and strong. [*Mystified, she smiles and exits to kitchen. He is weirdly elated, rubbing his fists into his palms. He strides to* MARCO.] You wait, Marco, you see some real fights here. You ever do any boxing?

MARCO: No, I never.

EDDIE [*to* RODOLPHO]: Betcha you have done some, heh?

RODOLPHO: No.

EDDIE: Well, come on, I'll teach you.

BEATRICE: What's he got to learn that for?

EDDIE: Ya can't tell, one a these days somebody's liable to step on his foot or sump'm. Come on, Rodolpho, I show you a couple a passes. [*He stands below table.*]

BEATRICE: Go ahead, Rodolpho. He's a good boxer, he could teach you.

RODOLPHO [*embarrassed*]: Well, I don't know how to – [*He moves down to* EDDIE.]

EDDIE: Just put your hands up. Like this, see? That's right. That's very good, keep your left up, because you lead with the left, see, like this. [*He gently moves his left into* RODOLPHO'S *face.*] See? Now what you gotta do is you gotta block me, so when I come in like that you – [RODOLPHO *parries his left.*] Hey, that's very good! [RODOLPHO *laughs.*] All right, now come into me. Come on.

RODOLPHO: I don't want to hit you, Eddie.

EDDIE: Don't pity me, come on. Throw it, I'll show you how to block it. *Rodolpho jabs at him, laughing. The others join.*] 'At's it. Come on again. For the jaw right here. [RODOLPHO *jabs with more assurance.*] Very good!

BEATRICE [*to* MARCO]: He's very good!

[EDDIE *crosses directly upstage of* RODOLPHO.]

EDDIE: Sure, he's great! Come on, kid, put sump'm behind it, you can't hurt me. [RODOLPHO, *more seriously, jabs at* EDDIE'S *jaw and grazes it.*] Attaboy. [CATHERINE *comes from the kitchen, watches.*] Now I'm gonna hit you, so block me, see?

CATHERINE [*with beginning alarm*]: What are they doin'?

[*They are lightly boxing now.*]

BEATRICE [*she senses only the comradeship in it now*]: He's teachin' him; he's very good!

EDDIE: Sure, he's terrific! Look at him go! [RODOLPHO *lands a blow.*] 'At's it! Now, watch out, here I come, Danish! [*He feints with his left hand and lands with his right. It mildly staggers* RODOLPHO. MARCO *rises.*]

CATHERINE [*rushing to* RODOLPHO]: Eddie!

EDDIE: Why? I didn't hurt him. Did I hurt you, kid? [*He rubs the back of his hand across his mouth.*]

RODOLPHO: No, no, he didn't hurt me. [*To* EDDIE *with a certain gleam and a smile*] I was only surprised.

BEATRICE [*pulling* EDDIE *down into the rocker*]: That's enough, Eddie; he did pretty good, though.

EDDIE: Yeah. [*Rubbing his fists together*] He could be very good, Marco. I'll teach him again.

[MARCO *nods at him dubiously.*]

RODOLPHO: Dance, Catherine. Come. [*He takes her hand; they go to phonograph and start it. It plays 'Paper Doll'.*]

[RODOLPHO *takes her in his arms. They dance.* EDDIE *in thought sits in his chair, and* MARCO *takes a chair, places it in front of* EDDIE, *and looks down at it.* BEATRICE *and* EDDIE *watch him.*]

MARCO: Can you lift this chair?

EDDIE: What do you mean?

MARCO: From here. [*He gets on one knee with one hand behind his back, and grasps the bottom of one of the chair legs but does not raise it.*]

EDDIE: Sure, why not? [*He comes to the chair, kneels, grasps the leg, raises the chair one inch, but it leans over to the floor.*] Gee, that's hard, I never knew that. [*He tries again, and again fails.*] It's on an angle, that's why, heh?

MARCO: Here. [*He kneels, grasps, and with strain slowly raises the chair higher and higher, getting to his feet now.* RODOLPHO *and* CATHERINE *have stopped dancing as* MARCO *raises the chair over his head.*

[MARCO *is face to face with* EDDIE, *a strained tension gripping his eyes and jaw, his neck stiff, the chair raised like a weapon over* EDDIE's *head – and he transforms what might appear like a glare of warning into a smile of triumph, and* EDDIE's *grin vanishes as he absorbs his look.*]

CURTAIN

Act Two

Light rises on ALFIERI *at his desk.*

ALFIERI: On the twenty-third of that December a case of Scotch whisky slipped from a net while being unloaded – as a case of Scotch whisky is inclined to do on the twenty-third of December on Pier Forty-one. There was no snow, but it was cold, his wife was out shopping. Marco was still at work. The boy had not been hired that day; Catherine told me later that this was the first time they had been alone together in the house.

[*Light is rising on* CATHERINE *in the apartment.* RODOLPHO *is watching as she arranges a paper pattern on cloth spread on the table.*]

CATHERINE: You hungry?

RODOLPHO: Not for anything to eat. [*Pause.*] I have nearly three hundred dollars. Catherine?

CATHERINE: I heard you.

RODOLPHO: You don't like to talk about it any more?

CATHERINE: Sure, I don't mind talkin' about it.

RODOLPHO: What worries you, Catherine?

CATHERINE: I been wantin' to ask you about something. Could I?

RODOLPHO: All the answers are in my eyes, Catherine. But you don't look in my eyes lately. You're full of secrets. [*She looks at him. She seems withdrawn.*] What is the question?

CATHERINE: Suppose I wanted to live in Italy.

RODOLPHO [*smiling at the incongruity*]: You going to marry somebody rich?

CATHERINE: No, I mean live there – you and me.

RODOLPHO [*his smile vanishing*]: When?

CATHERINE: Well . . . when we get married.

RODOLPHO [*astonished*]: You want to be an Italian?

CATHERINE: No, but I could live there without being Italian. Americans live there.

RODOLPHO: Forever?

CATHERINE: Yeah.

RODOLPHO [*crosses to rocker*]: You're fooling.

CATHERINE: No, I mean it.

RODOLPHO: Where do you get such an idea?

CATHERINE: Well, you're always saying it's so beautiful there, with the mountains and the ocean and all the –

RODOLPHO: You're fooling me.

CATHERINE: I mean it.

RODOLPHO [*goes to her slowly*]: Catherine, if I ever brought you home with no money, no business, nothing, they would call the priest and the doctor and they would say Rodolpho is crazy.

CATHERINE: I know, but I think we would be happier there.

RODOLPHO: Happier! What would you eat? You can't cook the view!

CATHERINE: Maybe you could be a singer, like in Rome or –

RODOLPHO: Rome! Rome is full of singers.

CATHERINE: Well, I could work then.

RODOLPHO: Where?

CATHERINE: God, there must be jobs somewhere!

RODOLPHO: There's nothing! Nothing, nothing, nothing. Now tell me what you're talking about. How can I bring you from a rich country to suffer in a poor country? What are you talking about? [*She searches for words.*] I would be a criminal stealing your face. In two years you would have an old, hungry face. When my brother's babies cry they give them water, water that boiled a bone. Don't you believe that?

CATHERINE [*quietly*]: I'm afraid of Eddie here.

[*Slight pause.*]

RODOLPHO [*steps closer to her*]: We wouldn't live here. Once I am a citizen I could work anywhere and I would find better jobs and we would have a house, Catherine. If I were not afraid to be arrested I would start to be something wonderful here!

CATHERINE [*steeling herself*]: Tell me something. I mean just tell me, Rodolpho – would you still want to do it if it turned out we had to go live in Italy? I mean just if it turned out that way.

RODOLPHO: This is your question or his question?

CATHERINE: I would like to know, Rodolpho. I mean it.

RODOLPHO: To go there with nothing.

CATHERINE: Yeah.

RODOLPHO: No. [*She looks at him wide-eyed.*] No.

CATHERINE: You wouldn't?

RODOLPHO: No; I will not marry you to live in Italy. I want you to be my wife, and I want to be a citizen. Tell him that, or I will. Yes. [*He moves about angrily.*] And tell him also, and tell yourself, please, that I am not a beggar, and you are not a horse, a gift, a favour for a poor immigrant.

CATHERINE: Well, don't get mad!

RODOLPHO: I am furious! [*Goes to her.*] Do you think I am so desperate? My brother is desperate, not me. You think I would carry on my back the rest of my life a woman I didn't love just to be an American? It's so wonderful? You think we have no tall buildings in Italy? Electric lights? No wide streets? No flags? No automobiles? Only work we don't have. I want to be an American so I can work, that is the only wonder here – work! How can you insult me, Catherine?

CATHERINE: I didn't mean that –

RODOLPHO: My heart dies to look at you. Why are you so afraid of him?

CATHERINE [*near tears*]: I don't know!

RODOLPHO: Do you trust me, Catherine? You?

CATHERINE: It's only that I – He was good to me, Rodolpho. You don't know him; he was always the sweetest guy to me. Good. He razzes me all the time but he don't mean it. I know. I would – just feel ashamed if I made him sad. 'Cause I always dreamt that when I got married he would be happy at the wedding, and laughin' – and now he's – mad all the time and nasty – [*She is weeping.*] Tell him you'd live in Italy – just tell him, and maybe he would start to trust you a little, see? Because I want him to be happy; I mean – I like him, Rodolpho – and I can't stand it!

RODOLPHO: Oh, Catherine – oh, little girl.

CATHERINE: I love you, Rodolpho, I love you.

RODOLPHO: Then why are you afraid? That he'll spank you?

CATHERINE: Don't, don't laugh at me! I've been here all my life . . . Every day I saw him when he left in the morning and when he came home at night. You think it's so easy to turn around and say to a man he's nothin' to you no more?

RODOLPHO: I know, but –

CATHERINE: You don't know; nobody knows! I'm not a baby, I know a lot more than people think I know. Beatrice says to be a woman, but –

RODOLPHO: Yes.

CATHERINE: Then why don't she be a woman? If I was a wife I would make a man happy instead of goin' at him all the time. I can tell a block away when he's blue in his mind and just wants to talk to somebody quiet and nice . . . I can tell when he's hungry or wants a beer before he even says anything. I know when his feet hurt him, I mean I *know* him and now I'm supposed to turn around and make a stranger out of him? I don't know why I have to do that, I mean.

RODOLPHO: Catherine. If I take in my hands a little bird. And she grows and wishes to fly. But I will not let her out of my hands because I love her so much, is that right for me to do? I don't say you must hate him; but anyway you must go, mustn't you? Catherine?

CATHERINE [*softly*]: Hold me.

RODOLPHO [*clasping her to him*]: Oh, my little girl.

CATHERINE: Teach me. [*She is weeping.*] I don't know anything, teach me, Rodolpho, hold me.

RODOLPHO: There's nobody here now. Come inside. Come. [*He is leading her toward the bedrooms.*] And don't cry any more.

[*Light rises on the street. In a moment* EDDIE *appears. He is unsteady, drunk. He mounts the stairs. He enters the apartment, looks around, takes out a bottle from one pocket, puts it on the table. Then another bottle from another pocket, and a third from an inside pocket. He sees the pattern and cloth, goes over to it and touches it, and turns toward upstage.*]

EDDIE: Beatrice? [*He goes to the open kitchen door and looks in.*] Beatrice? Beatrice?

[CATHERINE *enters from bedroom; under his gaze she adjusts her dress.*]

CATHERINE: You got home early.

EDDIE: Knocked off for Christmas early. [*Indicating the pattern*] Rodolpho makin' you a dress?

CATHERINE: No. I'm makin' a blouse.

[RODOLPHO *appears in the bedroom doorway.* EDDIE *sees him and his arm jerks slightly in shock.* RODOLPHO *nods to him testingly.*]

RODOLPHO: Beatrice went to buy presents for her mother.

[*Pause.*]

EDDIE: Pack it up. Go ahead. Get your stuff and get outa here. [CATHERINE *instantly turns and walks toward the bedroom, and* EDDIE *grabs her arm.*] Where you goin'?

CATHERINE [*trembling with fright*]: I think I have to get out of here, Eddie.

EDDIE: No, you ain't goin' nowhere, he's the one.

CATHERINE: I think I can't stay here no more. [*She frees her arm, steps back toward the bedroom.*] I'm sorry, Eddie. [*She sees the tears in his eyes.*] Well, don't cry. I'll be around the neighbourhood; I'll see you. I just can't stay here no more. You know I can't. [*Her sobs of pity and love for him break her composure.*] Don't you know I can't? You know that, don't you? [*She goes to him.*] Wish me luck. [*She clasps her hands prayerfully.*] Oh, Eddie, don't be like that!

EDDIE: You ain't goin' nowheres.

CATHERINE: Eddie, I'm not gonna be a baby any more! You –

[*He reaches out suddenly, draws her to him, and as she strives to free herself he kisses her on the mouth.*]

RODOLPHO: Don't! [*He pulls on* EDDIE*'s arm.*] Stop that! Have respect for her!

EDDIE [*spun round by* RODOLPHO]: You want something?

RODOLPHO: Yes! She'll be my wife. That is what I want. My wife!

EDDIE: But what're you gonna be?

RODOLPHO: I show you what I be!

CATHERINE: Wait outside; don't argue with him!

EDDIE: Come on, show me! What're you gonna be? Show me!

RODOLPHO [*with tears of rage*]: Don't say that to me!

[RODOLPHO *flies at him in attack.* EDDIE *pins his arms, laughing, and suddenly kisses him.*]

CATHERINE: Eddie! Let go, ya hear me! I'll kill you! Leggo of him!

[*She tears at* EDDIE*'s face and* EDDIE *releases* RODOLPHO. EDDIE *stands there with tears rolling down his face as he laughs mockingly at* RODOLPHO. *She is staring at him in horror.* RODOLPHO *is rigid. They are like animals that have torn at one another and broken up without a decision, each waiting for the other's mood.*]

EDDIE [*to* CATHERINE]: You see? [*To* RODOLPHO] I give you till tomorrow, kid. Get outa here. Alone. You hear me? Alone.

CATHERINE: I'm going with him, Eddie. [*She starts toward* RODOLPHO.]

EDDIE, [*indicating* RODOLPHO *with his head*] Not with that. [*She halts, frightened. He sits, still panting for breath, and they watch him helplessly as he leans toward them over the table.*] Don't make me do nuttin', Catherine. Watch your step, submarine. By rights they oughta throw you back in the water. But I got pity for you. [*He moves unsteadily toward the door, always facing* RODOLPHO.] Just get outa here and don't lay another hand on her unless you wanna go out feet first. [*He goes out of the apartment.*]

[*The lights go down, as they rise on* ALFIERI.]

ALFIERI: On December twenty-seventh I saw him next. I normally
go home well before six, but that day I sat around looking out my
window at the bay, and when I saw him walking through my
doorway, I knew why I had waited. And if I seem to tell this like
a dream, it was that way. Several moments arrived in the course
of the two talks we had when it occurred to me how – almost
transfixed I had come to feel. I had lost my strength somewhere.
[EDDIE *enters, removing his cap, sits in the chair, looks thoughtfully out.*]
I looked in his eyes more than I listened – in fact, I can hardly
remember the conversation. But I will never forget how dark the
room became when he looked at me; his eyes were like tunnels.
I kept wanting to call the police, but nothing had happened.
Nothing at all had really happened. [*He breaks off and looks down at
the desk. Then he turns to* EDDIE.] So in other words, he won't leave?
EDDIE: My wife is talkin' about renting a room upstairs for them.
An old lady on the top floor is got an empty room.
ALFIERI: What does Marco say?
EDDIE: He just sits there. Marco don't say much.
ALFIERI: I guess they didn't tell him, heh? What happened?
EDDIE: I don't know; Marco don't say much.
ALFIERI: What does your wife say?
EDDIE [*unwilling to pursue this*]: Nobody's talkin' much in the house.
So what about that?
ALFIERI: But you didn't prove anything about him. It sounds like he
just wasn't strong enough to break your grip.
EDDIE: I'm tellin' you I know – he ain't right. Somebody that don't
want it can break it. Even a mouse, if you catch a teeny mouse
and you hold it in your hand, that mouse can give you the right
kind of fight. He didn't give me the right kind of fight, I know it,
Mr Alfieri, the guy ain't right.
ALFIERI: What did you do that for, Eddie?
EDDIE: To show her what he is! So she would see, once and for all!
Her mother'll turn over in the grave! [*He gathers himself almost
peremptorily.*] So what do I gotta do now? Tell me what to do.

ALFIERI: She actually said she's marrying him?

EDDIE: She told me, yeah. So what do I do?

[*Slight pause.*]

ALFIERI: This is my last word, Eddie, take it or not, that's your business. Morally and legally you have no rights, you cannot stop it; she is a free agent.

EDDIE [*angering*]: Didn't you hear what I told you?

ALFIERI [*with a tougher tone*]: I heard what you told me, and I'm telling you what the answer is. I'm not only telling you now, I'm warning you – the law is nature. The law is only a word for what has a right to happen. When the law is wrong it's because it's unnatural, but in this case it is natural and a river will drown you if you buck it now. Let her go. And bless her. [*A phone booth begins to glow on the opposite side of the stage; a faint, lonely blue.* EDDIE *stands up, jaws clenched.*] Somebody had to come for her, Eddie, sooner or later. [EDDIE *starts turning to go and* ALFIERI *rises with new anxiety.*] You won't have a friend in the world, Eddie! Even those who understand will turn against you, even the ones who feel the same will despise you! [EDDIE *moves off.*] Put it out of your mind! Eddie! [*He follows into the darkness, calling desperately.*]

[EDDIE *is gone. The phone is glowing in light now. Light is out on* ALFIERI. EDDIE *has at the same time appeared beside the phone.*]

EDDIE: Give me the number of the Immigration Bureau. Thanks. [*He dials.*] I want to report something. Illegal immigrants. Two of them. That's right. Four-forty-one Saxon Street, Brooklyn, yeah. Ground floor. Heh? [*With greater difficulty*] I'm just around the neighbourhood, that's all. Heh?

[*Evidently he is being questioned further, and he slowly hangs up. He leaves the phone just as* LOUIS *and* MIKE *come down the street.*]

LOUIS: Go bowlin', Eddie?

EDDIE: No, I'm due home.

LOUIS: Well, take it easy.

EDDIE: I'll see yiz.

[*They leave him, exiting right, and he watches them go. He glances about, then goes up into the house. The lights go on in the apartment.* BEATRICE *is taking down Christmas decorations and packing them in a box.*]

EDDIE: Where is everybody? [BEATRICE *does not answer.*] I says where is everybody?

BEATRICE [*looking up at him, wearied with it, and concealing a fear of him*]: I decided to move them upstairs with Mrs Dondero.

EDDIE: Oh, they're all moved up there already?

BEATRICE: Yeah.

EDDIE: Where's Catherine? She up there?

BEATRICE: Only to bring pillow cases.

EDDIE: She ain't movin' in with them.

BEATRICE: Look, I'm sick and tired of it. I'm sick and tired of it!

EDDIE: All right, all right, take it easy.

BEATRICE: I don't wanna hear no more about it, you understand? Nothin'!

EDDIE: What're you blowin' off about? Who brought them in here?

BEATRICE: All right, I'm sorry; I wish I'd a drop dead before I told them to come. In the ground I wish I was.

EDDIE: Don't drop dead, just keep in mind who brought them in here, that's all. [*He moves about restlessly.*] I mean I got a couple of rights here. [*He moves, wanting to beat down her evident disapproval of him.*] This is my house here not their house.

BEATRICE: What do you want from me? They're moved out; what do you want now?

EDDIE: I want my respect!

BEATRICE: So I moved them out, what more do you want? You got your house now, you got your respect.

EDDIE [*he moves about biting his lip*]: I don't like the way you talk to me, Beatrice.

BEATRICE: I'm just tellin' you I done what you want!

EDDIE: I don't like it! The way you talk to me and the way you look at me. This is my house. And she is my niece and I'm responsible for her.

BEATRICE: So that's why you done that to him?

EDDIE: I done what to him?

BEATRICE: What you done to him in front of her; you know what I'm talkin' about. She goes around shakin' all the time, she can't go to sleep! That's what you call responsible for her?

EDDIE [*quietly*]: The guy ain't right, Beatrice. [*She is silent.*] Did you hear what I said?

BEATRICE: Look, I'm finished with it. That's all. [*She resumes her work.*]

EDDIE [*helping her to pack the tinsel*]: I'm gonna have it out with you one of these days, Beatrice.

BEATRICE: Nothin' to have out with me, it's all settled. Now we gonna be like it never happened, that's all.

EDDIE: I want my respect, Beatrice, and you know what I'm talkin' about.

BEATRICE: What?

[*Pause.*]

EDDIE [*finally his resolution hardens*]: What I feel like doin' in the bed and what I don't feel like doin'. I don't want no –

BEATRICE: When'd I say anything about that?

EDDIE: You said, you said, I ain't deaf. I don't want no more conversations about that, Beatrice. I do what I feel like doin' or what I don't feel like doin'.

BEATRICE: Okay.

[*Pause.*]

EDDIE: You used to be different, Beatrice. You had a whole different way.

BEATRICE: *I'm* no different.

EDDIE: You didn't used to jump me all the time about everything. The last year or two I come in the house I don't know what's gonna hit me. It's a shootin' gallery in here and I'm the pigeon.

BEATRICE: Okay, okay.

EDDIE: Don't tell me okay, okay, I'm tellin' you the truth. A wife is supposed to believe the husband. If I tell you that guy ain't right don't tell me he is right.

BEATRICE: But how do you know?

EDDIE: Because I know. I don't go around makin' accusations. He give me the heeby-jeebies the first minute I seen him. And I don't like you sayin' I don't want her marryin' anybody. I broke my back payin' her stenography lessons so she could go out and meet a better class of people. Would I do that if I didn't want her to get married? Sometimes you talk like I was a crazy man or sump'm.

BEATRICE: But she likes him.

EDDIE: Beatrice, she's a baby, how is she gonna know what she likes?

BEATRICE: Well, you kept her a baby, you wouldn't let her go out. I told you a hundred times.

[*Pause.*]

EDDIE: All right. Let her go out, then.

BEATRICE: She don't wanna go out now. It's too late, Eddie.

[*Pause.*]

EDDIE: Suppose I told her to go out. Suppose I –

BEATRICE: They're going to get married next week, Eddie.

EDDIE [*his head jerks around to her*]: She said that?

BEATRICE: Eddie, if you want my advice, go to her and tell her good luck. I think maybe now that you had it out you learned better.

EDDIE: What's the hurry next week?

BEATRICE: Well, she's been worried about him bein' picked up; this way he could start to be a citizen. She loves him, Eddie. [*He gets up, moves about uneasily, restlessly.*] Why don't you give her a good word? Because I still think she would like you to be a friend, y'know? [*He is standing, looking at the floor.*] I mean like if you told her you'd go to the wedding.

EDDIE: She asked you that?

BEATRICE: I know she would like it. I'd like to make a party here for her. I mean there oughta be some kinda send-off. Heh? I mean she'll have trouble enough in her life, let's start it off happy. What do you say? 'Cause in her heart she still loves you, Eddie. I know it. [*He presses his fingers against his eyes.*] What're you, cryin'? [*She goes to him, holds his face.*] Go . . . whyn't you go tell her you're sorry? [CATHERINE *is seen on the upper landing of the stairway, and they hear her descending.*] There . . . she's comin' down. Come on, shake hands with her.

EDDIE [*moving with suppressed suddenness*]: No, I can't, I can't talk to her.

BEATRICE: Eddie, give her a break; a wedding should be happy!

EDDIE: I'm goin', I'm goin' for a walk.

[*He goes upstage for his jacket.* CATHERINE *enters and starts for the bedroom door.*]

BEATRICE: Katie? . . . Eddie, don't go, wait a minute. [*She embraces* EDDIE's *arm with warmth.*] Ask him, Katie. Come on, honey.

EDDIE: It's all right, I'm – [*He starts to go and she holds him.*]

BEATRICE: No, she wants to ask you. Come on, Katie, ask him. We'll have a party! What're we gonna do, hate each other? Come on!

CATHERINE: I'm gonna get married, Eddie. So if you wanna come, the wedding be on Saturday.

[*Pause.*]

EDDIE: Okay. I only wanted the best for you, Katie. I hope you know that.

CATHERINE: Okay. [*She starts out again.*]

EDDIE: Catherine? [*She turns to him.*] I was just tellin' Beatrice . . . if you wanna go out, like . . . I mean I realize maybe I kept you home too much. Because he's the first guy you ever knew, y'know? I mean now that you got a job, you might meet some fellas, and you get a different idea, y'know? I mean you could always come back to him, you're still only kids, the both of yiz. What's the hurry? Maybe you'll get around a little bit, you grow up a little more, maybe you'll see different in a couple of months. I mean you be surprised, it don't have to be him.

CATHERINE: No, we made it up already.

EDDIE [*with increasing anxiety*]: Katie, wait a minute.

CATHERINE: No, I made up my mind.

EDDIE: But you never knew no other fella, Katie! How could you make up your mind?

CATHERINE: 'Cause I did. I don't want nobody else.

EDDIE: But, Katie, suppose he gets picked up.

CATHERINE: That's why we gonna do it right away. Soon as we finish the wedding he's goin' right over and start to be a citizen. I made up my mind, Eddie. I'm sorry. [*To* BEATRICE] Could I take two more pillow cases for the other guys?

BEATRICE: Sure, go ahead. Only don't let her forget where they came from.

[CATHERINE *goes into a bedroom.*]

EDDIE: She's got other boarders up there?

BEATRICE: Yeah, there's two guys that just came over.

EDDIE: What do you mean, came over?

BEATRICE: From Italy. Lipari the butcher – his nephew. They come from Bari, they just got here yesterday. I didn't even know till Marco and Rodolpho moved up there before. [CATHERINE *enters, going toward exit with two pillow cases.*] It'll be nice, they could all talk together.

EDDIE: Catherine! [*She halts near the exit door. He takes in* BEATRICE *too.*] What're you, got no brains? You put them up there with two other submarines?

CATHERINE: Why?

EDDIE [*in a driving fright and anger*]: Why! How do you know they're not trackin' these guys? They'll come up for them and find Marco and Rodolpho! Get them out of the house!

BEATRICE: But they been here so long already –

EDDIE: How do you know what enemies Lipari's got? Which they'd love to stab him in the back?

CATHERINE: Well what'll I do with them?

EDDIE: The neighbourhood is full of rooms. Can't you stand to live a couple of blocks away from him? Get them out of the house!

CATHERINE: Well maybe tomorrow night I'll –

EDDIE: Not tomorrow, do it now. Catherine, you never mix yourself with somebody else's family! These guys get picked up, Lipari's liable to blame you or me and we got his whole family on our head. They got a temper, that family.

[*Two men in overcoats appear outside, start into the house.*]

CATHERINE: How'm I gonna find a place tonight?

EDDIE: Will you stop arguin' with me and get them out! You think I'm always tryin' to fool you or sump'm? What's the matter with you, don't you believe I could think of your good? Did I ever ask sump'm for myself? You think I got no feelin's? I never told you nothin' in my life that wasn't for your good. Nothin'! And look at the way you talk to me! Like I was an enemy! Like I – [*A knock on the door. His head swerves. They all stand motionless. Another knock.* EDDIE, *in a whisper, pointing upstage.*] Go up the fire escape, get them out over the back fence.

[CATHERINE *stands motionless, uncomprehending.*]

FIRST OFFICER [*in the hall*]: Immigration! Open up in there!

EDDIE: Go, go. Hurry up! [*She stands a moment staring at him in a real-ized horror.*] Well, what're you lookin' at!

FIRST OFFICER: Open up!

EDDIE [*calling toward door*]: Who's that there?

FIRST OFFICER: Immigration, open up.

[EDDIE *turns, looks at* BEATRICE. *She sits. Then he looks at* CATHER-INE. *With a sob of fury* CATHERINE *streaks into a bedroom.*
    Knock is repeated.]

EDDIE: All right, take it easy, take it easy. [*He goes and opens the door. The* OFFICER *steps inside.*] What's all this?

FIRST OFFICER: Where are they?

[SECOND OFFICER *sweeps past and, glancing about, goes into the kitchen.*]

EDDIE: Where's who?

FIRST OFFICER: Come on, come on, where are they? [*He hurries into the bedrooms.*]

EDDIE: Who? We got nobody here. [*He looks at* BEATRICE, *who turns her head away. Pugnaciously, furious, he steps toward* BEATRICE.] What's the matter with *you*?

[FIRST OFFICER *enters from the bedroom, calls to the kitchen.*]

FIRST OFFICER: Dominick?

[*Enter* SECOND OFFICER *from kitchen.*]

SECOND OFFICER: Maybe it's a different apartment.

FIRST OFFICER: There's only two more floors up there. I'll take the front, you go up the fire escape. I'll let you in. Watch your step up there.

SECOND OFFICER: Okay, right, Charley. [FIRST OFFICER *goes out apartment door and runs up the stairs.*] This is Four-forty-one, isn't it?

EDDIE: That's right.

[SECOND OFFICER *goes out into the kitchen.*
    EDDIE *turns to* BEATRICE. *She looks at him now and sees his terror.*]

BEATRICE [*weakened with fear*]: Oh, Jesus, Eddie.

EDDIE: What's the matter with *you*?

BEATRICE [*pressing her palms against her face*]: Oh, my God, my God.

EDDIE: What're you, accusin' me?

BEATRICE [*her final thrust is to turn toward him instead of running from him*]: My God, what did you do?

[*Many steps on the outer stair draw his attention. We see the* FIRST OFFICER *descending, with* MARCO, *behind him* RODOLPHO, *and* CATHERINE *and the two strange immigrants, followed by* SECOND OFFICER. BEATRICE *hurries to door.*]

CATHERINE [*backing down stairs, fighting with* FIRST OFFICER; *as they appear on the stairs*]: What do yiz want from them? They work, that's all. They're boarders upstairs, they work on the piers.

BEATRICE [*to* FIRST OFFICER]: Ah, Mister, what do you want from them, who do they hurt?

CATHERINE [*pointing to* RODOLPHO]: They ain't no submarines, he was born in Philadelphia.

FIRST OFFICER: Step aside, lady.

CATHERINE: What do you mean? You can't just come in a house and –

FIRST OFFICER: All right, take it easy. [*To* RODOLPHO] What street were you born in Philadelphia?

CATHERINE: What do you mean, what street? Could you tell me what street you were born?

FIRST OFFICER: Sure. Four blocks away, One-eleven Union Street. Let's go fellas.

CATHERINE [*fending him off* RODOLPHO]: No, you can't! Now, get outa here!

FIRST OFFICER: Look, girlie, if they're all right they'll be out tomorrow. If they're illegal they go back where they came from. If you want, get yourself a lawyer, although I'm tellin' you now you're wasting your money. Let's get them in the car, Dom. [*To the men*] Andiamo, andiamo, let's go.

[*The men start, but* MARCO *hangs back.*]

BEATRICE [*from doorway*]: Who're they hurtin', for God's sake, what do you want from them? They're starvin' over there, what do you want! Marco!

[MARCO *suddenly breaks from the group and dashes into the room and faces* EDDIE; BEATRICE *and* FIRST OFFICER *rush in as* MARCO *spits into* EDDIE'*s face.*

CATHERINE *runs into hallway and throws herself into* RODOLPHO'*s arms.* EDDIE, *with an enraged cry, lunges for* MARCO.]

EDDIE: Oh, you mother's – !

[FIRST OFFICER *quickly intercedes and pushes* EDDIE *from* MARCO, *who stands there accusingly.*]

FIRST OFFICER [*between them, pushing* EDDIE *from* MARCO]: Cut it out!

EDDIE [*over the* FIRST OFFICER'*s shoulder, to* MARCO]: I'll kill you for that, you son of a bitch!

FIRST OFFICER: Hey! [*Shakes him.*] Stay in here now, don't come out, don't bother him. You hear me? Don't come out, fella.

[*For an instant there is silence. Then* FIRST OFFICER *turns and takes* MARCO'*s arm and then gives a last, informative look at* EDDIE. *As he and* MARCO *are going out into the hall,* EDDIE *erupts.*]

EDDIE: I don't forget that, Marco! You hear what I'm sayin'?

[*Out in the hall,* FIRST OFFICER *and* MARCO *go down the stairs. Now, in the street,* LOUIS, MIKE, *and several neighbours including the butcher,* LIPARI – *a stout, intense, middle-aged man – are gathering around the stoop.*

LIPARI, *the butcher, walks over to the two strange men and kisses them. His wife, keening, goes and kisses their hands.* EDDIE *is emerging from the house shouting after* MARCO. BEATRICE *is trying to restrain him.*]

EDDIE: That's the thanks I get? Which I took the blankets off my bed for yiz? You gonna apologize to me, Marco! *Marco!*

FIRST OFFICER [*in the doorway with* MARCO]: All right, lady, let them go. Get in the car, fellas, it's over there.

[RODOLPHO *is almost carrying the sobbing* CATHERINE *off up the street, left.*]

CATHERINE: He was born in Philadelphia! What do you want from him?

FIRST OFFICER: Step aside, lady, come on now . . .

[*The* SECOND OFFICER *has moved off with the two strange men.*

MARCO, *taking advantage of the* FIRST OFFICER's *being occupied with* CATHERINE, *suddenly frees himself and points back at* EDDIE.]

MARCO: That one! I accuse that one!

[EDDIE *brushes* BEATRICE *aside and rushes out to the stoop.*]

FIRST OFFICER [*grabbing him and moving him quickly off up the left street*]: Come on!

MARCO [*as he is taken off, pointing back at* EDDIE]: That one! He killed my children! That one stole the food from my children!

[MARCO *is gone. The crowd has turned to* EDDIE.]

EDDIE [*to* LIPARI *and wife*]: He's crazy! I give them the blankets off my bed. Six months I kept them like my own brothers!

[LIPARI, *the butcher, turns and starts up left with his arm around his wife.*]

EDDIE: Lipari! [*He follows* LIPARI *up left.*] For Christ's sake, I kept them, I give them the blankets off my bed!

[LIPARI *and wife exit.* EDDIE *turns and starts crossing down right to* LOUIS *and* MIKE.]

EDDIE: Louis! *Louis!*

[LOUIS *barely turns, then walks off and exits down right with* MIKE. *Only* BEATRICE *is left on the stoop.* CATHERINE *now returns, blank-eyed, from offstage and the car.* EDDIE *calls after* LOUIS *and* MIKE.]

EDDIE: He's gonna take that back. He's gonna take that back or I'll kill him! You hear me? I'll kill him! I'll kill him! [*He exits up street calling.*]

[*There is a pause of darkness before the lights rise, on the reception room of a prison.* MARCO *is seated;* ALFIERI, CATHERINE, *and* RODOLPHO *standing.*]

ALFIERI: I'm waiting, Marco, what do you say?

RODOLPHO: Marco never hurt anybody.

ALFIERI: I can bail you out until your hearing comes up. But I'm not going to do it, you understand me? Unless I have your promise. You're an honourable man, I will believe your promise. Now what do you say?

MARCO: In my country he would be dead now. He would not live this long.

ALFIERI: All right, Rodolpho – you come with me now.

RODOLPHO: No! Please, Mister. Marco – promise the man. Please, I want you to watch the wedding. How can I be married and you're in here? Please, you're not going to do anything; you know you're not.

[MARCO *is silent.*]

CATHERINE [*kneeling left of* MARCO]: Marco, don't you understand? He can't bail you out if you're gonna do something bad. To hell with Eddie. Nobody is gonna talk to him again if he lives to a hundred. Everybody knows you spit in his face, that's enough, isn't it? Give me the satisfaction – I want you at the wedding. You got a wife and kids, Marco. You could be workin' till the hearing comes up, instead of layin' around here.

MARCO [*to* ALFIERI]: I have no chance?

ALFIERI [*crosses to behind* MARCO]: No, Marco. You're going back. The hearing is a formality, that's all.

MARCO: But him? There is a chance, eh?

ALFIERI: When she marries him he can start to become an American. They permit that, if the wife is born here.

MARCO [*looking at* RODOLPHO]: Well – we did something. [*He lays a palm on* RODOLPHO's *arm and* RODOLPHO *covers it.*]

RODOLPHO: Marco, tell the man.

MARCO [*pulling his hand away*]: What will I tell him? He knows such a promise is dishonourable.

ALFIERI: To promise not to kill is not dishonourable.

MARCO [*looking at* ALFIERI]: No?

ALFIERI: No.

MARCO [*gesturing with his head – this is a new idea*]: Then what is done with such a man?

ALFIERI: Nothing. If he obeys the law, he lives. That's all.

MARCO [*rises, turns to* ALFIERI]: The law? All the law is not in a book.

ALFIERI: Yes. In a book. There is no other law.

MARCO [*his anger rising*]: He degraded my brother. My blood. He robbed my children, he mocks my work. I work to come here, mister!

ALFIERI: I know, Marco –

MARCO: There is no law for that? Where is the law for that?

ALFIERI: There is none.

MARCO [*shaking his head, sitting*]: I don't understand this country.

ALFIERI: Well? What is your answer? You have five or six weeks you could work. Or else you sit here. What do you say to me?

MARCO [*lowers his eyes. It almost seems he is ashamed.*] All right.

ALFIERI: You won't touch him. This is your promise.

[*Slight pause.*]

MARCO: Maybe he wants to apologize to me.

[MARCO *is staring away.* ALFIERI *takes one of his hands.*]

ALFIERI: This is not God, Marco. You hear? Only God makes justice.

MARCO: All right.

ALFIERI [*nodding, not with assurance*]: Good! Catherine, Rodolpho, Marco, let us go.

[CATHERINE *kisses* RODOLPHO *and* MARCO, *then kisses* ALFIERI'S *hand.*]

CATHERINE: I'll get Beatrice and meet you at the church. [*She leaves quickly.*]

[MARCO *rises.* RODOLPHO *suddenly embraces him.* MARCO *pats him on the back and* RODOLPHO *exits after* CATHERINE. MARCO *faces* ALFIERI.]

ALFIERI: Only God, Marco.

[MARCO *turns and walks out.* ALFIERI *with a certain processional tread leaves the stage. The lights dim out.*

The lights rise in the apartment. EDDIE *is alone in the rocker, rocking back and forth in little surges. Pause. Now* BEATRICE *emerges from a bedroom. She is in her best clothes, wearing a hat.*]

BEATRICE [*with fear, going to* EDDIE]: I'll be back in an hour, Eddie. All right?

EDDIE [*quietly, almost inaudibly, as though drained*]: What, have I been talkin' to myself?

BEATRICE: Eddie, for God's sake, it's her wedding.

EDDIE: Didn't you hear what I told you? You walk out that door to that wedding you ain't comin' back here, Beatrice.

BEATRICE: Why! What do you want?

EDDIE: I want my respect. Didn't you ever hear of that? From my wife?

[CATHERINE *enters from bedroom.*]

CATHERINE: It's after three; we're supposed to be there already, Beatrice. The priest won't wait.

BEATRICE: Eddie. It's her wedding. There'll be nobody there from her family. For my sister let me go. I'm goin' for my sister.

EDDIE [*as though hurt*]: Look, I been arguin' with you all day already, Beatrice, and I said what I'm gonna say. He's gonna come here and apologize to me or nobody from this house is goin' into that church today. Now if that's more to you than I am, then go. But don't come back. You be on my side or on their side, that's all.

CATHERINE [*suddenly*]: Who the hell do you think you are?

BEATRICE: Sssh!

CATHERINE: You got no more right to tell nobody nothin'! Nobody! The rest of your life, nobody!

BEATRICE: Shut up, Katie! [*She turns* CATHERINE *around.*]

CATHERINE: You're gonna come with me!

BEATRICE: I can't Katie, I can't . . .

CATHERINE: How can you listen to him? This rat!

BEATRICE [*shaking* CATHERINE]: Don't you call him that!

CATHERINE [*clearing from* BEATRICE]: What're you scared of? He's a rat! He belongs in the sewer!

BEATRICE: Stop it!

CATHERINE [*weeping*]: He bites people when they sleep! He comes when nobody's lookin' and poisons decent people. In the garbage he belongs!

[EDDIE *seems about to pick up the table and fling it at her.*]

BEATRICE: No, Eddie! Eddie! [*To* CATHERINE] Then we all belong in the garbage. You, and me too. Don't say that. Whatever happened we all done it, and don't you ever forget it, Catherine. [*She goes to* CATHERINE.] Now go, go to your wedding, Katie, I'll stay home. Go. God bless you, God bless your children.

[*Enter* RODOLPHO.]

RODOLPHO: Eddie?

EDDIE: Who said you could come in here? Get outa here!

RODOLPHO: Marco is coming, Eddie. [*Pause.* BEATRICE *raises her hands in terror.*] He's praying in the church. You understand? [*Pause.* RODOLPHO *advances into the room.*] Catherine, I think it is better we go. Come with me.

CATHERINE: Eddie, go away, please.

BEATRICE [*quietly*]: Eddie. Let's go someplace. Come. You and me. [*He has not moved.*] I don't want you to be here when he comes. I'll get your coat.

EDDIE: Where? Where am I goin'? This is my house.

BEATRICE [*crying out*]: What's the use of it! He's crazy now, you know the way they get, what good is it! You got nothin' against Marco, you always liked Marco!

EDDIE: I got nothin' against Marco? Which he called me a rat in front of the whole neighbourhood? Which he said I killed his children! Where you been?

RODOLPHO [*quite suddenly, stepping up to* EDDIE]: It is my fault, Eddie. Everything. I wish to apologize. It was wrong that I do not ask your permission. I kiss your hand. [*He reaches for* EDDIE*'s hand, but* EDDIE *snaps it away from him.*]

BEATRICE: Eddie, he's apologizing!

RODOLPHO: I have made all our troubles. But you have insult me too. Maybe God understand why you did that to me. Maybe you did not mean to insult me at all –

BEATRICE: Listen to him! Eddie, listen what he's tellin' you!

RODOLPHO: I think, maybe when Marco comes, if we can tell him we are comrades now, and we have no more argument between us. Then maybe Marco will not –

EDDIE: Now, listen –

CATHERINE: Eddie, give him a chance!

BEATRICE: What do you want! Eddie, what do you want!

EDDIE: I want my name! He didn't take my name; he's only a punk. Marco's got my name – [*to* RODOLPHO] and you can run tell him, kid, that he's gonna give it back to me in front of this neighbourhood, or we have it out. [*Hoisting up his pants*] Come on, where is he? Take me to him.

BEATRICE: Eddie, listen –

EDDIE: I heard enough! Come on, let's go!

BEATRICE: Only blood is good? He kissed your hand!

EDDIE: What he does don't mean nothin' to nobody! [*To* RODOLPHO] Come on!

BEATRICE [*barring his way to the stairs*]: What's gonna mean somethin'? Eddie, listen to me. Who could give you your name? Listen to me, I love you, I'm talkin' to you, I love you; if Marco'll kiss your hand outside, if he goes on his knees, what is he got to give you? That's not what you want.

EDDIE: Don't bother me!

BEATRICE: You want somethin' else, Eddie, and you can never have her!

CATHERINE [*in horror*]: B.!

EDDIE [*shocked, horrified, his fist clenching*]: Beatrice!

[MARCO *appears outside, walking toward the door from a distant point.*]

BEATRICE [*crying out, weeping*]: The truth is not as bad as blood, Eddie! I'm tellin' you the truth – tell her good-bye forever!

EDDIE [*crying out in agony*]: That's what you think of me – that I would have such a thought? [*His fists clench his head as though it will burst.*]

MARCO [*calling near the door outside*]: Eddie Carbone!

[EDDIE *swerves about; all stand transfixed for an instant. People appear outside.*]

EDDIE [*as though flinging his challenge*]: Yeah, Marco! Eddie Carbone. Eddie Carbone. Eddie Carbone. [*He goes up the stairs and emerges from the apartment.* RODOLPHO *streaks up and out past him and runs to* MARCO.]

RODOLPHO: No, Marco, please! Eddie, please, he has children! You will kill a family!

BEATRICE: Go in the house! Eddie, go in the house!

EDDIE [*he gradually comes to address the people*]: Maybe he come to apologize to me. Heh, Marco? For what you said about me in front of the neighbourhood? [*He is incensing himself and little bits of laughter even escape him as his eyes are murderous and he cracks his knuckles in his hands with a strange sort of relaxation.*] He knows that ain't right. To do like that? To a man? Which I put my roof over their head and my food in their mouth? Like in the Bible? Strangers I never seen in my whole life? To come out of the water and grab a girl for a passport? To go and take from your own family like from the stable – and never a word to me? And now accusations in the bargain! [*Directly to* MARCO] Wipin' the neighbourhood with my name like a dirty rag! I want my name, Marco. [*He is moving now, carefully, toward* MARCO.] Now gimme my name and we go together to the wedding.

BEATRICE *and* CATHERINE [*keening*]: Eddie! Eddie, don't! Eddie!

EDDIE: No, Marco knows what's right from wrong. Tell the people, Marco, tell them what a liar you are! [*He has his arms spread and* MARCO *is spreading his.*] Come on, liar, you know what you done! [*He lunges for* MARCO *as a great hushed shout goes up from the people.*]

[MARCO *strikes* EDDIE *beside the neck.*]

MARCO: Animal! You go on your knees to me!

[EDDIE *goes down with the blow and* MARCO *starts to raise a foot to stomp him when* EDDIE *springs a knife into his hand and* MARCO *steps back.* LOUIS *rushes in toward* EDDIE.]

LOUIS: Eddie, for Christ's sake!

[EDDIE *raises the knife and* LOUIS *halts and steps back.*]

EDDIE: You lied about me, Marco. Now say it. Come on now, say it!
MARCO: Anima-a-a-l!

[EDDIE *lunges with the knife.* MARCO *grabs his arm, turning the blade inward and pressing it home as the women and* LOUIS *and* MIKE *rush in and separate them, and* EDDIE, *the knife still in his hand, falls to his knees before* MARCO. *The two women support him for a moment, calling his name again and again.*]

CATHERINE: Eddie I never meant to do nothing bad to you.
EDDIE: Then why – Oh, B.!
BEATRICE: Yes, yes!
EDDIE: My B.!

[*He dies in her arms, and* BEATRICE *covers him with her body.* ALFIERI, *who is in the crowd, turns out to the audience. The lights have gone down, leaving him in a glow, while behind him the dull prayers of the people and the keening of the women continue.*]

ALFIERI: Most of the time now we settle for half and I like it better. But the truth is holy, and even as I know how wrong he was, and his death useless, I tremble, for I confess that something perversely pure calls to me from his memory – not purely good, but himself purely, for he allowed himself to be wholly known and for that I think I will love him more than all my sensible clients. And yet, it is better to settle for half, it must be! And so I mourn him – I admit it – with a certain . . . alarm.

CURTAINpenguin CLASSICS

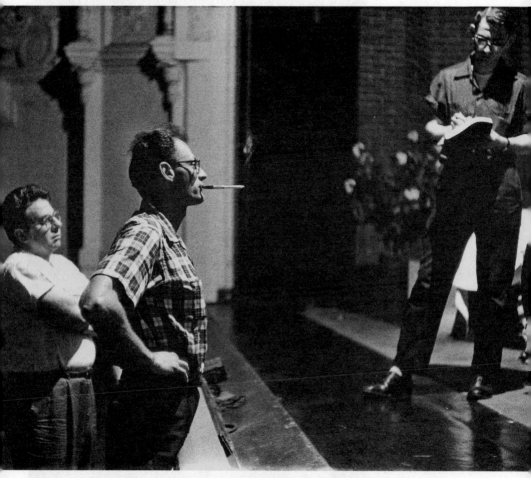

1. Arthur Miller during a rehearsal for the first production of *A View from the Bridge* at the Coronet Theatre in New York, 1955. Photograph by Dan Weiner.

2. Van Heflin and the cast of the original production at The Coronet Theatre. Photograph by Alfredo Valente.

3. Miller with Mary Ure and Anthony Quayle in rehearsals for Peter Brook's 1956 production in London. After the New York run, Miller revised the play to contain two acts, and the two–act play premiered in London. Photograph by Charles Hewitt.

4. (*above*) Miller arriving at the London premiere with his wife Marilyn Monroe, 11 October 1956. The Lord Chamberlain had originally banned the production, so the producers leased the Comedy Theatre and turned it into a club – 'The New Watergate Theatre Club'. Because audience members had paid a membership fee, it was considered a private performance, and the production evaded censorship. Photograph by Brian Seed.

5. (*left*) Miller and Monroe with Sir Laurence Olivier and Vivian Leigh, waiting for the start of the play.

6. (*top*) Raf Vallone in Peter Brook's production at the Theatre Antoine, Paris, 1958.

7. (*bottom*) Vallone, who also starred in the film version directed by Sidney Lumet, on set, Brooklyn, 1961. Photographs 7 and 8 by Inge Morath.

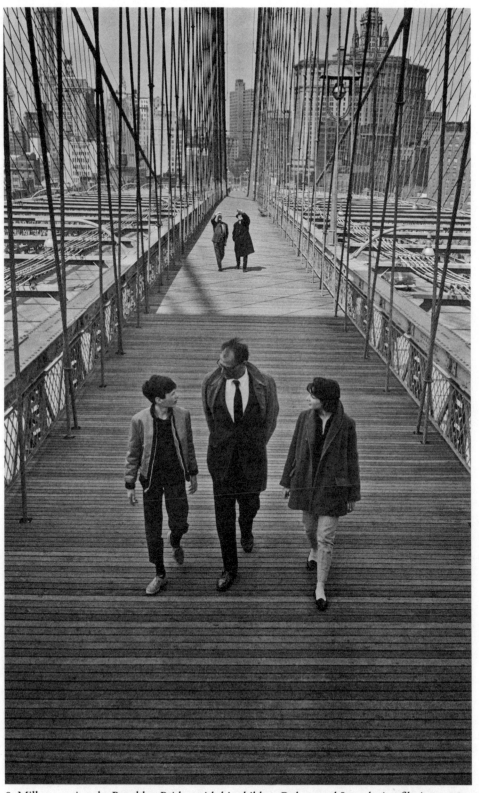

8. Miller crossing the Brooklyn Bridge with his children Robert and Jane during filming, 1961.

9. The theatrical poster for a 1965 off–Broadway revival designed by Ben Shahn.

10. (*above*) Michael Gambon, Elizabeth Bell and Suzan Sylvester in Alan Ayckbourn's National Theatre production, 1987. Photograph by Nobby Clark.

11. (*left*) Ken Stott and Hayley Atwell in Lindsay Posner's production at the Duke of York's Theatre, London, 2009. Photograph by Robbie Jack.

12. (*top*) Scarlett Johansson and Liev Schreiber in rehearsal for a 2010 Broadway revival, directed by Gregory Mosher. Photograph by Jennifer S. Altman.

13. (*bottom*) Phoebe Fox, Mark Strong and Nicola Walker in Ivo Van Hove's production at the Young Vic, London, 2014.

Illustration Credits

All My Sons

1. Eileen Darby/The LIFE Images Collection/Getty Images;
2. Photofest; 3. Courtesy of the Arthur Miller Archive; 4. Victoria &
Albert Museum Theatre Collection/V & A Images; 5. Arnold
Newman/Mander & Mitchenson Theatre Collection/Bristol
University Archives/ArenaPAL/Topfoto; 6. Kobal Collection;
7. Frazer Ashford/ArenaPAL; 8. Chris Parker/ArenaPAL; 9. Colin
Willoughby/ArenaPAL; 10. ArenaPAL/Topfoto; 11. Joan Marcus/
ArenaPAL; 12. Joan Marcus/ArenaPAL; 13. Tristram Kenton;
14. Robbie Jack/Corbis; 15. Jonathan Keenan

Death of a Salesman

1. W. Eugene Smith/The LIFE Picture Collection/Getty Images;
2. Jo Meilziner/Photofest; 3. Eileen Darby; 4. Eileen Darby/
Keystone Features/Getty Images; 5. Granger Collection/Topfoto;
6. Bert Hardy/Picture Post/Hulton Archive/Getty Images; 7. John
Swope/The LIFE Picture Collection/Getty Images; 8. Daniel
Bernstein; 9–13. Inge Morath/The Inge Morath Foundation/
Magnum Photos; 14. Brigitte Lacombe; 15. Robbie Jack/Corbis

The Crucible

1. Eve Arnold/Magnum Photos; 2. Gjon Mili/The LIFE Picture
Collection/Getty Images; 3. Paul Berg/Courtesy of the Arthur
Miller Archives; 4. Roger-Viollet/Topfoto; 5. Mander & Mitchenson Theatre Collection/University of Bristol/ArenaPAL/Topfoto;
6. Inge Morath/The Inge Morath Foundation/Magnum Photos;
7. Keystone Pictures USA/Alamy; 8. Richard Mildenhall; 9–14. Inge
Morath/The Inge Morath Foundation/Magnum Photos

A View from the Bridge

1. Dan Weiner © John Broderick; 2. Alfredo Valente. Courtesy of Richard Valente; 3. Charles Hewitt/Picture Post/Getty Images; 4. Brian Seed/Lebrecht Music & Arts/Corbis; 5. Express/Archive Photos/Getty Images; 6. Roger-Viollet/Topfoto; 7–8. Inge Morath/ The Inge Morath Foundation/Magnum Photos; 9. Granger Collection/Topfoto; 10. Nobby Clark/ArenaPAL/Topfoto; 11. Robbie Jack/Corbis; 12. Jennifer S. Altman/Contour by Getty Images; 13. Robbie Jack/Corbis